Kamisama Kiss

Story & Art by

Julietta Suzuki

CHARACTERS

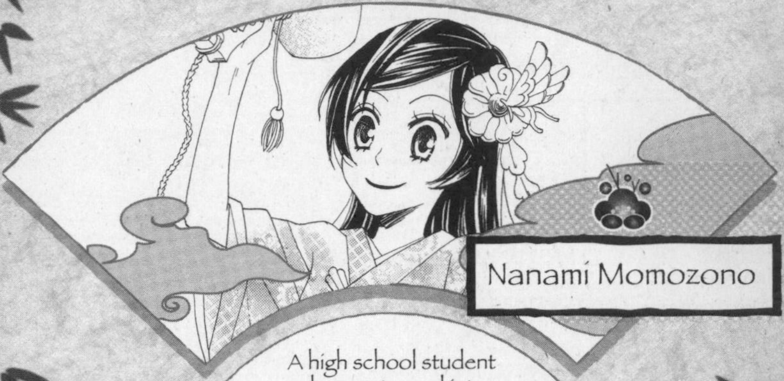

Nanami Momozono

A high school student who was turned into a kamisama by the tochigami Mikage.

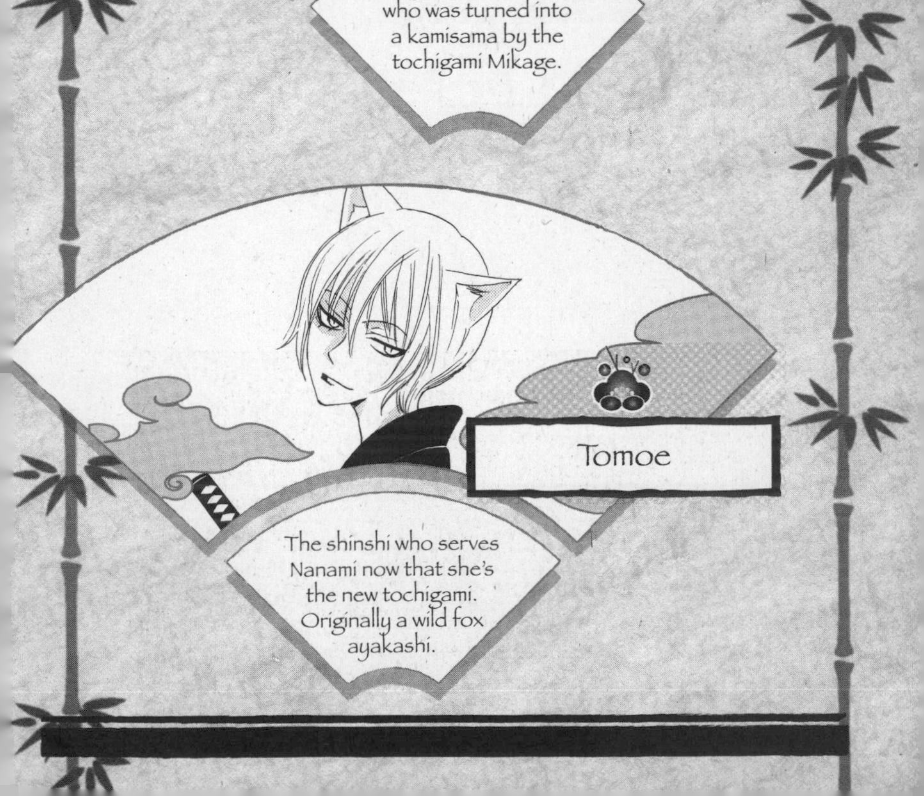

Tomoe

The shinshi who serves Nanami now that she's the new tochigami. Originally a wild fox ayakashi.

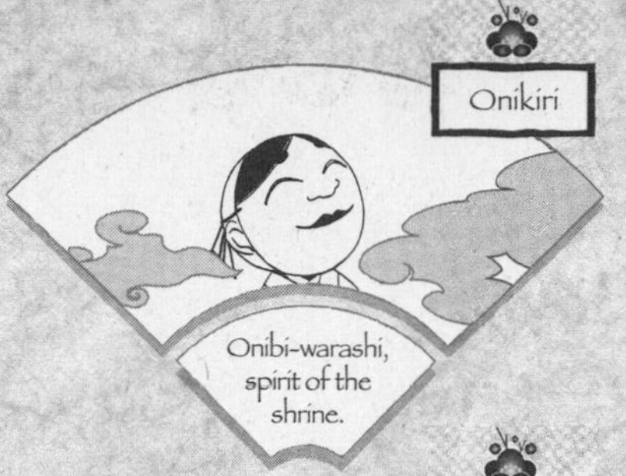
Onikiri
Onibi-warashi, spirit of the shrine.

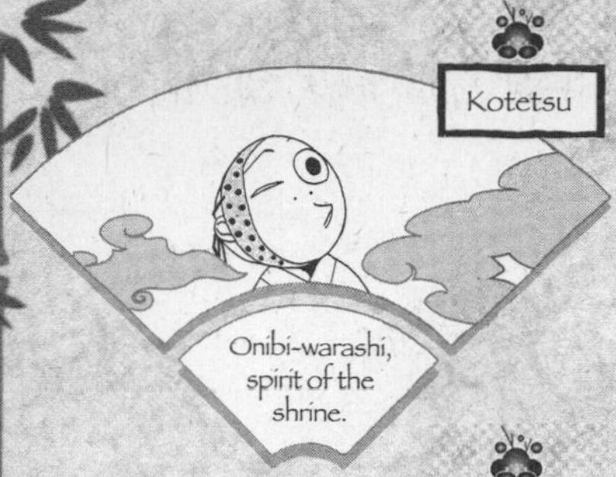
Kotetsu
Onibi-warashi, spirit of the shrine.

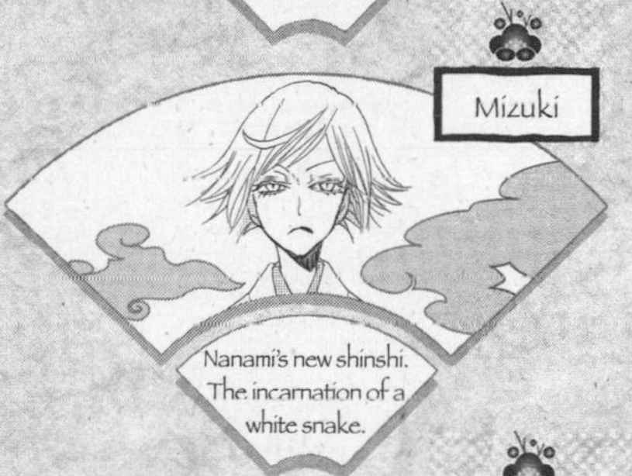
Mizuki
Nanami's new shinshi. The incarnation of a white snake.

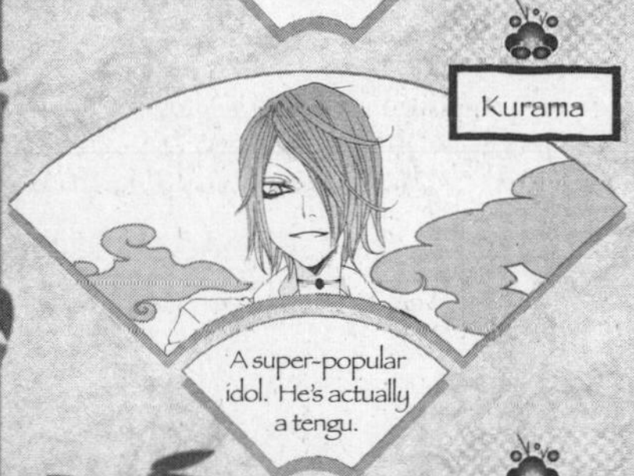
Kurama
A super-popular idol. He's actually a tengu.

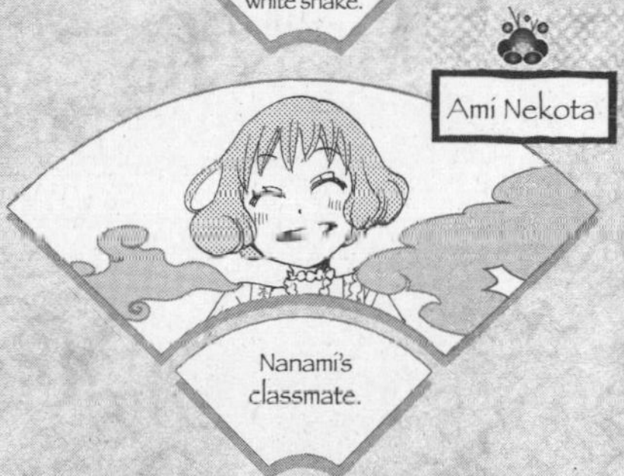
Ami Nekota
Nanami's classmate.

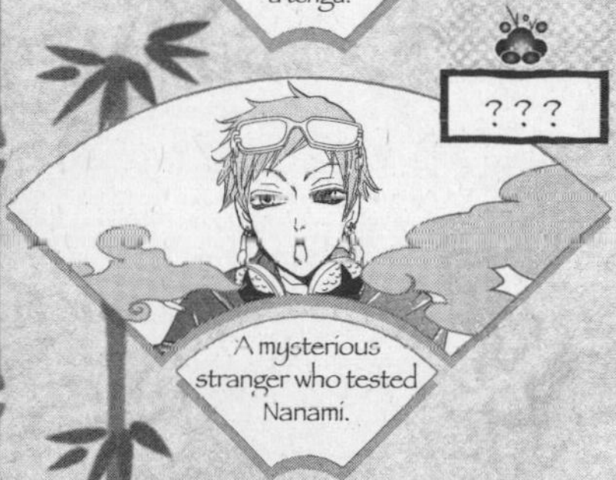
???
A mysterious stranger who tested Nanami.

Story so far

Nanami Momozono is a high school student who was evicted from her home when her dad skipped town.
She rescued a strange man in a park, and in thanks he offered her his home. But when she got there, it turned out to be a ruined shrine. The man she rescued was the tochigami Mikage, who ran away from his shrine.
Now Nanami must fulfill the shrine duties of the kamisama. She spends her days with Tomoe (her shinshi) and with Onikiri and Kotetsu (the onibi-warashi spirits of the shrine).
Nanami grants the prayers of those who come to her shrine. Less pleasantly, she's also attacked by supernatural creatures that want to become the kamisama themselves. She can't catch a break.
When the Mikage Shrine holds a summer festival, Nanami dances the kagura, which somehow attracts a miracle and a swarm of otherworldly butterflies!

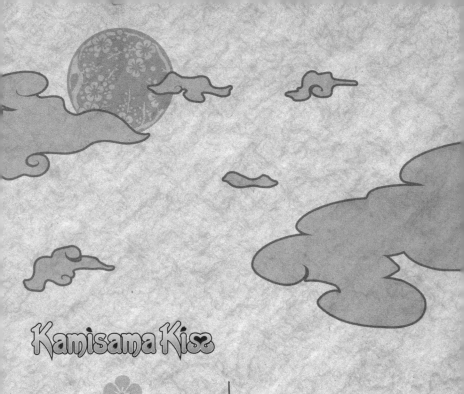

Kamisama Kiss

Volume 6
CONTENTS

Chapter 31   005

Chapter 32   037

Chapter 33   067

Chapter 34   097

Chapter 35   129

Chapter 36   159

End Notes   192

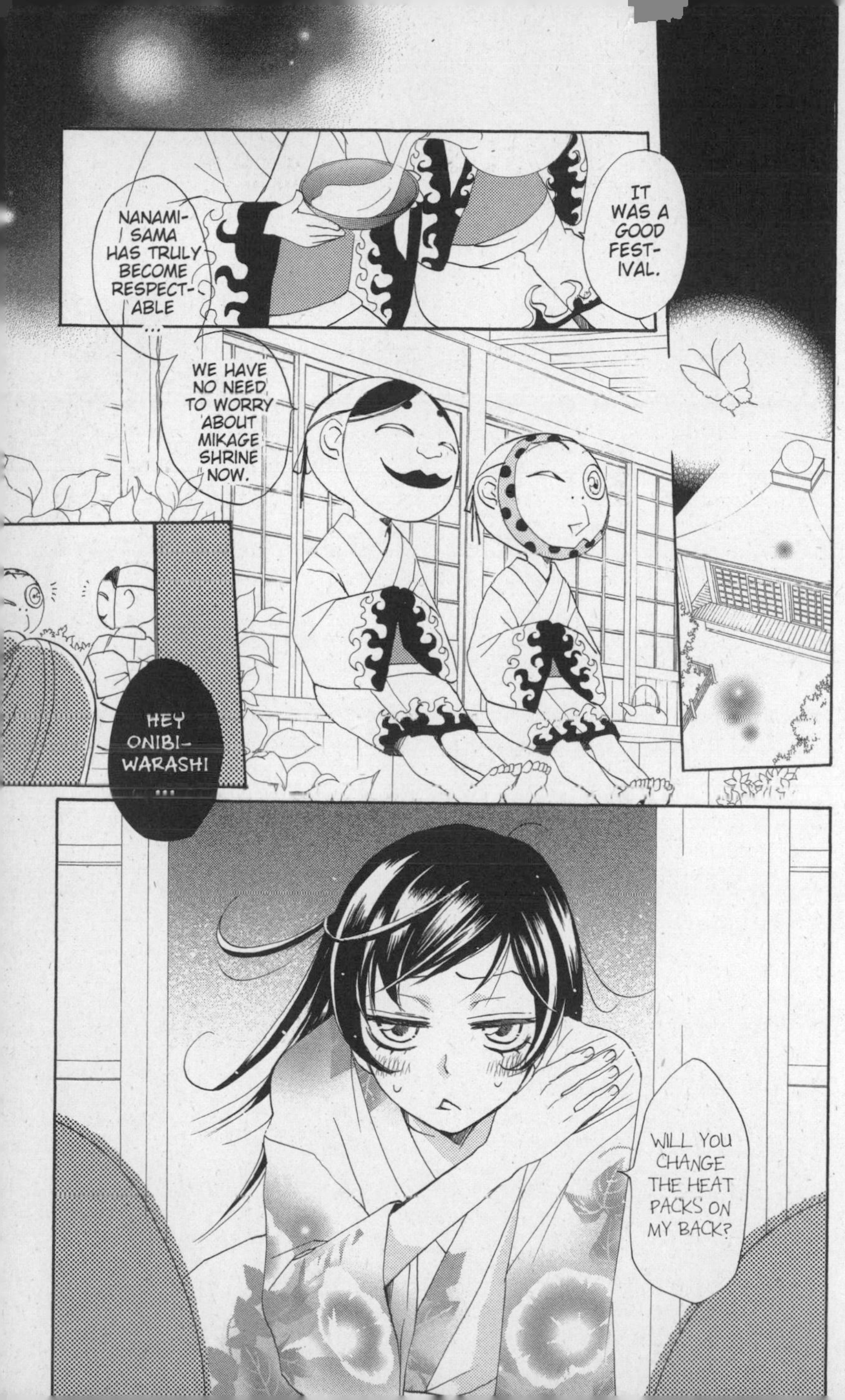
IT WAS A GOOD FEST-IVAL.
NANAMI-SAMA HAS TRULY BECOME RESPECT-ABLE ...
WE HAVE NO NEED TO WORRY ABOUT MIKAGE SHRINE NOW.
HEY ONIBI-WARASHI ...
WILL YOU CHANGE THE HEAT PACKS ON MY BACK?

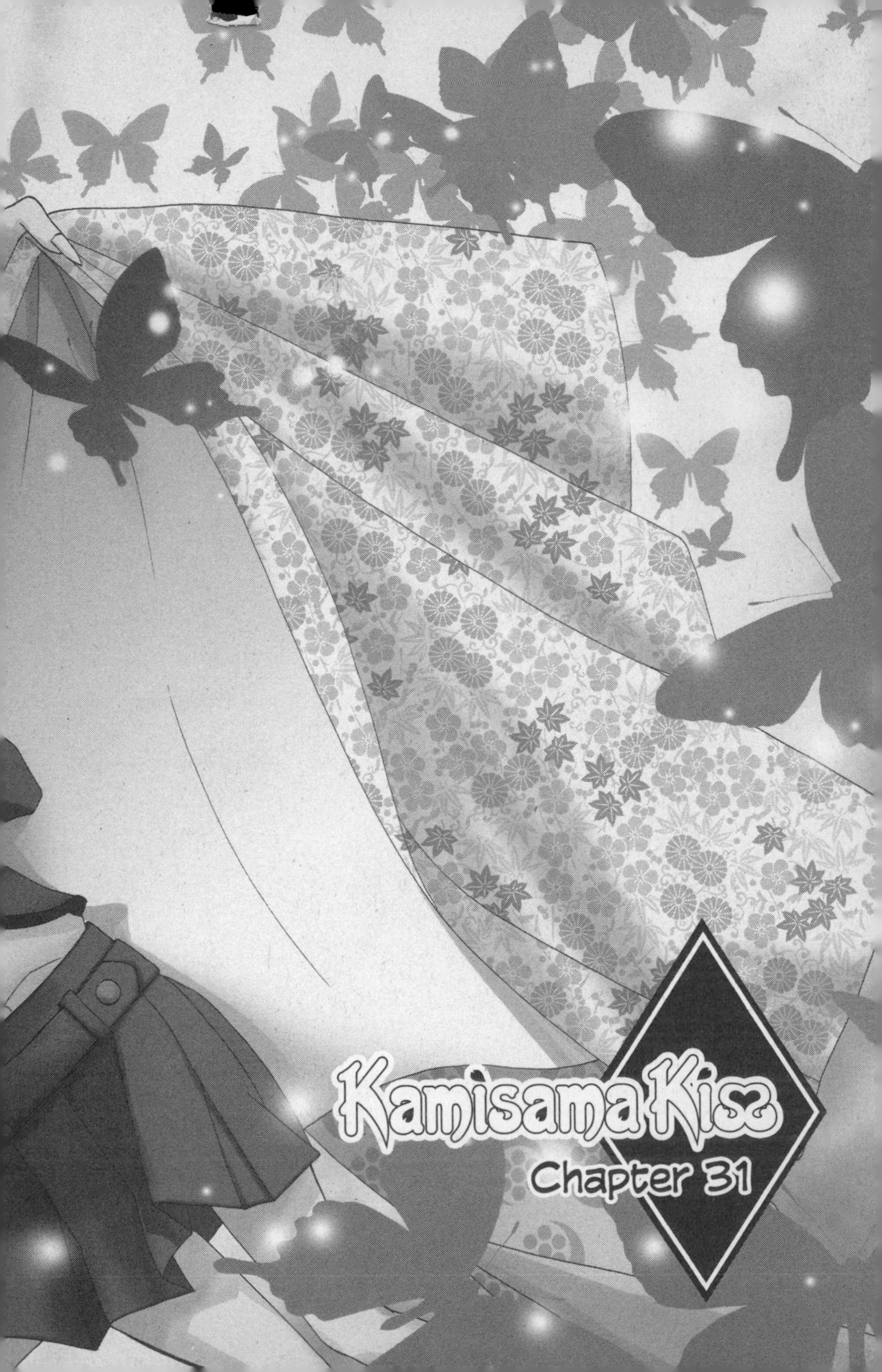
Kamisama Kiss
Chapter 31

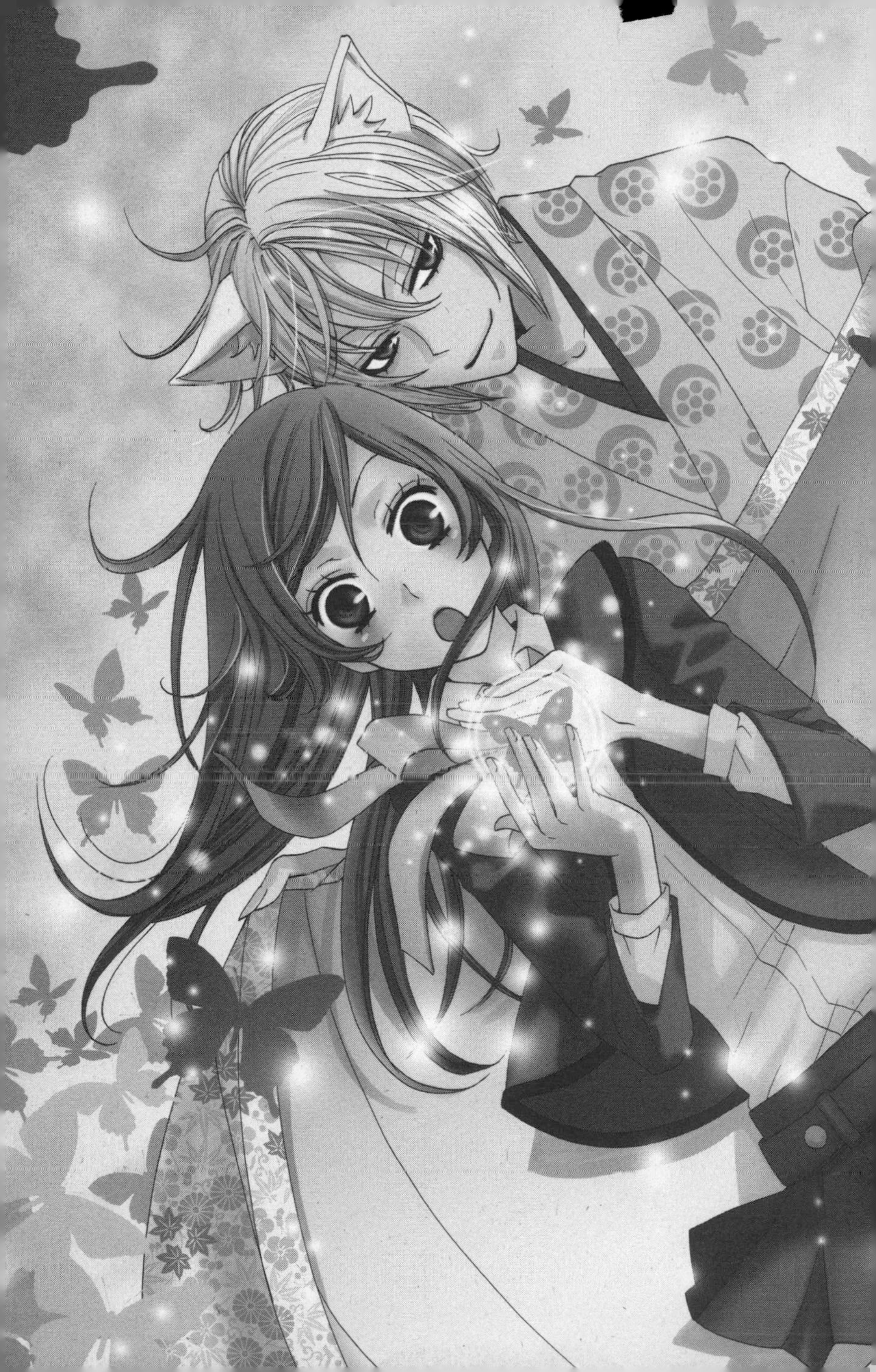

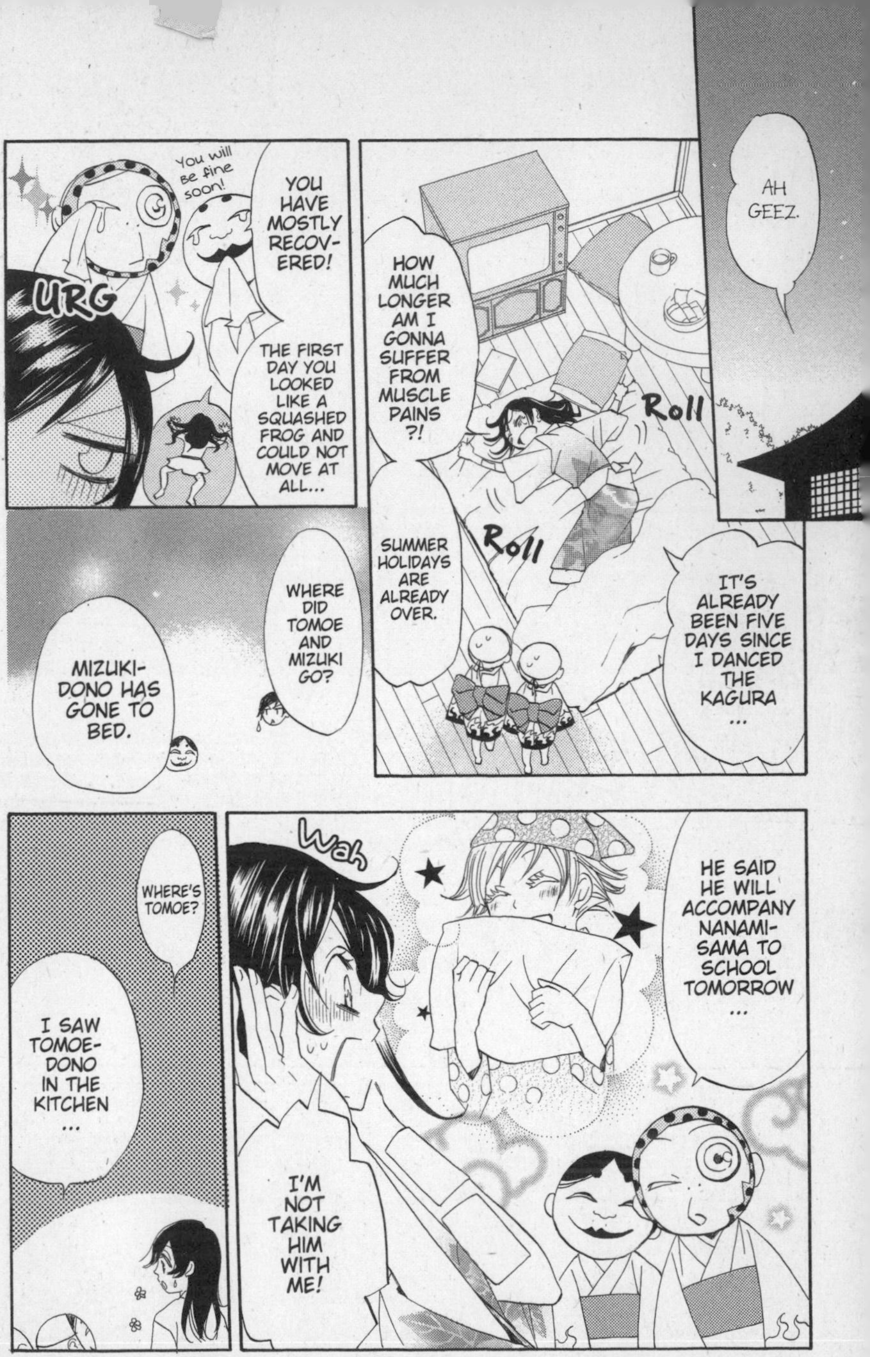
AH GEEZ.
IT'S ALREADY BEEN FIVE DAYS SINCE I DANCED THE KAGURA ...
HOW MUCH LONGER AM I GONNA SUFFER FROM MUSCLE PAINS ?!
Roll
Roll
SUMMER HOLIDAYS ARE ALREADY OVER.
YOU HAVE MOSTLY RECOVERED!
You will be fine soon!
THE FIRST DAY YOU LOOKED LIKE A SQUASHED FROG AND COULD NOT MOVE AT ALL...
URG
WHERE DID TOMOE AND MIZUKI GO?
MIZUKI-DONO HAS GONE TO BED.
HE SAID HE WILL ACCOMPANY NANAMI-SAMA TO SCHOOL TOMORROW ...
Wah
I'M NOT TAKING HIM WITH ME!
WHERE'S TOMOE?
I SAW TOMOE-DONO IN THE KITCHEN ...

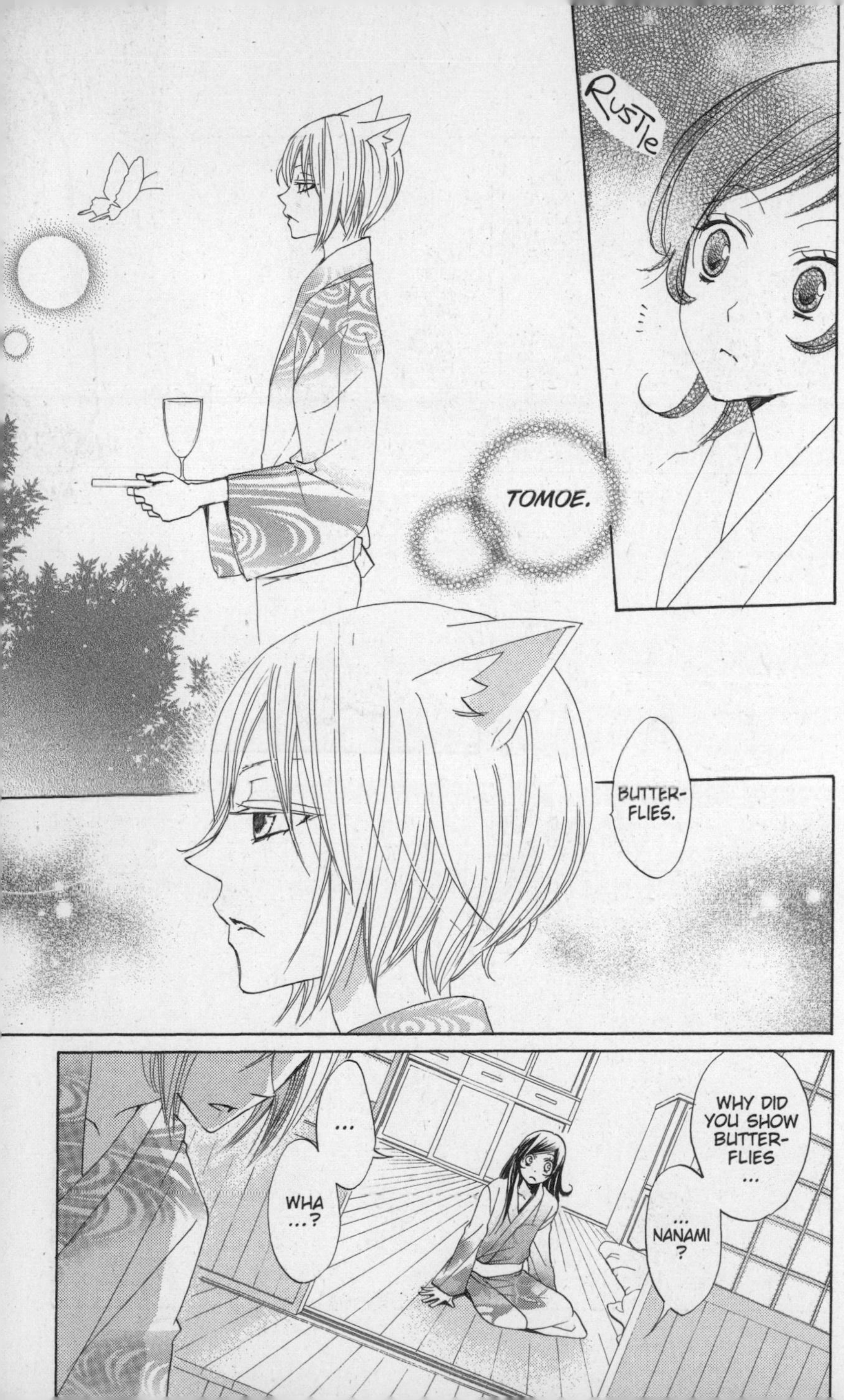
RUSTLE
TOMOE.
BUTTER-FLIES.
WHY DID YOU SHOW BUTTER-FLIES ...
... NANAMI ?
...
WHA ...?

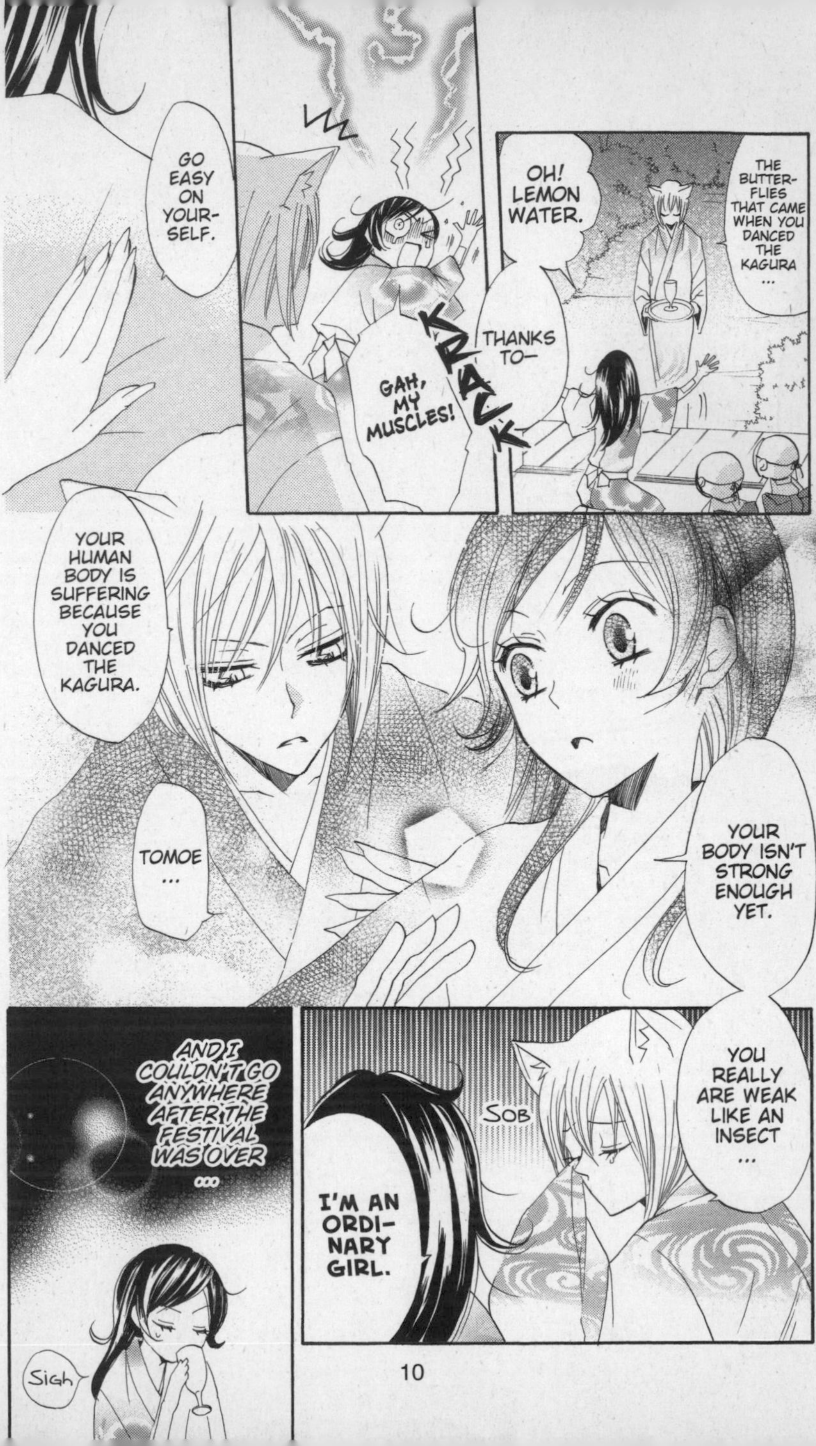
THE BUTTERFLIES THAT CAME WHEN YOU DANCED THE KAGURA ...
OH! LEMON WATER.
THANKS TO—
KRACK
GAH, MY MUSCLES!
GO EASY ON YOURSELF.
YOUR HUMAN BODY IS SUFFERING BECAUSE YOU DANCED THE KAGURA.
YOUR BODY ISN'T STRONG ENOUGH YET.
TOMOE ...
YOU REALLY ARE WEAK LIKE AN INSECT ...
SOB
I'M AN ORDINARY GIRL.
AND I COULDN'T GO ANYWHERE AFTER THE FESTIVAL WAS OVER ...
SIGH

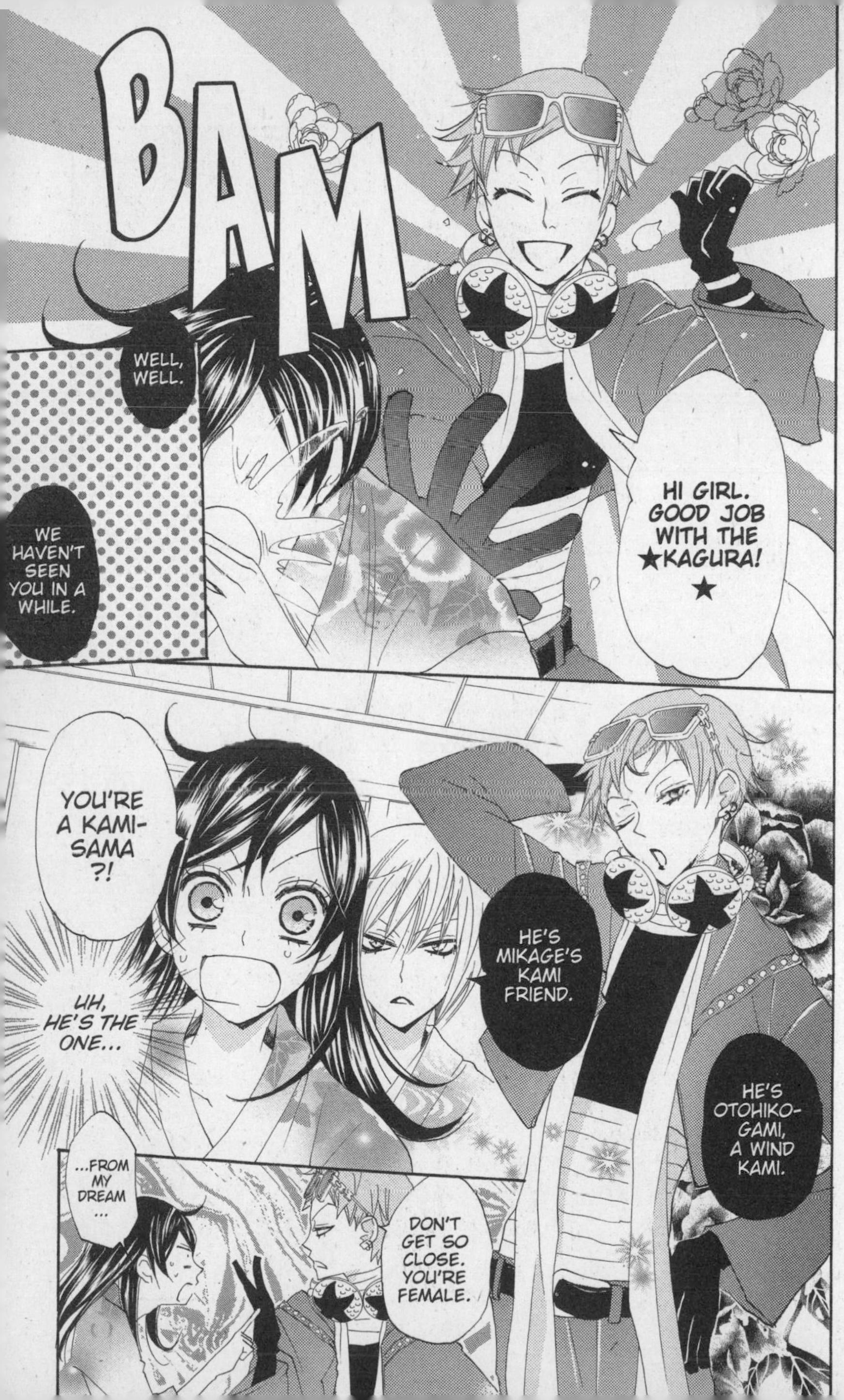
BAM
HI GIRL. GOOD JOB WITH THE ★KAGURA! ★
WELL, WELL.
WE HAVEN'T SEEN YOU IN A WHILE.
HE'S MIKAGE'S KAMI FRIEND.
HE'S OTOHIKO-GAMI, A WIND KAMI.
YOU'RE A KAMI-SAMA ?!
UH, HE'S THE ONE...
...FROM MY DREAM ...
DON'T GET SO CLOSE. YOU'RE FEMALE.

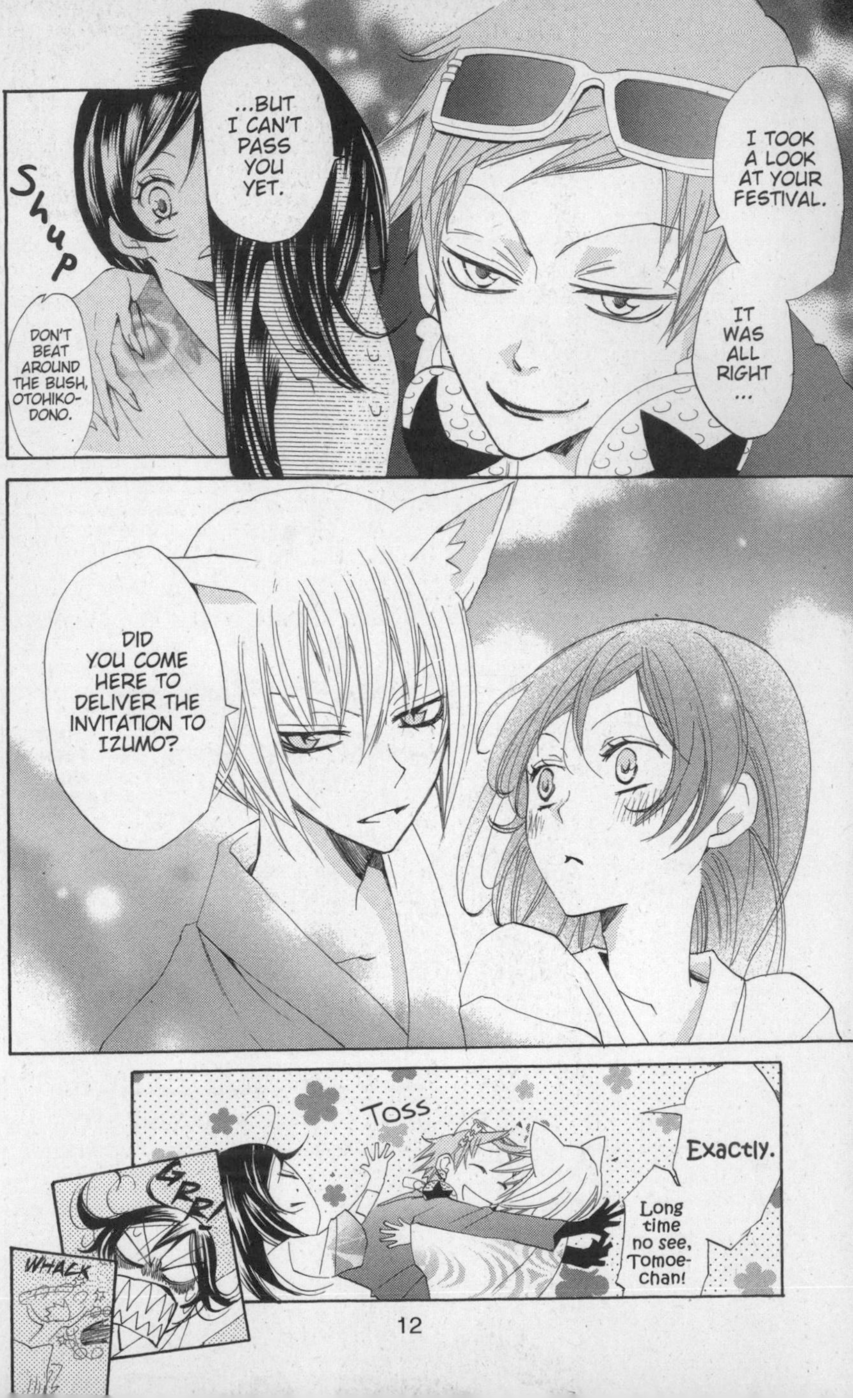
I TOOK A LOOK AT YOUR FESTIVAL.
IT WAS ALL RIGHT ...
...BUT I CAN'T PASS YOU YET.
Shup
DON'T BEAT AROUND THE BUSH, OTOHIKO-DONO.
DID YOU COME HERE TO DELIVER THE INVITATION TO IZUMO?
Exactly.
Long time no see, Tomoe-chan!
TOSS
GRR!
WHACK

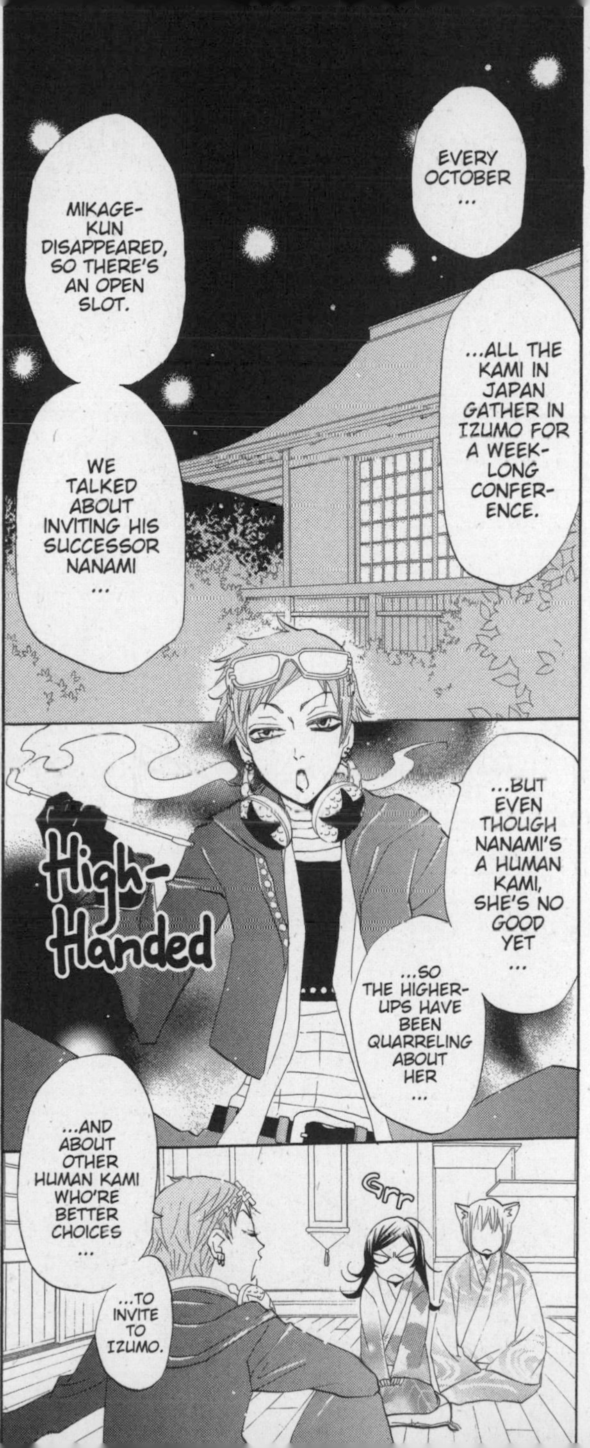
EVERY OCTOBER...
...ALL THE KAMI IN JAPAN GATHER IN IZUMO FOR A WEEK-LONG CONFERENCE.
MIKAGE-KUN DISAPPEARED, SO THERE'S AN OPEN SLOT.
WE TALKED ABOUT INVITING HIS SUCCESSOR NANAMI...
High-Handed
...BUT EVEN THOUGH NANAMI'S A HUMAN KAMI, SHE'S NO GOOD YET...
...SO THE HIGHER-UPS HAVE BEEN QUARRELING ABOUT HER...
...AND ABOUT OTHER HUMAN KAMI WHO'RE BETTER CHOICES...
Grr
...TO INVITE TO IZUMO.

A Break

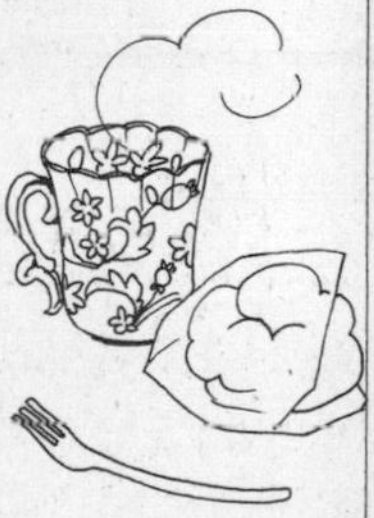

Thank you for picking up Volume 6 of Kamisama Kiss!

I hope you enjoy reading it just like you enjoy tea at three o'clock.

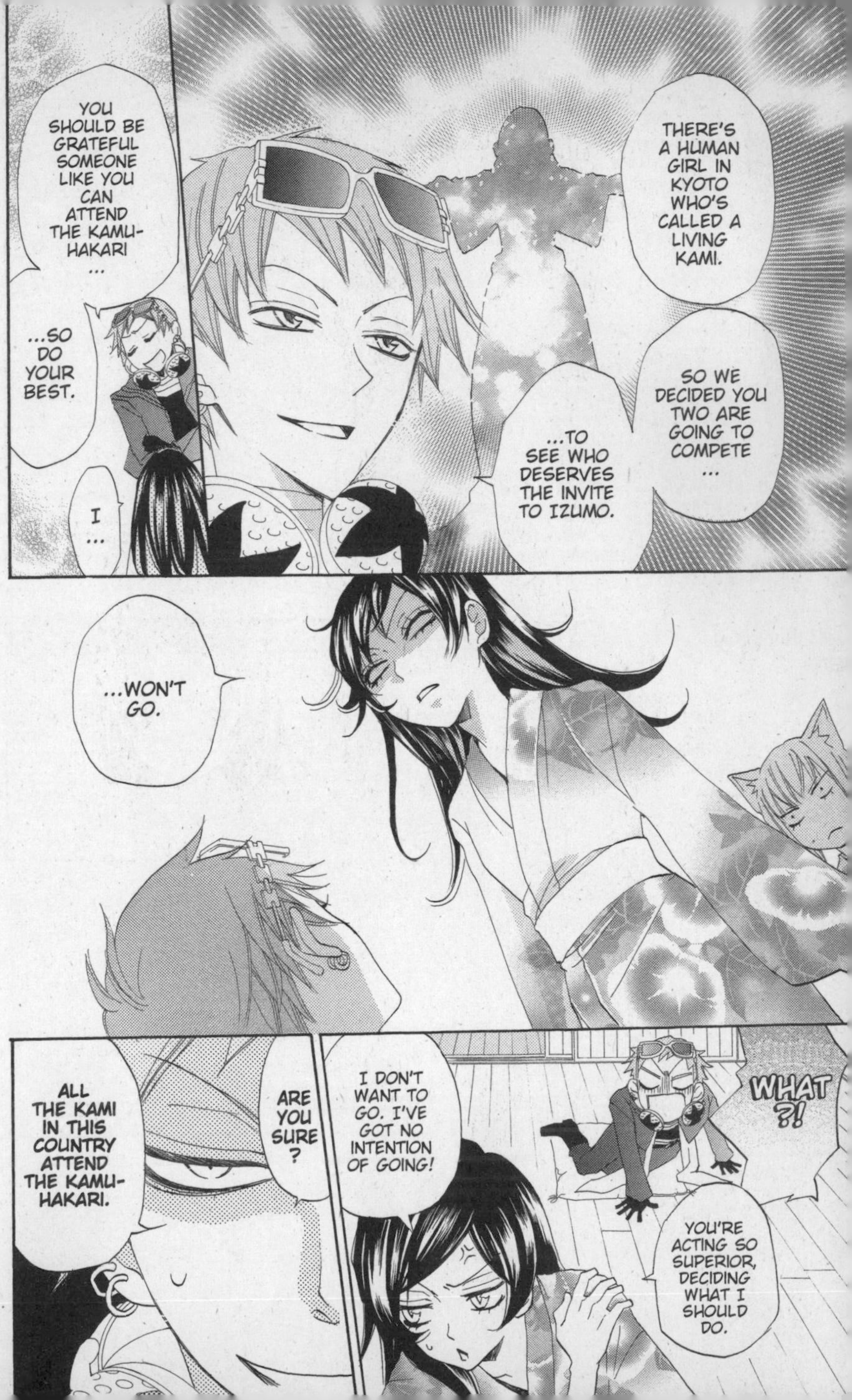

THERE'S A HUMAN GIRL IN KYOTO WHO'S CALLED A LIVING KAMI.
SO WE DECIDED YOU TWO ARE GOING TO COMPETE ...
...TO SEE WHO DESERVES THE INVITE TO IZUMO.
YOU SHOULD BE GRATEFUL SOMEONE LIKE YOU CAN ATTEND THE KAMU-HAKARI ...
...SO DO YOUR BEST.
I ...
...WON'T GO.
I DON'T WANT TO GO. I'VE GOT NO INTENTION OF GOING!
WHAT?!
YOU'RE ACTING SO SUPERIOR, DECIDING WHAT I SHOULD DO.
ARE YOU SURE?
ALL THE KAMI IN THIS COUNTRY ATTEND THE KAMU-HAKARI.

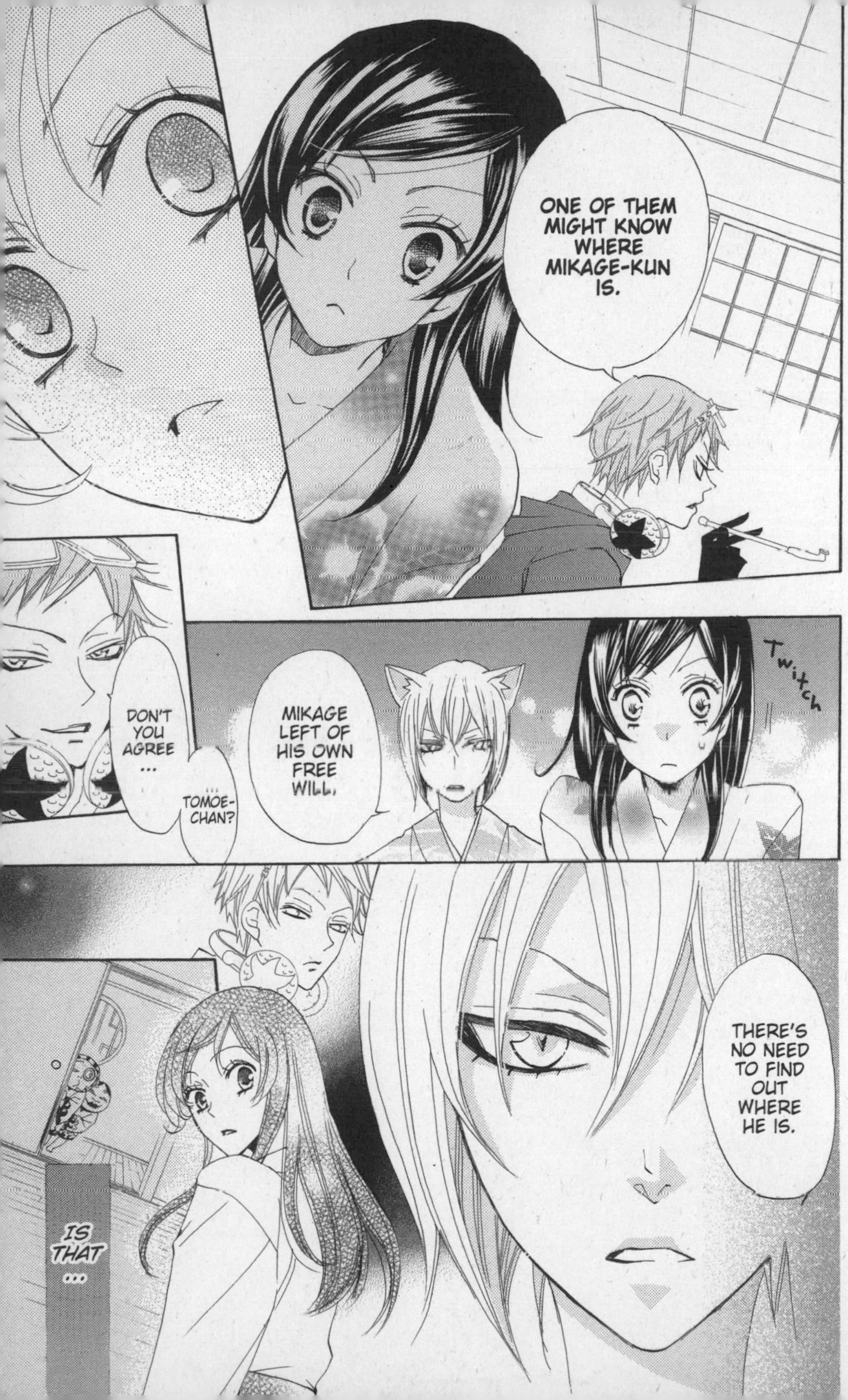
ONE OF THEM MIGHT KNOW WHERE MIKAGE-KUN IS.
Twitch
MIKAGE LEFT OF HIS OWN FREE WILL,
DON'T YOU AGREE ...
... TOMOE-CHAN?
THERE'S NO NEED TO FIND OUT WHERE HE IS.
IS THAT ...

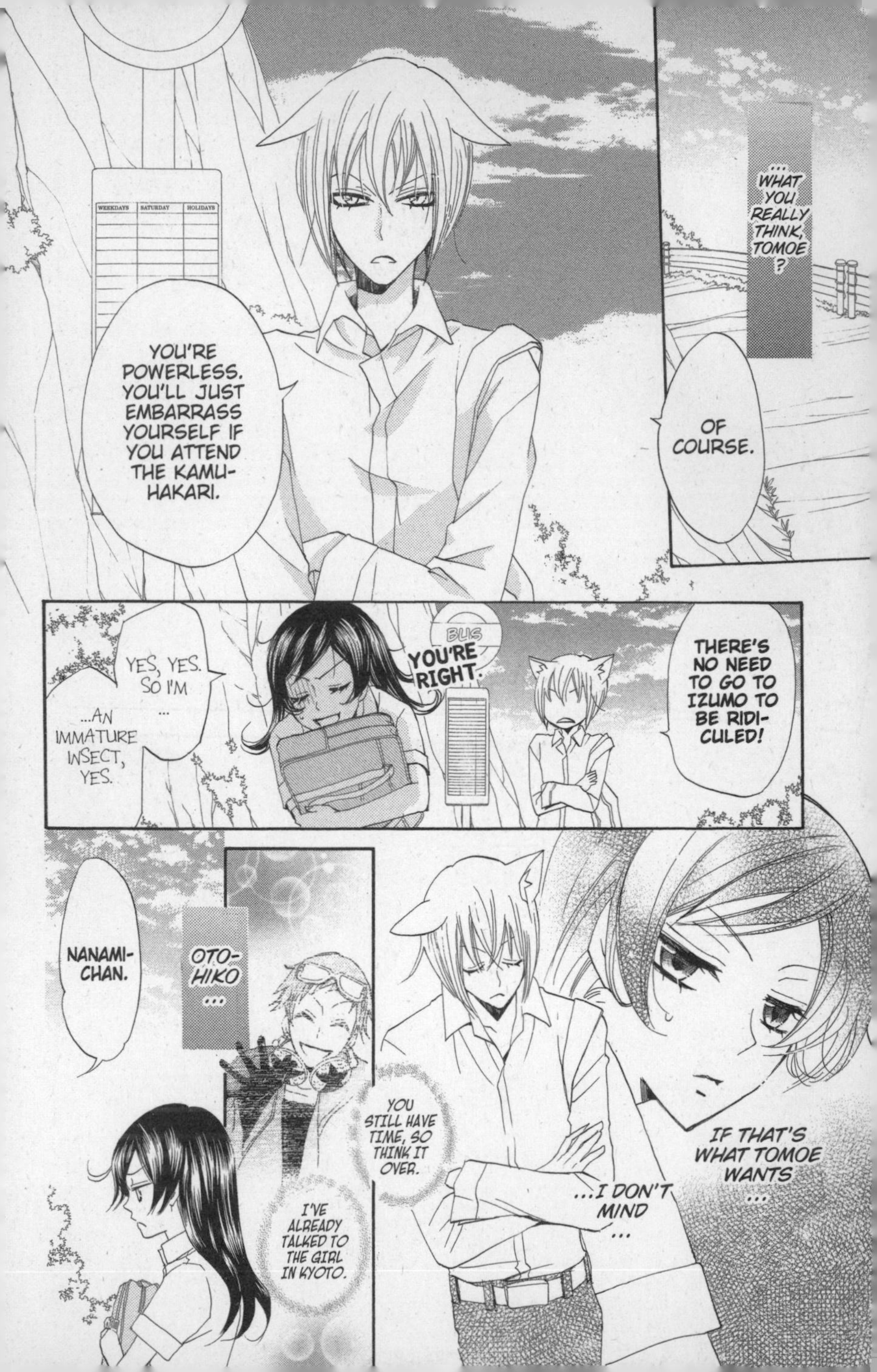
...WHAT YOU REALLY THINK, TOMOE ?
OF COURSE.
WEEKDAYS SATURDAY HOLIDAYS
YOU'RE POWERLESS. YOU'LL JUST EMBARRASS YOURSELF IF YOU ATTEND THE KAMU-HAKARI.
THERE'S NO NEED TO GO TO IZUMO TO BE RIDICULED!
BUS
YOU'RE RIGHT.
YES, YES. SO I'M ...
...AN IMMATURE INSECT, YES.
IF THAT'S WHAT TOMOE WANTS ...
...I DON'T MIND ...
YOU STILL HAVE TIME, SO THINK IT OVER.
I'VE ALREADY TALKED TO THE GIRL IN KYOTO.
NANAMI-CHAN.
OTO-HIKO ...

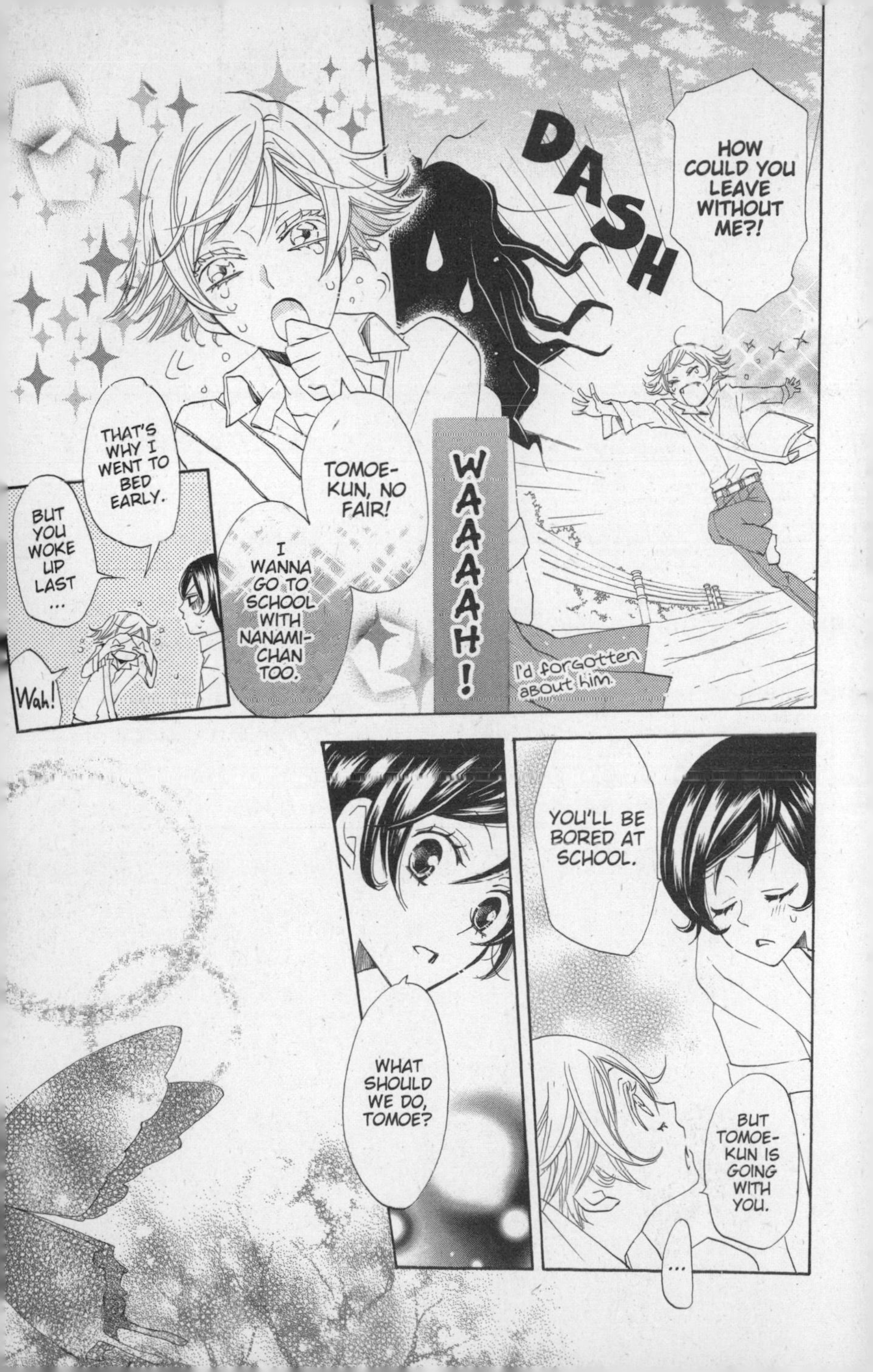
HOW COULD YOU LEAVE WITHOUT ME?!
DASH
WAAAAAH!
I'd forgotten about him.
TOMOE-KUN, NO FAIR!
I WANNA GO TO SCHOOL WITH NANAMI-CHAN TOO.
THAT'S WHY I WENT TO BED EARLY.
BUT YOU WOKE UP LAST ...
Wah!
YOU'LL BE BORED AT SCHOOL.
BUT TOMOE-KUN IS GOING WITH YOU.
...
WHAT SHOULD WE DO, TOMOE?

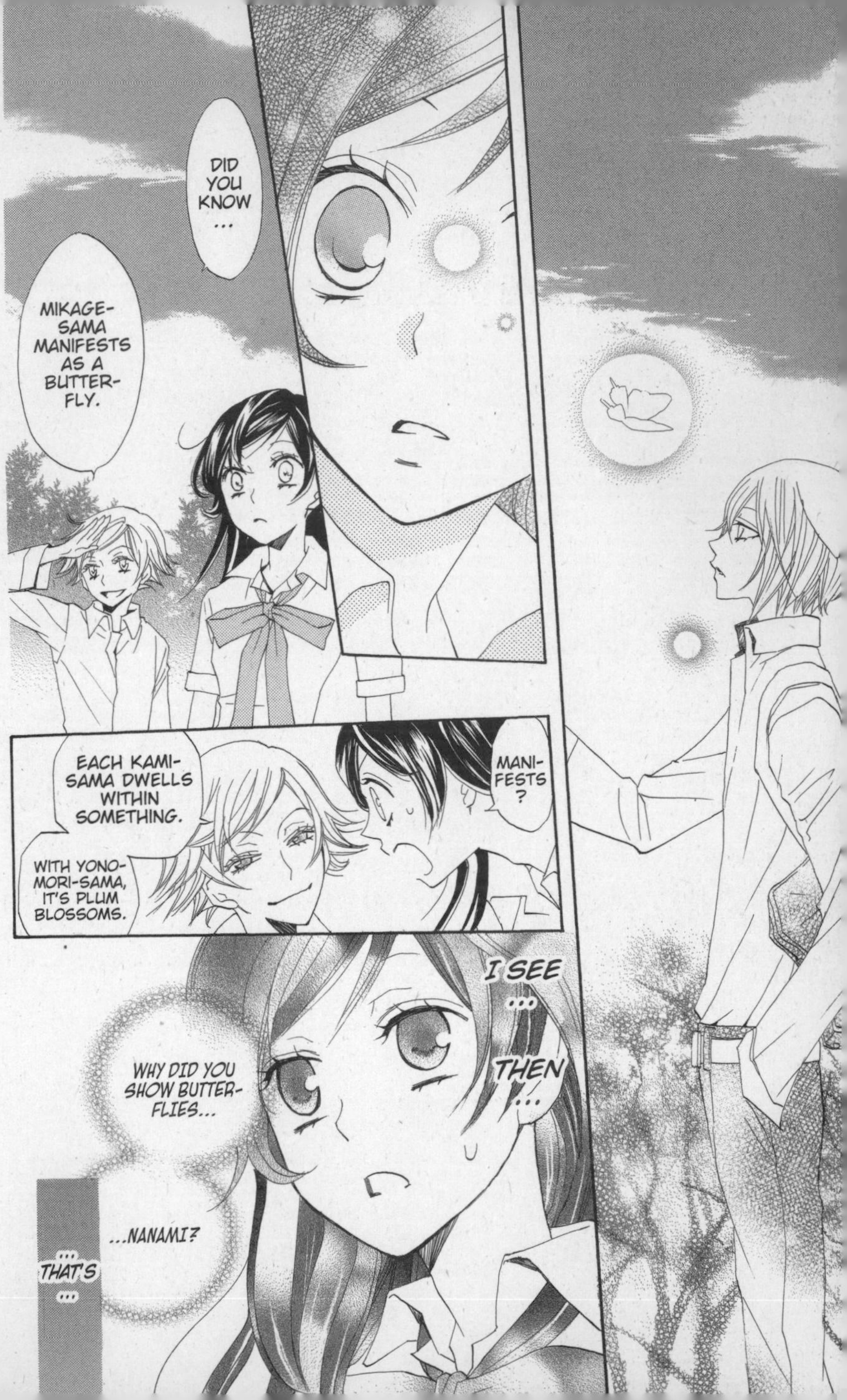
DID YOU KNOW ...
MIKAGE-SAMA MANIFESTS AS A BUTTERFLY.
MANI-FESTS?
EACH KAMI-SAMA DWELLS WITHIN SOMETHING.
WITH YONO-MORI-SAMA, IT'S PLUM BLOSSOMS.
I SEE ... THEN ...
WHY DID YOU SHOW BUTTER-FLIES...
...NANAMI?
... THAT'S ...

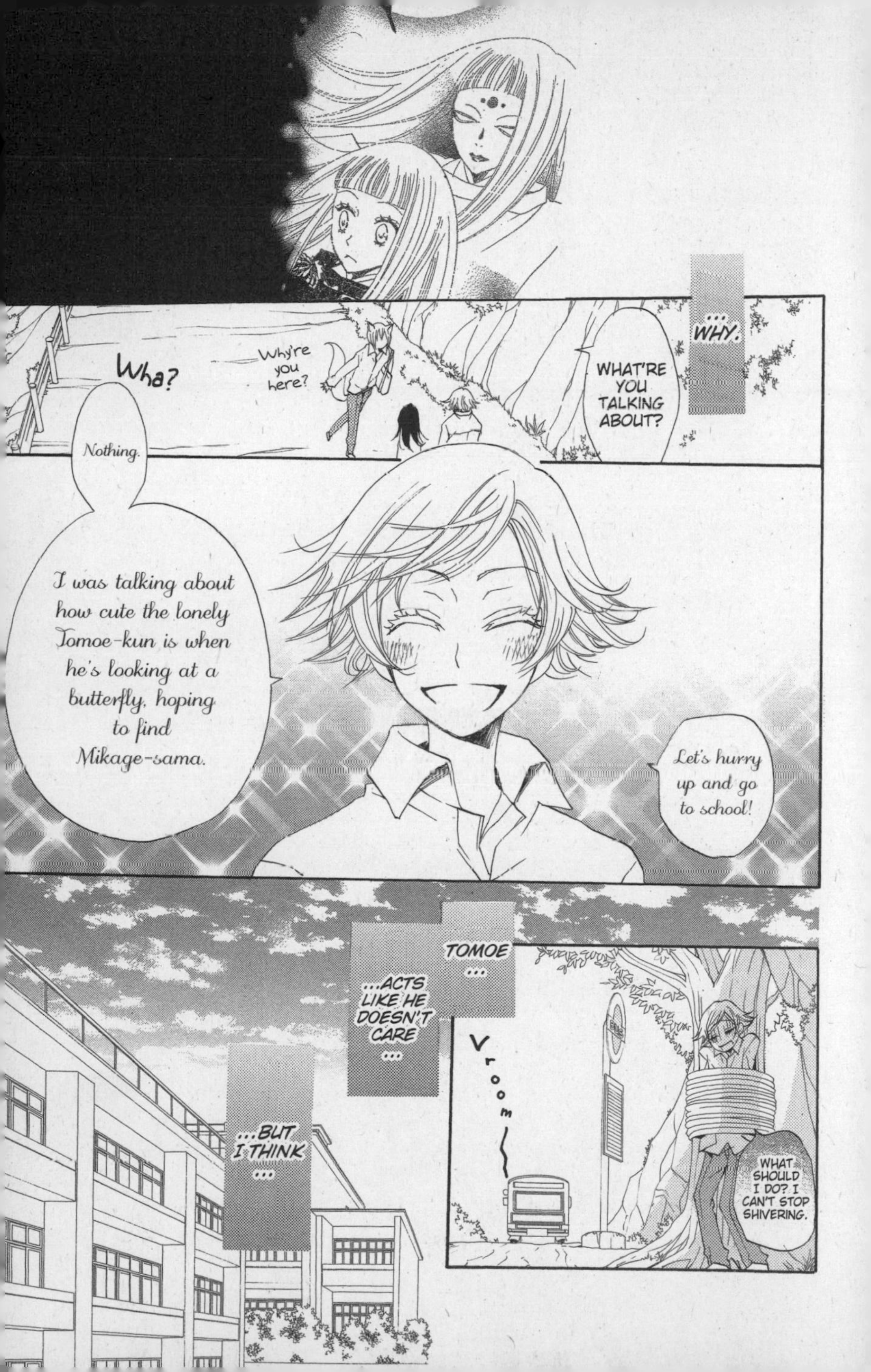
...WHY.
WHAT'RE YOU TALKING ABOUT?
Why're you here?
Wha?
Nothing.
I was talking about how cute the lonely Tomoe-kun is when he's looking at a butterfly, hoping to find Mikage-sama.
Let's hurry up and go to school!
TOMOE...
...ACTS LIKE HE DOESN'T CARE...
Vroom
WHAT SHOULD I DO? I CAN'T STOP SHIVERING.
...BUT I THINK...

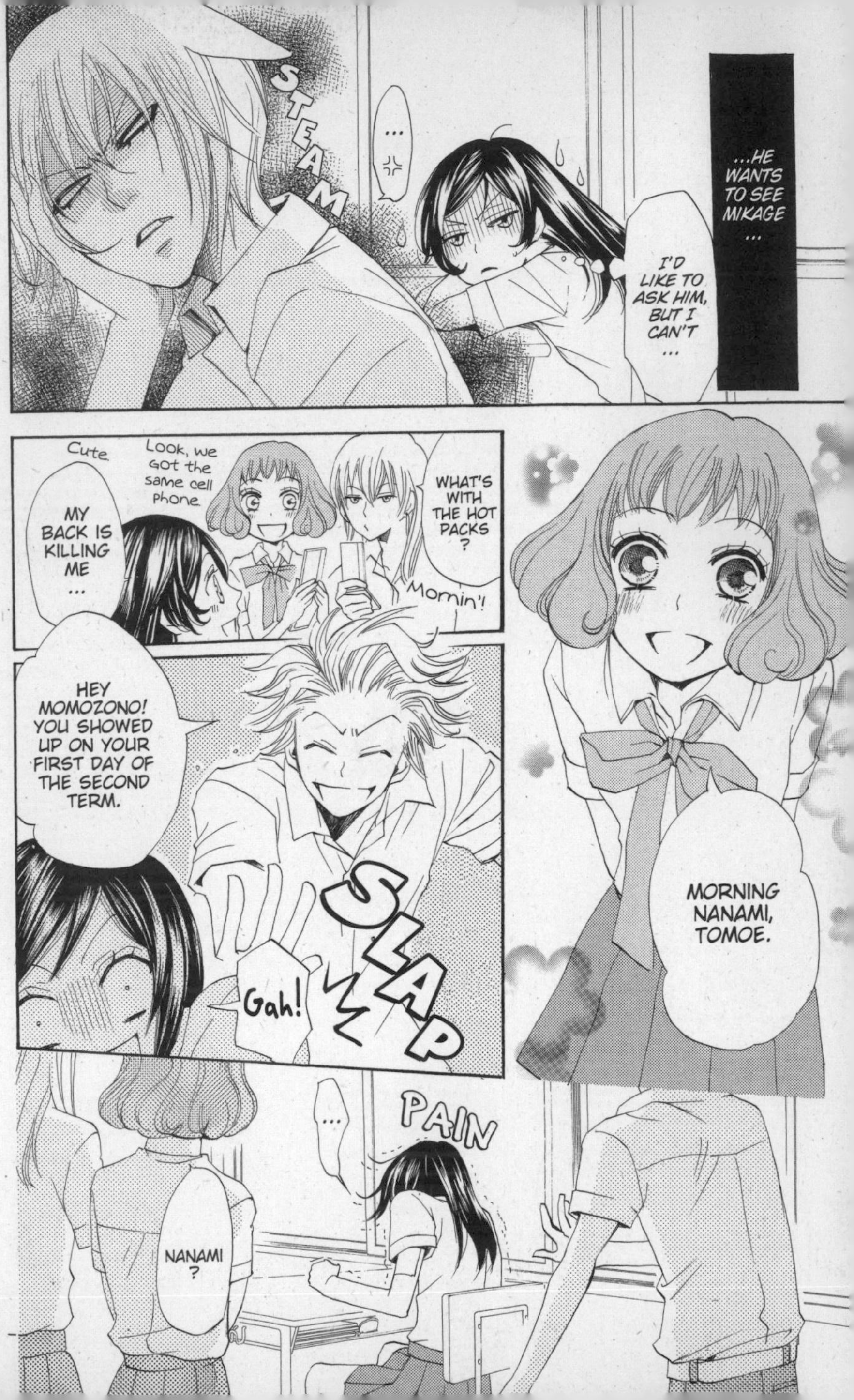
...HE WANTS TO SEE MIKAGE ...
I'D LIKE TO ASK HIM, BUT I CAN'T ...
...
STEAM
MORNING NANAMI, TOMOE.
WHAT'S WITH THE HOT PACKS ?
Mornin'!
Look, we got the same cell phone.
Cute.
MY BACK IS KILLING ME ...
HEY MOMOZONO! YOU SHOWED UP ON YOUR FIRST DAY OF THE SECOND TERM.
SLAP
Gah!
PAIN
...
NANAMI ?

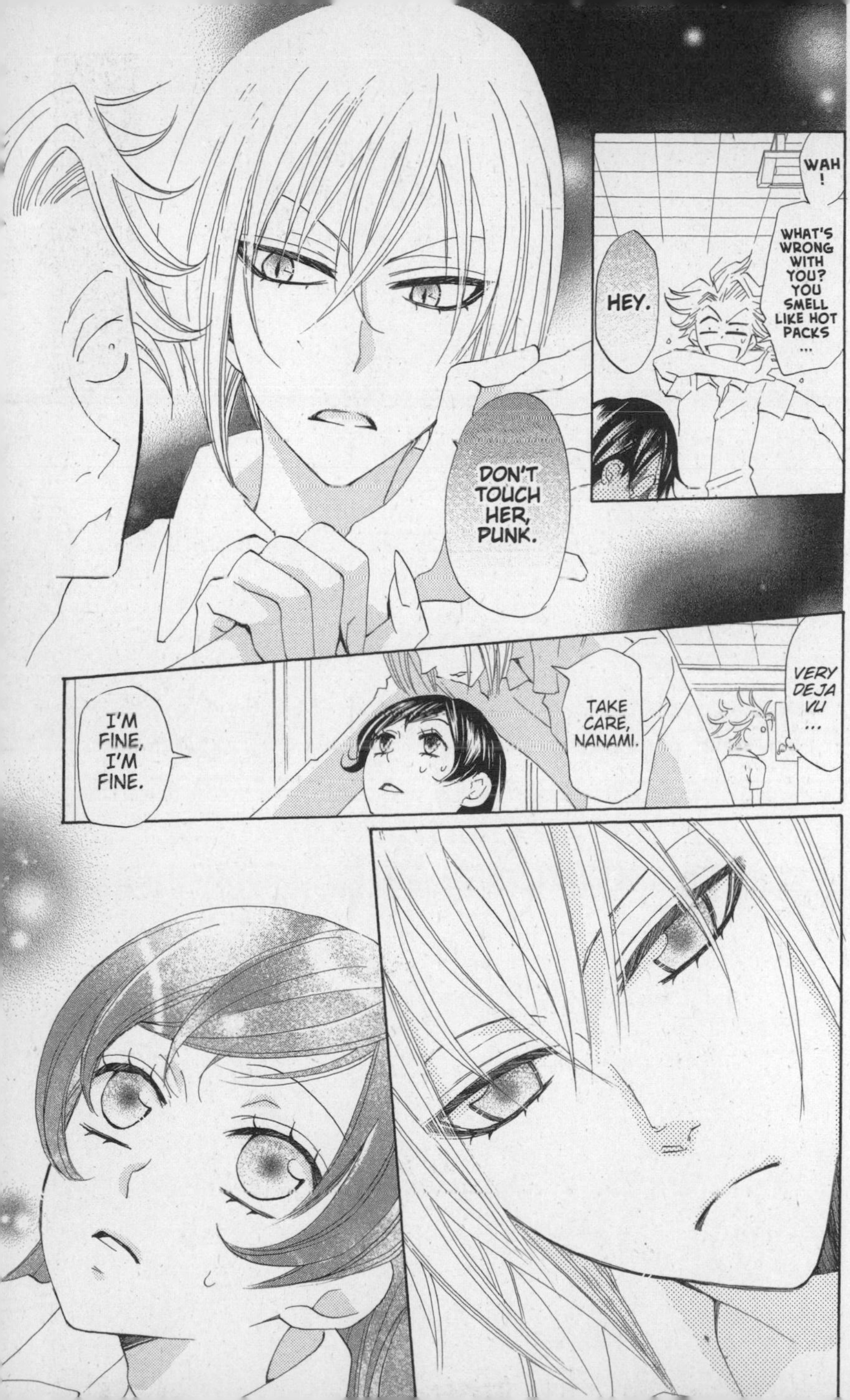
WAH!
WHAT'S WRONG WITH YOU? YOU SMELL LIKE HOT PACKS...
HEY.
DON'T TOUCH HER, PUNK.
VERY DEJA VU...
TAKE CARE, NANAMI.
I'M FINE, I'M FINE.

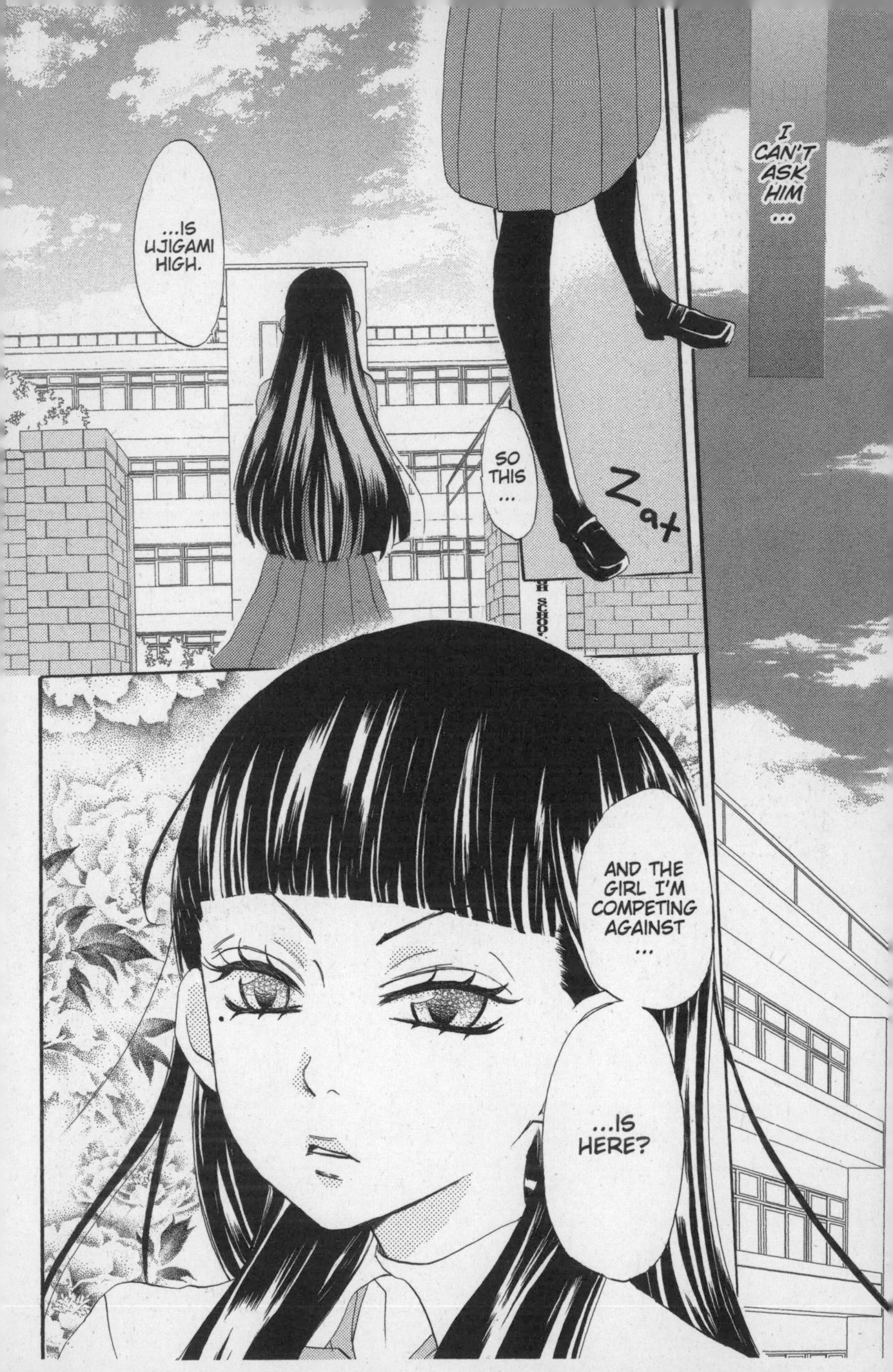
I CAN'T ASK HIM ...
SO THIS ...
Zax
...IS UJIGAMI HIGH.
AND THE GIRL I'M COMPETING AGAINST ...
...IS HERE?

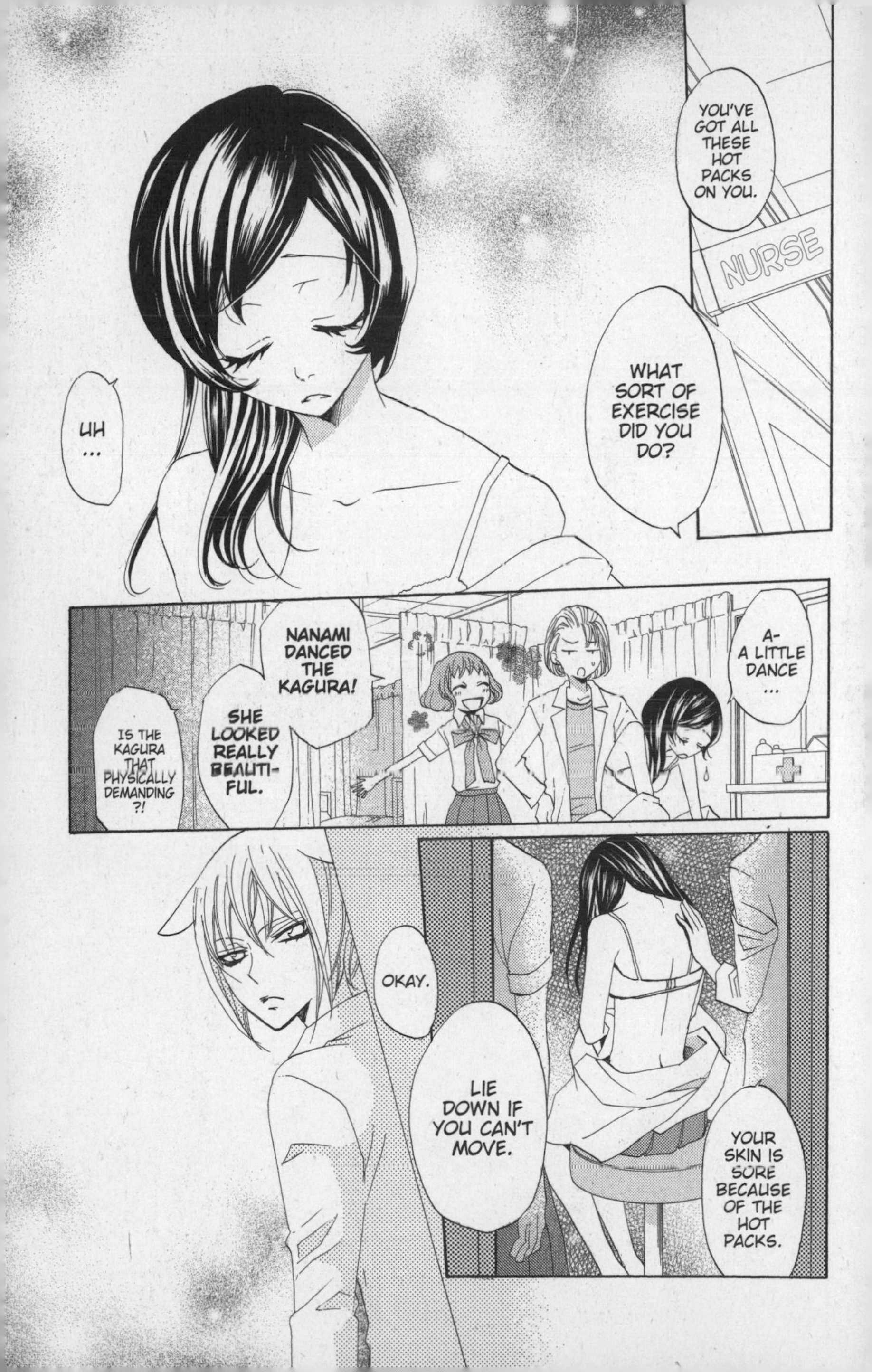
YOU'VE GOT ALL THESE HOT PACKS ON YOU.
NURSE
WHAT SORT OF EXERCISE DID YOU DO?
UH ...
A- A LITTLE DANCE ...
NANAMI DANCED THE KAGURA!
SHE LOOKED REALLY BEAUTI-FUL.
IS THE KAGURA THAT PHYSICALLY DEMANDING ?!
YOUR SKIN IS SORE BECAUSE OF THE HOT PACKS.
LIE DOWN IF YOU CAN'T MOVE.
OKAY.

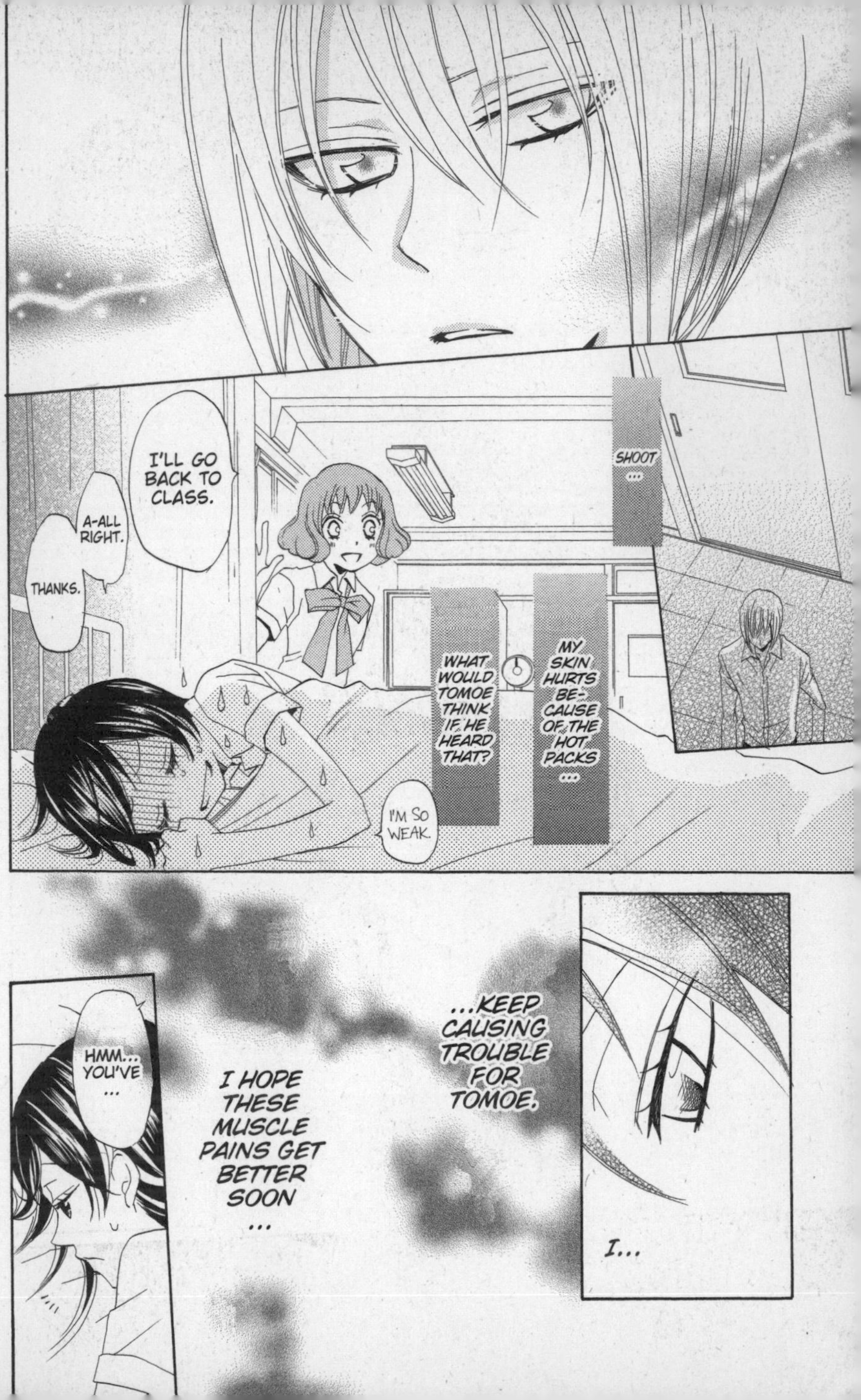
SHOOT...
MY SKIN HURTS BE-CAUSE OF THE HOT PACKS...
WHAT WOULD TOMOE THINK IF HE HEARD THAT?
I'LL GO BACK TO CLASS.
A-ALL RIGHT.
THANKS.
I'M SO WEAK.
I...
...KEEP CAUSING TROUBLE FOR TOMOE.
I HOPE THESE MUSCLE PAINS GET BETTER SOON...
HMM... YOU'VE...

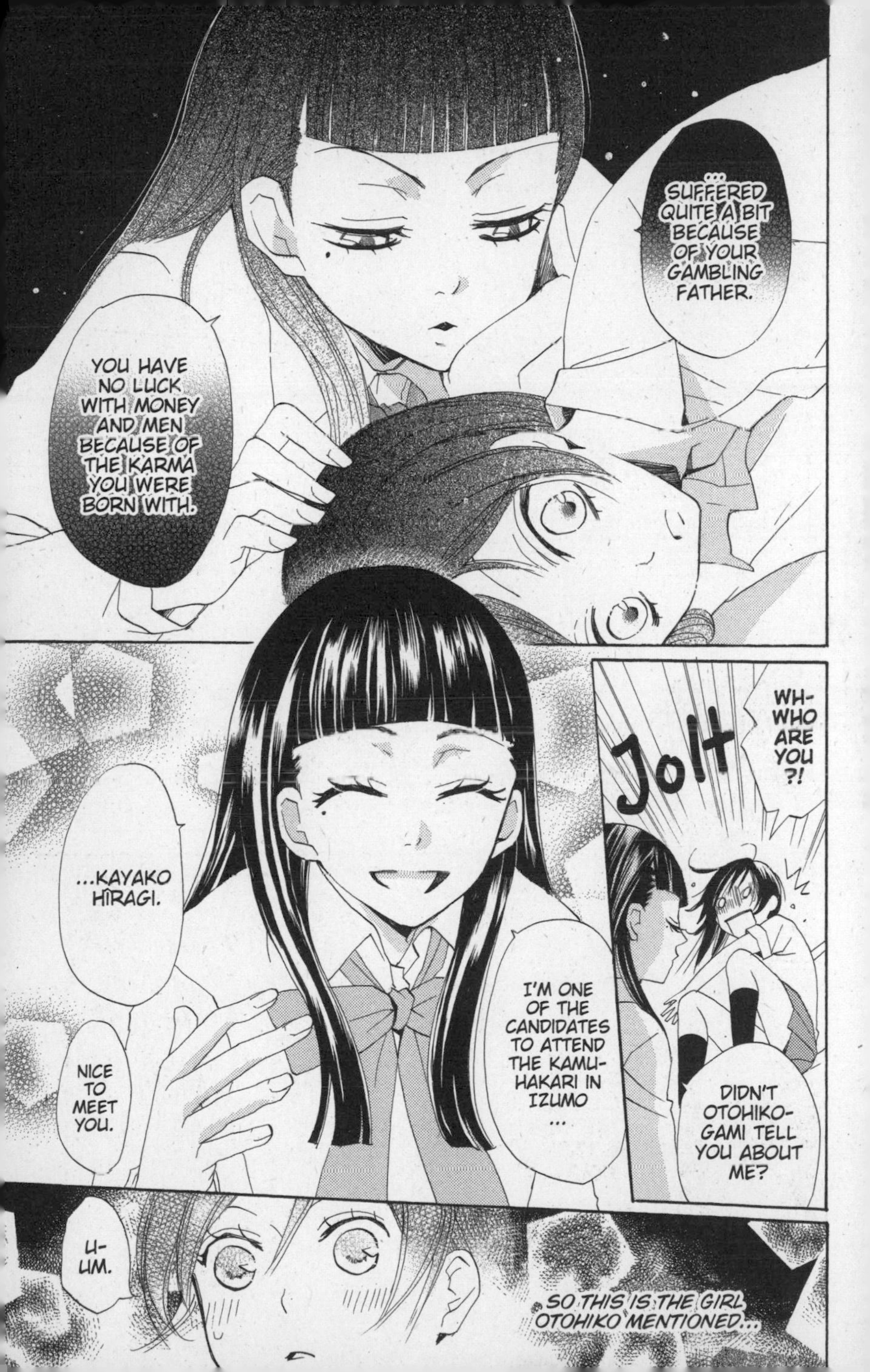
...SUFFERED QUITE A BIT BECAUSE OF YOUR GAMBLING FATHER.
YOU HAVE NO LUCK WITH MONEY AND MEN BECAUSE OF THE KARMA YOU WERE BORN WITH.
Jolt
WH-WHO ARE YOU?!
DIDN'T OTOHIKO-GAMI TELL YOU ABOUT ME?
I'M ONE OF THE CANDIDATES TO ATTEND THE KAMU-HAKARI IN IZUMO...
...KAYAKO HĪRAGI.
NICE TO MEET YOU.
U-UM.
SO THIS IS THE GIRL OTOHIKO MENTIONED...

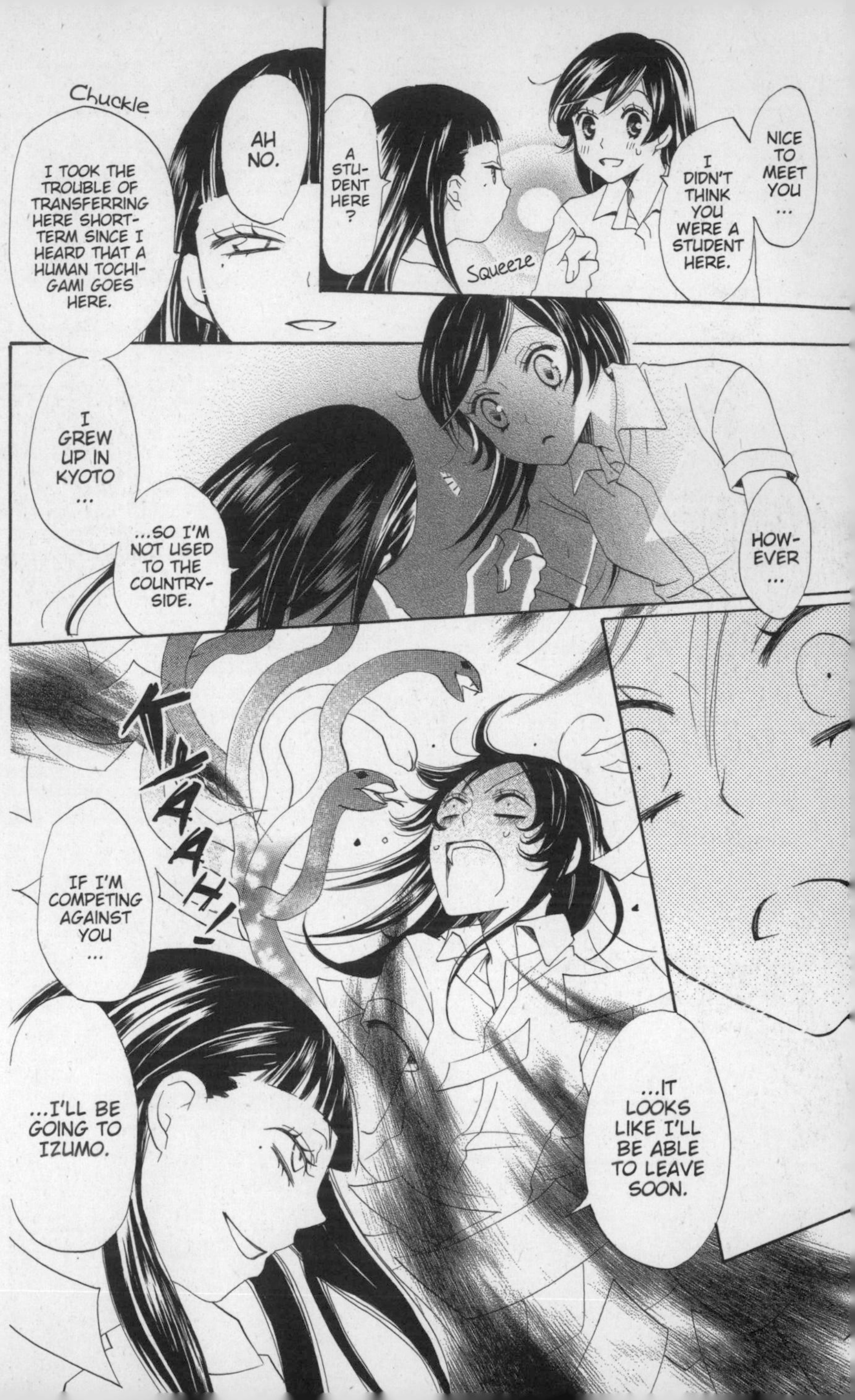
NICE TO MEET YOU ...
I DIDN'T THINK YOU WERE A STUDENT HERE.
Squeeze
A STUDENT HERE?
AH NO.
Chuckle
I TOOK THE TROUBLE OF TRANSFERRING HERE SHORT-TERM SINCE I HEARD THAT A HUMAN TOCHIGAMI GOES HERE.
HOWEVER ...
I GREW UP IN KYOTO ...
...SO I'M NOT USED TO THE COUNTRYSIDE.
KYAAAH!
IF I'M COMPETING AGAINST YOU ...
...IT LOOKS LIKE I'LL BE ABLE TO LEAVE SOON.
...I'LL BE GOING TO IZUMO.

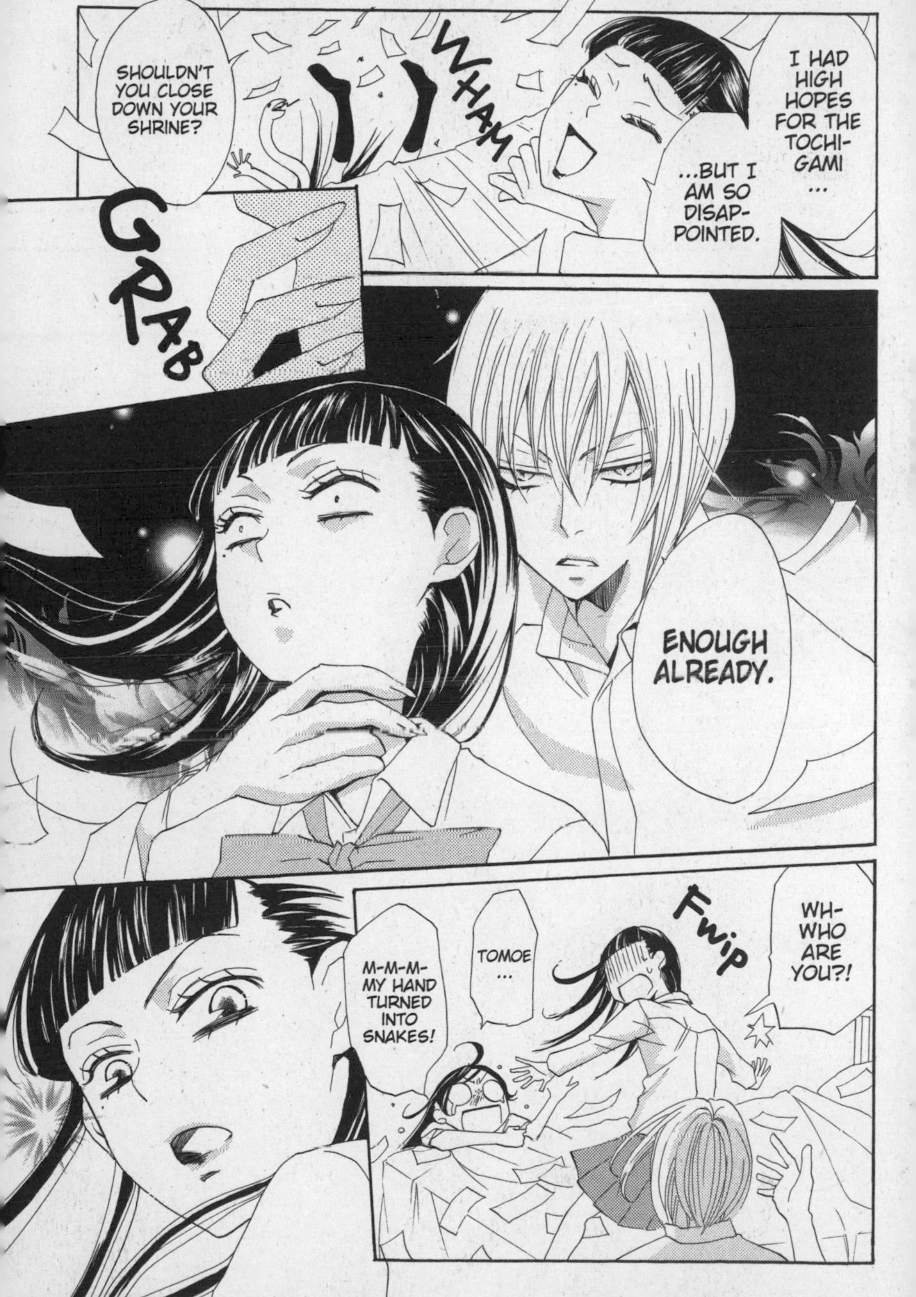
I HAD HIGH HOPES FOR THE TOCHI-GAMI ...
...BUT I AM SO DISAP-POINTED.
WHAM
SHOULDN'T YOU CLOSE DOWN YOUR SHRINE?
GRAB
ENOUGH ALREADY.
WH-WHO ARE YOU?!
Fwip
TOMOE ...
M-M-M-MY HAND TURNED INTO SNAKES!

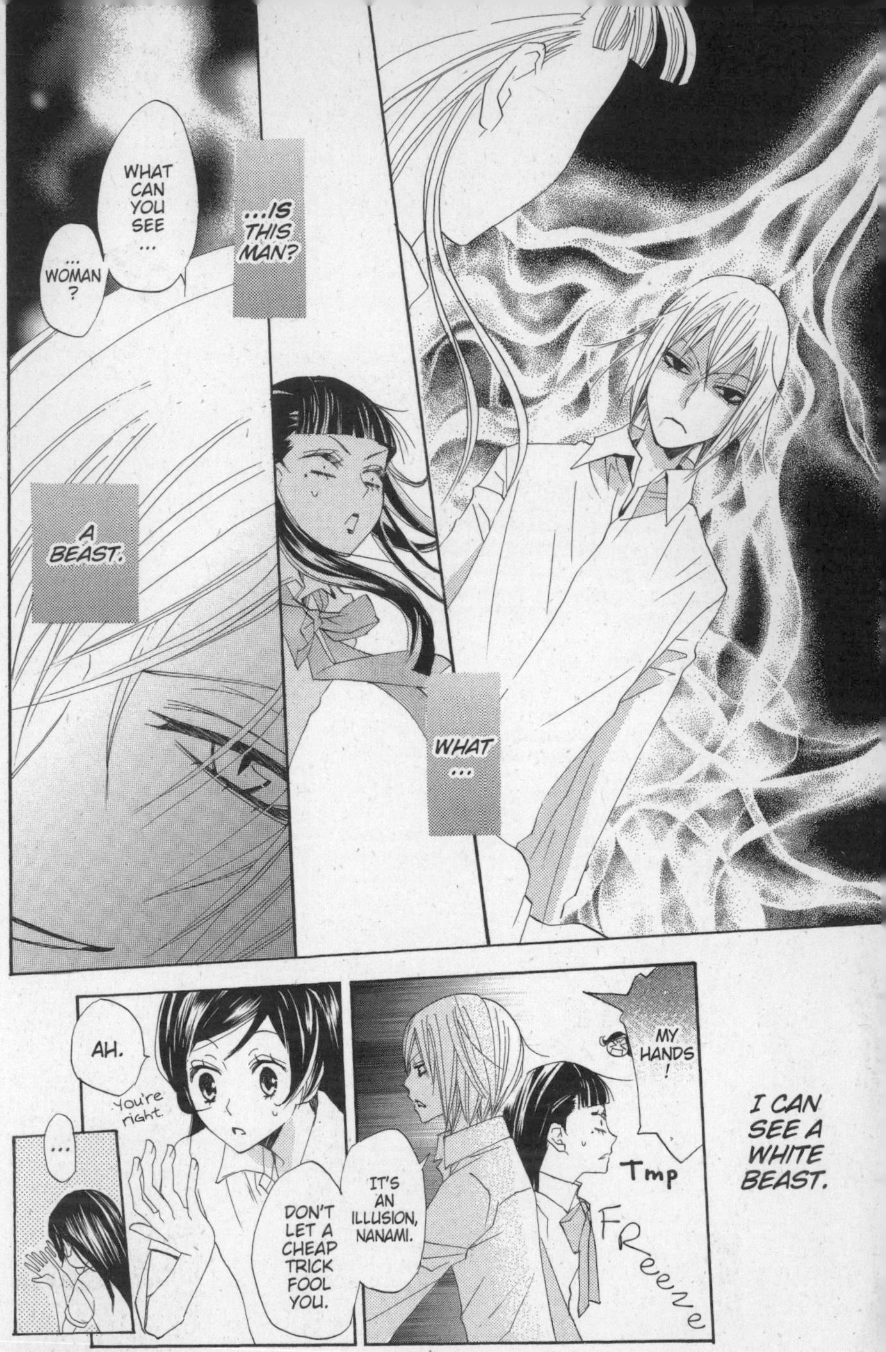
WHAT ...
...IS THIS MAN?
WHAT CAN YOU SEE ...
... WOMAN?
A BEAST.
I CAN SEE A WHITE BEAST.
MY HANDS!
Tmp
Freeze
IT'S AN ILLUSION, NANAMI.
DON'T LET A CHEAP TRICK FOOL YOU.
AH.
You're right.
...

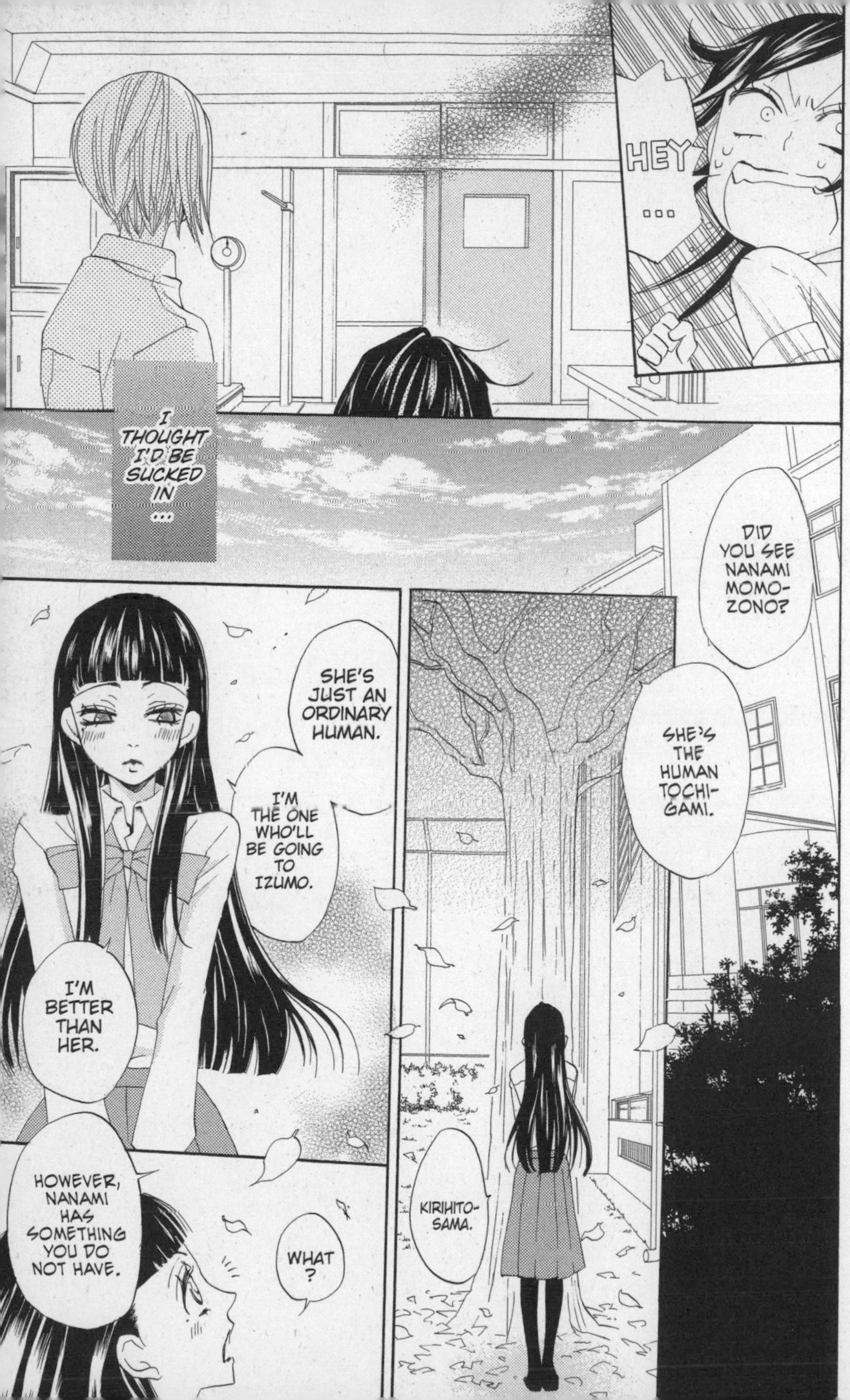
HEY
...
I THOUGHT I'D BE SUCKED IN ...
DID YOU SEE NANAMI MOMO-ZONO?
SHE'S THE HUMAN TOCHI-GAMI.
KIRIHITO-SAMA.
SHE'S JUST AN ORDINARY HUMAN.
I'M THE ONE WHO'LL BE GOING TO IZUMO.
I'M BETTER THAN HER.
HOWEVER, NANAMI HAS SOMETHING YOU DO NOT HAVE.
WHAT?

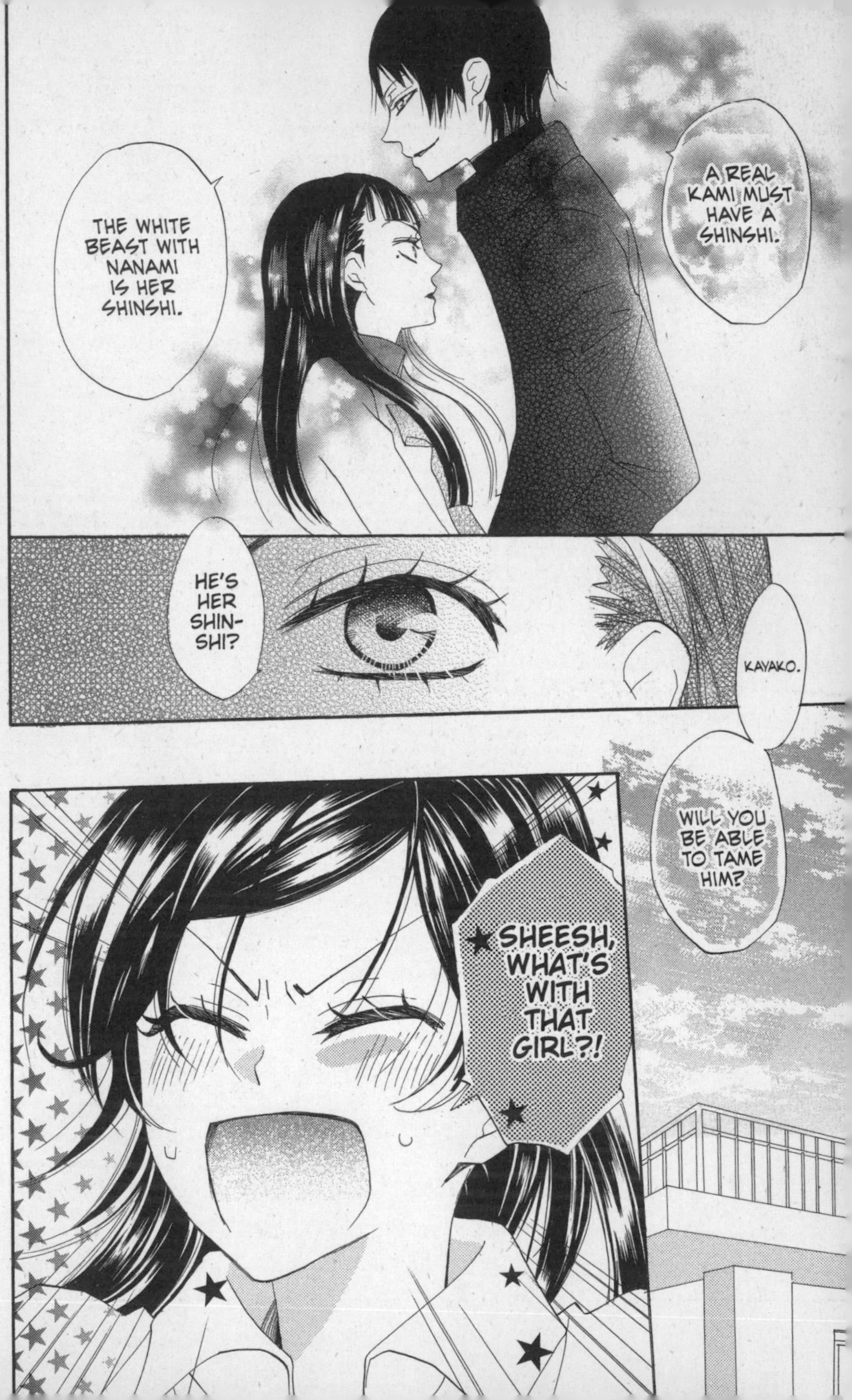
A REAL KAMI MUST HAVE A SHINSHI.
THE WHITE BEAST WITH NANAMI IS HER SHINSHI.
HE'S HER SHIN-SHI?
KAYAKO.
WILL YOU BE ABLE TO TAME HIM?
SHEESH, WHAT'S WITH THAT GIRL?!

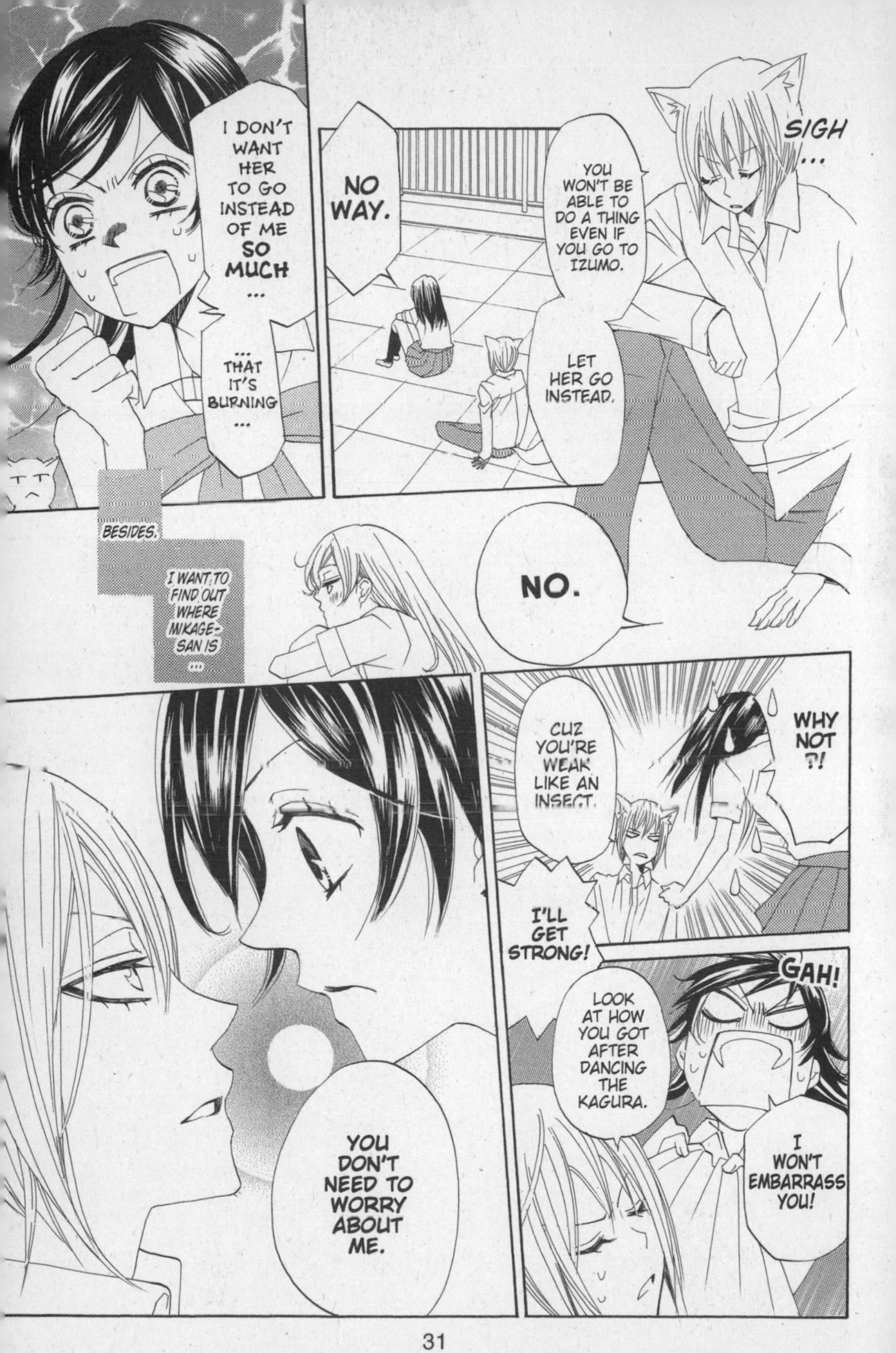
SIGH...
YOU WON'T BE ABLE TO DO A THING EVEN IF YOU GO TO IZUMO.
LET HER GO INSTEAD.
NO.
NO WAY.
I DON'T WANT HER TO GO INSTEAD OF ME SO MUCH...
...THAT IT'S BURNING...
BESIDES.
I WANT TO FIND OUT WHERE MIKAGE-SAN IS...
WHY NOT?!
CUZ YOU'RE WEAK LIKE AN INSECT.
I'LL GET STRONG!
GAH!
LOOK AT HOW YOU GOT AFTER DANCING THE KAGURA.
I WON'T EMBARRASS YOU!
YOU DON'T NEED TO WORRY ABOUT ME.

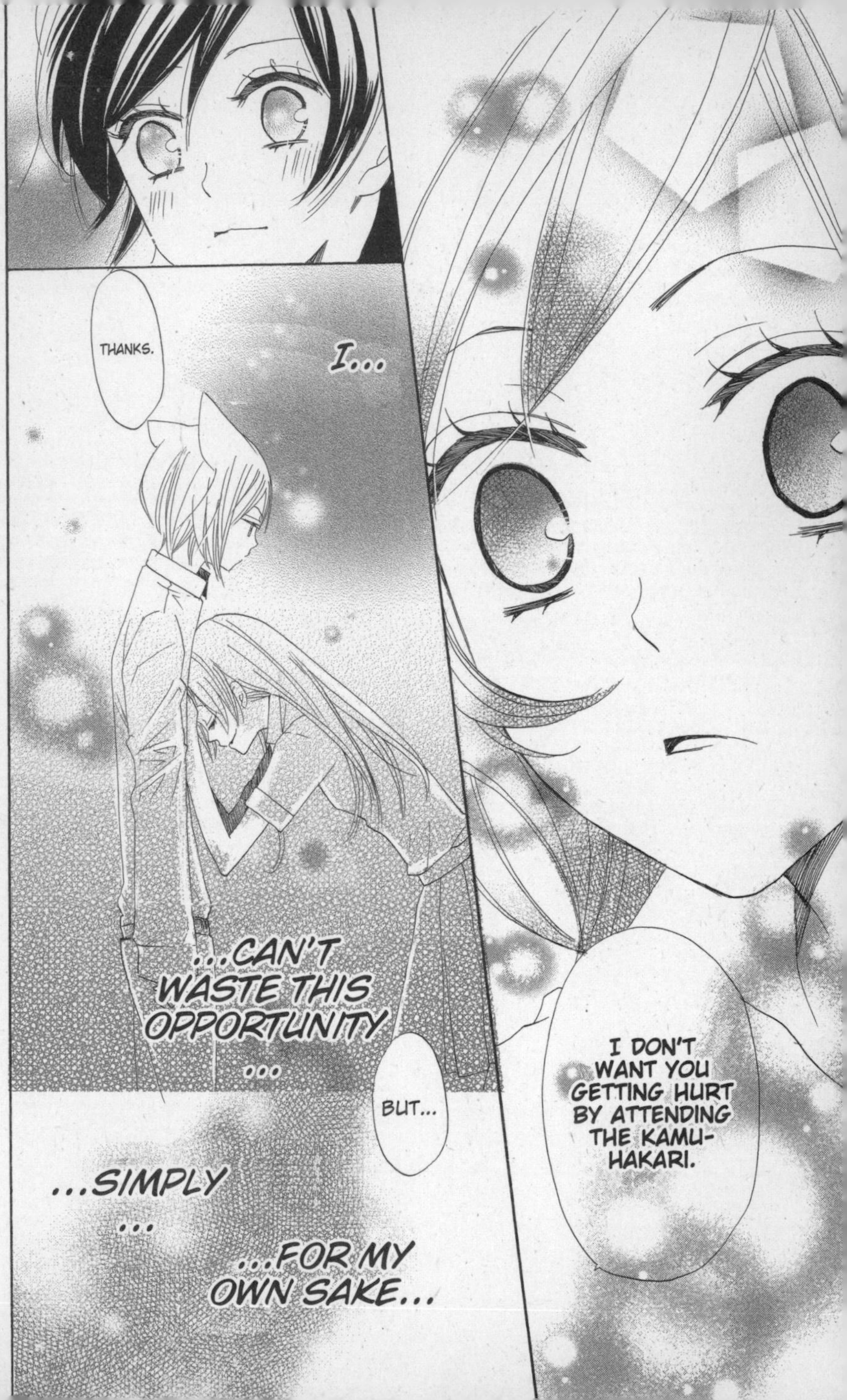
I DON'T WANT YOU GETTING HURT BY ATTENDING THE KAMU-HAKARI.
THANKS.
I...
...CAN'T WASTE THIS OPPORTUNITY...
BUT...
...SIMPLY...
...FOR MY OWN SAKE...

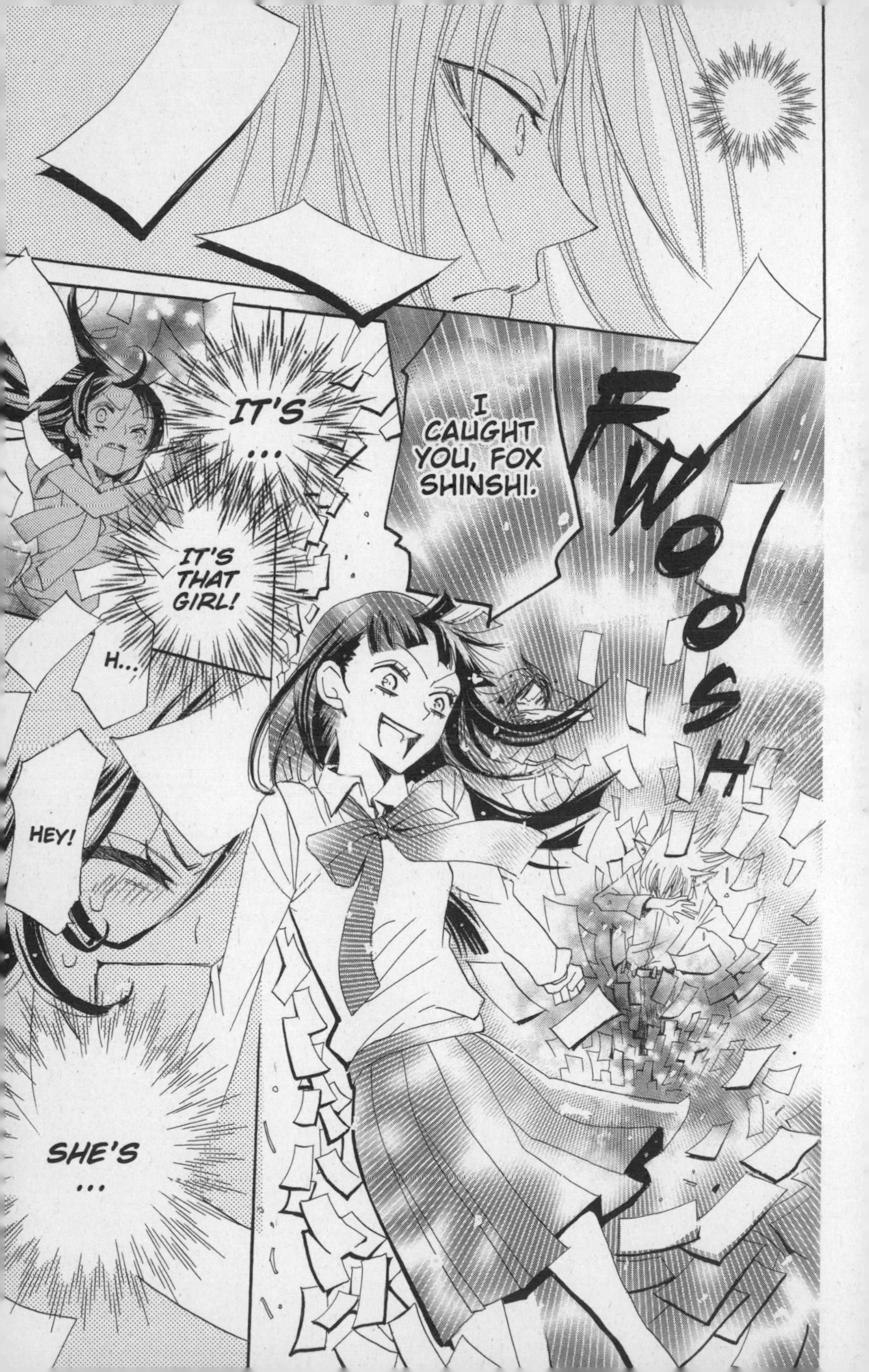
I CAUGHT YOU, FOX SHINSHI.
FWOOSH
IT'S ...
IT'S THAT GIRL!
H...
HEY!
SHE'S ...

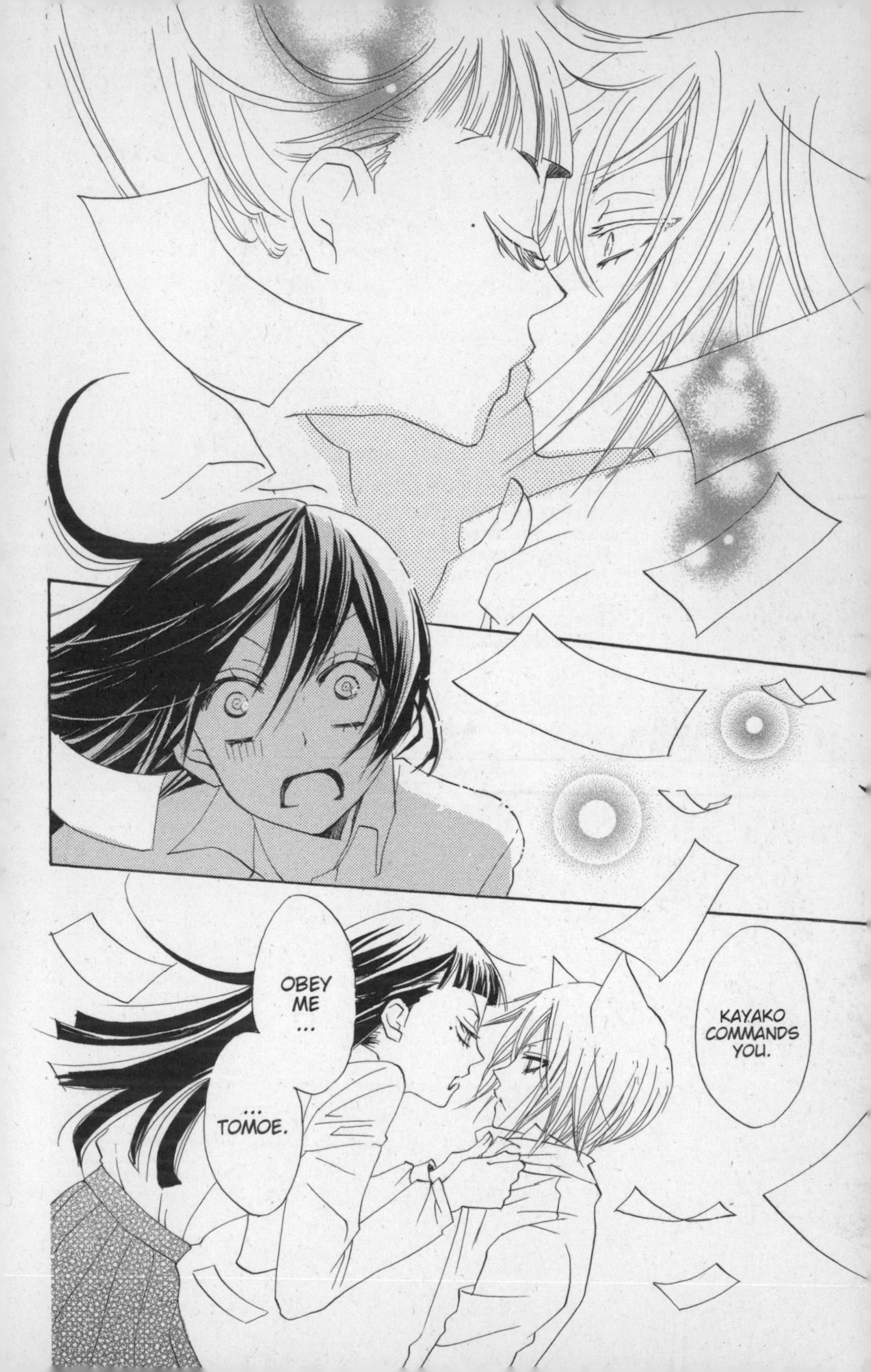
KAYAKO COMMANDS YOU.
OBEY ME ...
... TOMOE.

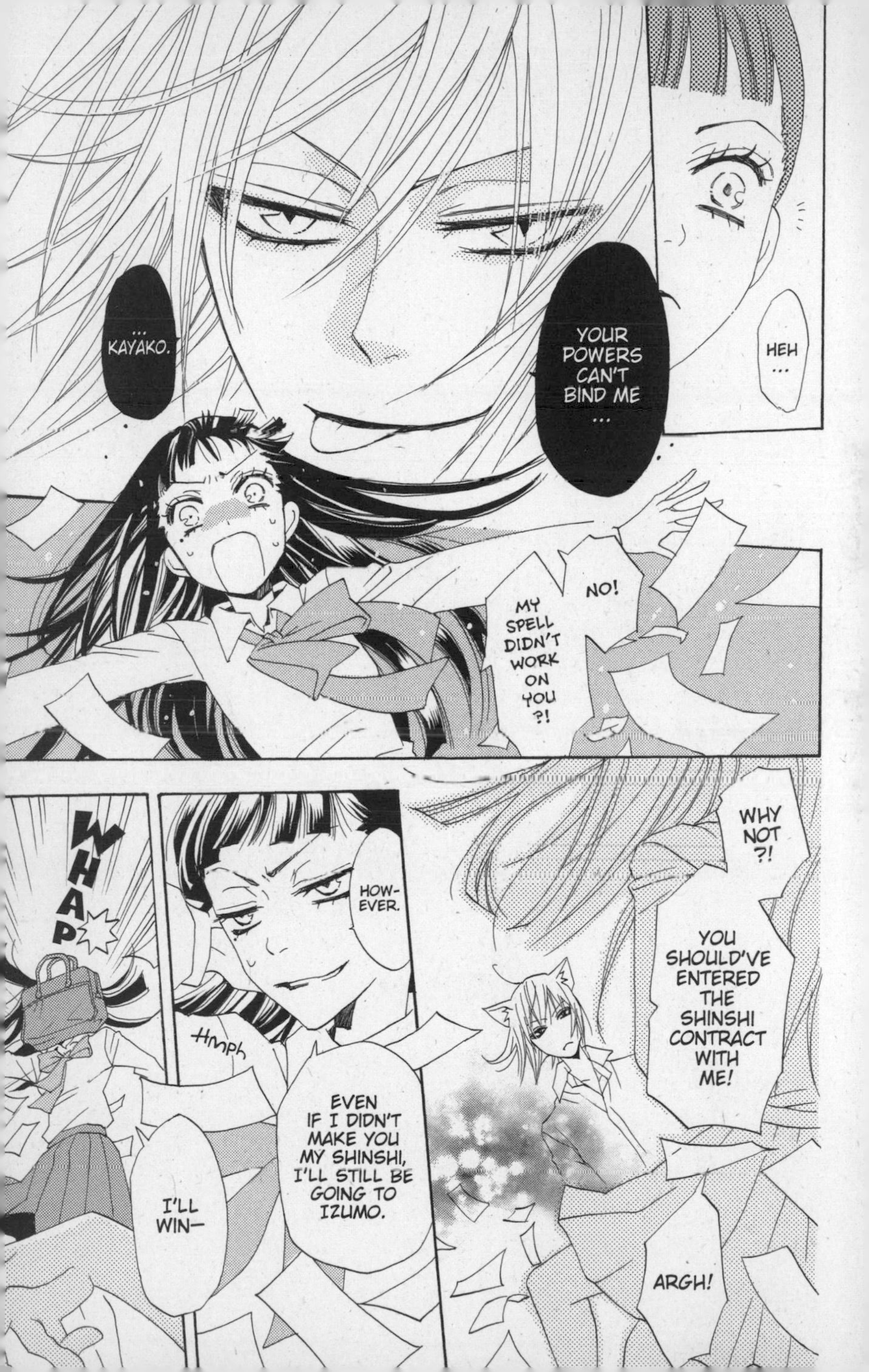
HEH...
YOUR POWERS CAN'T BIND ME...
...KAYAKO.
NO!
MY SPELL DIDN'T WORK ON YOU?!
WHY NOT?!
YOU SHOULD'VE ENTERED THE SHINSHI CONTRACT WITH ME!
ARGH!
HOW-EVER.
Hmph
EVEN IF I DIDN'T MAKE YOU MY SHINSHI, I'LL STILL BE GOING TO IZUMO.
I'LL WIN—
WHAP

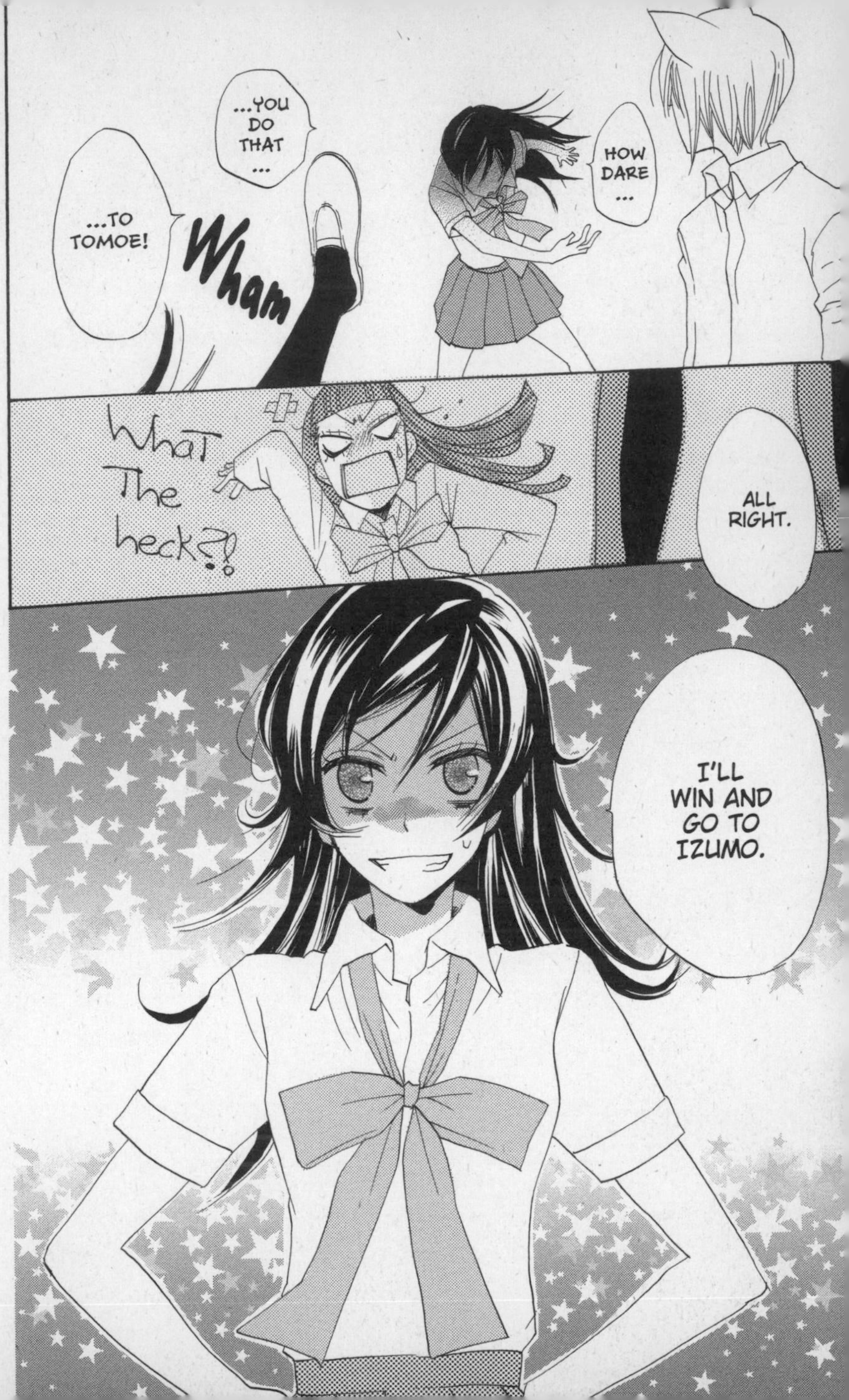
HOW DARE ...
...YOU DO THAT ...
...TO TOMOE!
Wham
ALL RIGHT.
What The heck?!
I'LL WIN AND GO TO IZUMO.

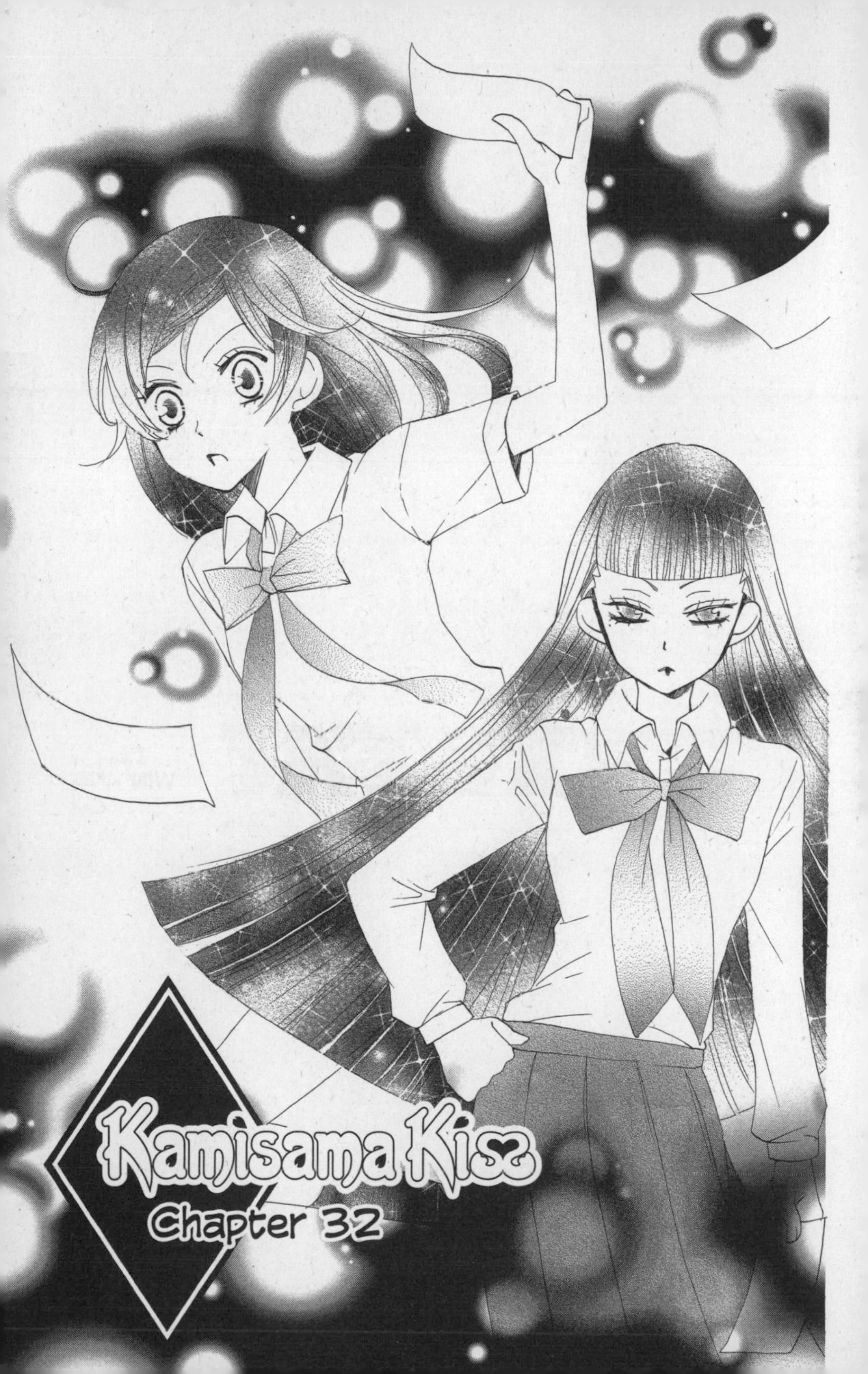
Kamisama Kiss
Chapter 32

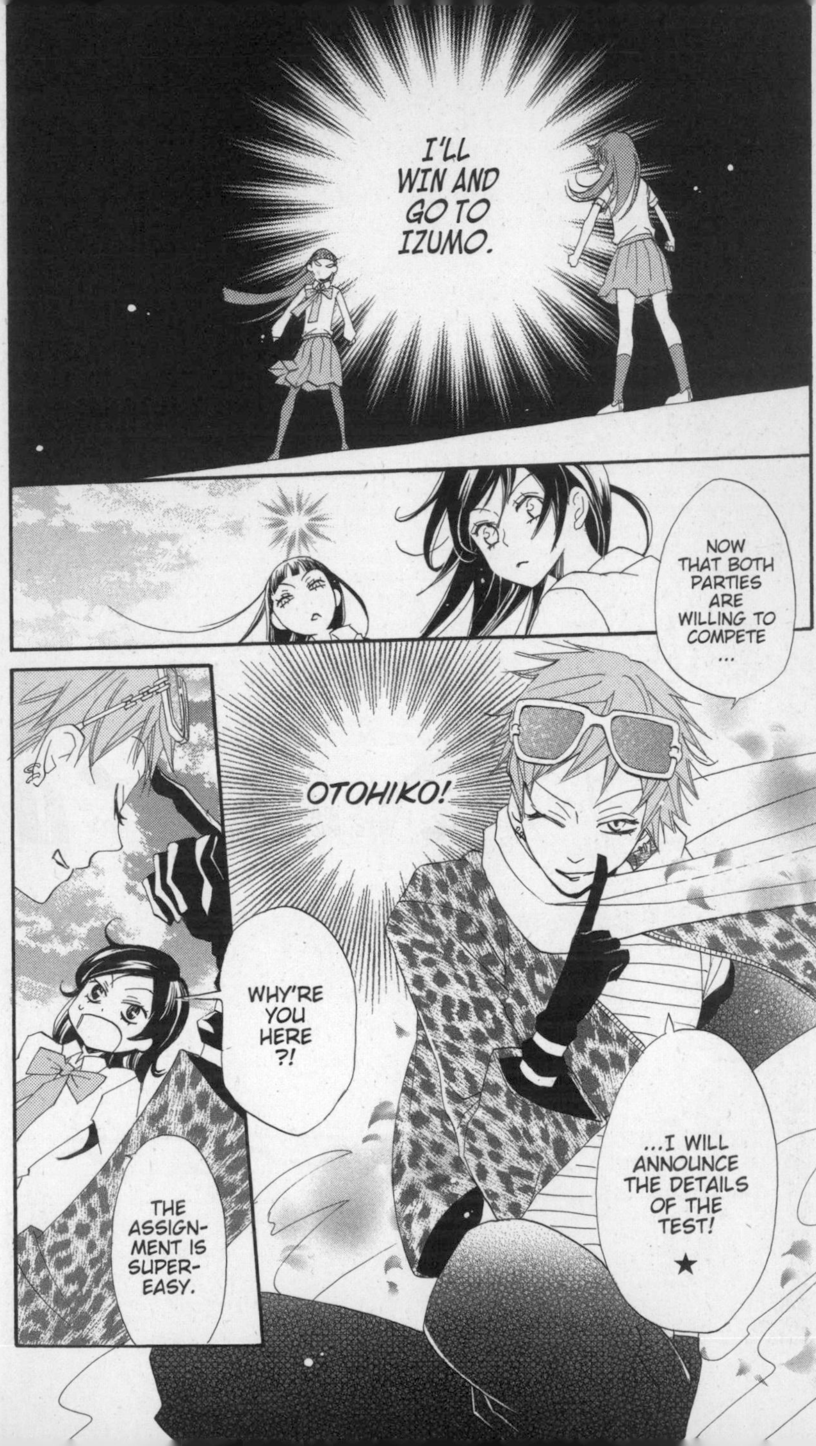
I'LL WIN AND GO TO IZUMO.
NOW THAT BOTH PARTIES ARE WILLING TO COMPETE ...
...I WILL ANNOUNCE THE DETAILS OF THE TEST! ★
OTOHIKO!
WHY'RE YOU HERE ?!
THE ASSIGNMENT IS SUPER-EASY.

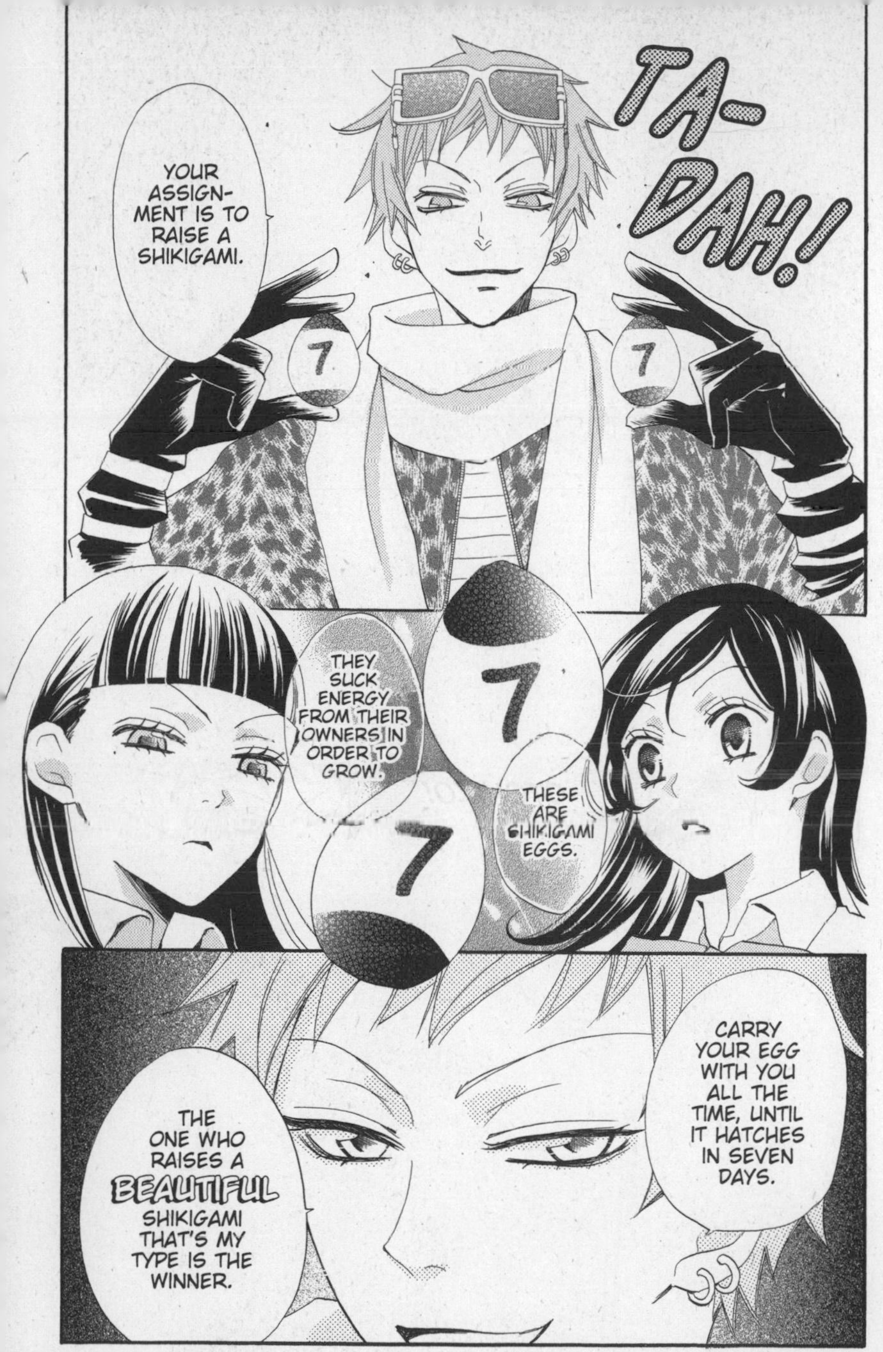
TA-DAH!
YOUR ASSIGN-MENT IS TO RAISE A SHIKIGAMI.
THESE ARE SHIKIGAMI EGGS.
THEY SUCK ENERGY FROM THEIR OWNERS IN ORDER TO GROW.
7
CARRY YOUR EGG WITH YOU ALL THE TIME, UNTIL IT HATCHES IN SEVEN DAYS.
THE ONE WHO RAISES A BEAUTIFUL SHIKIGAMI THAT'S MY TYPE IS THE WINNER.

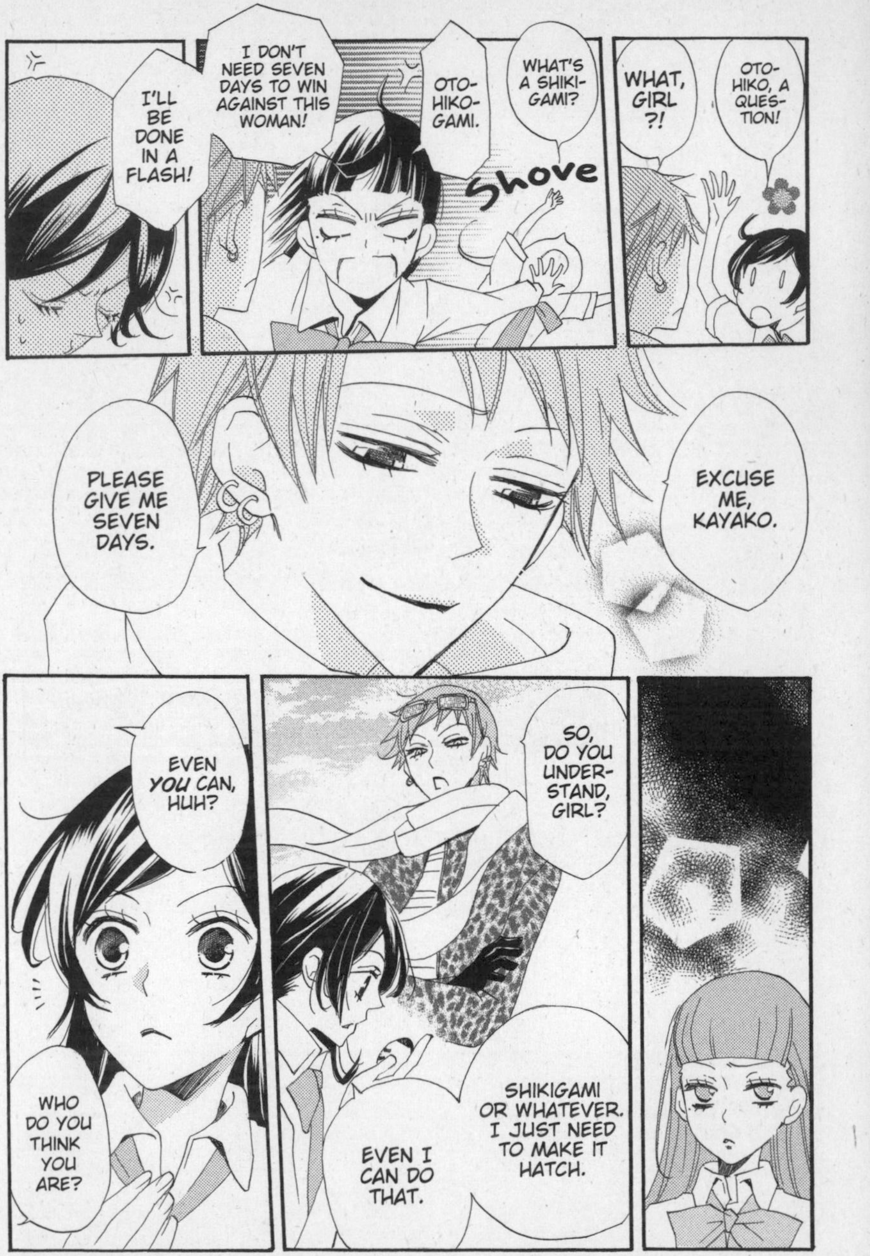
OTO-HIKO, A QUES-TION!
WHAT, GIRL ?!
WHAT'S A SHIKI-GAMI?
OTO-HIKO-GAMI.
Shove
I DON'T NEED SEVEN DAYS TO WIN AGAINST THIS WOMAN!
I'LL BE DONE IN A FLASH!
EXCUSE ME, KAYAKO.
PLEASE GIVE ME SEVEN DAYS.
SO, DO YOU UNDER-STAND, GIRL?
SHIKIGAMI OR WHATEVER. I JUST NEED TO MAKE IT HATCH.
EVEN I CAN DO THAT.
EVEN *YOU* CAN, HUH?
WHO DO YOU THINK YOU ARE?

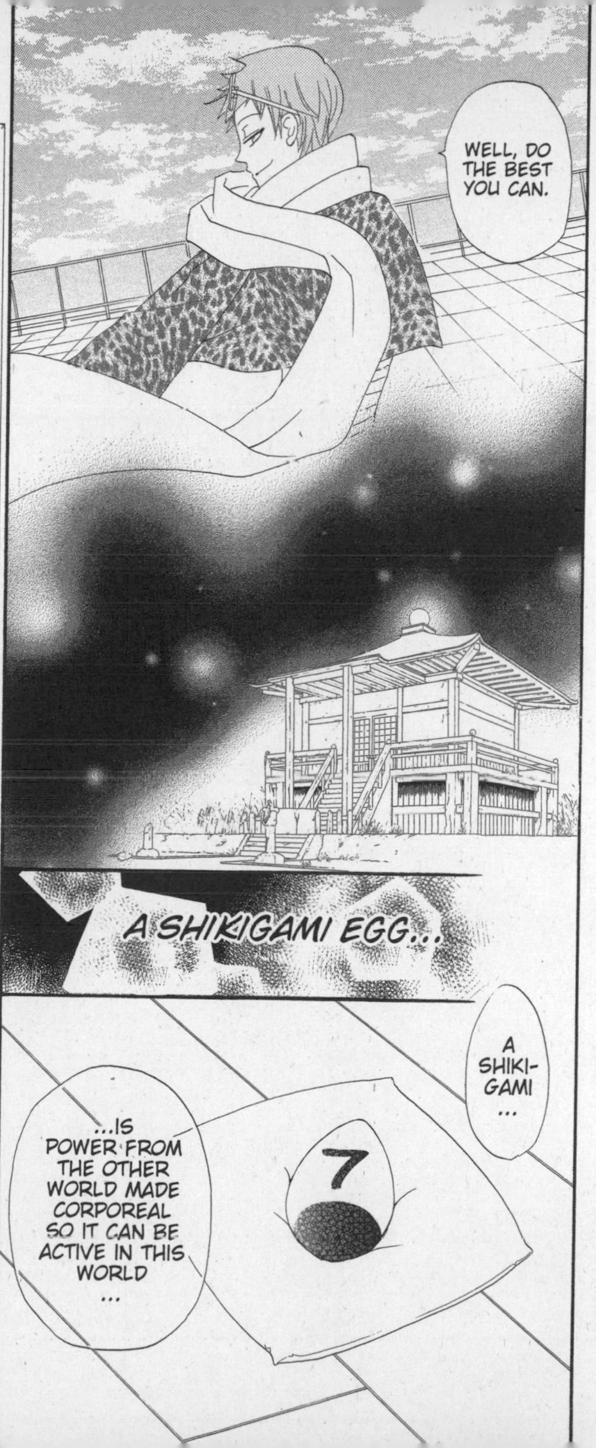
WELL, DO THE BEST YOU CAN.
A SHIKIGAMI EGG...
A SHIKI-GAMI...
...IS POWER FROM THE OTHER WORLD MADE CORPOREAL SO IT CAN BE ACTIVE IN THIS WORLD...
7

I try to write sidebars and extra pages properly for readers who follow the series in the magazine, but I always end up doing things halfway. So this time I'd like to write about the manga.

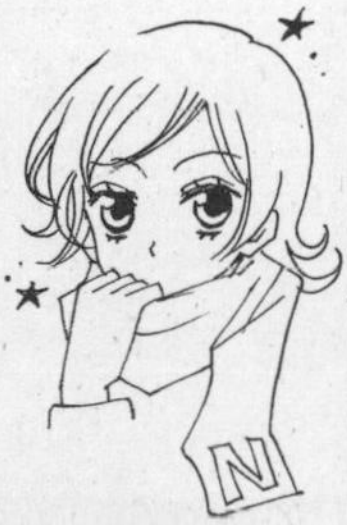
N

Nanami Momozono

I named her so girls would like her, as I heard that girls supposedly prefer the sounds M and N. Nanami Momozono contains lots of Ms and Ns! Kamisama Kiss has taught me that female characters are no good unless I'm trying to draw them cutely. Oh my.

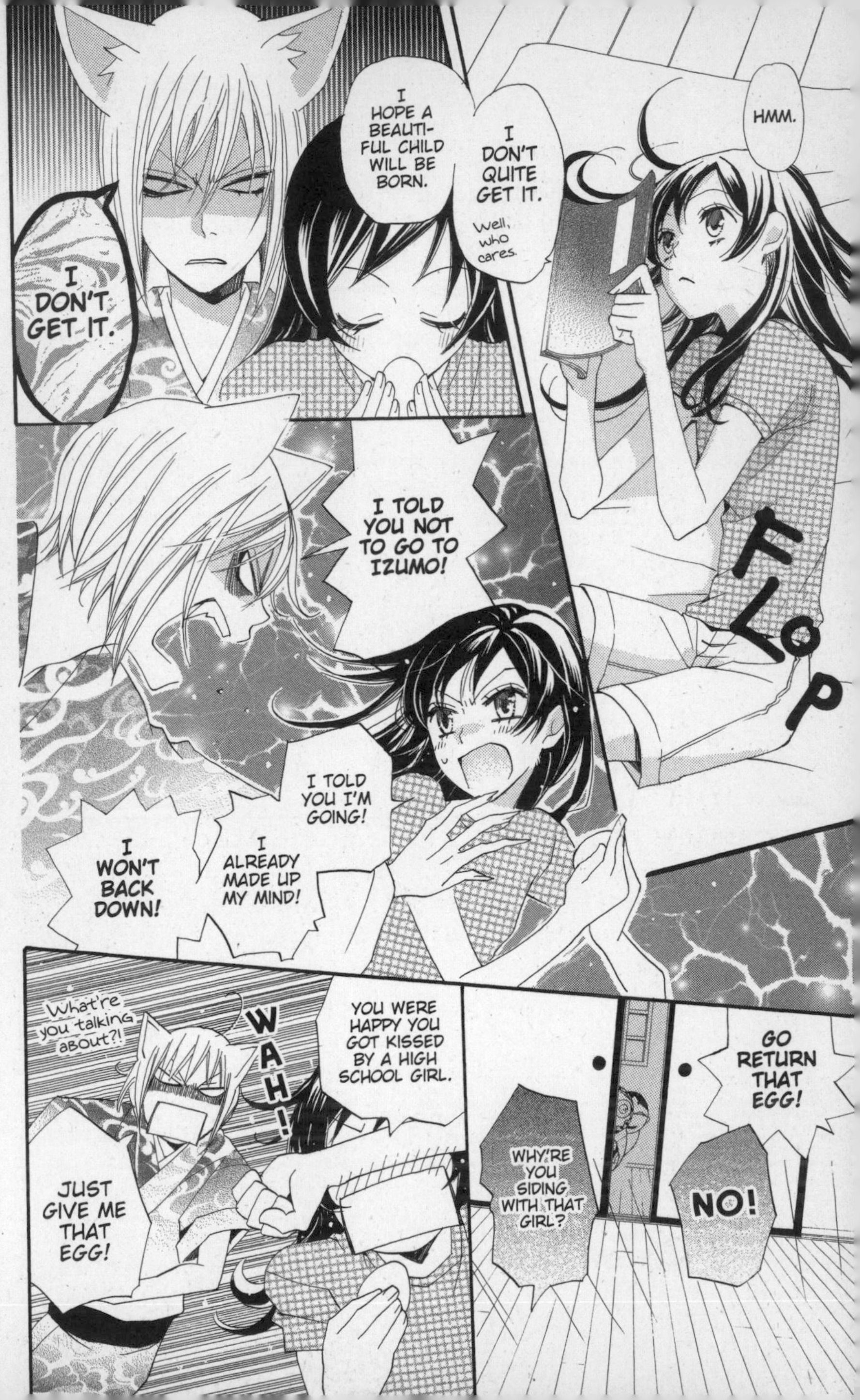
HMM.
FLOP
I HOPE A BEAUTIFUL CHILD WILL BE BORN.
I DON'T QUITE GET IT.
Well, who cares.
I DON'T GET IT.
I TOLD YOU NOT TO GO TO IZUMO!
I TOLD YOU I'M GOING!
I ALREADY MADE UP MY MIND!
I WON'T BACK DOWN!
GO RETURN THAT EGG!
NO!
WHY'RE YOU SIDING WITH THAT GIRL?
YOU WERE HAPPY YOU GOT KISSED BY A HIGH SCHOOL GIRL.
WAH!
What're you talking about?!
JUST GIVE ME THAT EGG!

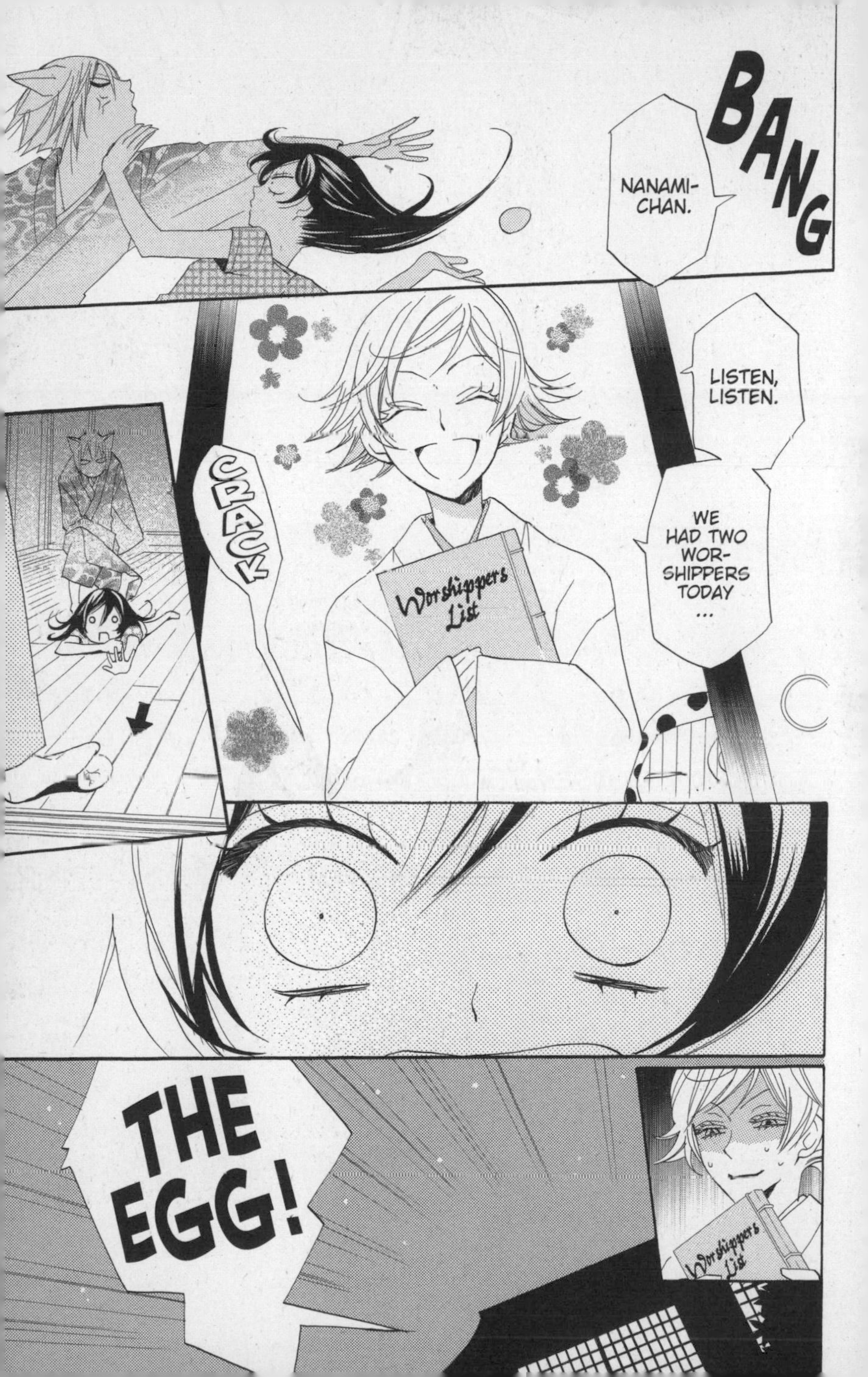
BANG
NANAMI-CHAN.
LISTEN, LISTEN.
WE HAD TWO WOR-SHIPPERS TODAY ...
Worshippers List
CRACK
Worshippers List
THE EGG!

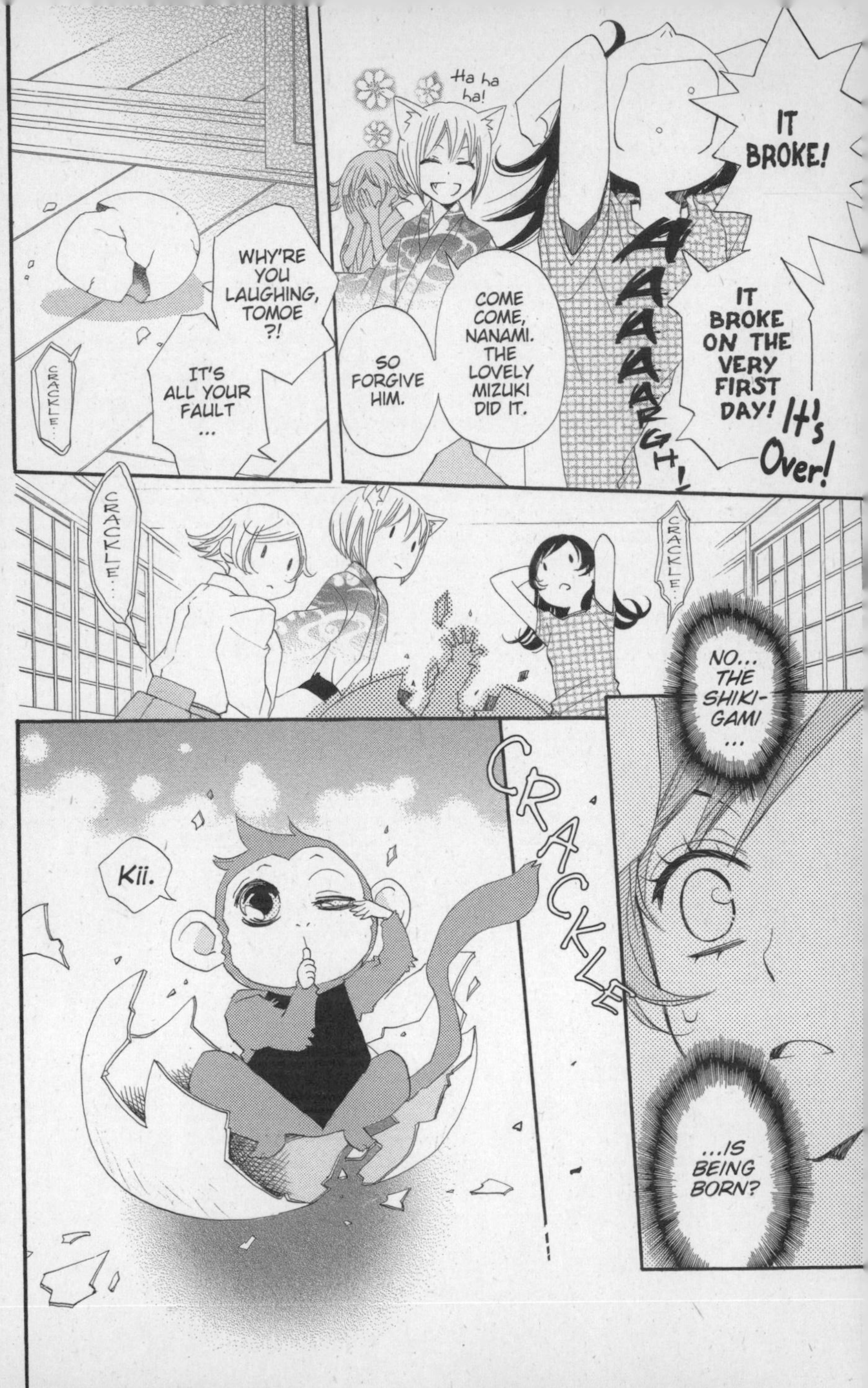
IT BROKE!
AAAAAARGH!
IT BROKE ON THE VERY FIRST DAY!
It's Over!
Ha ha ha!
COME COME, NANAMI. THE LOVELY MIZUKI DID IT.
SO FORGIVE HIM.
WHY'RE YOU LAUGHING, TOMOE?!
IT'S ALL YOUR FAULT...
CRACKLE...
CRACKLE...
CRACKLE...
NO... THE SHIKIGAMI...
...IS BEING BORN?
CRACKLE
Kii.

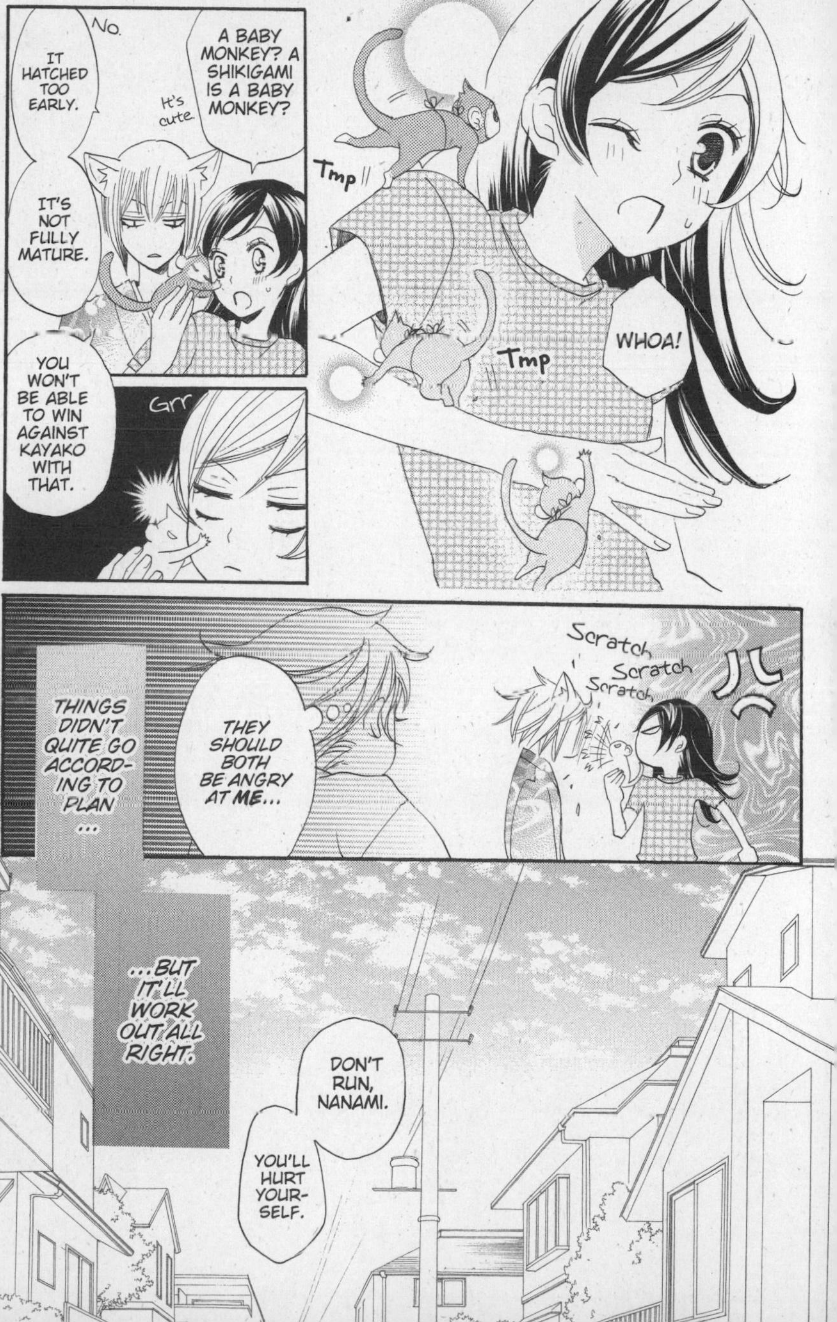
Tmp
WHOA!
Tmp
A BABY MONKEY? A SHIKIGAMI IS A BABY MONKEY?
It's cute.
No.
IT HATCHED TOO EARLY.
IT'S NOT FULLY MATURE.
YOU WON'T BE ABLE TO WIN AGAINST KAYAKO WITH THAT.
Grr
Scratch
Scratch
Scratch
THEY SHOULD BOTH BE ANGRY AT ME...
THINGS DIDN'T QUITE GO ACCORD-ING TO PLAN ...
...BUT IT'LL WORK OUT ALL RIGHT.
DON'T RUN, NANAMI.
YOU'LL HURT YOUR-SELF.

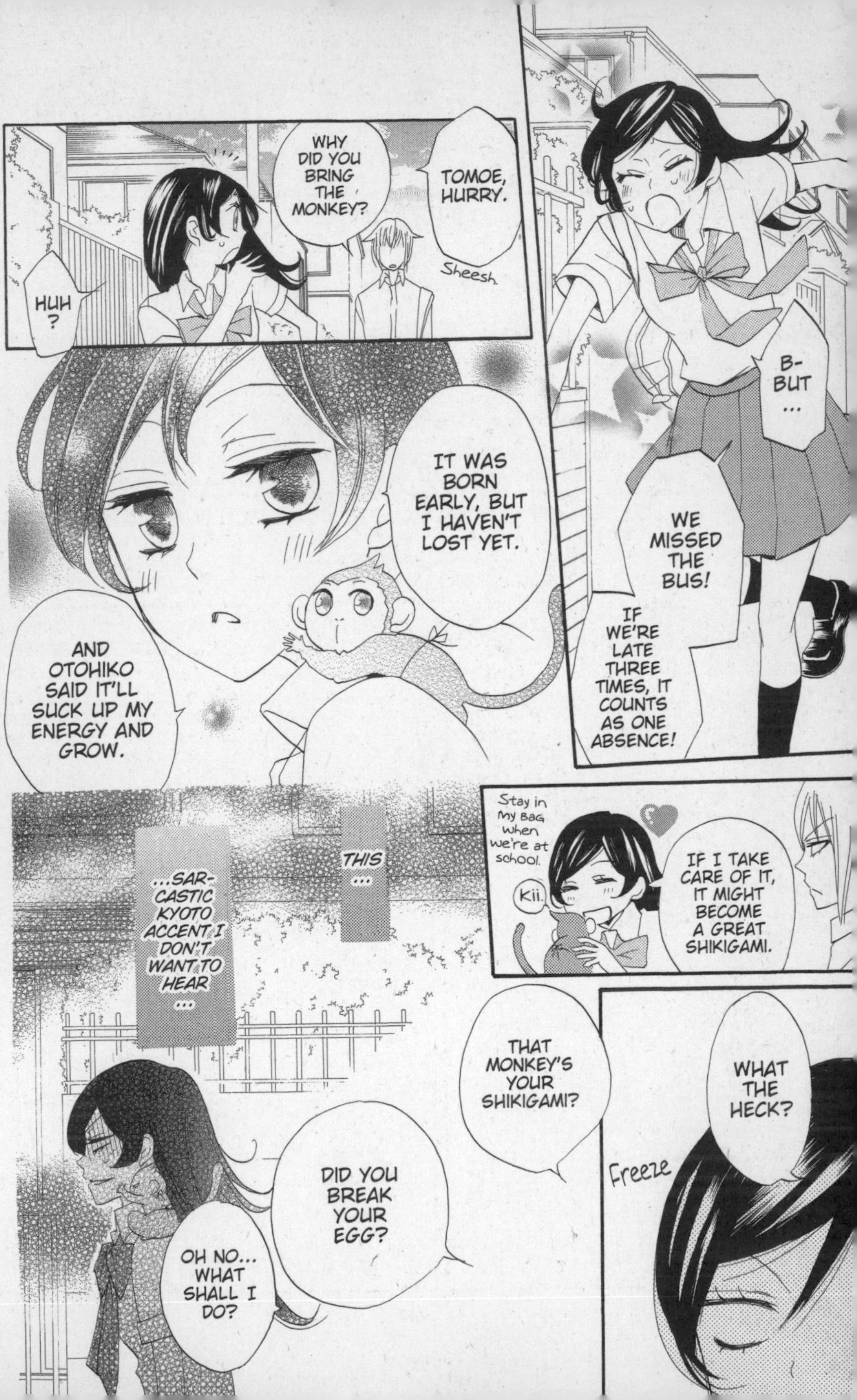

B-BUT ...
WE MISSED THE BUS!
IF WE'RE LATE THREE TIMES, IT COUNTS AS ONE ABSENCE!
TOMOE, HURRY.
WHY DID YOU BRING THE MONKEY?
Sheesh.
HUH?
IT WAS BORN EARLY, BUT I HAVEN'T LOST YET.
AND OTOHIKO SAID IT'LL SUCK UP MY ENERGY AND GROW.
Stay in my bag when we're at school.
IF I TAKE CARE OF IT, IT MIGHT BECOME A GREAT SHIKIGAMI.
Kii.
WHAT THE HECK?
THAT MONKEY'S YOUR SHIKIGAMI?
Freeze
THIS ...
...SAR-CASTIC KYOTO ACCENT I DON'T WANT TO HEAR ...
DID YOU BREAK YOUR EGG?
OH NO... WHAT SHALL I DO?

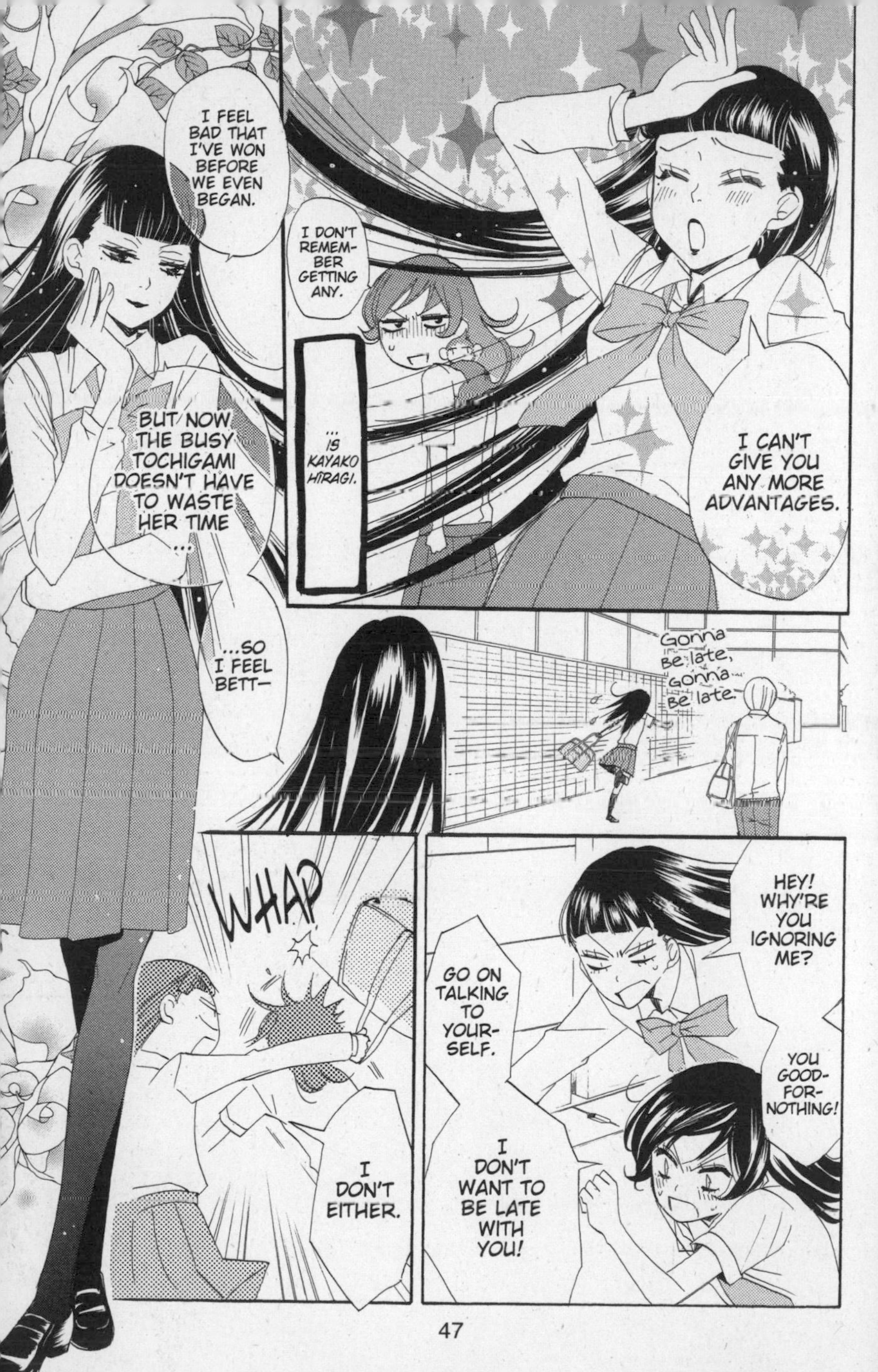
I CAN'T GIVE YOU ANY MORE ADVANTAGES.
I DON'T REMEMBER GETTING ANY.
...IS KAYAKO HIRAGI.
Gonna be late, gonna be late.
HEY! WHY'RE YOU IGNORING ME?
GO ON TALKING TO YOURSELF.
YOU GOOD-FOR-NOTHING!
I DON'T WANT TO BE LATE WITH YOU!
WHAP
I DON'T EITHER.
I FEEL BAD THAT I'VE WON BEFORE WE EVEN BEGAN.
BUT NOW THE BUSY TOCHIGAMI DOESN'T HAVE TO WASTE HER TIME...
...SO I FEEL BETT-

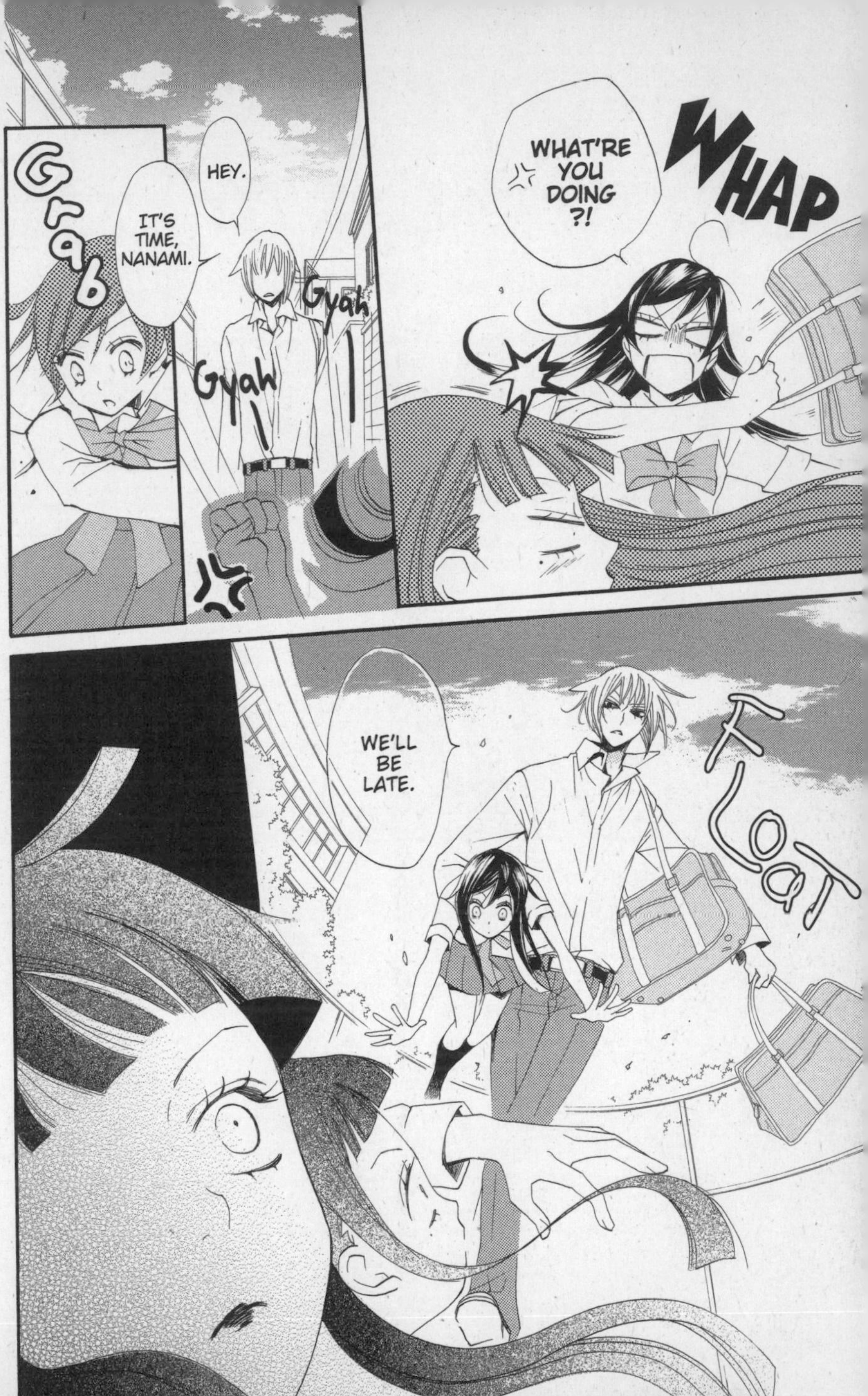
WHAP
WHAT'RE YOU DOING?!
HEY.
Gyah
Gyah
Grab
IT'S TIME, NANAMI.
WE'LL BE LATE.
FLoat

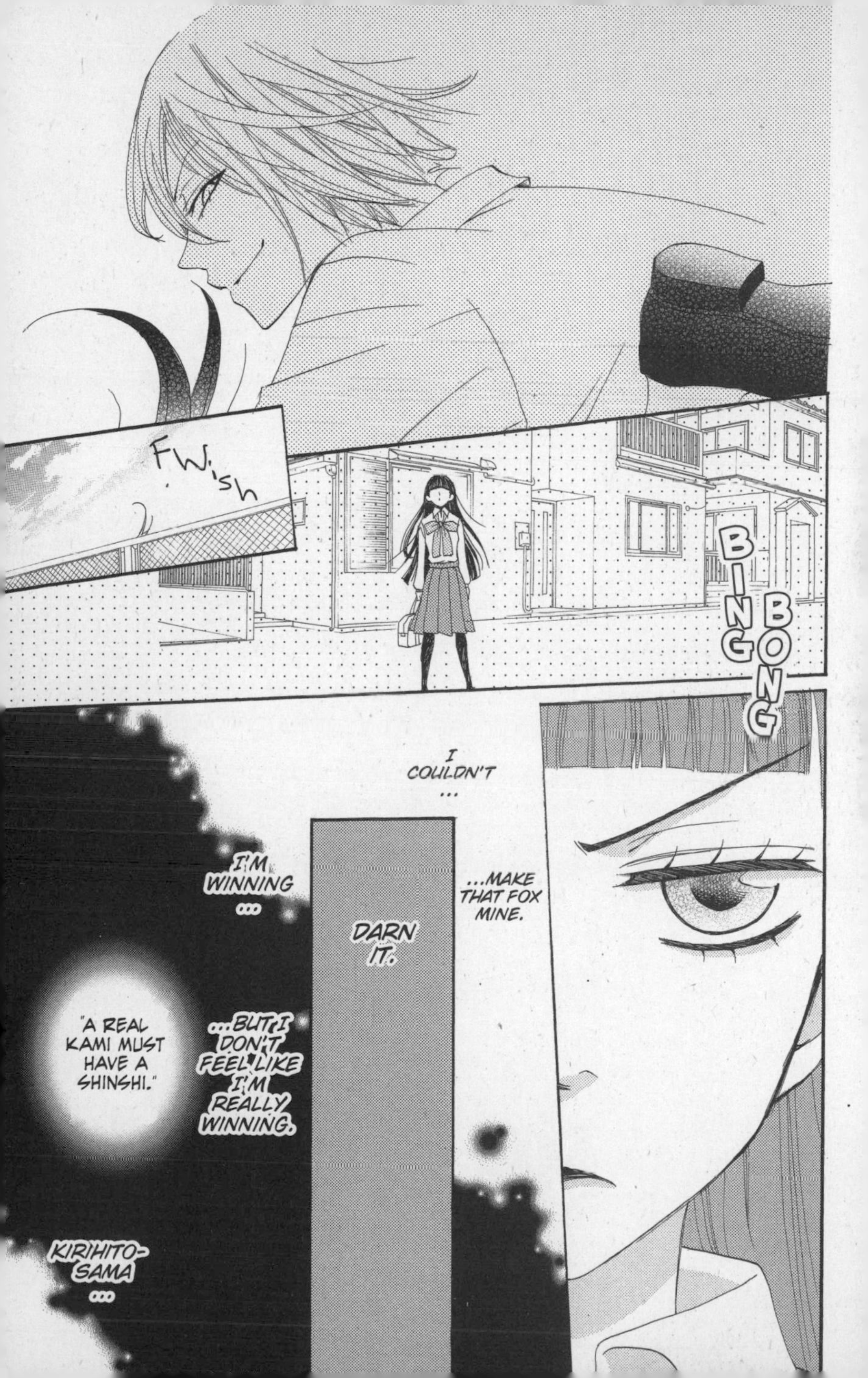
BING BONG
FWISH
I COULDN'T ...
...MAKE THAT FOX MINE.
DARN IT.
I'M WINNING...
...BUT I DON'T FEEL LIKE I'M REALLY WINNING.
"A REAL KAMI MUST HAVE A SHINSHI."
KIRIHITO-SAMA...

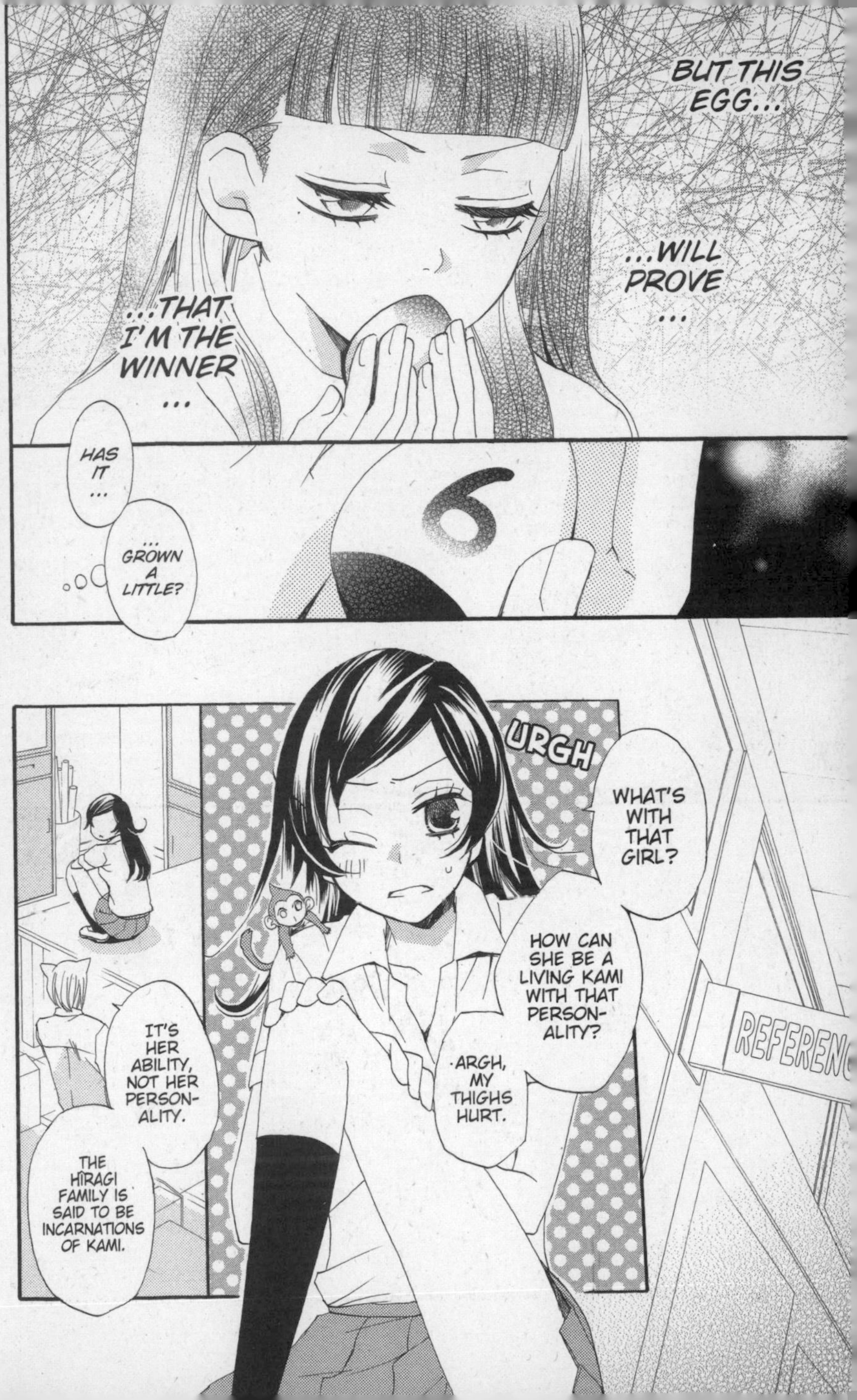
BUT THIS EGG...
...WILL PROVE ...
...THAT I'M THE WINNER ...
HAS IT ...
... GROWN A LITTLE?
URGH
WHAT'S WITH THAT GIRL?
HOW CAN SHE BE A LIVING KAMI WITH THAT PERSON-ALITY?
ARGH, MY THIGHS HURT.
REFERENC
IT'S HER ABILITY, NOT HER PERSON-ALITY.
THE HIRAGI FAMILY IS SAID TO BE INCARNATIONS OF KAMI.

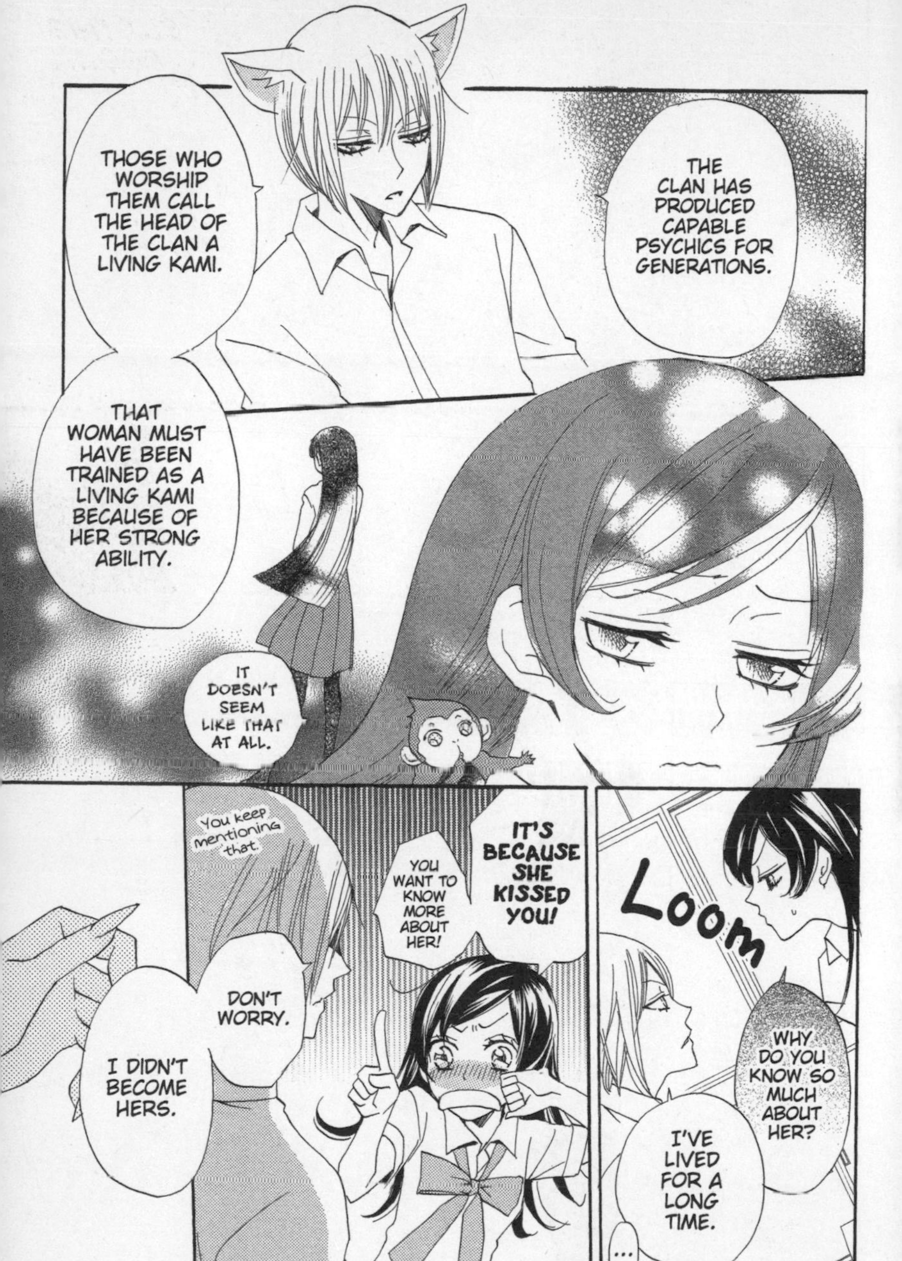
THE CLAN HAS PRODUCED CAPABLE PSYCHICS FOR GENERATIONS.
THOSE WHO WORSHIP THEM CALL THE HEAD OF THE CLAN A LIVING KAMI.
THAT WOMAN MUST HAVE BEEN TRAINED AS A LIVING KAMI BECAUSE OF HER STRONG ABILITY.
IT DOESN'T SEEM LIKE THAT AT ALL.
Loom
WHY DO YOU KNOW SO MUCH ABOUT HER?
I'VE LIVED FOR A LONG TIME.
...
IT'S BECAUSE SHE KISSED YOU!
YOU WANT TO KNOW MORE ABOUT HER!
You keep mentioning that.
DON'T WORRY.
I DIDN'T BECOME HERS.

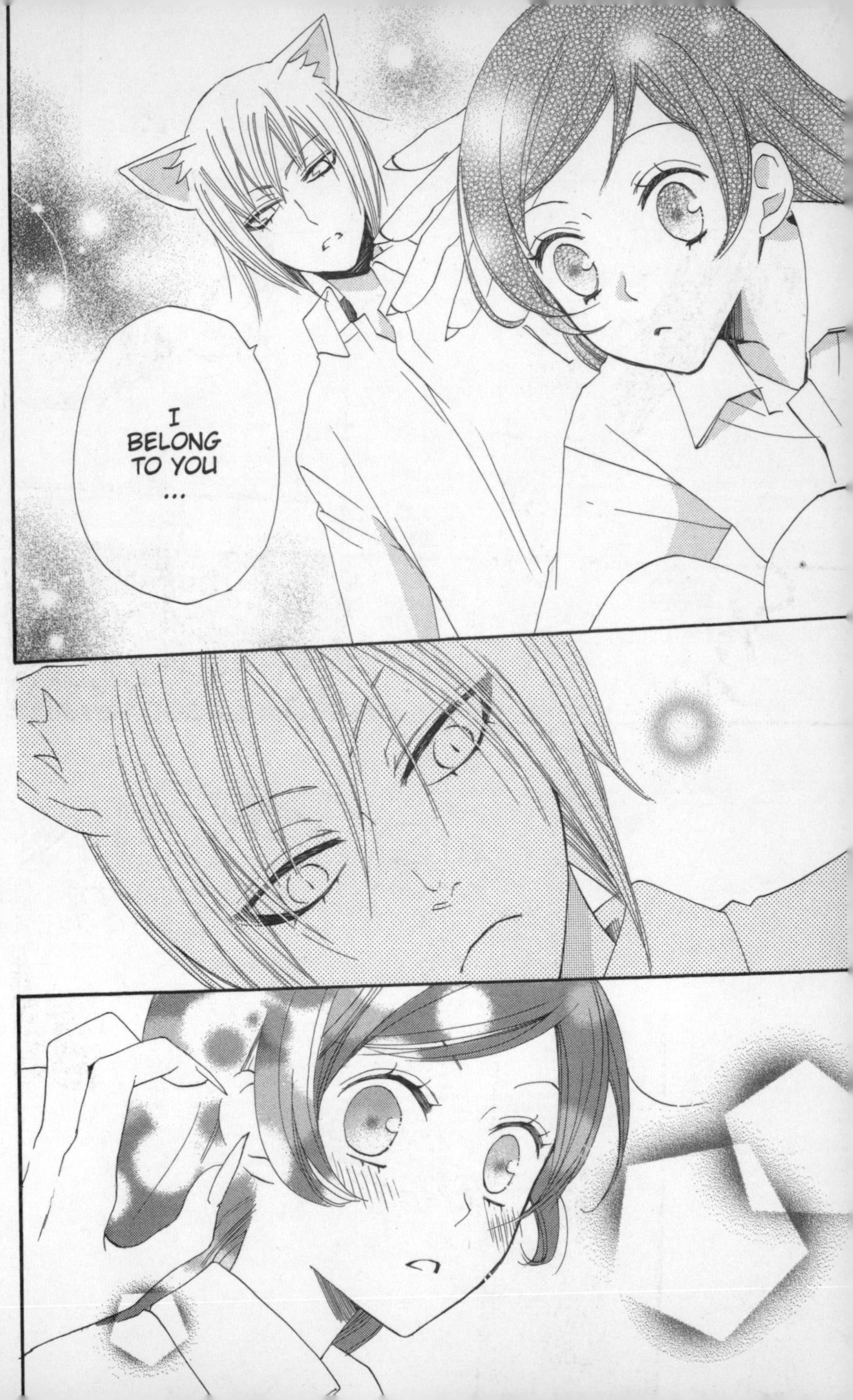
I BELONG TO YOU ...

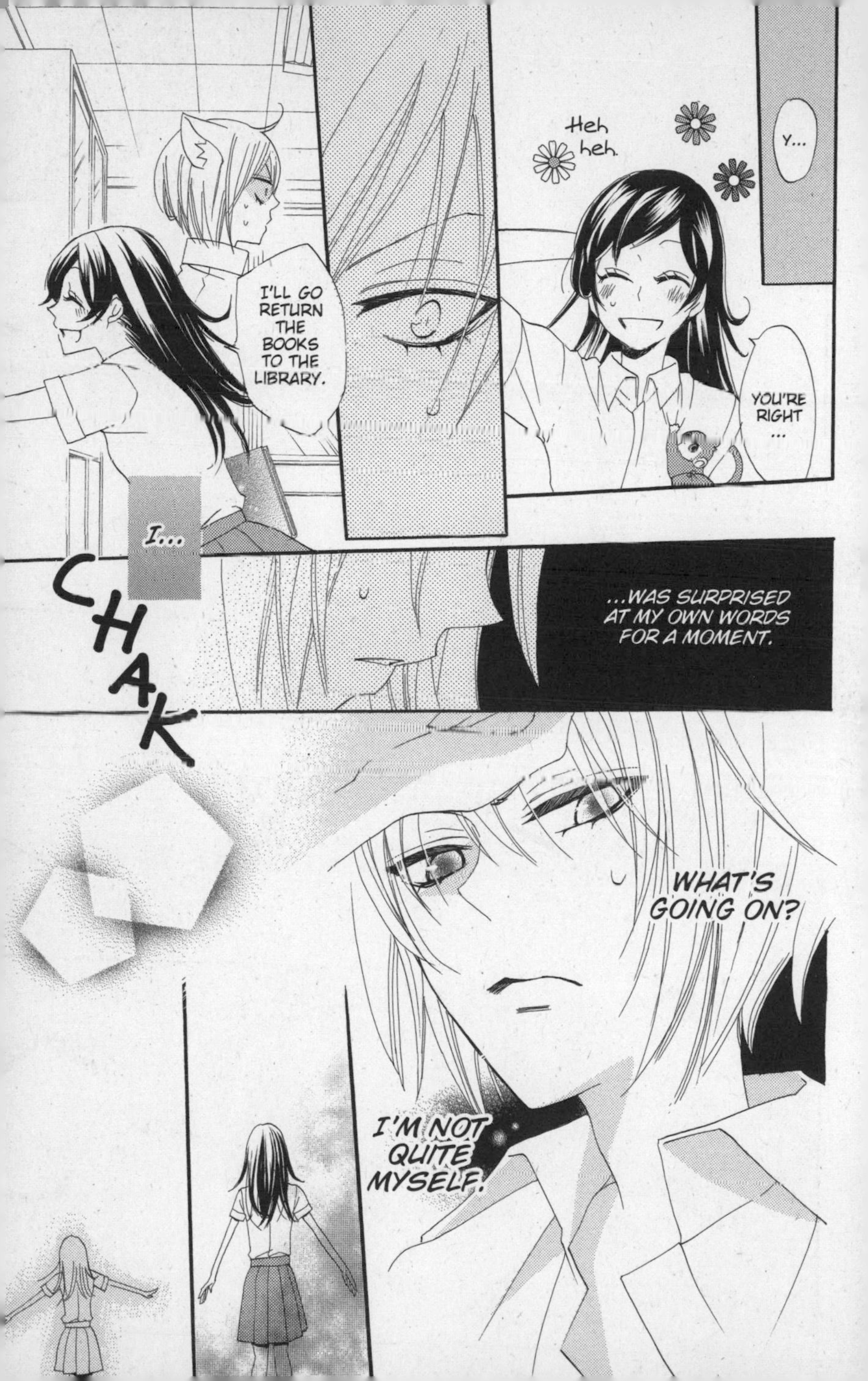
Y...
Heh heh.
YOU'RE RIGHT ...
I'LL GO RETURN THE BOOKS TO THE LIBRARY.
I...
...WAS SURPRISED AT MY OWN WORDS FOR A MOMENT.
CHAK
WHAT'S GOING ON?
I'M NOT QUITE MYSELF.

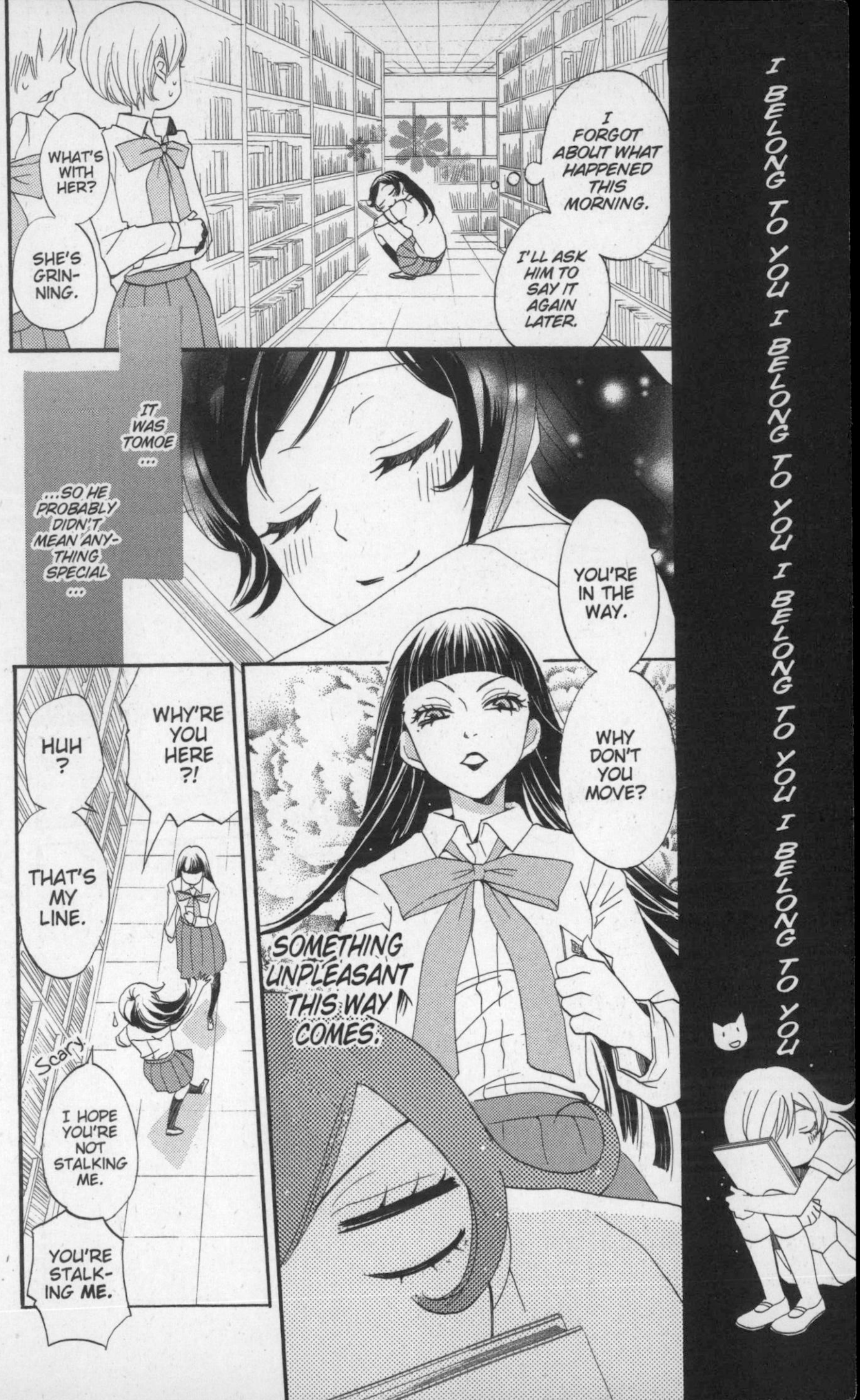
I FORGOT ABOUT WHAT HAPPENED THIS MORNING.
I'LL ASK HIM TO SAY IT AGAIN LATER.
WHAT'S WITH HER?
SHE'S GRIN-NING.
IT WAS TOMOE...
...SO HE PROBABLY DIDN'T MEAN ANY-THING SPECIAL...
YOU'RE IN THE WAY.
WHY DON'T YOU MOVE?
SOMETHING UNPLEASANT THIS WAY COMES.
WHY'RE YOU HERE?!
HUH?
THAT'S MY LINE.
Scary
I HOPE YOU'RE NOT STALKING ME.
YOU'RE STALK-ING ME.
I BELONG TO YOU I BELONG TO YOU I BELONG TO YOU I BELONG TO YOU

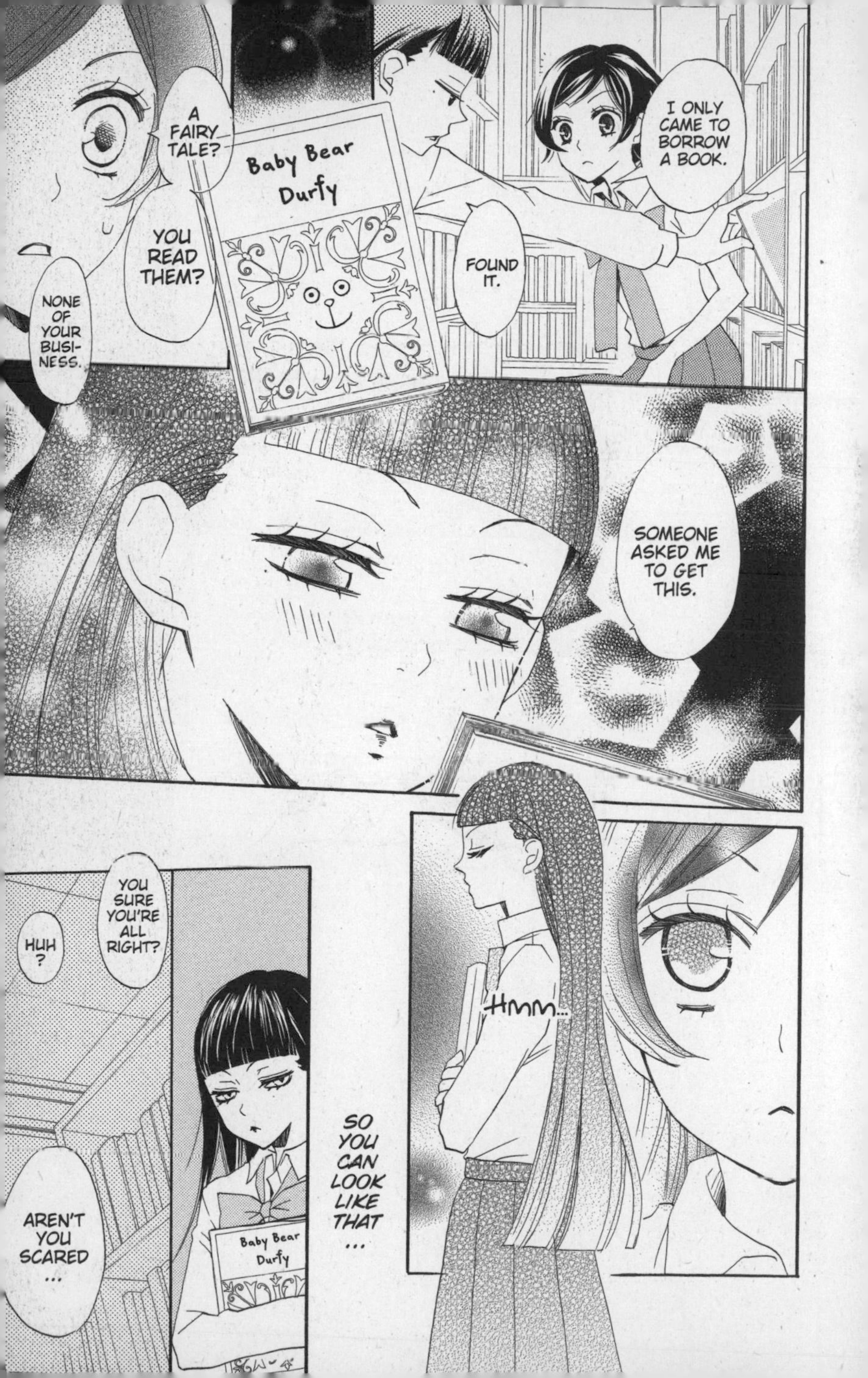
I ONLY CAME TO BORROW A BOOK.
FOUND IT.
A FAIRY TALE?
Baby Bear Durfy
YOU READ THEM?
NONE OF YOUR BUSI-NESS.
SOMEONE ASKED ME TO GET THIS.
Hmm...
SO YOU CAN LOOK LIKE THAT...
YOU SURE YOU'RE ALL RIGHT?
HUH?
Baby Bear Durfy
AREN'T YOU SCARED...

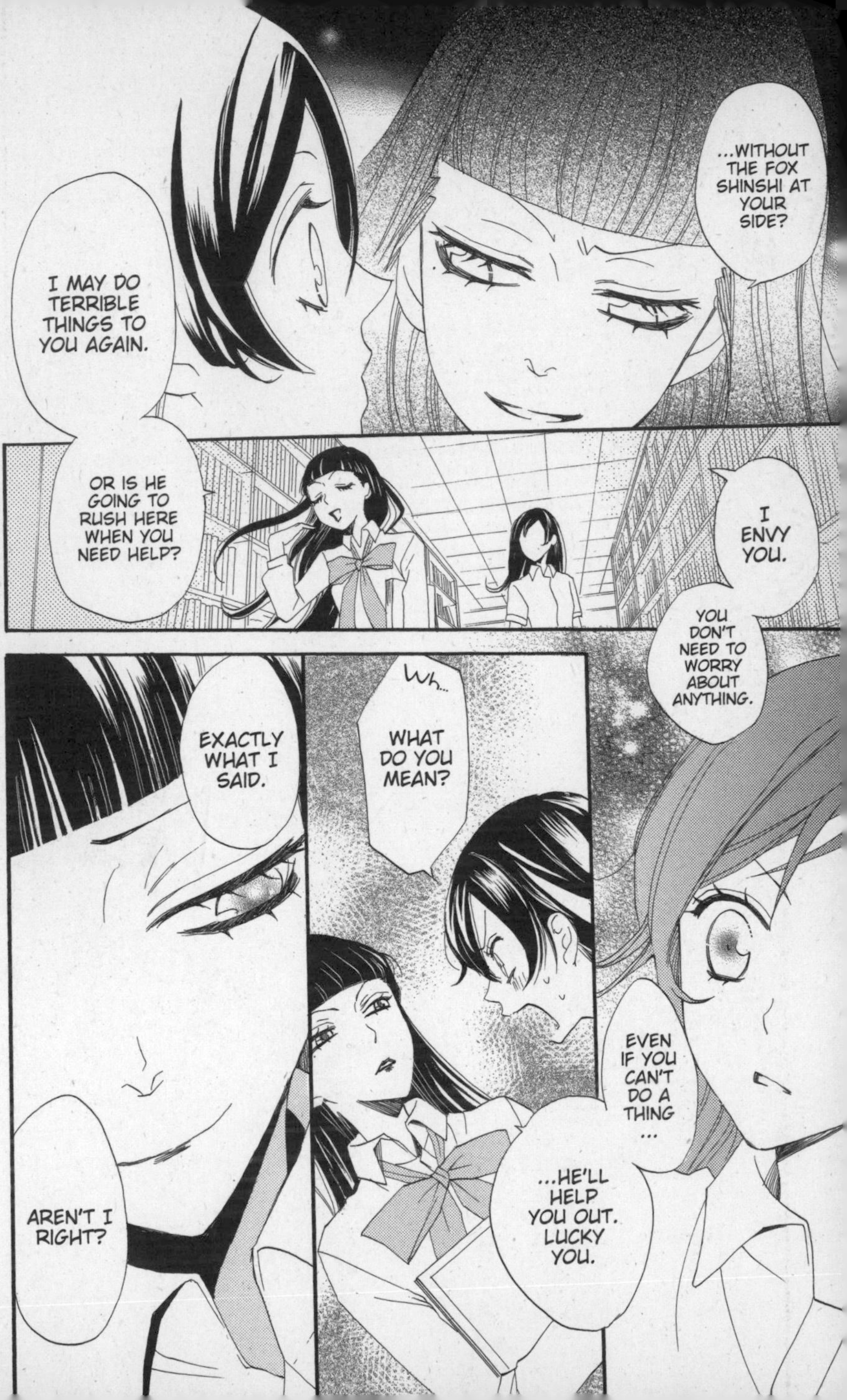
...WITHOUT THE FOX SHINSHI AT YOUR SIDE?
I MAY DO TERRIBLE THINGS TO YOU AGAIN.
OR IS HE GOING TO RUSH HERE WHEN YOU NEED HELP?
I ENVY YOU.
YOU DON'T NEED TO WORRY ABOUT ANYTHING.
EVEN IF YOU CAN'T DO A THING...
...HE'LL HELP YOU OUT. LUCKY YOU.
Wh...
WHAT DO YOU MEAN?
EXACTLY WHAT I SAID.
AREN'T I RIGHT?

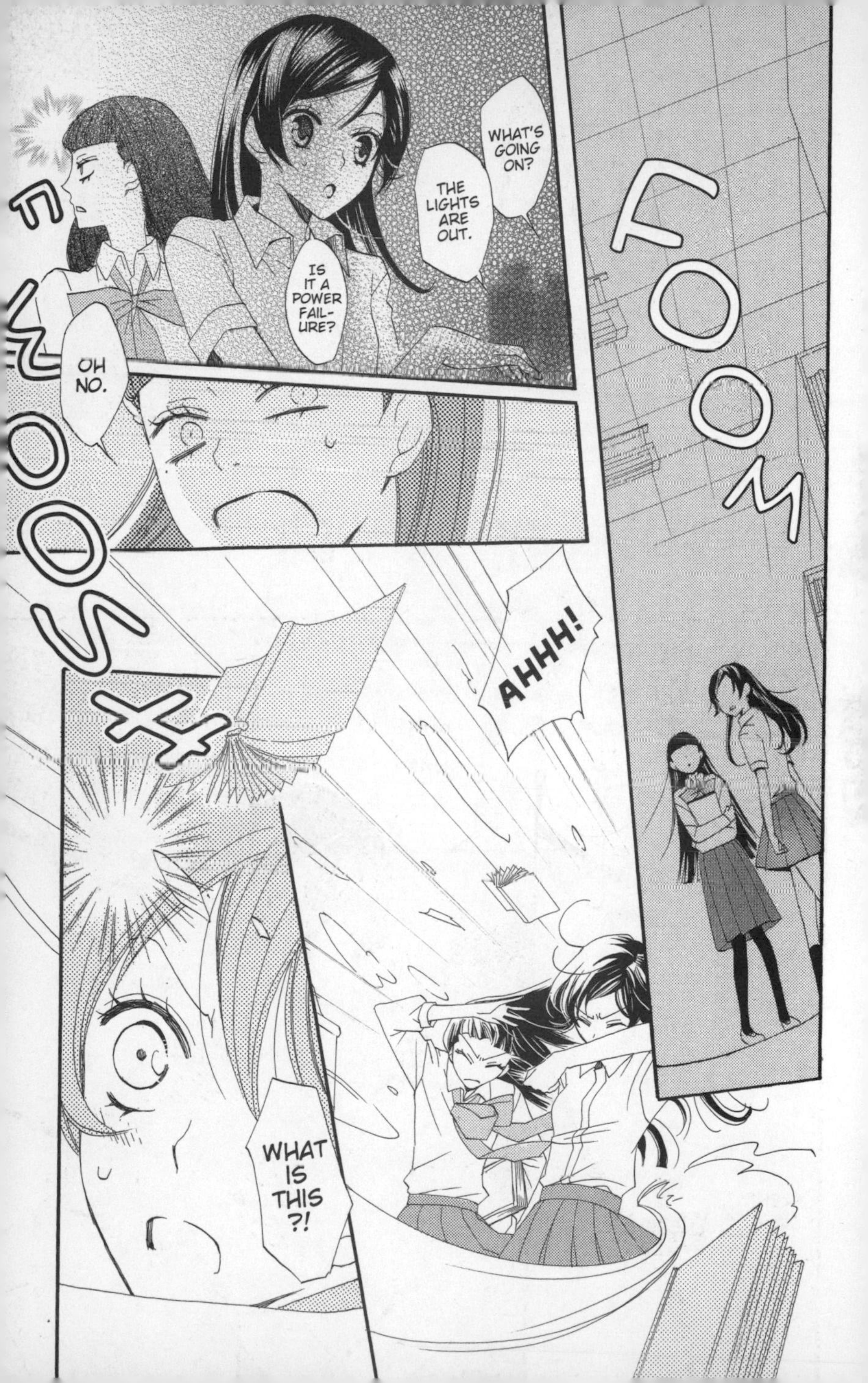
WHAT'S GOING ON?
THE LIGHTS ARE OUT.
IS IT A POWER FAILURE?
OH NO.
AHHH!
WHAT IS THIS ?!

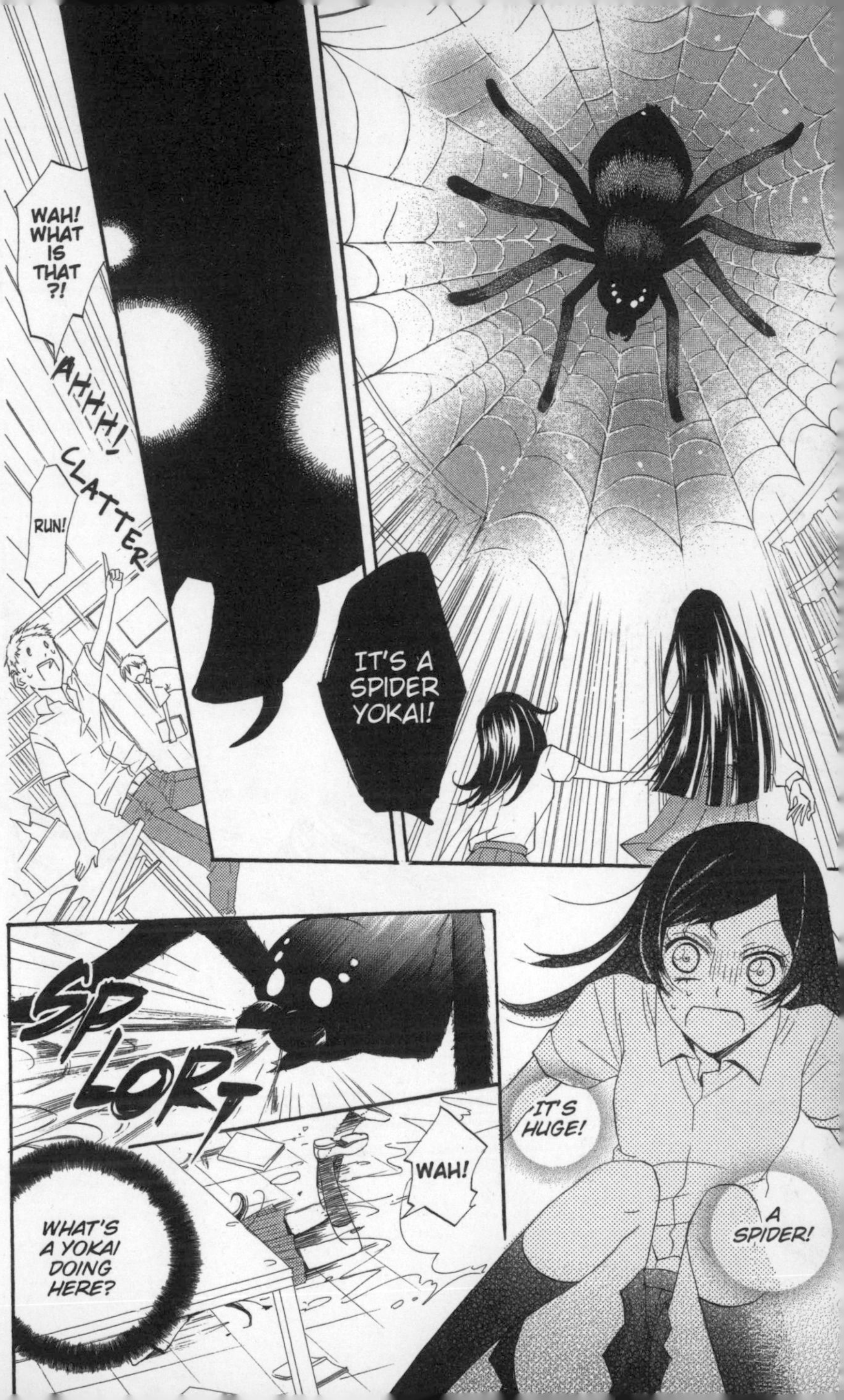
IT'S A SPIDER YOKAI!
WAH! WHAT IS THAT?!
AHHH!
CLATTER
RUN!
A SPIDER!
IT'S HUGE!
SPLORT
WAH!
WHAT'S A YOKAI DOING HERE?

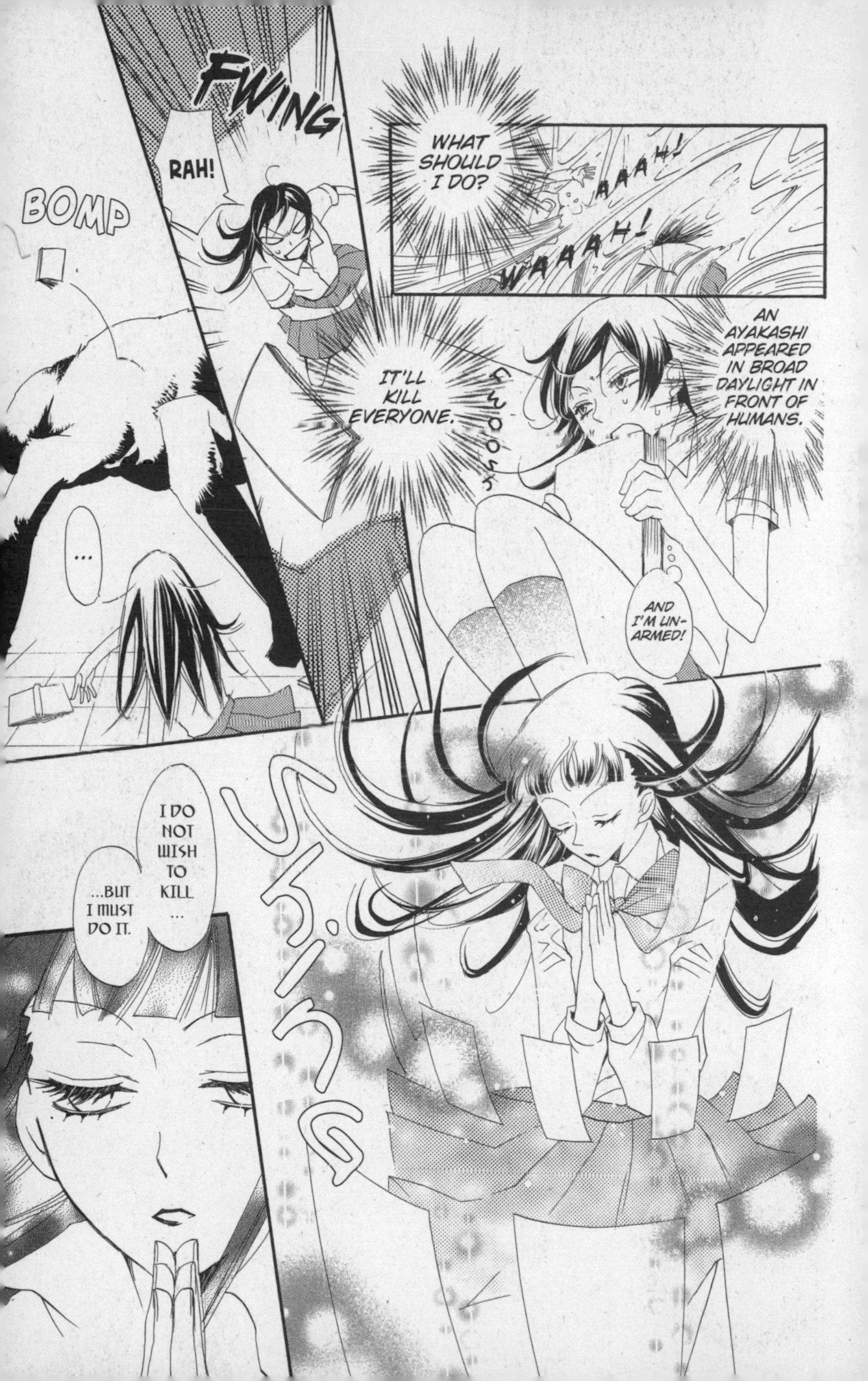
WHAT SHOULD I DO?
AAAAH!
WAAAAH!
AN AYAKASHI APPEARED IN BROAD DAYLIGHT IN FRONT OF HUMANS.
IT'LL KILL EVERYONE.
AND I'M UN-ARMED!
FWING
RAH!
BOMP
...
I DO NOT WISH TO KILL ...
...BUT I MUST DO IT.

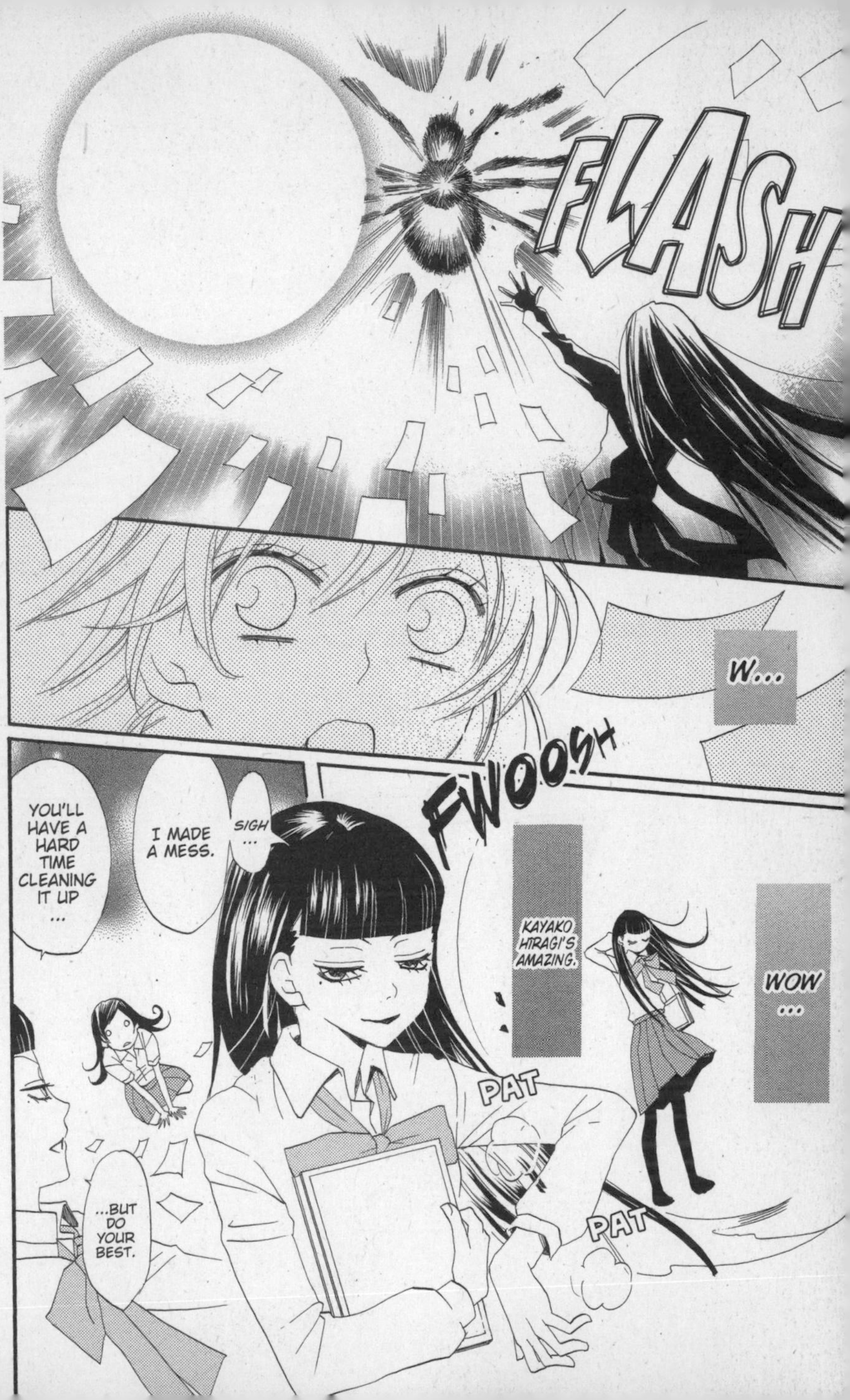
FLASH
W...
FWOOSH
WOW...
KAYAKO HIRAGI'S AMAZING.
PAT
PAT
SIGH...
I MADE A MESS.
YOU'LL HAVE A HARD TIME CLEANING IT UP...
...BUT DO YOUR BEST.

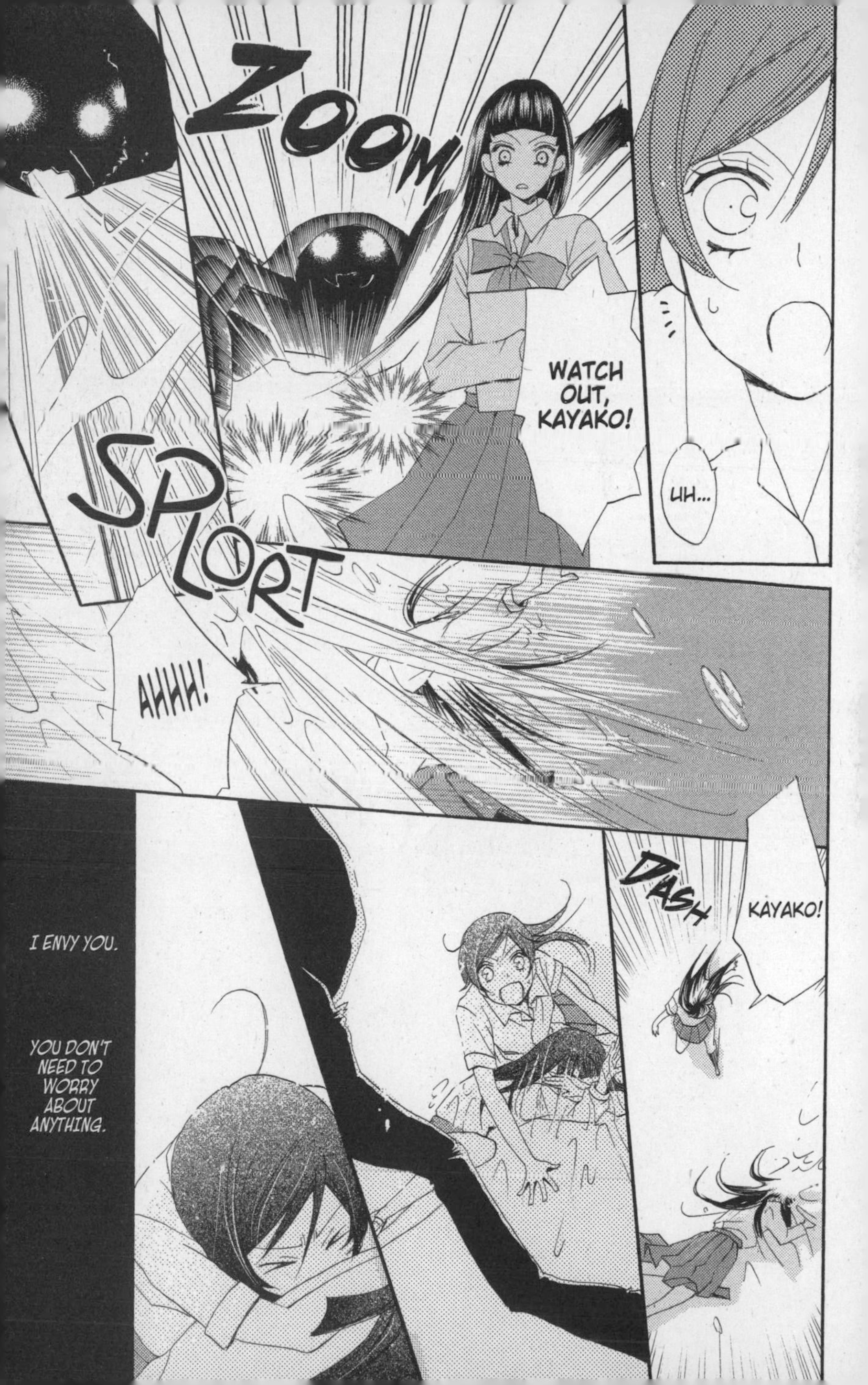
UH...
ZOOM
WATCH OUT, KAYAKO!
SPLORT
AHHH!
DASH
KAYAKO!
I ENVY YOU.
YOU DON'T NEED TO WORRY ABOUT ANYTHING.

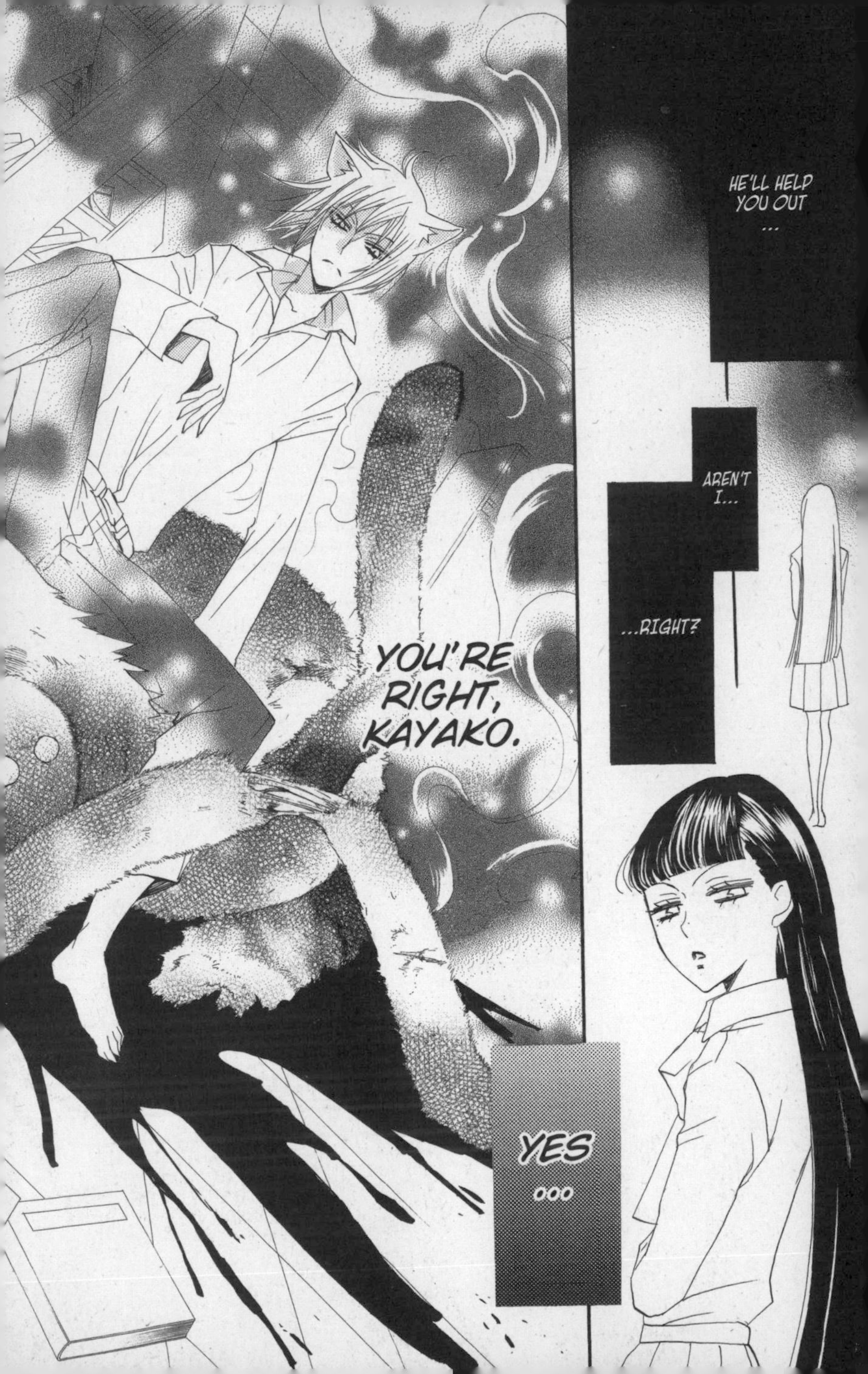
HE'LL HELP YOU OUT ...
AREN'T I...
...RIGHT?
YOU'RE RIGHT, KAYAKO.
YES ...

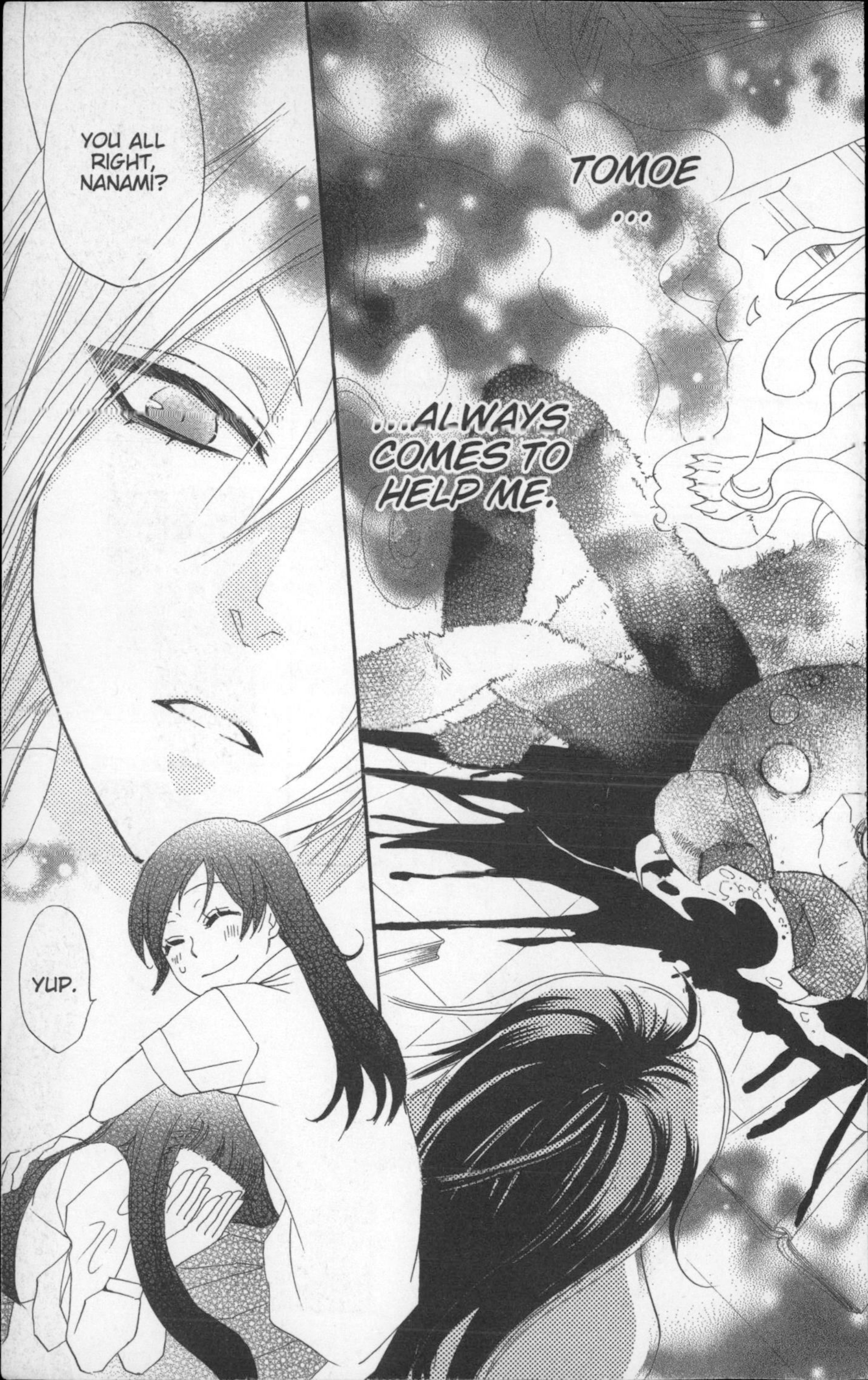
TOMOE ...
...ALWAYS COMES TO HELP ME.
YOU ALL RIGHT, NANAMI?
YUP.

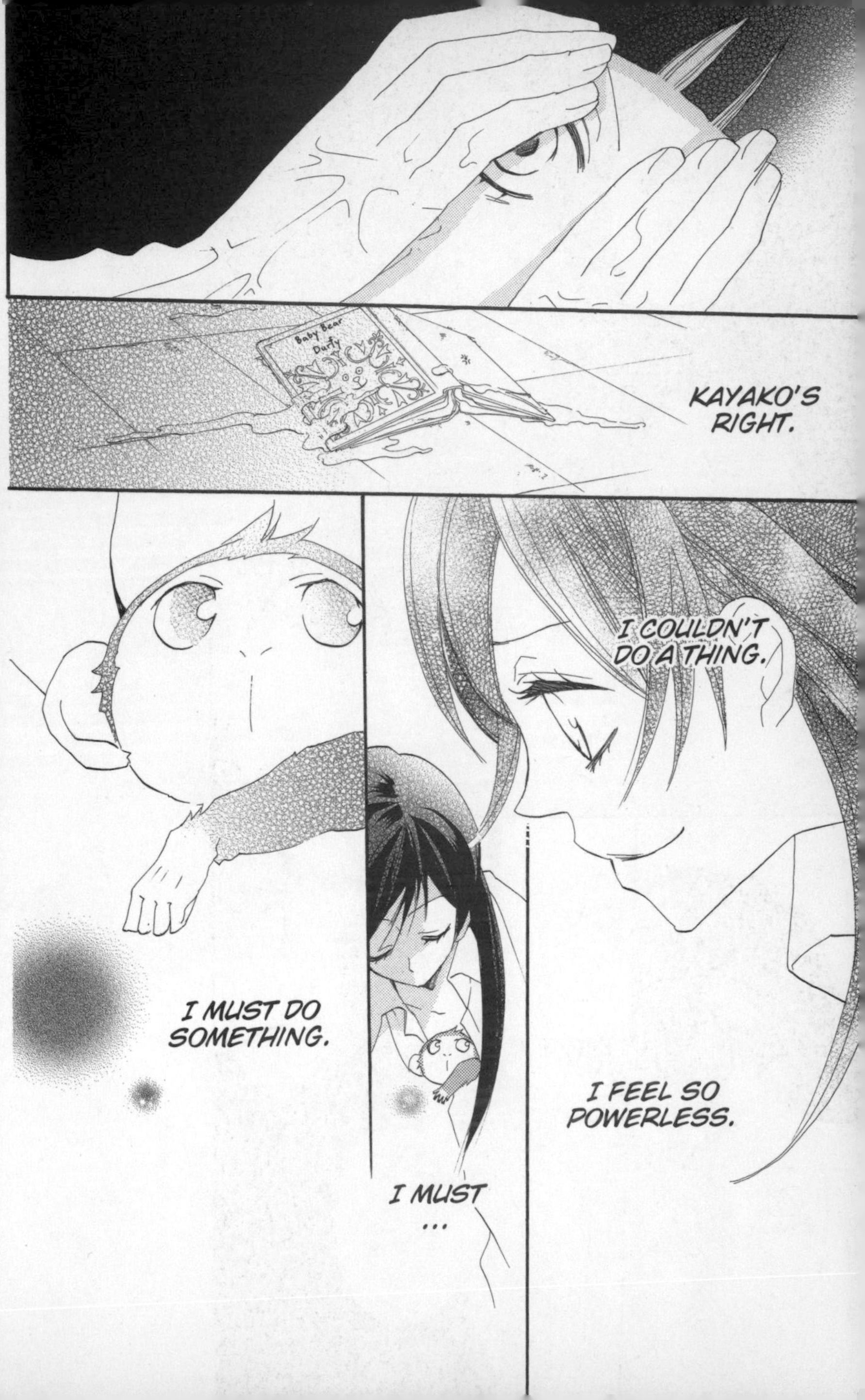
Baby Bear Durfy
KAYAKO'S RIGHT.
I COULDN'T DO A THING.
I FEEL SO POWERLESS.
I MUST ...
I MUST DO SOMETHING.

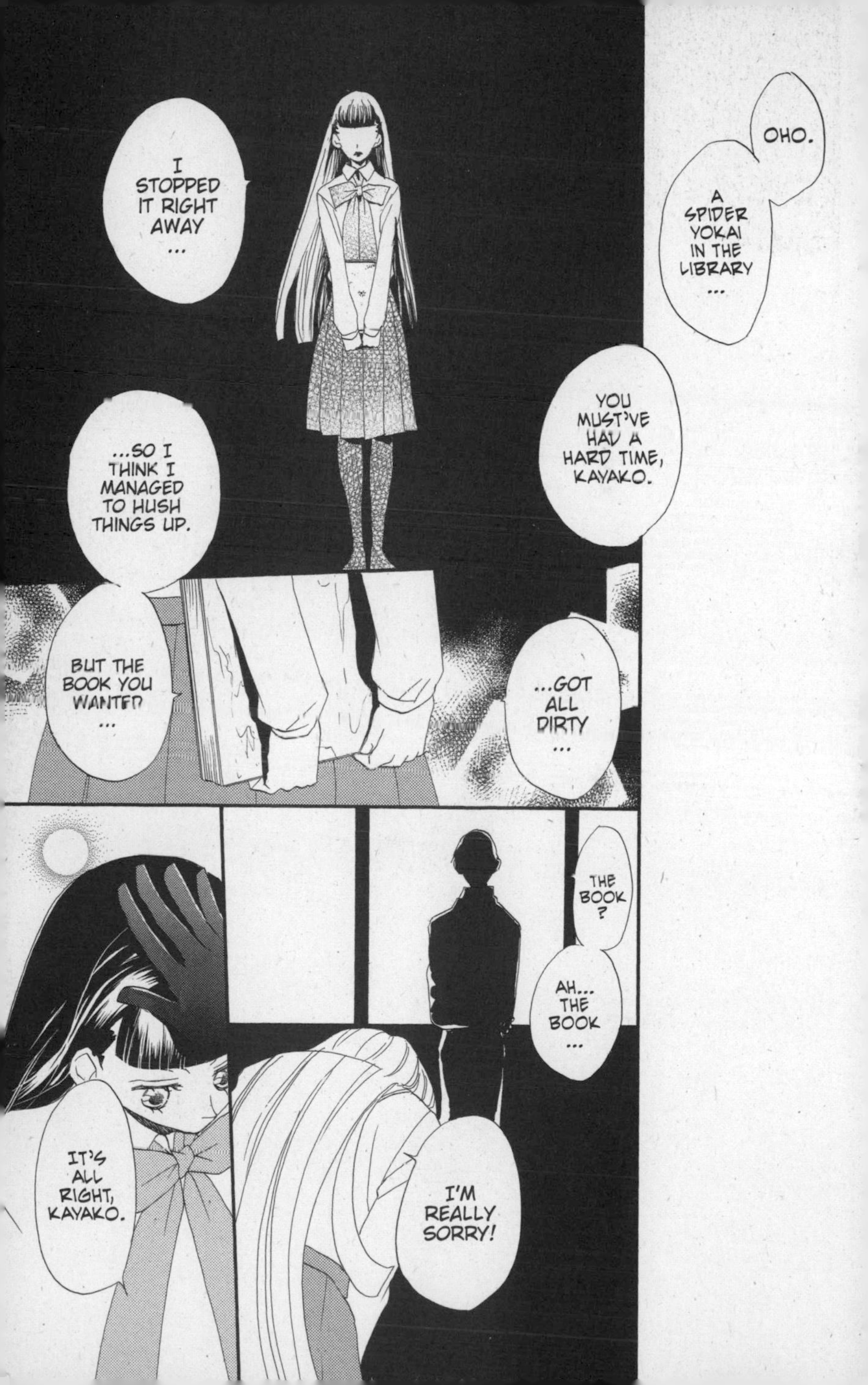
OHO.
A SPIDER YOKAI IN THE LIBRARY ...
YOU MUST'VE HAD A HARD TIME, KAYAKO.
I STOPPED IT RIGHT AWAY ...
...SO I THINK I MANAGED TO HUSH THINGS UP.
BUT THE BOOK YOU WANTED ...
...GOT ALL DIRTY ...
THE BOOK ?
AH... THE BOOK ...
I'M REALLY SORRY!
IT'S ALL RIGHT, KAYAKO.

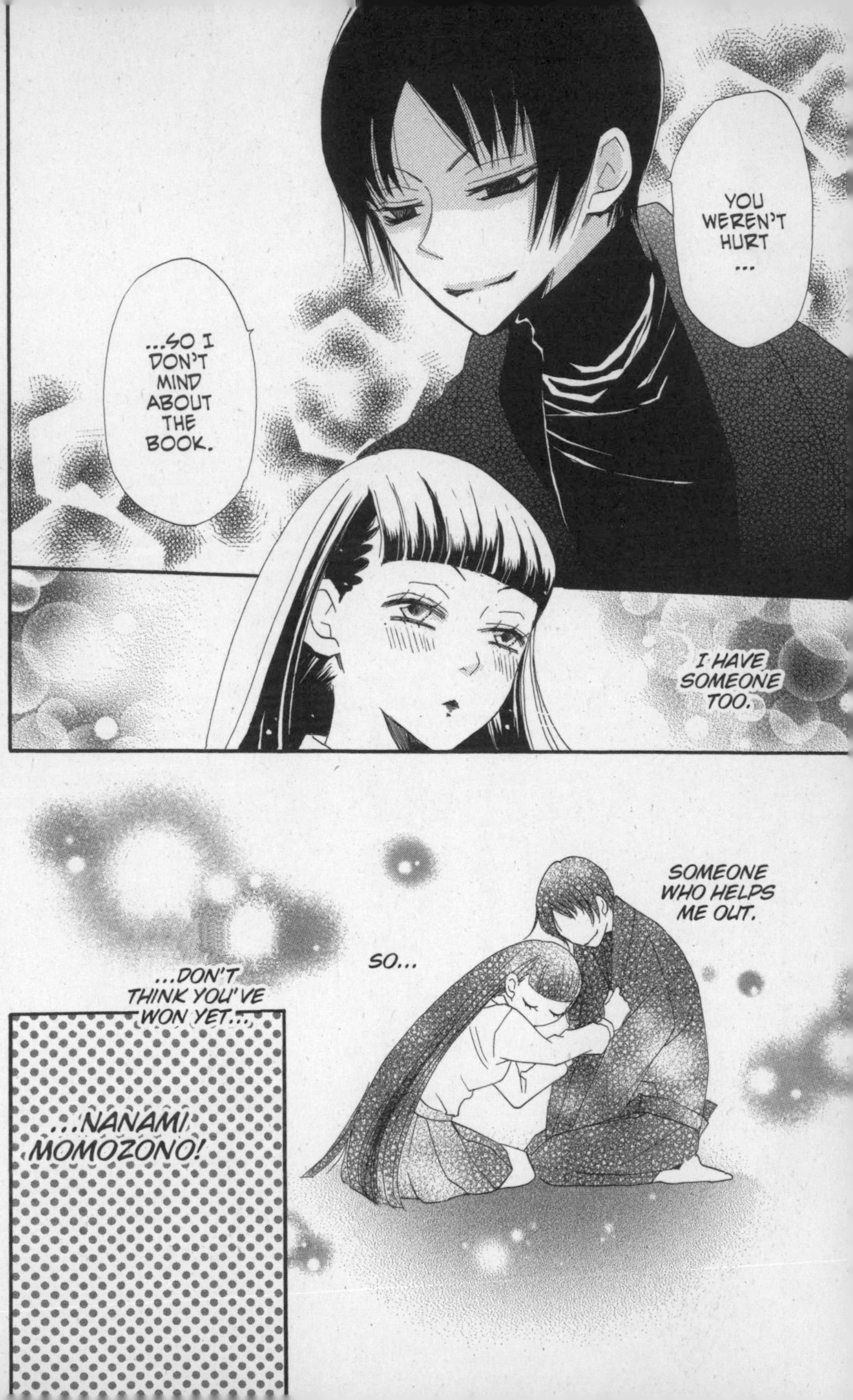
YOU WEREN'T HURT ...
...SO I DON'T MIND ABOUT THE BOOK.
I HAVE SOMEONE TOO.
SOMEONE WHO HELPS ME OUT.
SO...
...DON'T THINK YOU'VE WON YET...
...NANAMI MOMOZONO!

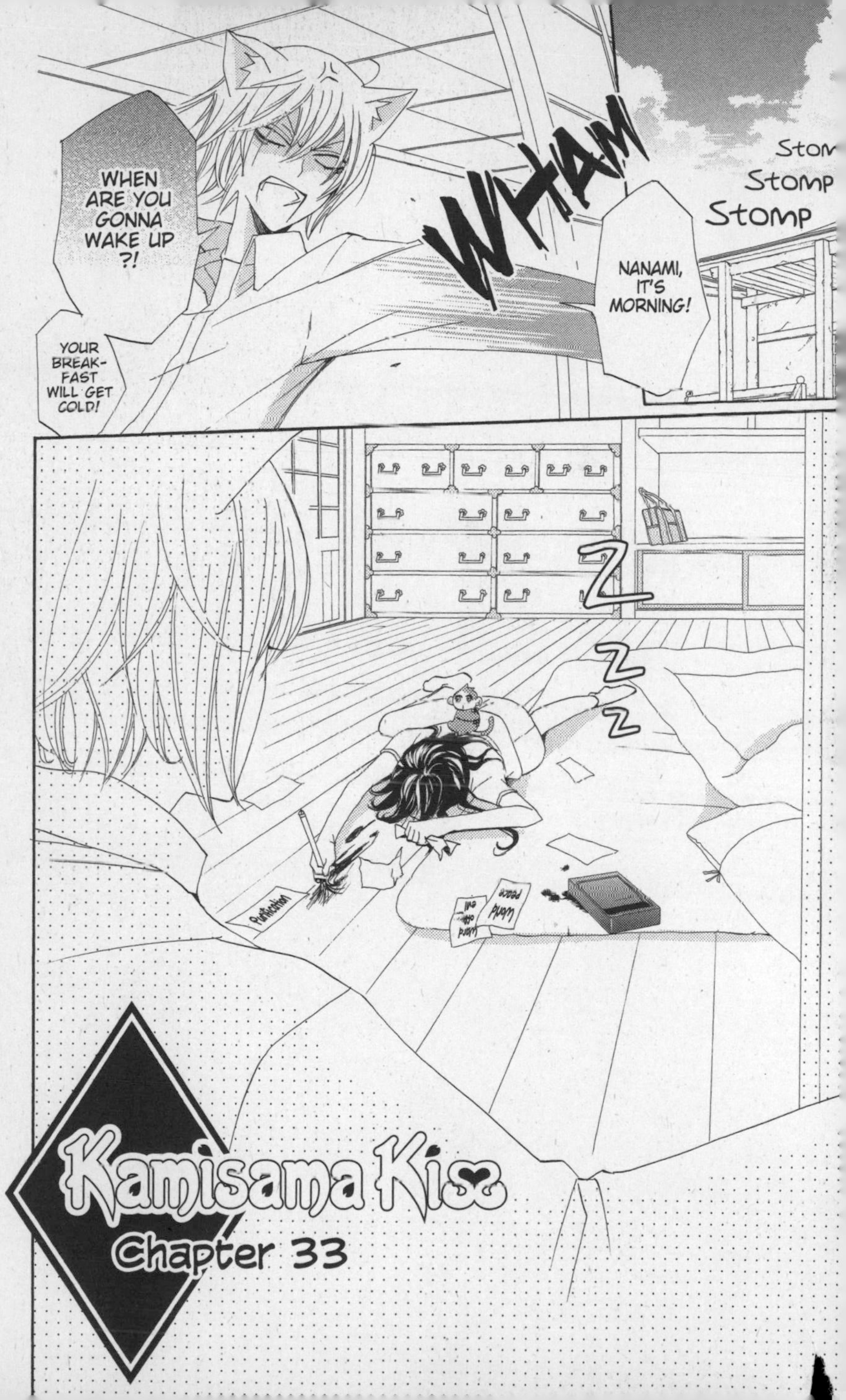
Stomp Stomp Stomp
NANAMI, IT'S MORNING!
WHAM
WHEN ARE YOU GONNA WAKE UP ?!
YOUR BREAKFAST WILL GET COLD!
Z Z Z
World peace
Ward off evil
Purification
Kamisama Kiss
Chapter 33

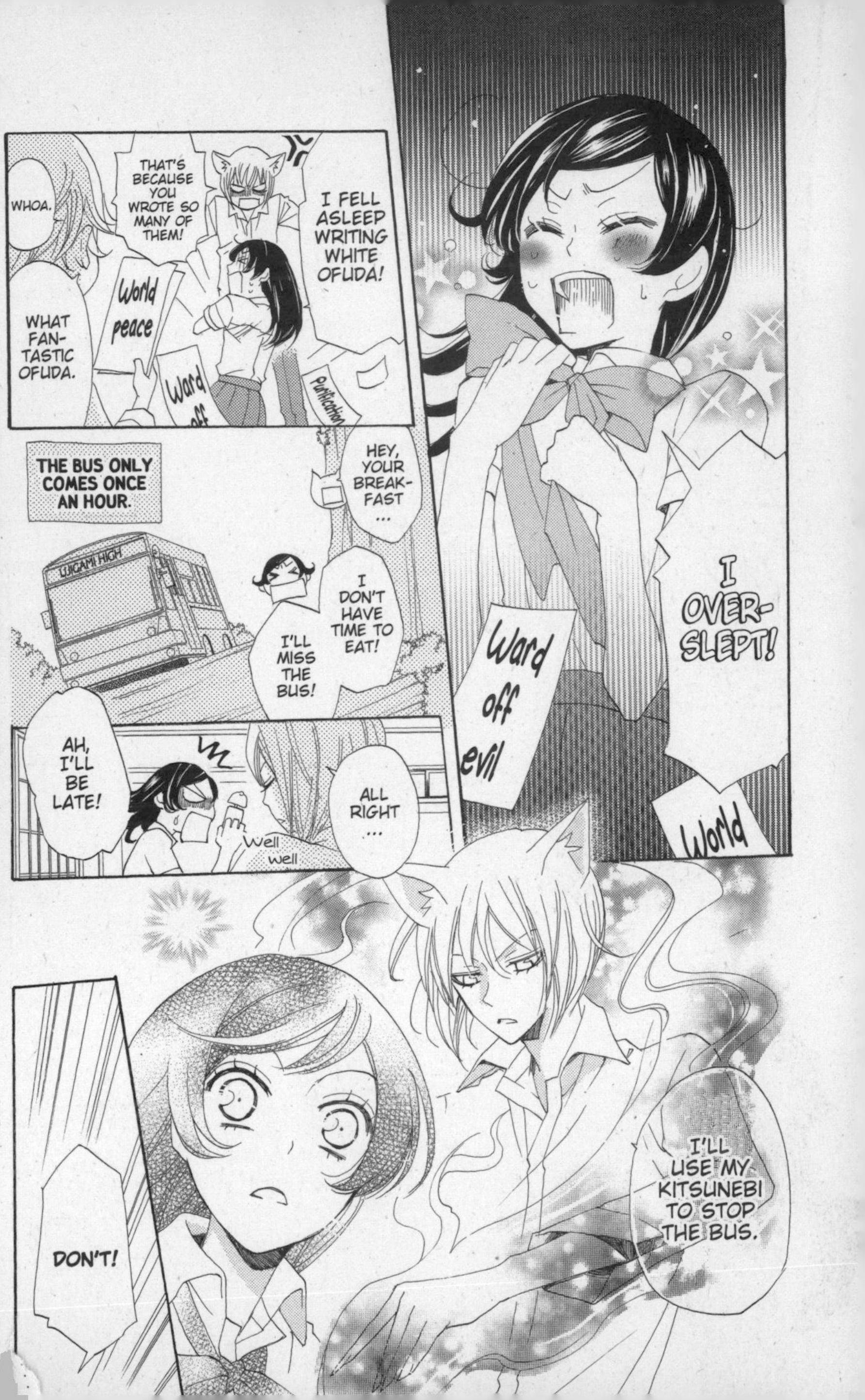

I OVER-SLEPT!
Ward off evil
World
I FELL ASLEEP WRITING WHITE OFUDA!
THAT'S BECAUSE YOU WROTE SO MANY OF THEM!
WHOA.
WHAT FAN-TASTIC OFUDA.
World peace
Purification
Ward off
HEY, YOUR BREAK-FAST ...
THE BUS ONLY COMES ONCE AN HOUR.
I DON'T HAVE TIME TO EAT!
I'LL MISS THE BUS!
ALL RIGHT ...
Well well
AH, I'LL BE LATE!
I'LL USE MY KITSUNEBI TO STOP THE BUS.
DON'T!

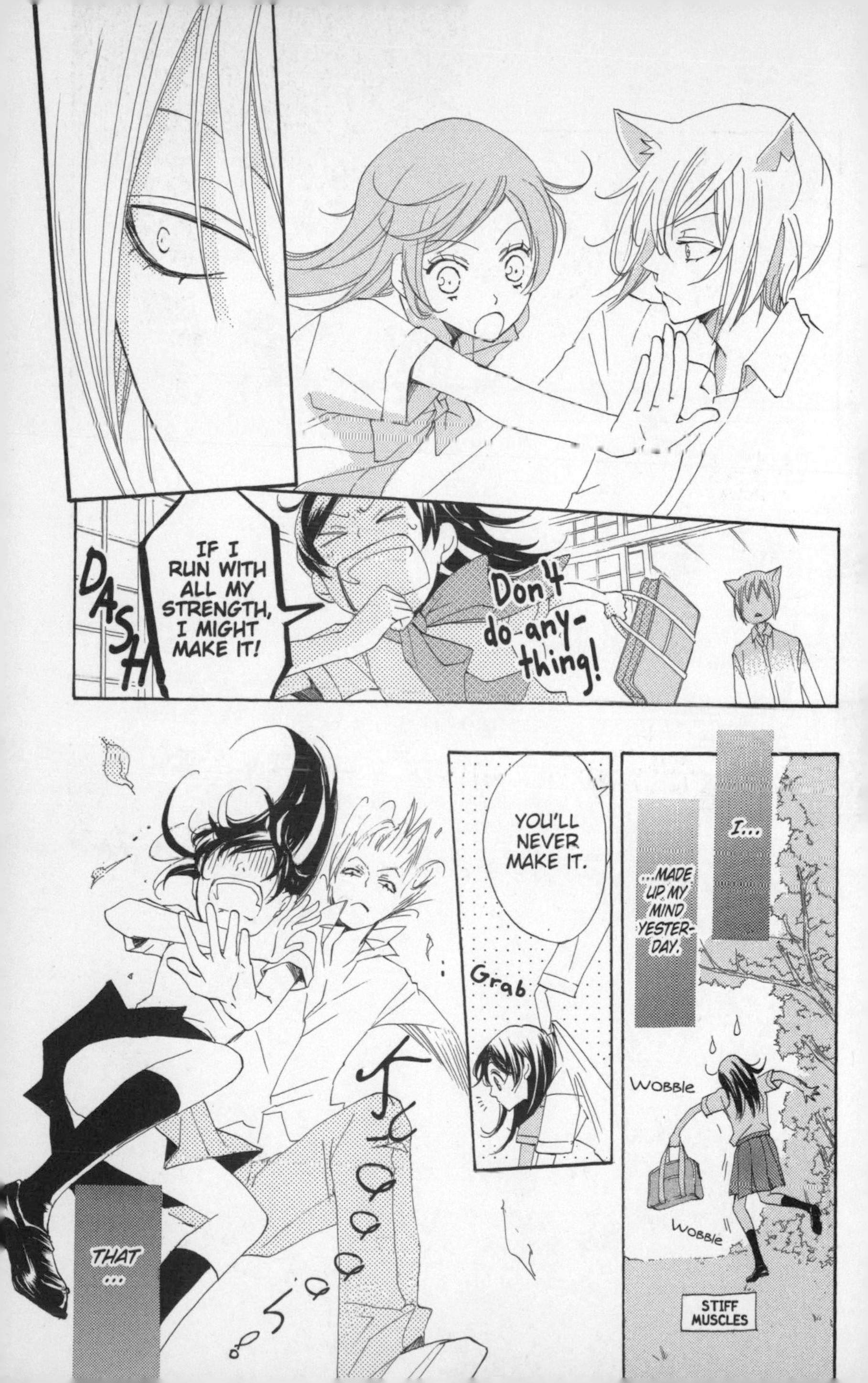

Don't do-anything!
IF I RUN WITH ALL MY STRENGTH, I MIGHT MAKE IT!
DASH
I...
...MADE UP MY MIND YESTERDAY.
Wobble
Wobble
STIFF MUSCLES
YOU'LL NEVER MAKE IT.
Grab
THAT ...

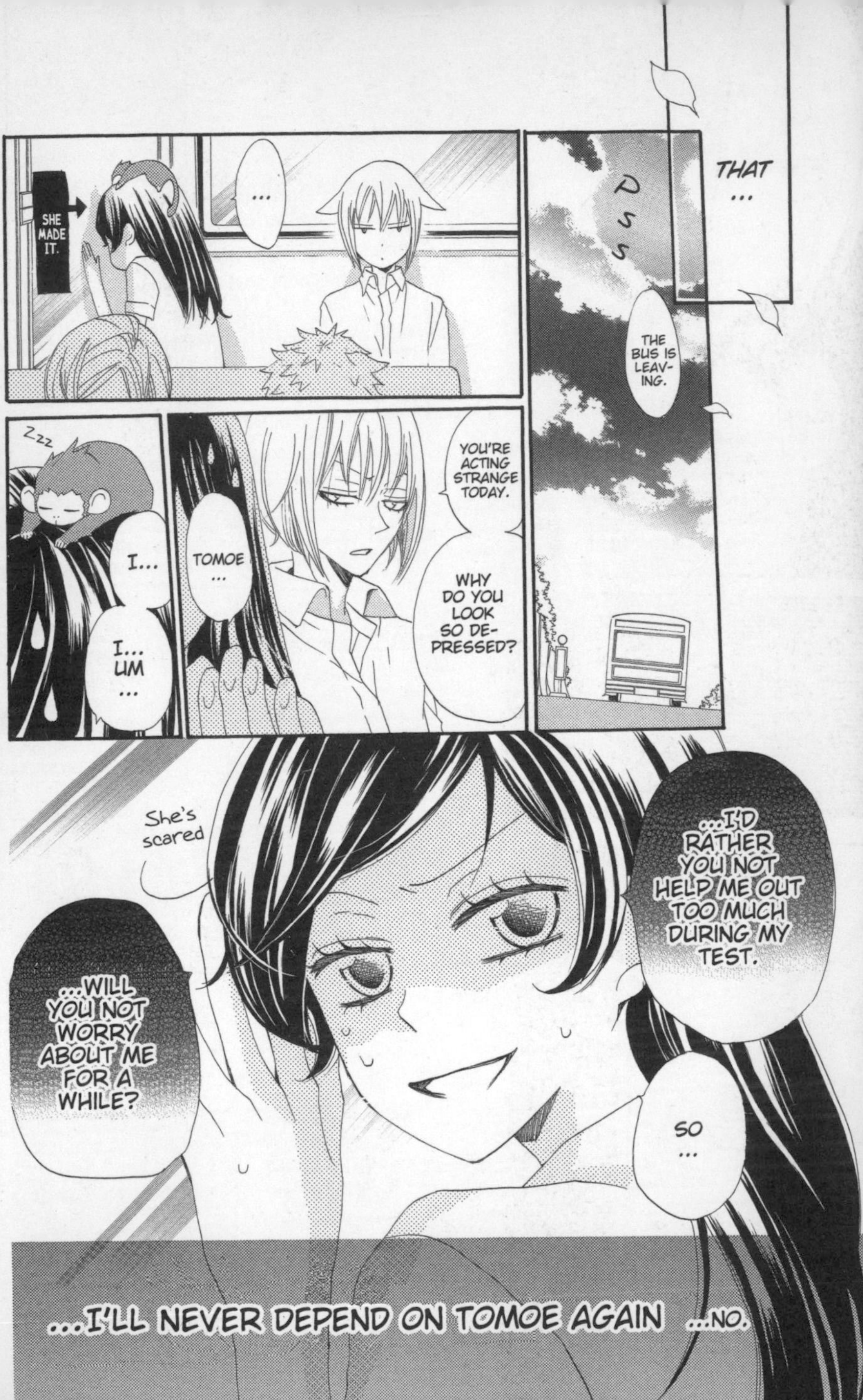
THAT ...
PSS
THE BUS IS LEAVING.
...
SHE MADE IT.
YOU'RE ACTING STRANGE TODAY.
WHY DO YOU LOOK SO DEPRESSED?
TOMOE ...
I...
I... UM ...
...I'D RATHER YOU NOT HELP ME OUT TOO MUCH DURING MY TEST.
SO ...
She's scared
...WILL YOU NOT WORRY ABOUT ME FOR A WHILE?
...I'LL NEVER DEPEND ON TOMOE AGAIN ...NO.

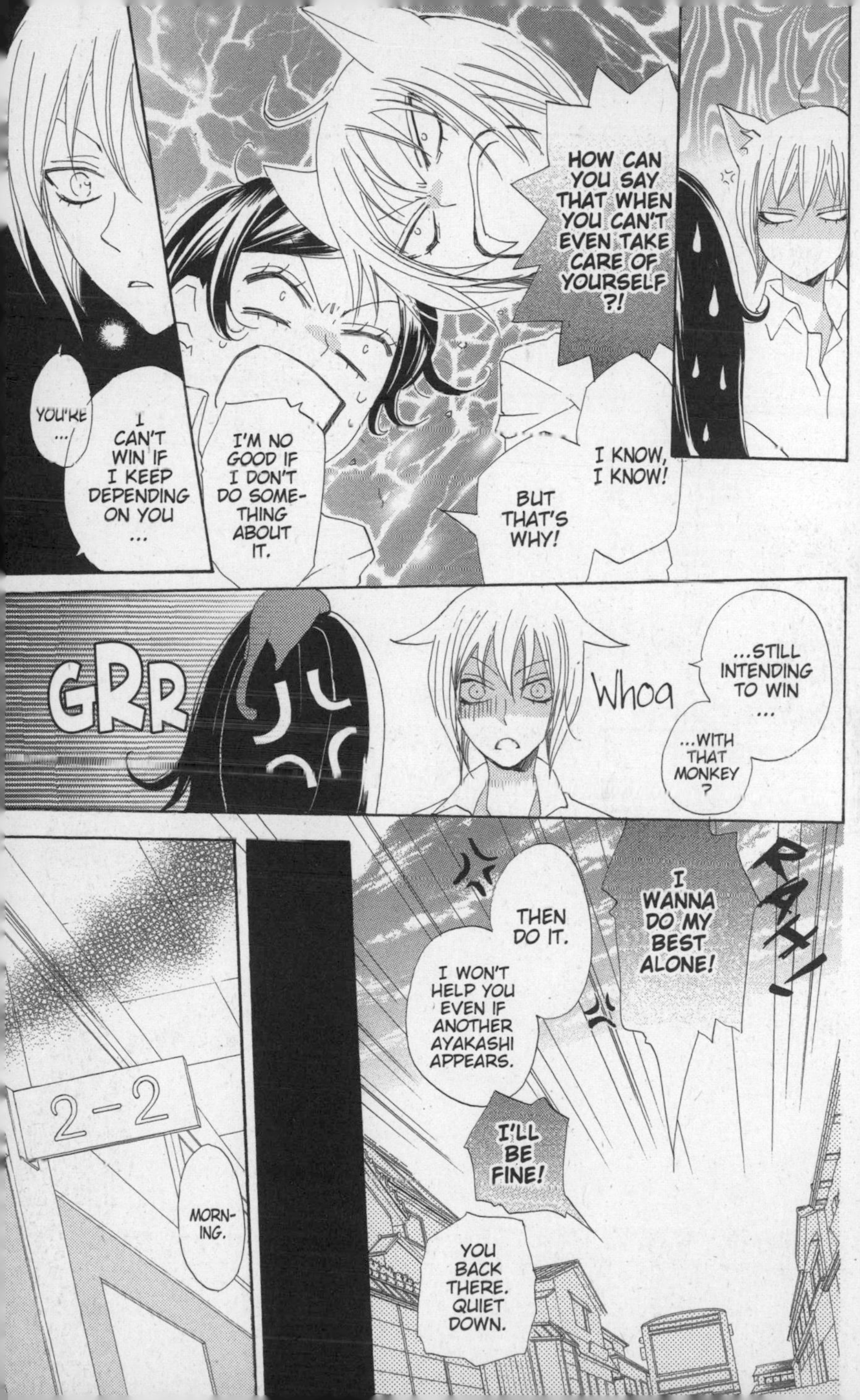
HOW CAN YOU SAY THAT WHEN YOU CAN'T EVEN TAKE CARE OF YOURSELF ?!
I KNOW, I KNOW!
BUT THAT'S WHY!
I'M NO GOOD IF I DON'T DO SOME-THING ABOUT IT.
I CAN'T WIN IF I KEEP DEPENDING ON YOU ...
YOU'RE ...
...STILL INTENDING TO WIN ...
...WITH THAT MONKEY ?
Whoa
GRR
RAH!
I WANNA DO MY BEST ALONE!
THEN DO IT.
I WON'T HELP YOU EVEN IF ANOTHER AYAKASHI APPEARS.
I'LL BE FINE!
YOU BACK THERE. QUIET DOWN.
2-2
MORN-ING.

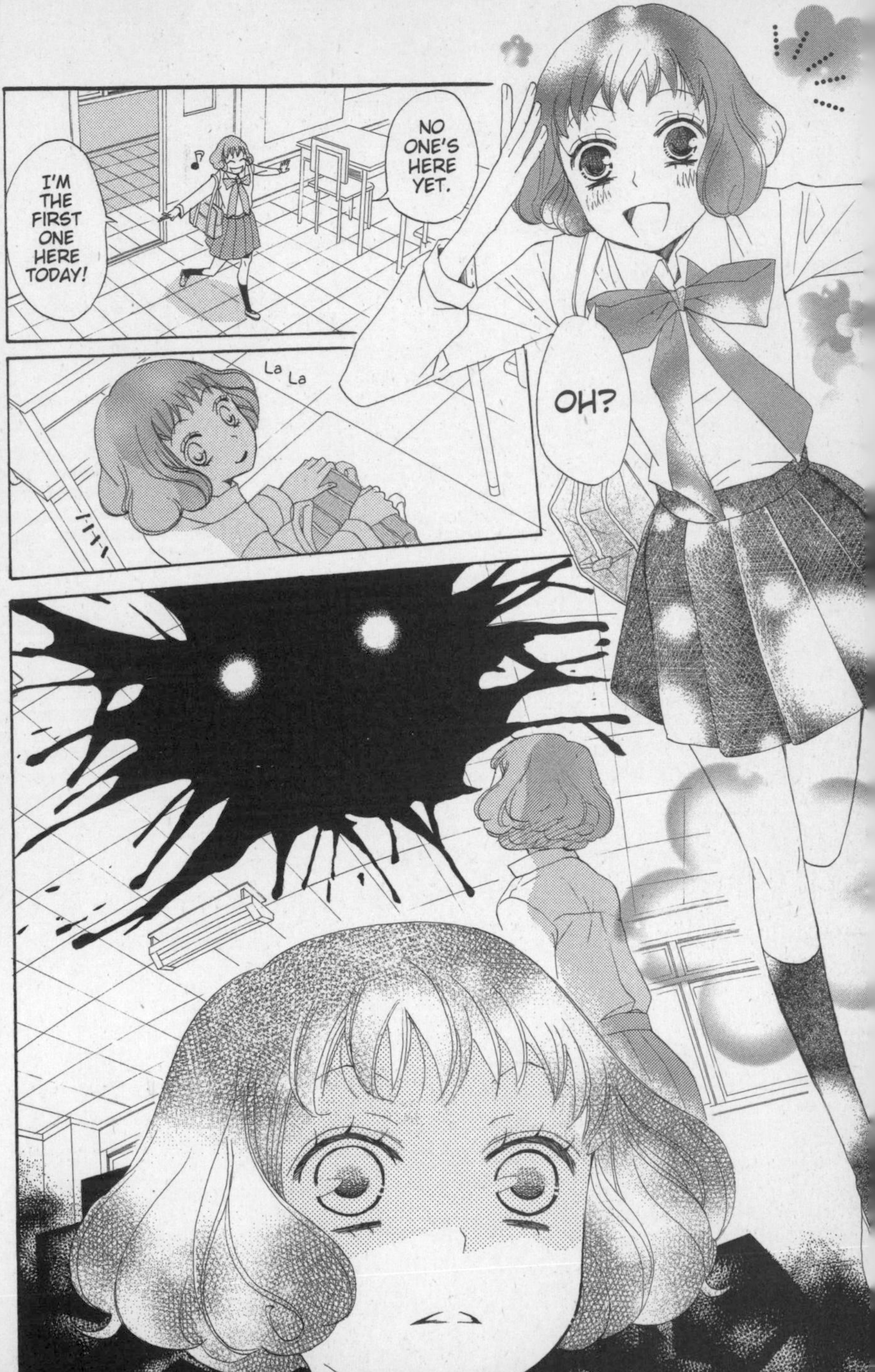
NO ONE'S HERE YET.
I'M THE FIRST ONE HERE TODAY!
La La
OH?

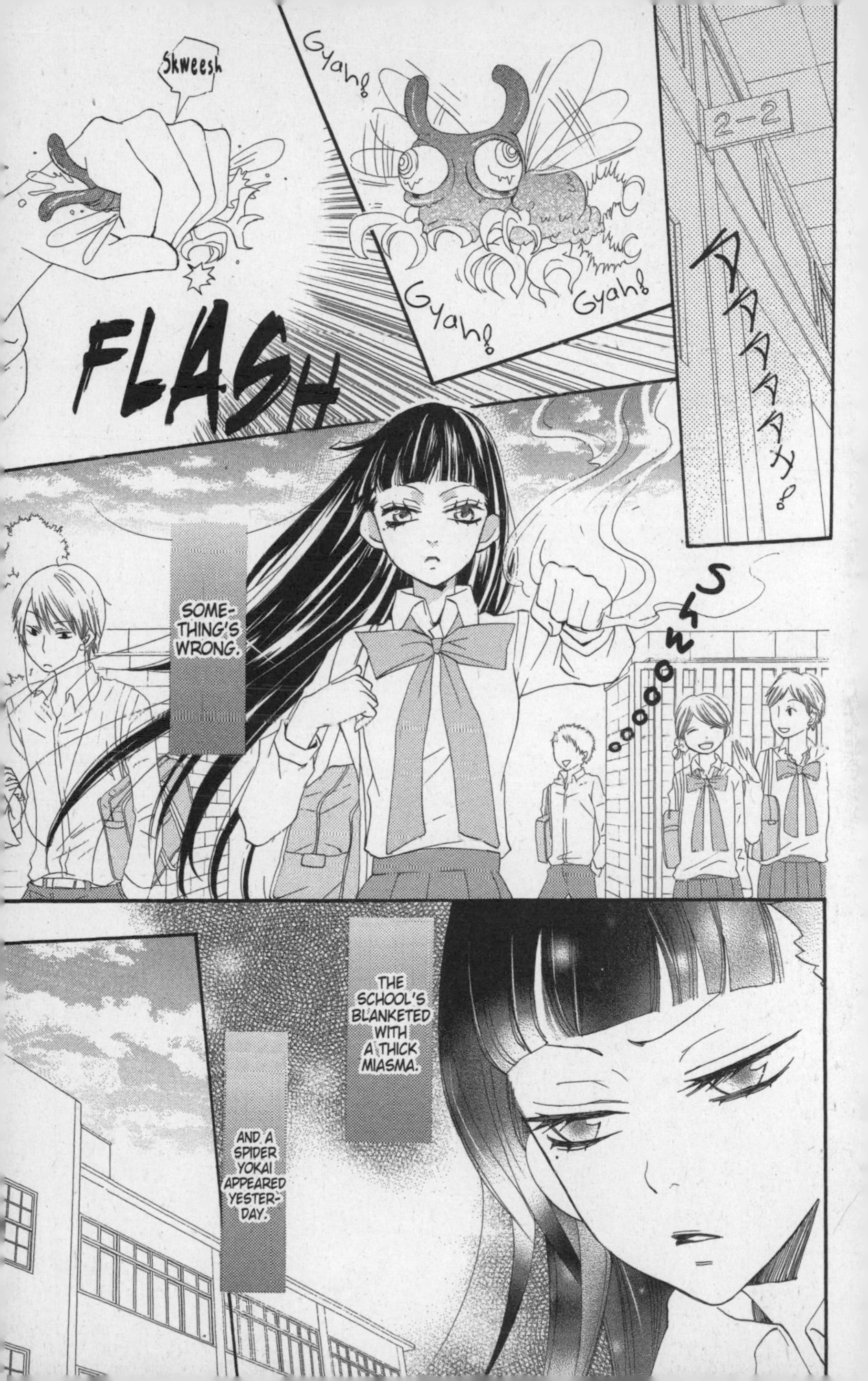
2-2
AAAAAAH!
Gyah!
Gyah!
Gyah!
Skweesh
FLASH
SHWOOOOO
SOME-THING'S WRONG.
THE SCHOOL'S BLANKETED WITH A THICK MIASMA.
AND A SPIDER YOKAI APPEARED YESTER-DAY.

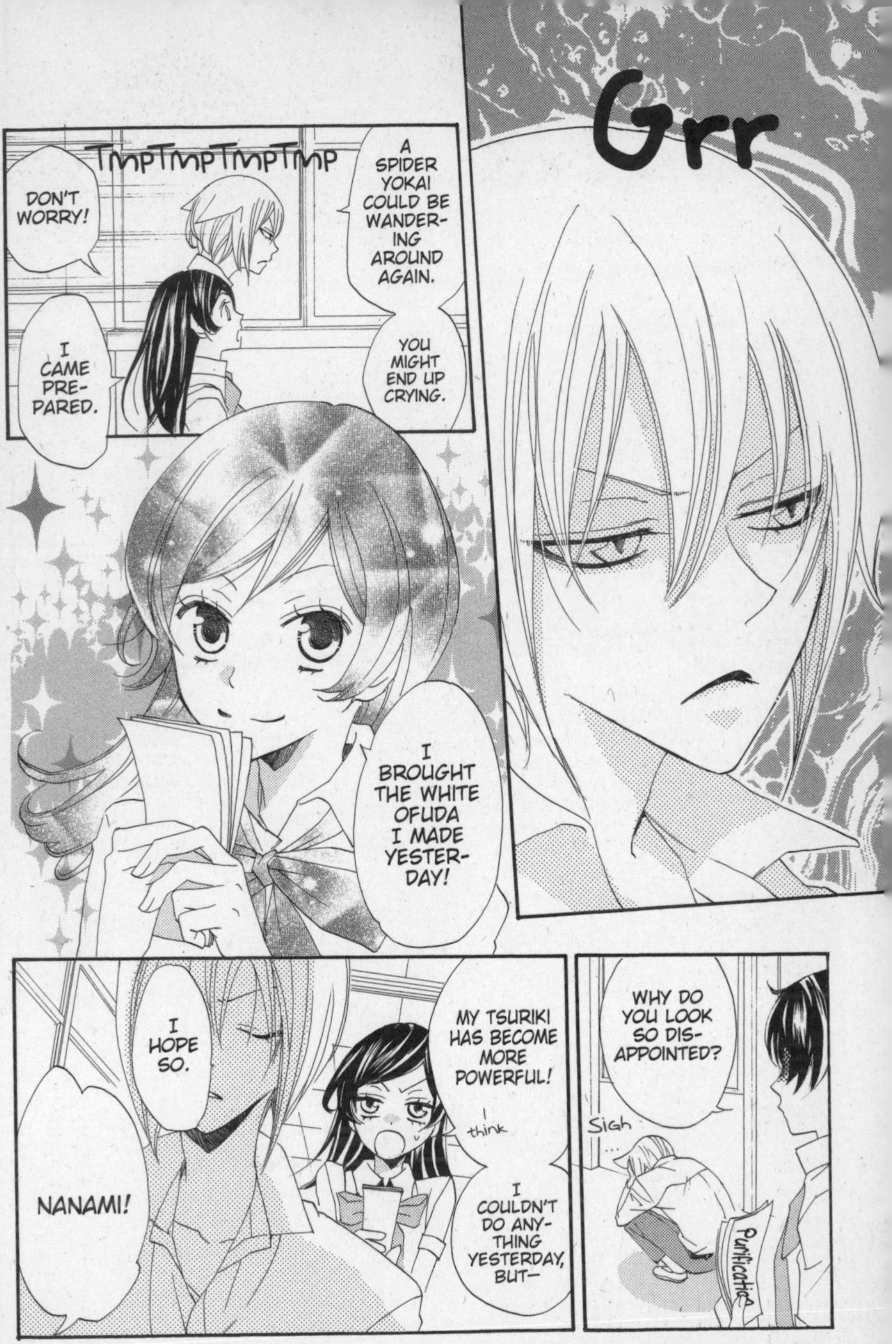
Grr
A SPIDER YOKAI COULD BE WANDERING AROUND AGAIN.
YOU MIGHT END UP CRYING.
TMPTMPTMPTMP
DON'T WORRY!
I CAME PREPARED.
I BROUGHT THE WHITE OFUDA I MADE YESTERDAY!
WHY DO YOU LOOK SO DISAPPOINTED?
Sigh...
Purification
MY TSURIKI HAS BECOME MORE POWERFUL!
I think
I COULDN'T DO ANYTHING YESTERDAY, BUT—
I HOPE SO.
NANAMI!

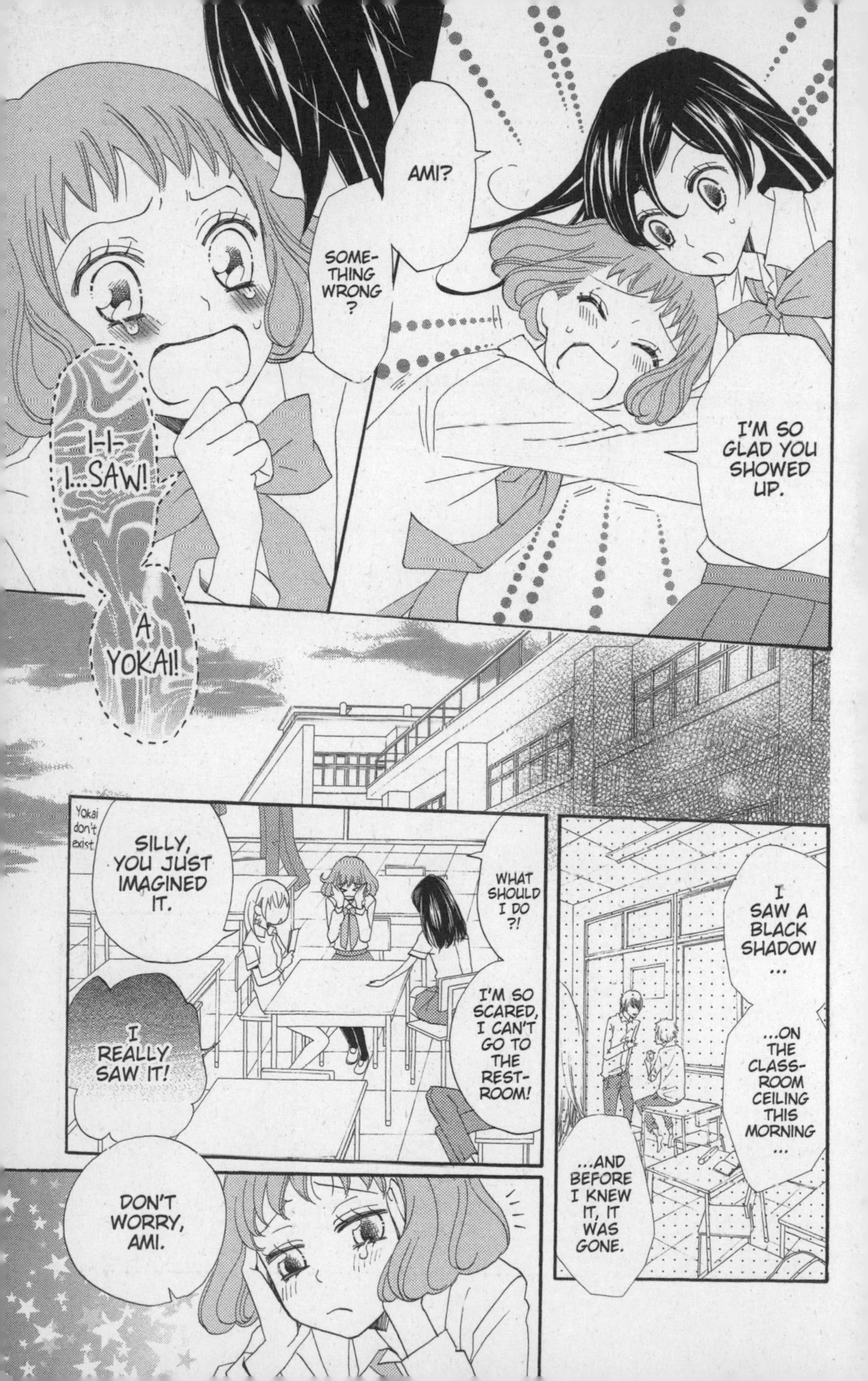
I'M SO GLAD YOU SHOWED UP.
AMI?
SOMETHING WRONG?
I-I-I...SAW!
A YOKAI!
I SAW A BLACK SHADOW...
...ON THE CLASSROOM CEILING THIS MORNING...
...AND BEFORE I KNEW IT, IT WAS GONE.
WHAT SHOULD I DO?!
I'M SO SCARED, I CAN'T GO TO THE RESTROOM!
SILLY, YOU JUST IMAGINED IT.
Yokai don't exist
I REALLY SAW IT!
DON'T WORRY, AMI.

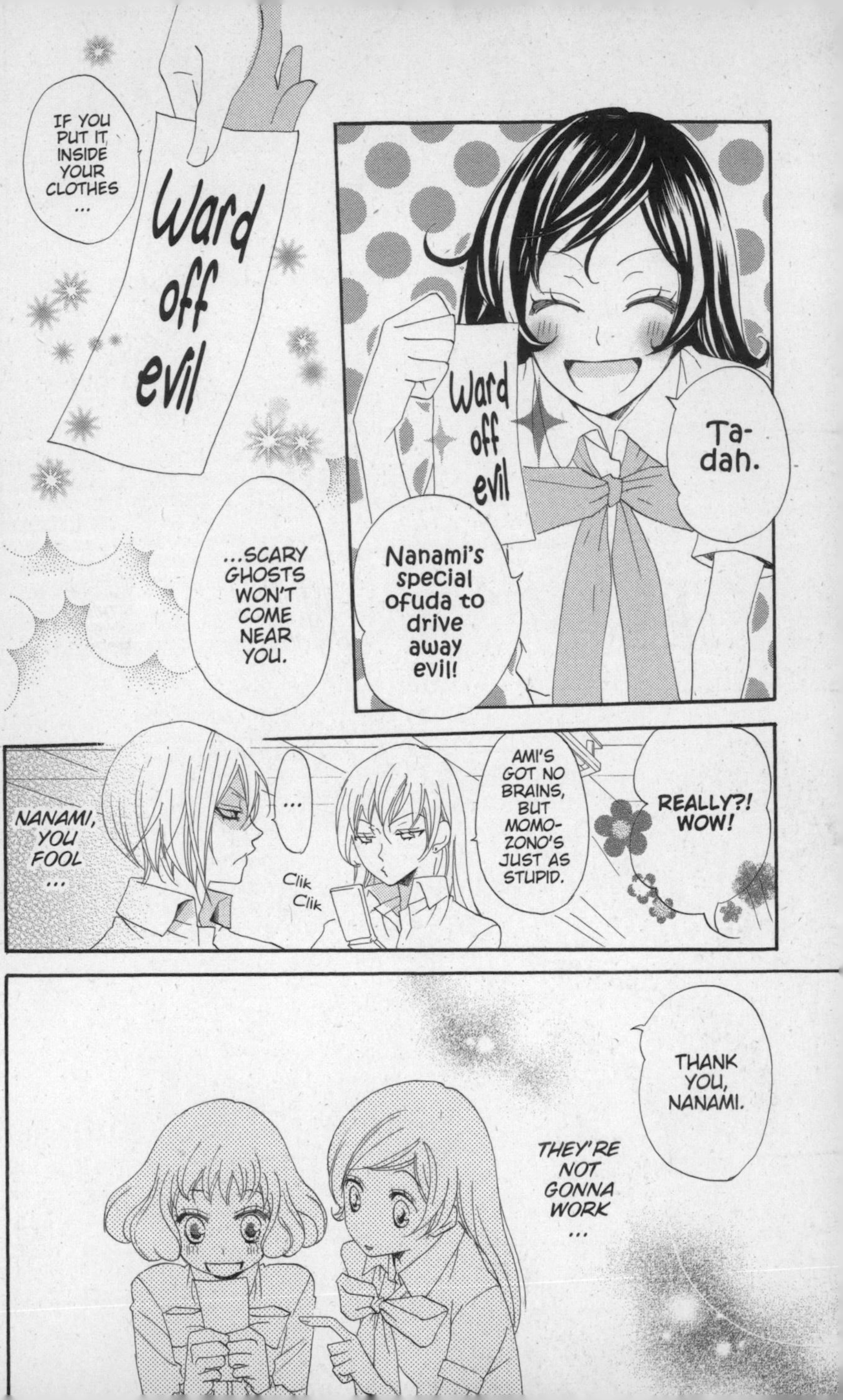
Ta-dah.
Ward off evil
Nanami's special ofuda to drive away evil!
Ward off evil
IF YOU PUT IT INSIDE YOUR CLOTHES ...
...SCARY GHOSTS WON'T COME NEAR YOU.
REALLY?! WOW!
AMI'S GOT NO BRAINS, BUT MOMOZONO'S JUST AS STUPID.
Clik Clik
...
NANAMI, YOU FOOL ...
THANK YOU, NANAMI.
THEY'RE NOT GONNA WORK ...

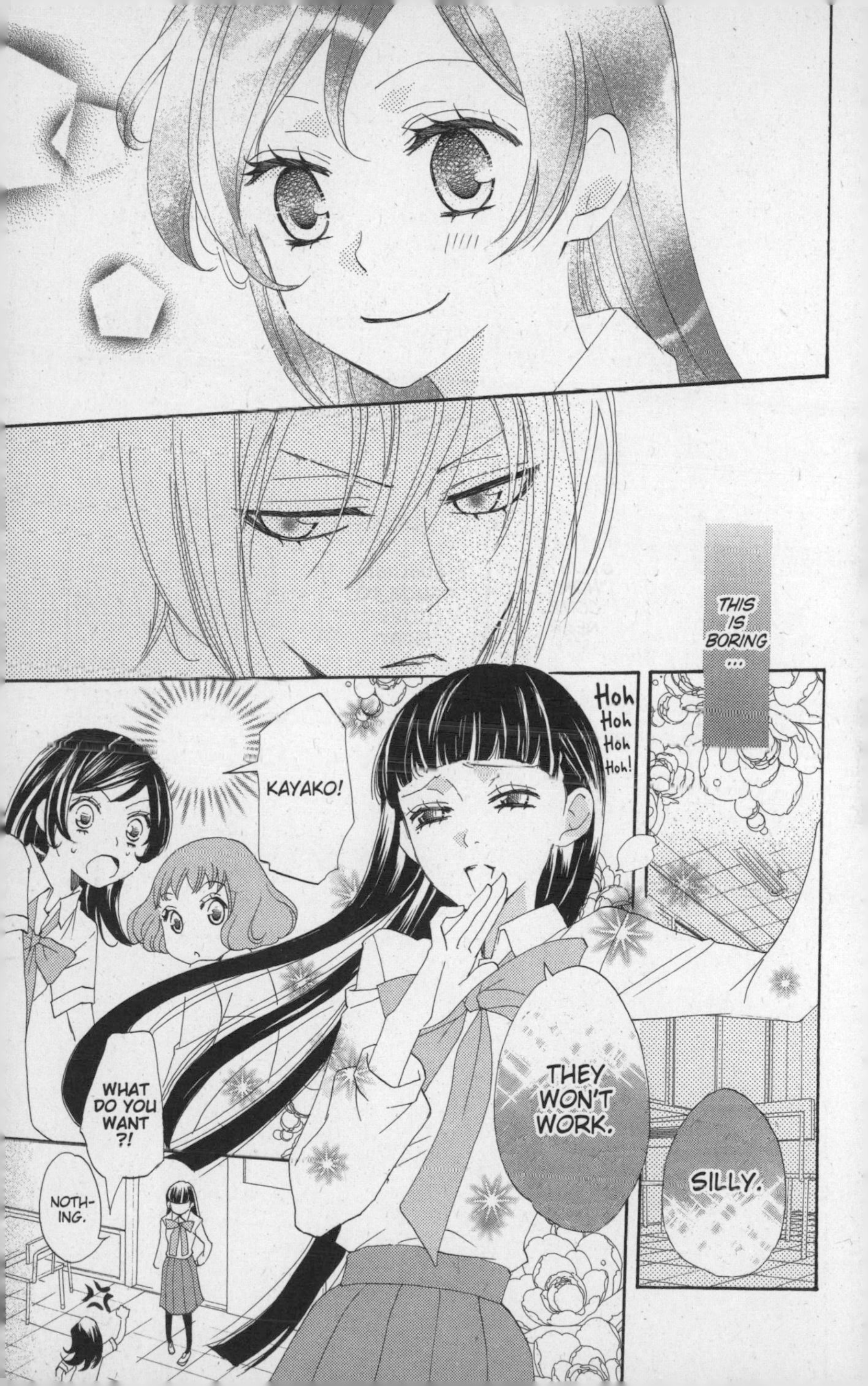
THIS IS BORING...
Hoh Hoh Hoh Hoh!
KAYAKO!
WHAT DO YOU WANT?!
NOTH-ING.
THEY WON'T WORK.
SILLY.

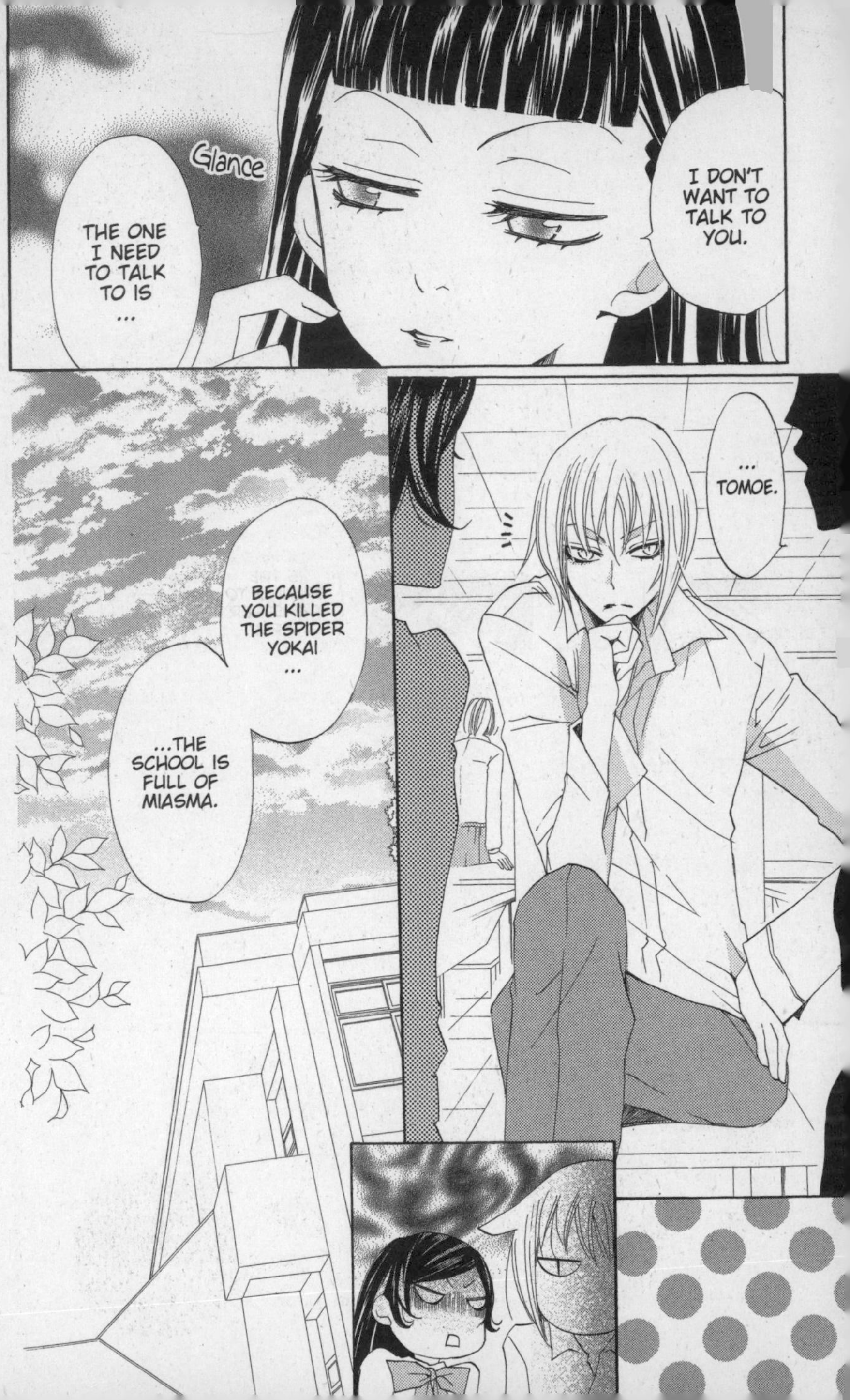
I DON'T WANT TO TALK TO YOU.
Glance
THE ONE I NEED TO TALK TO IS ...
... TOMOE.
BECAUSE YOU KILLED THE SPIDER YOKAI ...
...THE SCHOOL IS FULL OF MIASMA.

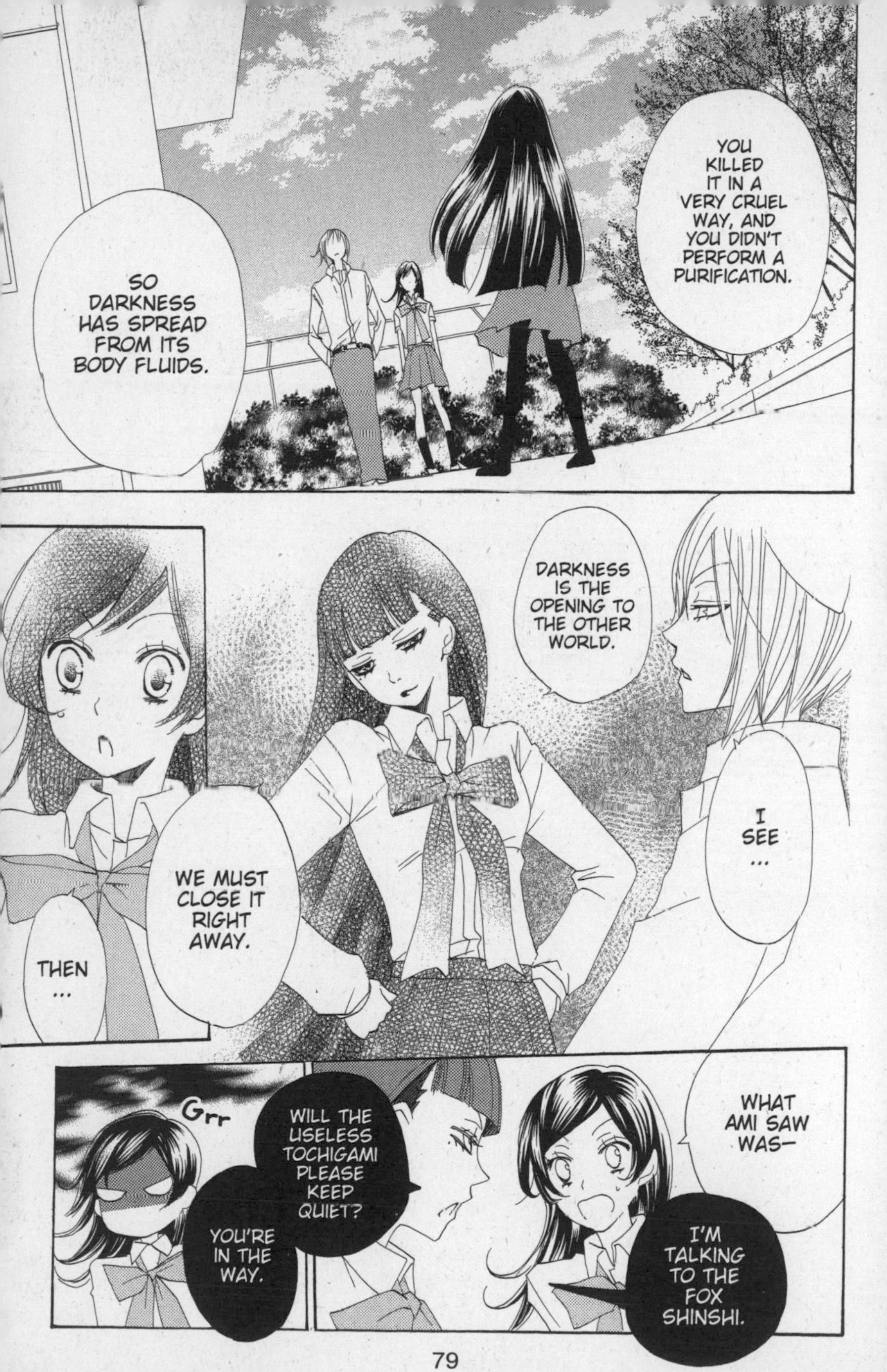
YOU KILLED IT IN A VERY CRUEL WAY, AND YOU DIDN'T PERFORM A PURIFICATION.
SO DARKNESS HAS SPREAD FROM ITS BODY FLUIDS.
DARKNESS IS THE OPENING TO THE OTHER WORLD.
I SEE ...
WE MUST CLOSE IT RIGHT AWAY.
THEN ...
WHAT AMI SAW WAS—
I'M TALKING TO THE FOX SHINSHI.
WILL THE USELESS TOCHIGAMI PLEASE KEEP QUIET?
YOU'RE IN THE WAY.
Grr

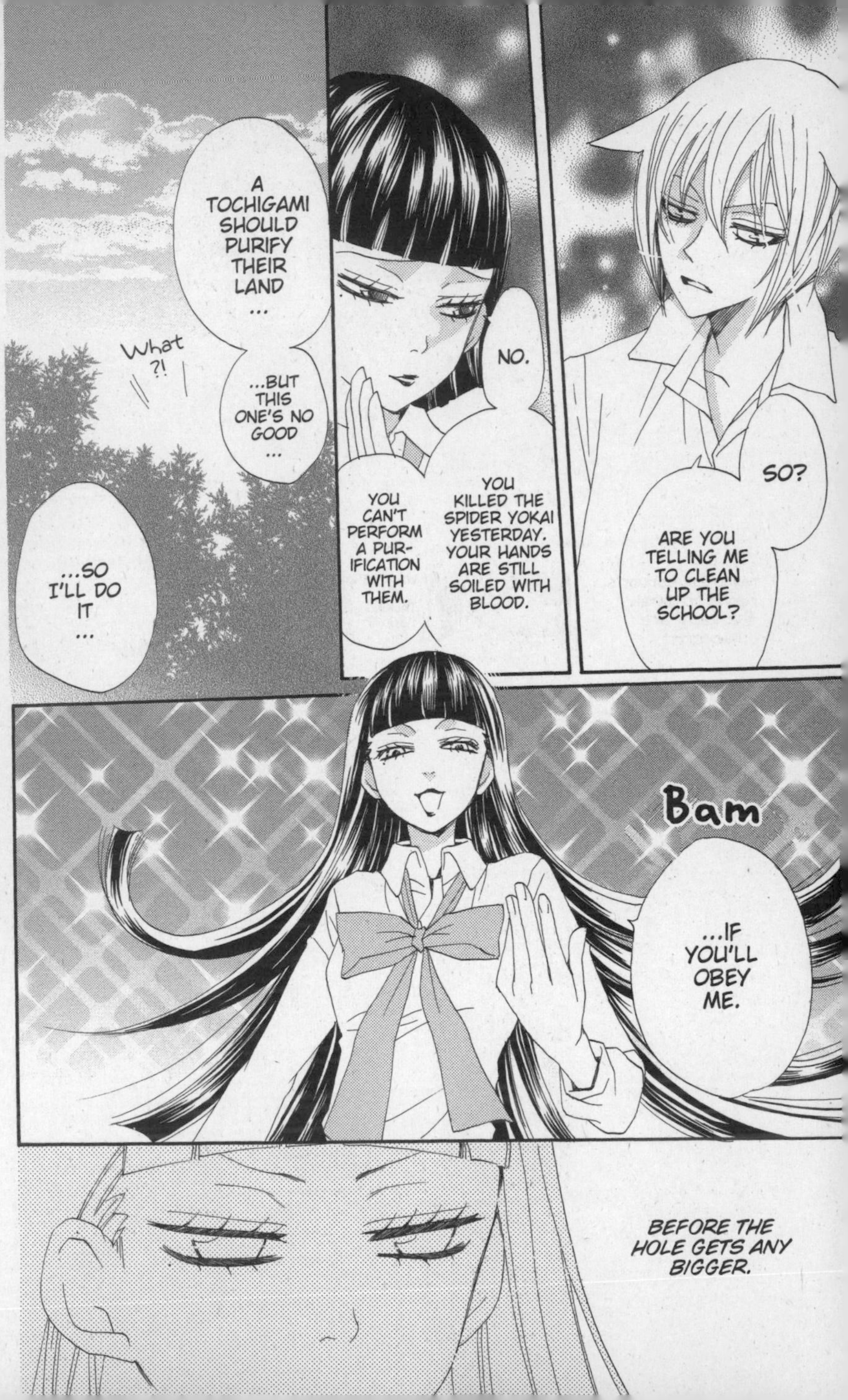
SO?
ARE YOU TELLING ME TO CLEAN UP THE SCHOOL?
NO.
YOU KILLED THE SPIDER YOKAI YESTERDAY. YOUR HANDS ARE STILL SOILED WITH BLOOD.
YOU CAN'T PERFORM A PURIFICATION WITH THEM.
A TOCHIGAMI SHOULD PURIFY THEIR LAND...
...BUT THIS ONE'S NO GOOD...
What ?!
...SO I'LL DO IT...
Bam
...IF YOU'LL OBEY ME.
BEFORE THE HOLE GETS ANY BIGGER.

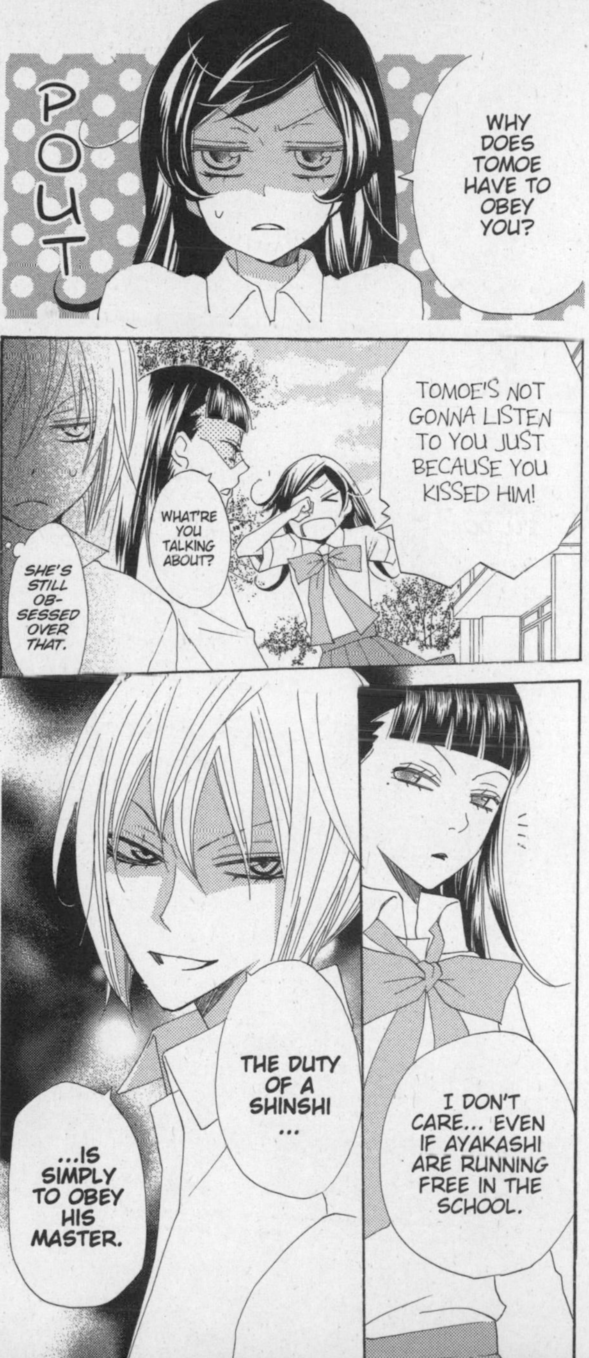
POUT
WHY DOES TOMOE HAVE TO OBEY YOU?
TOMOE'S NOT GONNA LISTEN TO YOU JUST BECAUSE YOU KISSED HIM!
WHAT'RE YOU TALKING ABOUT?
SHE'S STILL OB-SESSED OVER THAT.
I DON'T CARE... EVEN IF AYAKASHI ARE RUNNING FREE IN THE SCHOOL.
THE DUTY OF A SHINSHI ...
...IS SIMPLY TO OBEY HIS MASTER.

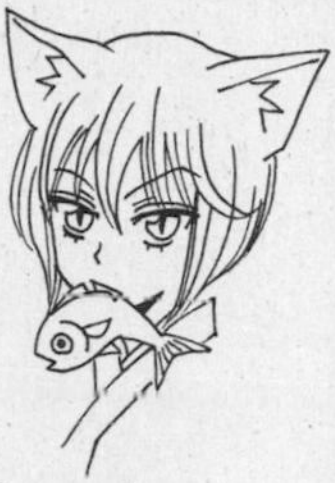

Tomoe has the same name as the boy in "Tsubaki Ori", a one-shot I wrote a long time ago. I took his name from my then editor's name (though the kanji are different).

I wanted to use the kanji for "looking at the moon" for Mizuki so he's looking at the moon in Yonomori, but it didn't feel quite right, so I changed the kanji.

Kurama was originally named Yukiya, but I made it Kurama to make things more obvious.

I took Onikiri and Kotetsu from names of Japanese swords.

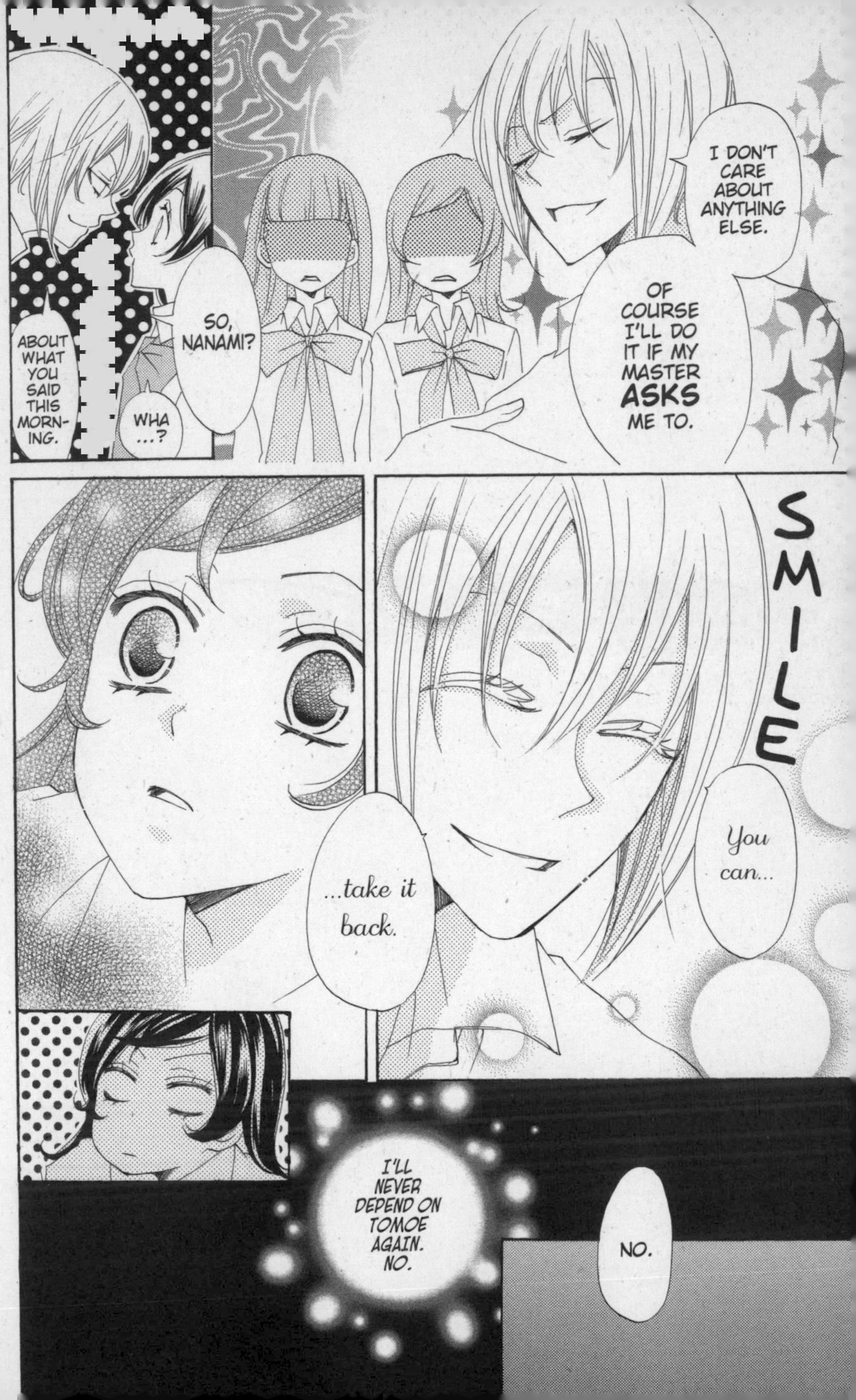
I DON'T CARE ABOUT ANYTHING ELSE.
OF COURSE I'LL DO IT IF MY MASTER **ASKS** ME TO.
SO, NANAMI?
ABOUT WHAT YOU SAID THIS MORNING.
WHA...?
SMILE
You can...
...take it back.
I'LL NEVER DEPEND ON TOMOE AGAIN. NO.
NO.

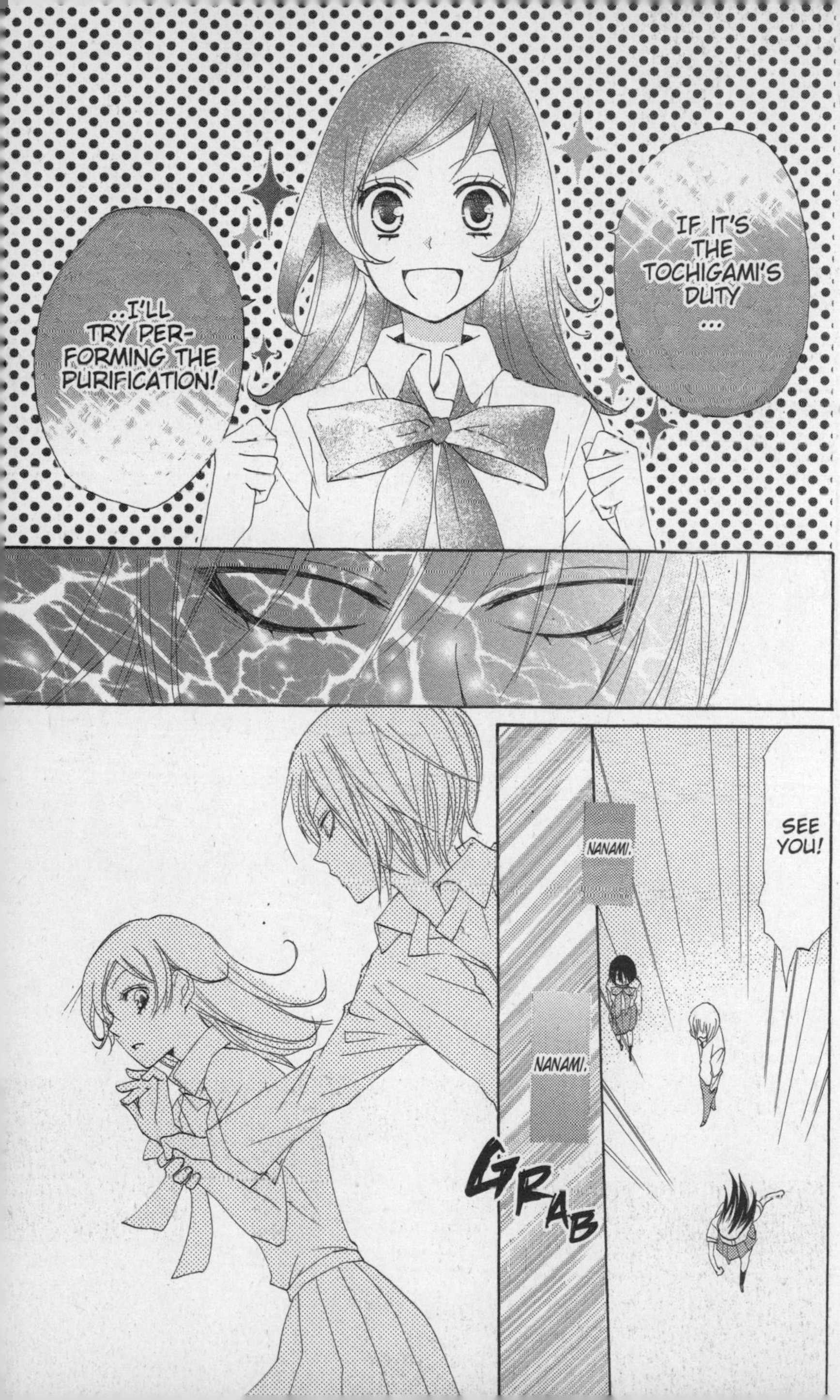
IF IT'S THE TOCHIGAMI'S DUTY ...
..I'LL TRY PER-FORMING THE PURIFICATION!
SEE YOU!
NANAMI.
NANAMI.
GRAB

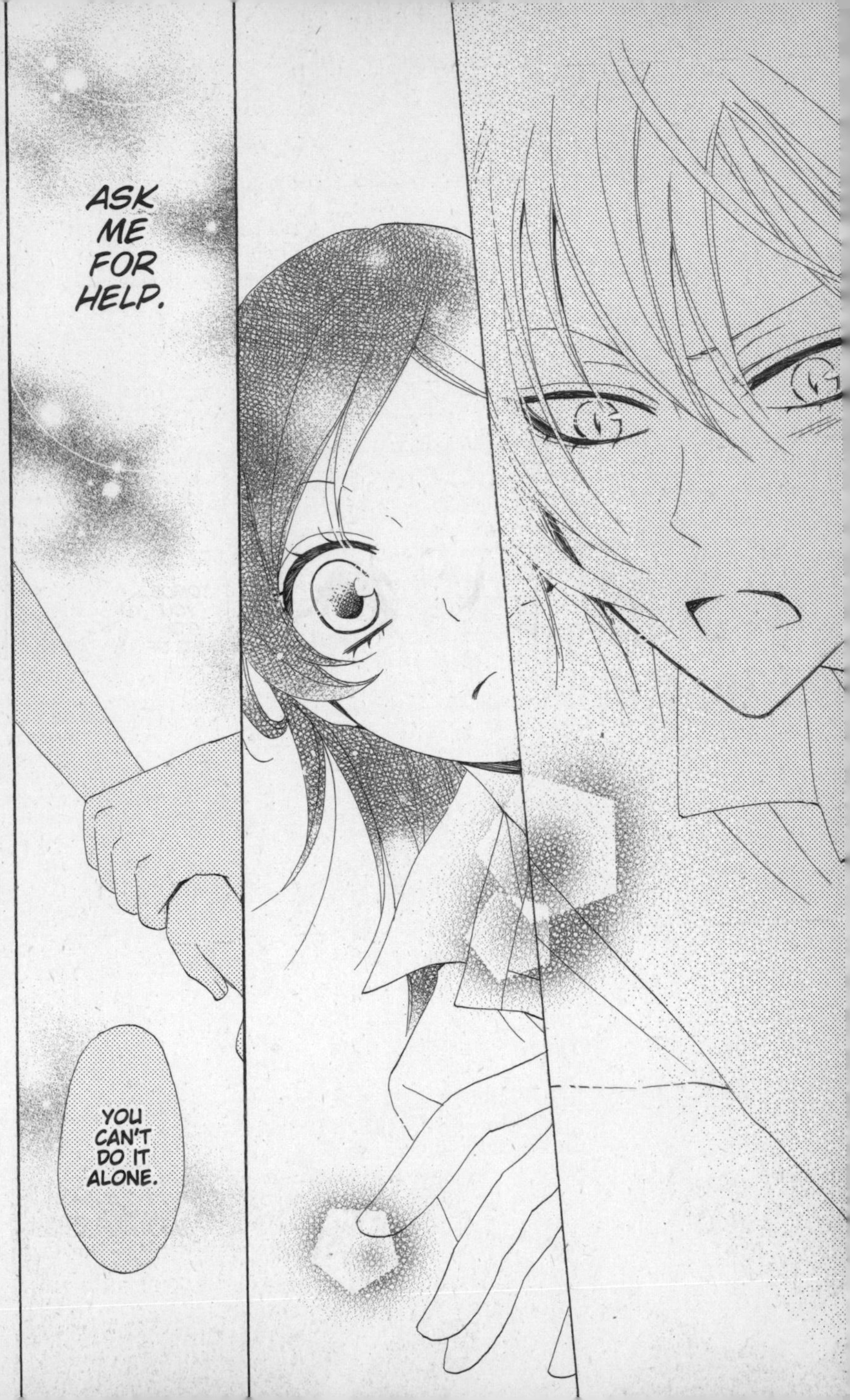
ASK ME FOR HELP.
YOU CAN'T DO IT ALONE.

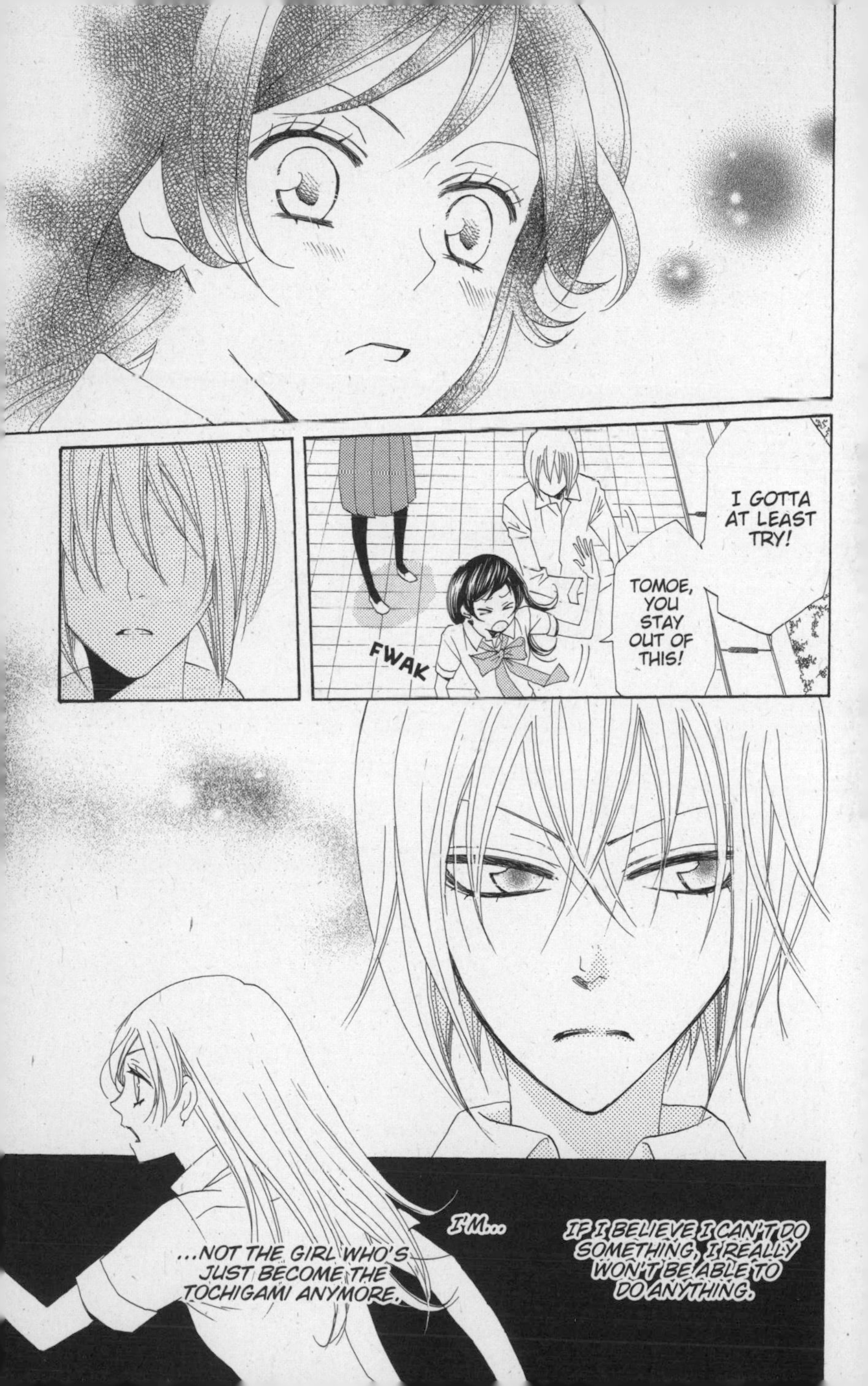
I GOTTA AT LEAST TRY!
TOMOE, YOU STAY OUT OF THIS!
FWAK
IF I BELIEVE I CAN'T DO SOMETHING, I REALLY WON'T BE ABLE TO DO ANYTHING.
I'M...
...NOT THE GIRL WHO'S JUST BECOME THE TOCHIGAMI ANYMORE.

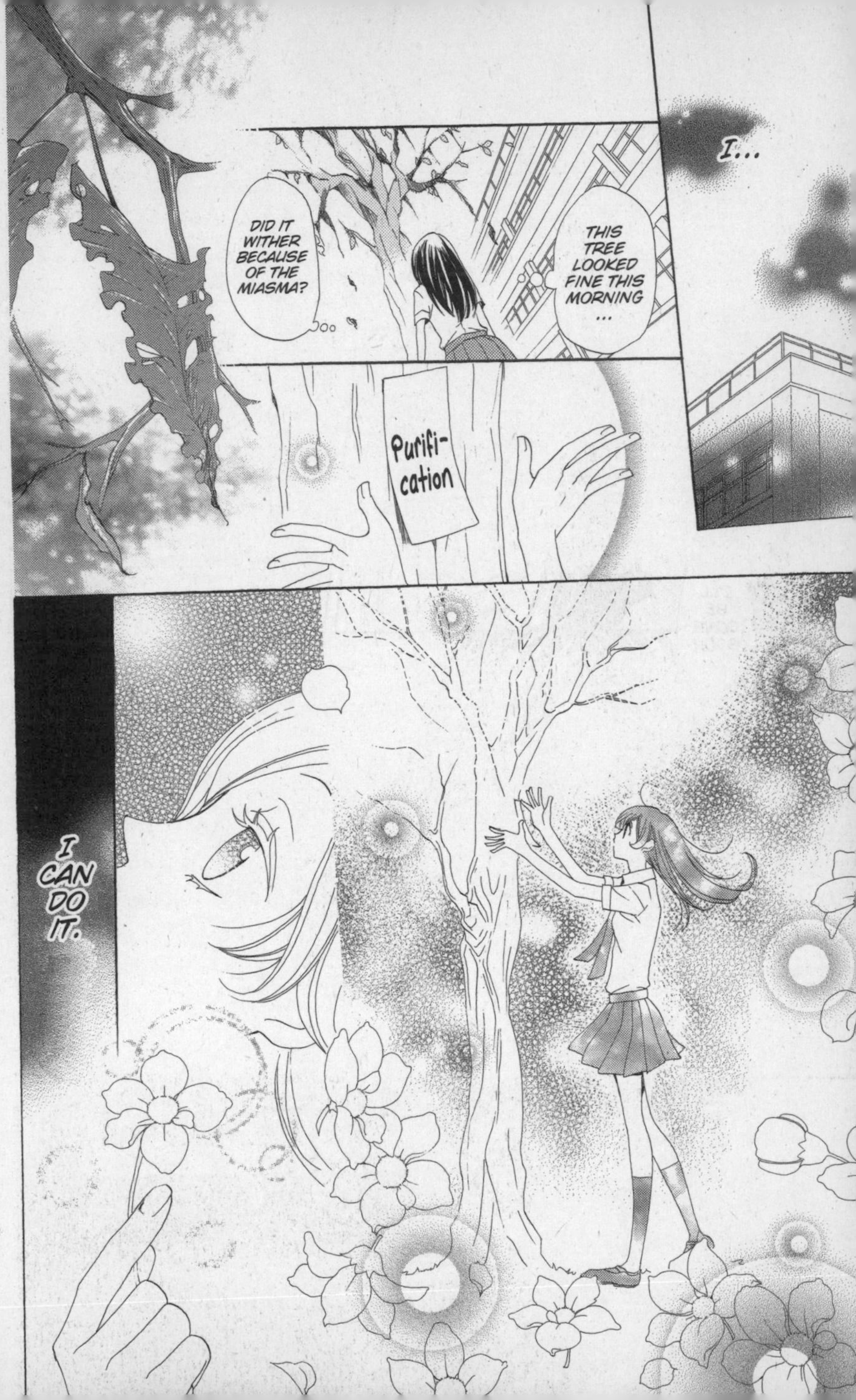
I...
THIS TREE LOOKED FINE THIS MORNING ...
DID IT WITHER BECAUSE OF THE MIASMA?
Purifi-cation
I CAN DO IT.

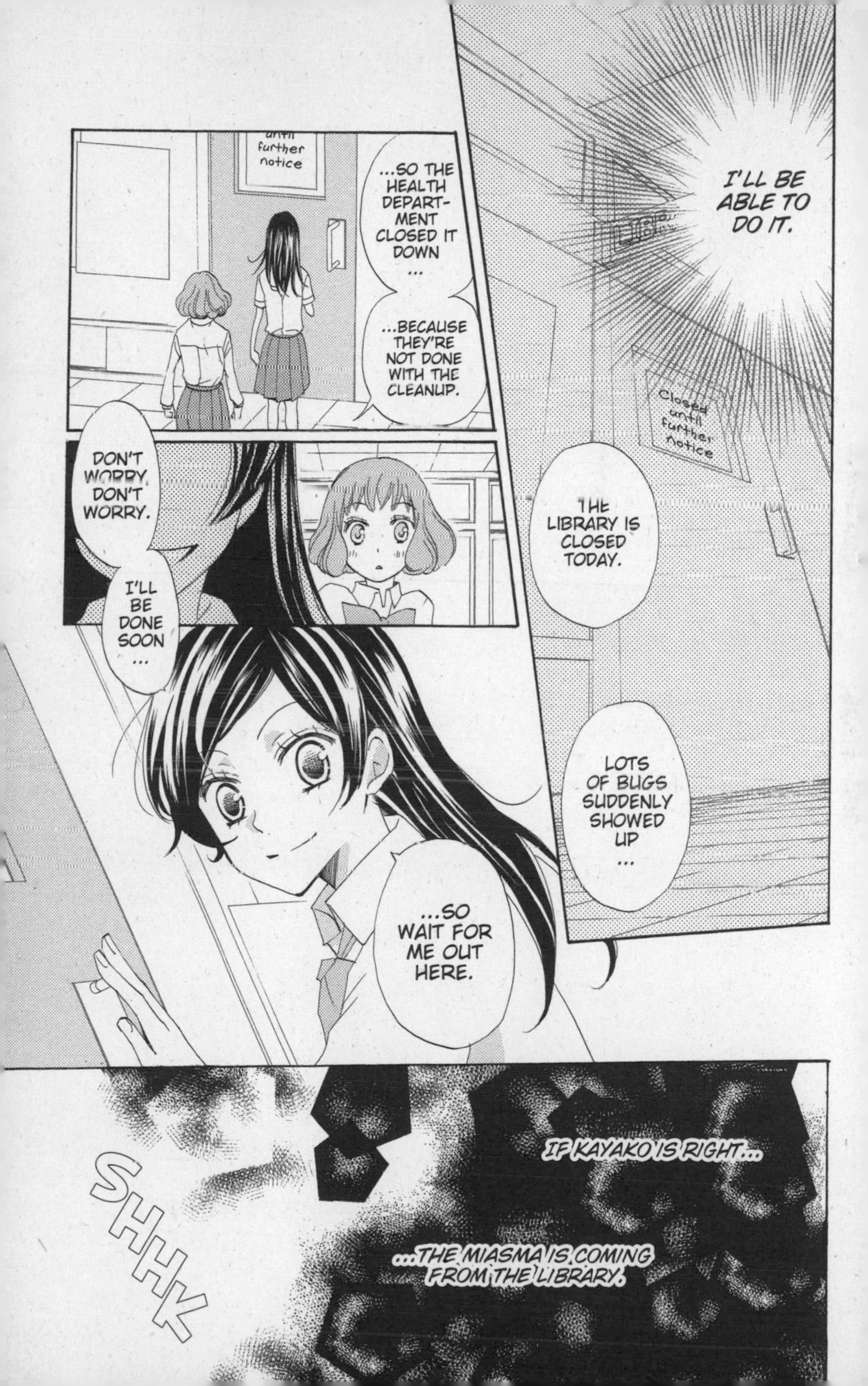

I'LL BE ABLE TO DO IT.
Closed until further notice
THE LIBRARY IS CLOSED TODAY.
LOTS OF BUGS SUDDENLY SHOWED UP...
until further notice
...SO THE HEALTH DEPARTMENT CLOSED IT DOWN...
...BECAUSE THEY'RE NOT DONE WITH THE CLEANUP.
DON'T WORRY, DON'T WORRY.
I'LL BE DONE SOON...
...SO WAIT FOR ME OUT HERE.
IF KAYAKO IS RIGHT...
...THE MIASMA IS COMING FROM THE LIBRARY.
SHHK

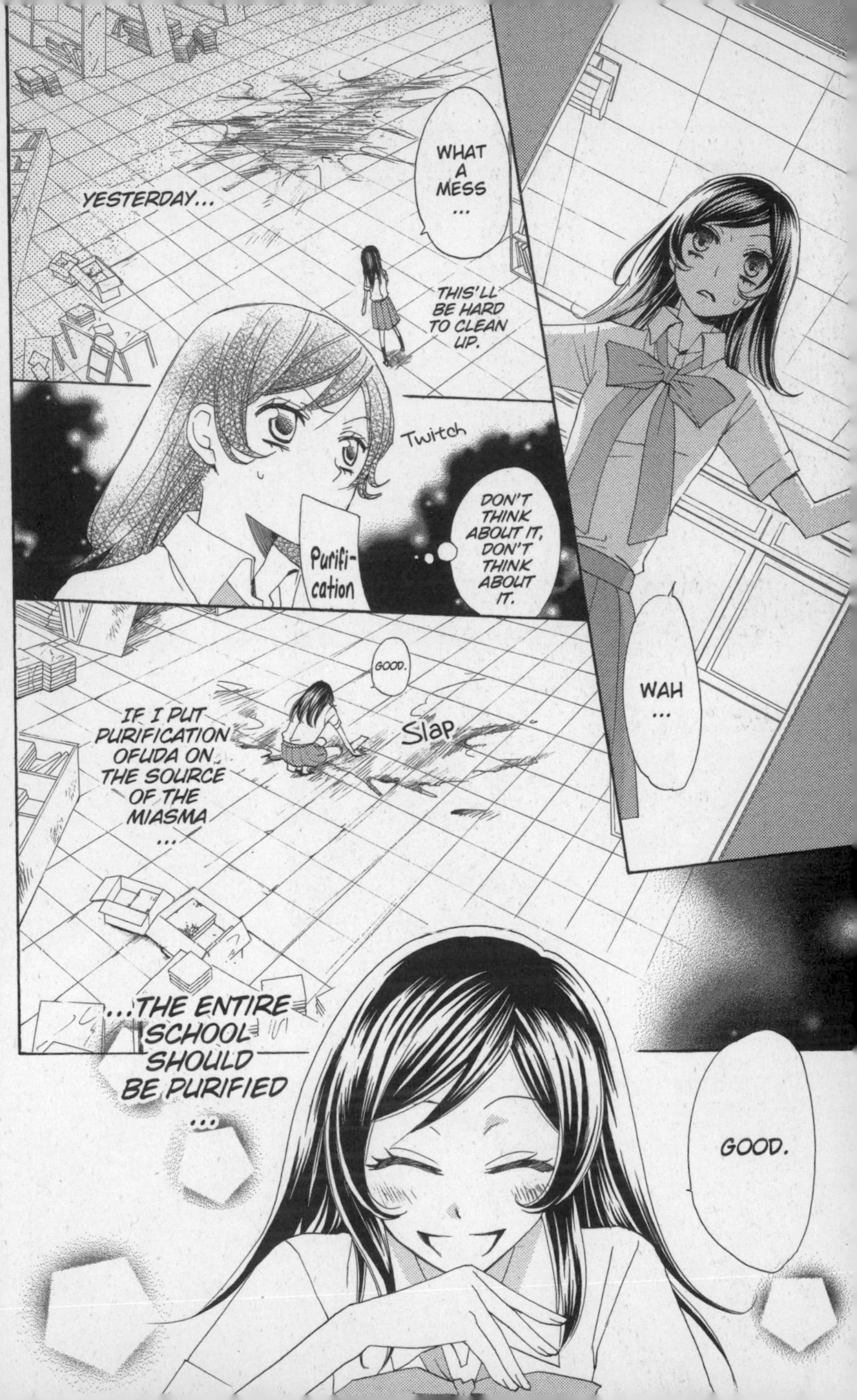
WAH...
WHAT A MESS...
YESTERDAY...
THIS'LL BE HARD TO CLEAN UP.
Twitch
DON'T THINK ABOUT IT, DON'T THINK ABOUT IT.
Purification
GOOD.
Slap
IF I PUT PURIFICATION OFUDA ON THE SOURCE OF THE MIASMA...
...THE ENTIRE SCHOOL SHOULD BE PURIFIED...
GOOD.

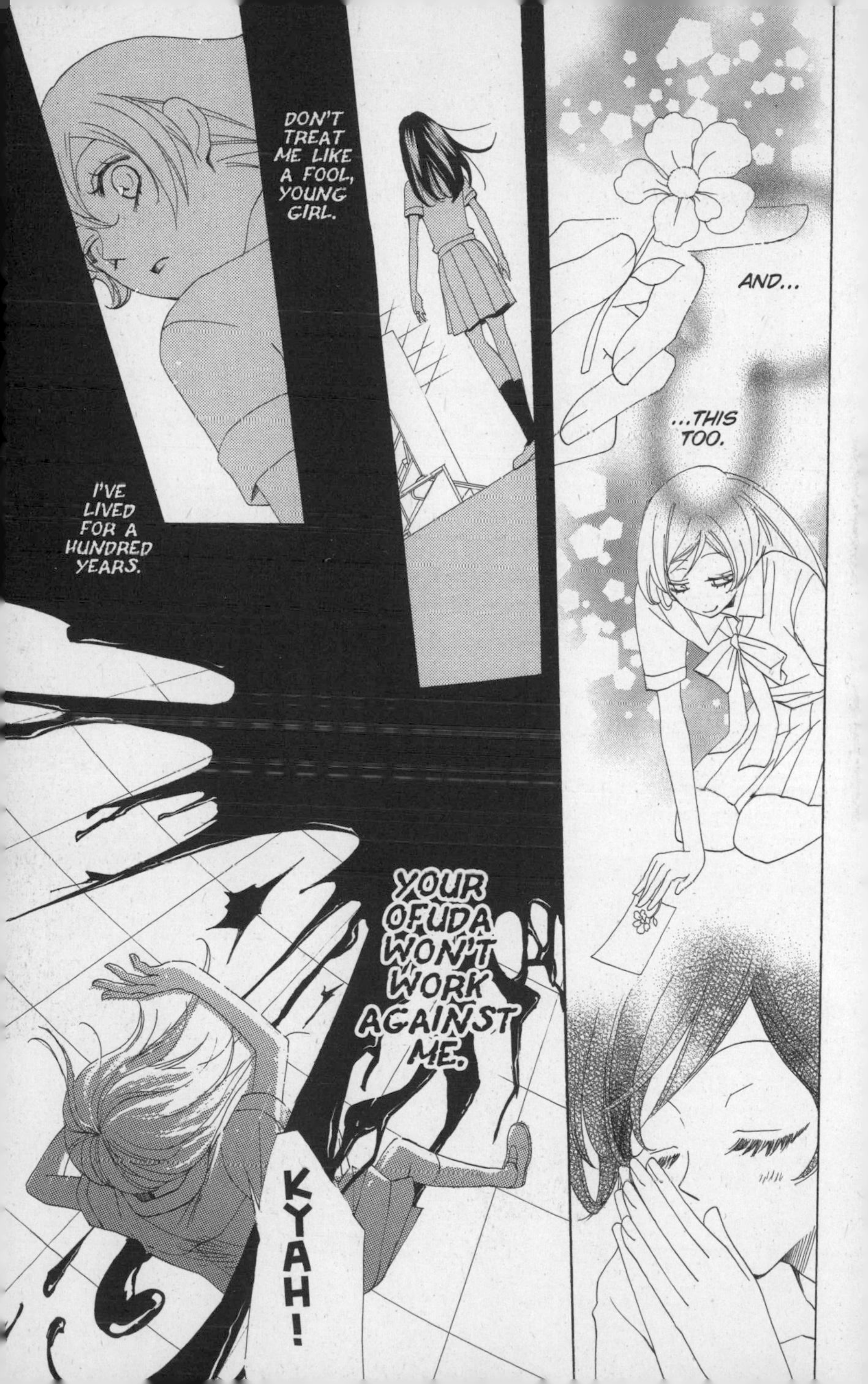
AND...
...THIS TOO.
DON'T TREAT ME LIKE A FOOL, YOUNG GIRL.
I'VE LIVED FOR A HUNDRED YEARS.
YOUR OFUDA WON'T WORK AGAINST ME.
KYAH!

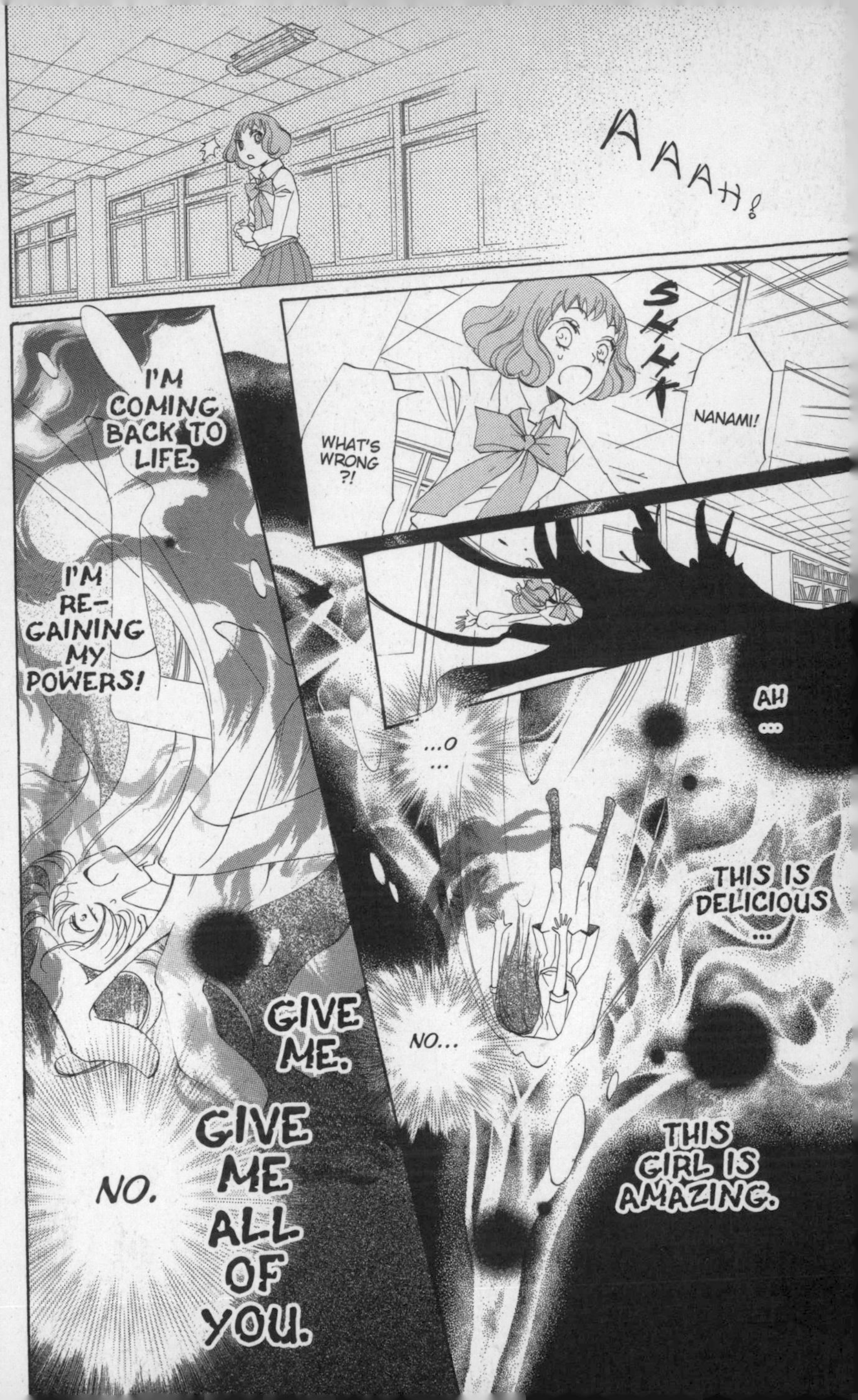
AAAAH!
SHHK
NANAMI!
WHAT'S WRONG?!
AH...
...O...
THIS IS DELICIOUS...
NO...
THIS GIRL IS AMAZING.
I'M COMING BACK TO LIFE.
I'M RE-GAINING MY POWERS!
GIVE ME.
GIVE ME ALL OF YOU.
NO.

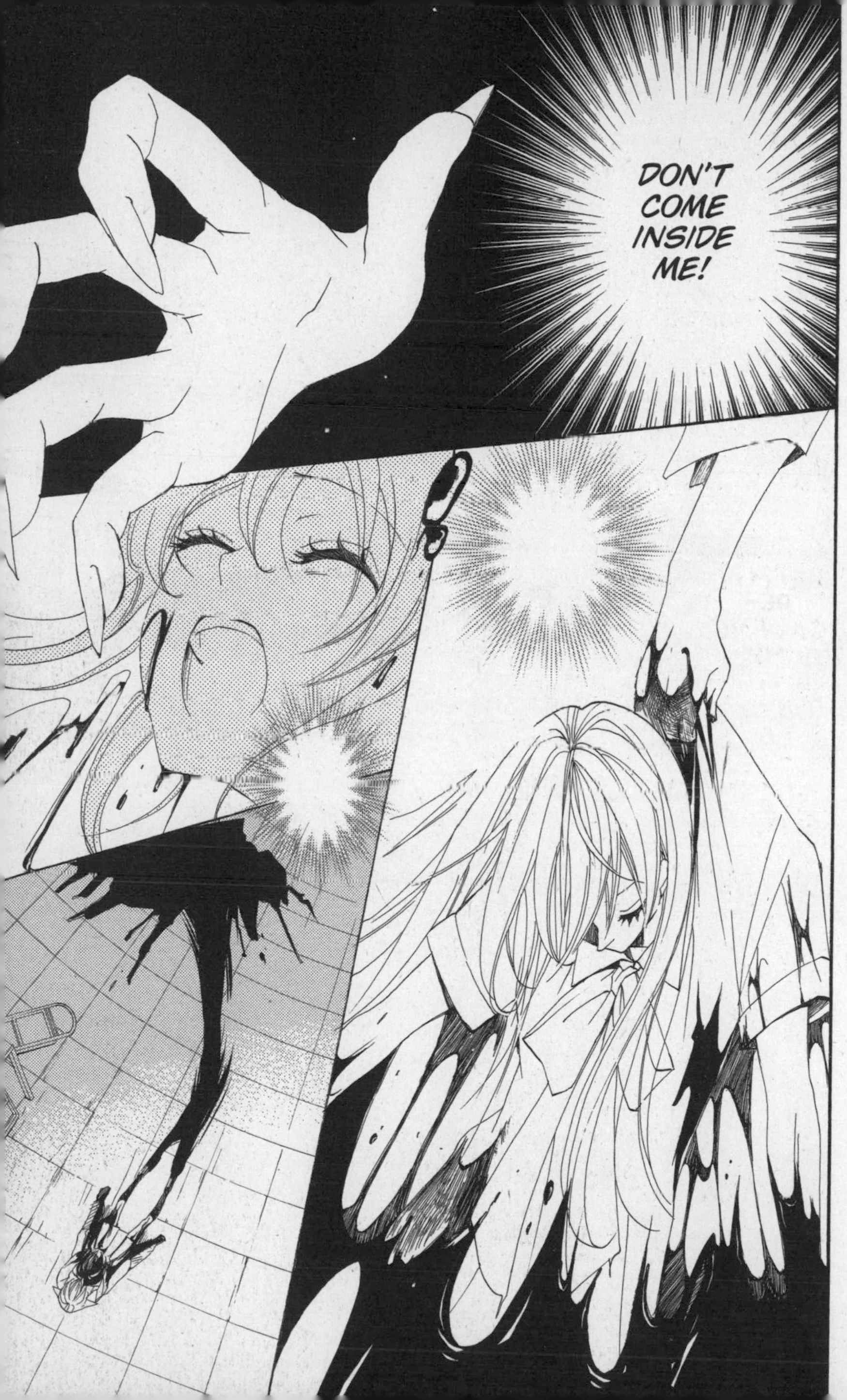
DON'T COME INSIDE ME!

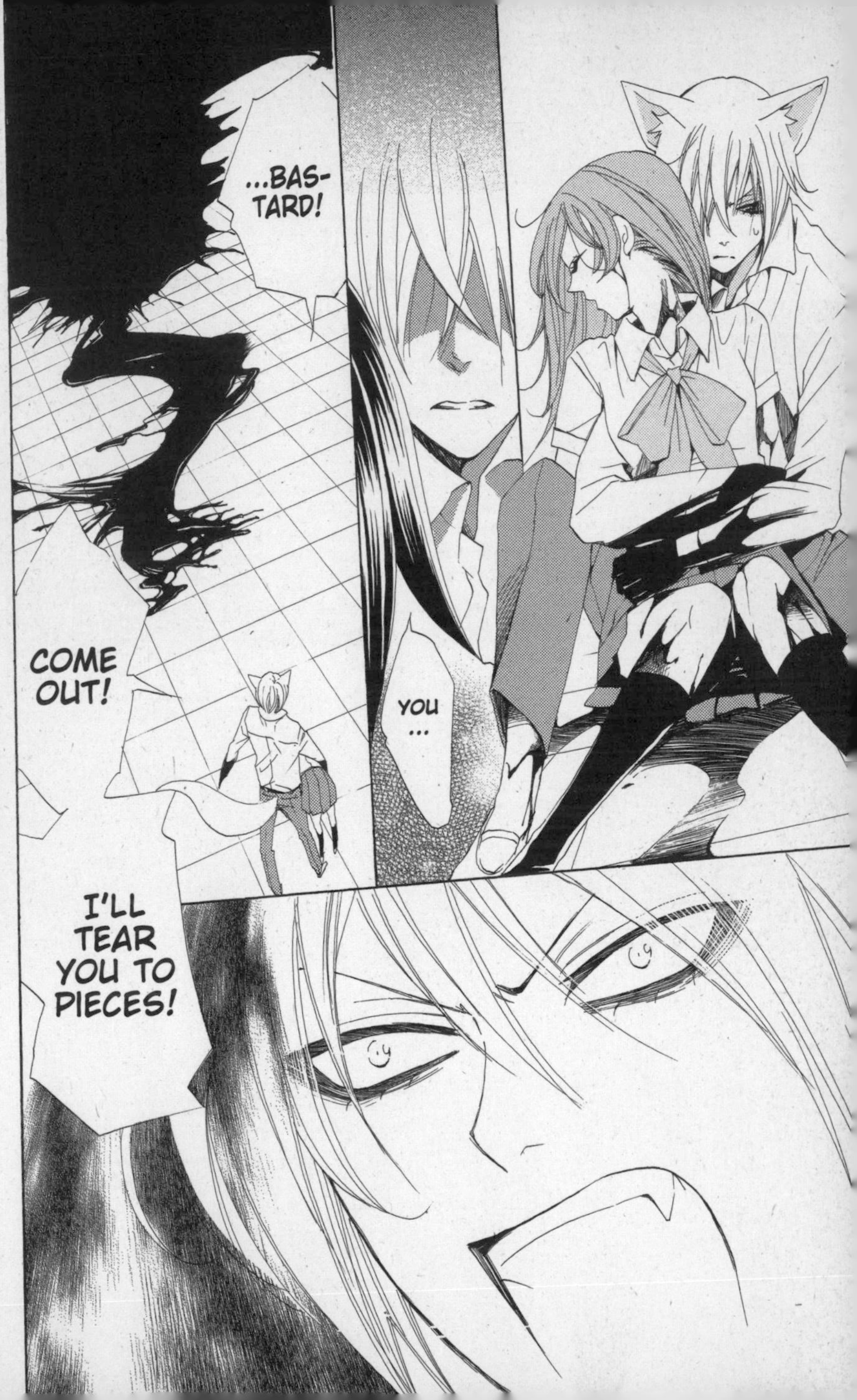
YOU ...
...BAS-TARD!
COME OUT!
I'LL TEAR YOU TO PIECES!

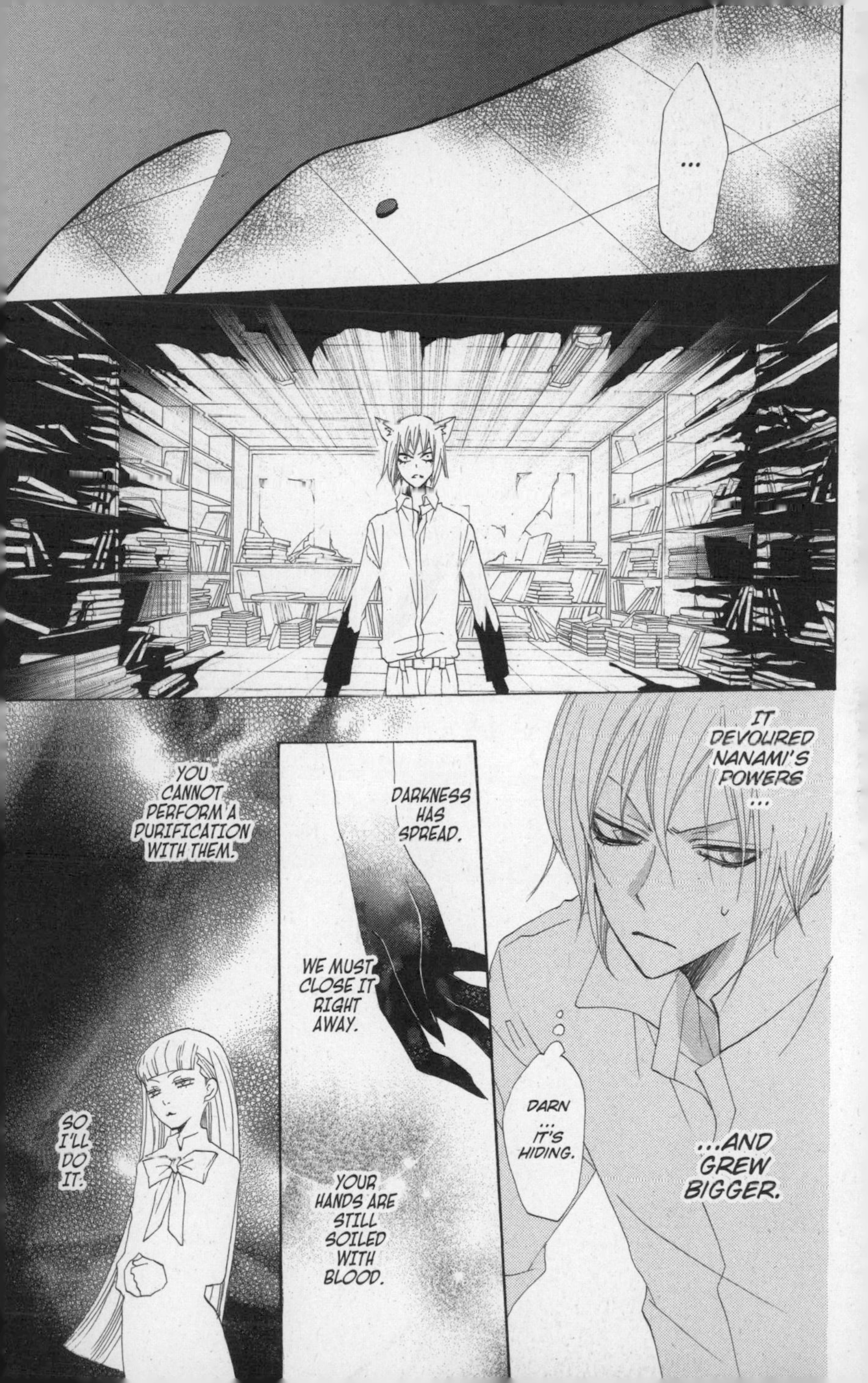
...
IT DEVOURED NANAMI'S POWERS ...
...AND GREW BIGGER.
DARN ... IT'S HIDING.
DARKNESS HAS SPREAD.
WE MUST CLOSE IT RIGHT AWAY.
YOUR HANDS ARE STILL SOILED WITH BLOOD.
YOU CANNOT PERFORM A PURIFICATION WITH THEM.
SO I'LL DO IT.

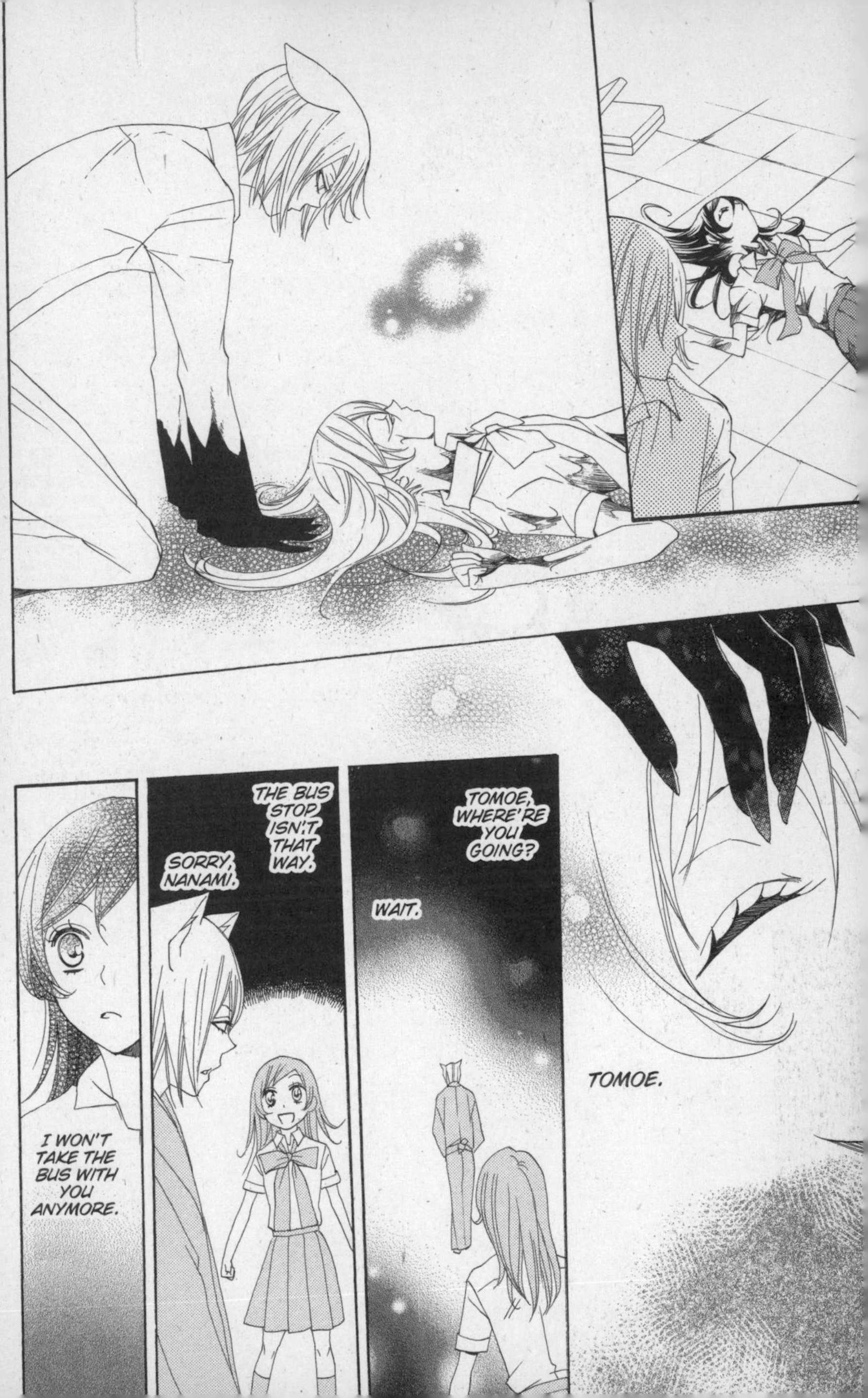
TOMOE.
TOMOE, WHERE'RE YOU GOING?
WAIT.
THE BUS STOP ISN'T THAT WAY.
SORRY, NANAMI.
I WON'T TAKE THE BUS WITH YOU ANYMORE.

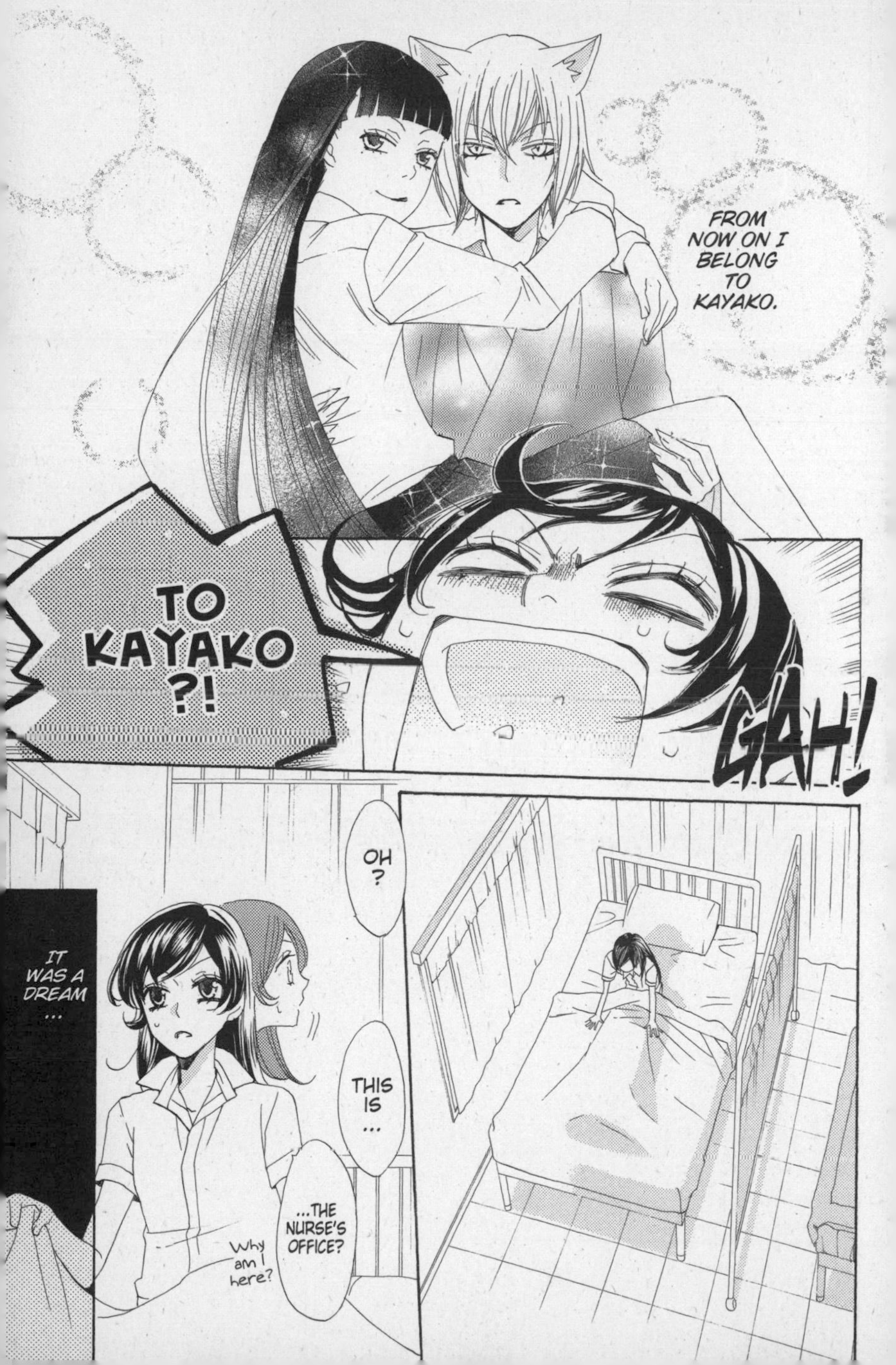
FROM NOW ON I BELONG TO KAYAKO.
TO KAYAKO ?!
GAH!
OH ?
THIS IS ...
...THE NURSE'S OFFICE?
Why am I here?
IT WAS A DREAM ...

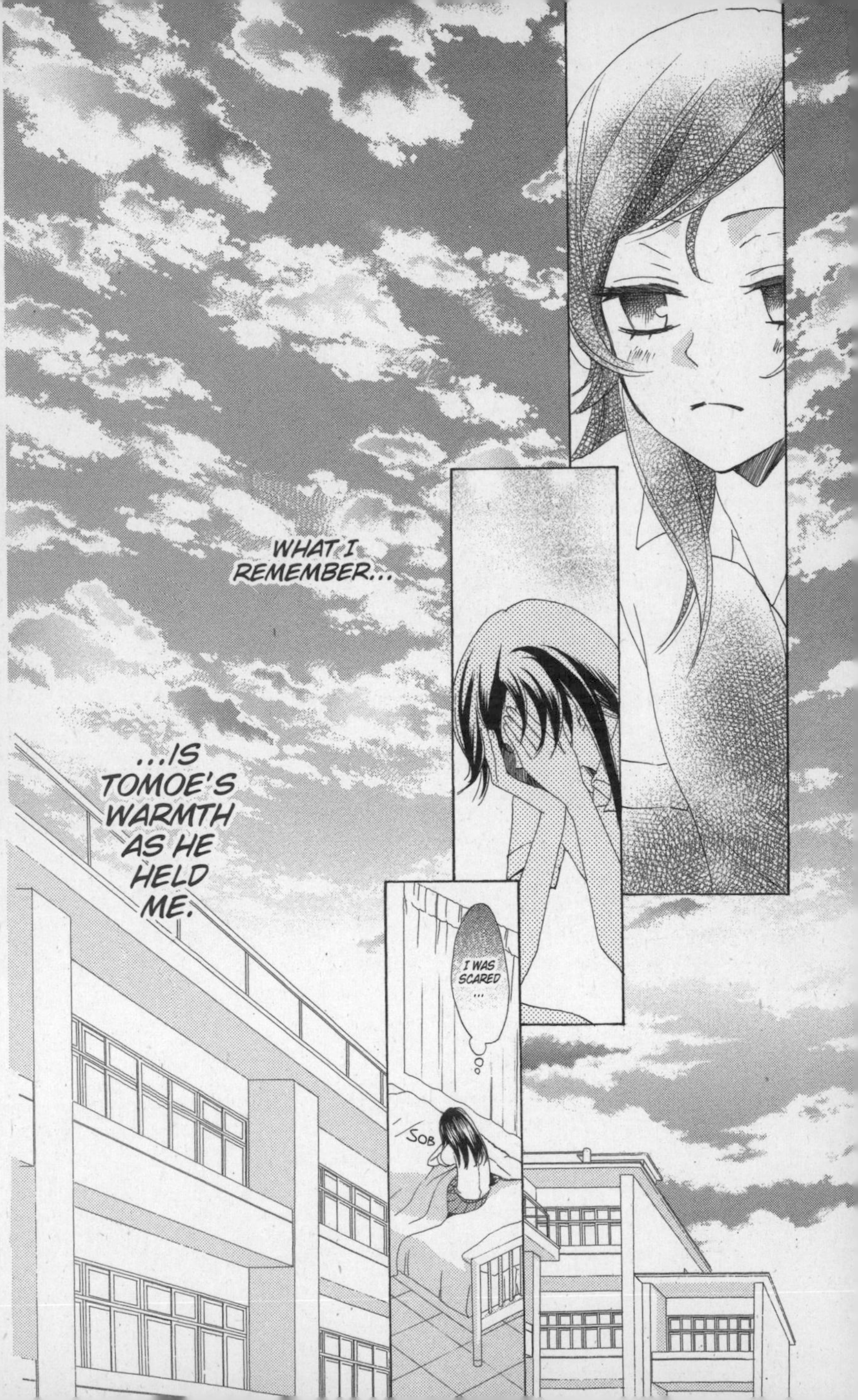
WHAT I REMEMBER...
I WAS SCARED...
SOB
...IS TOMOE'S WARMTH AS HE HELD ME.

Kamisama Kiss

Chapter 34

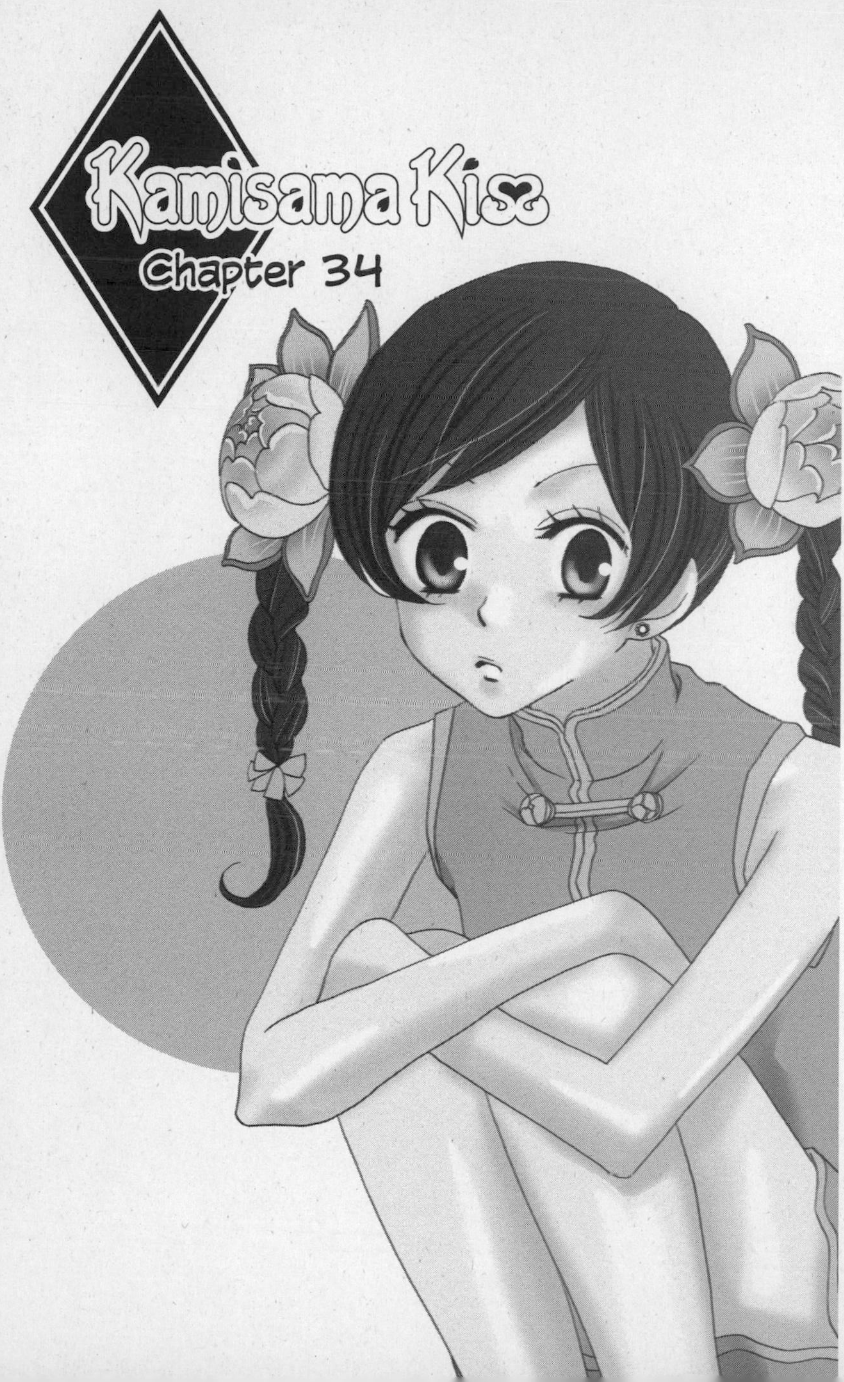

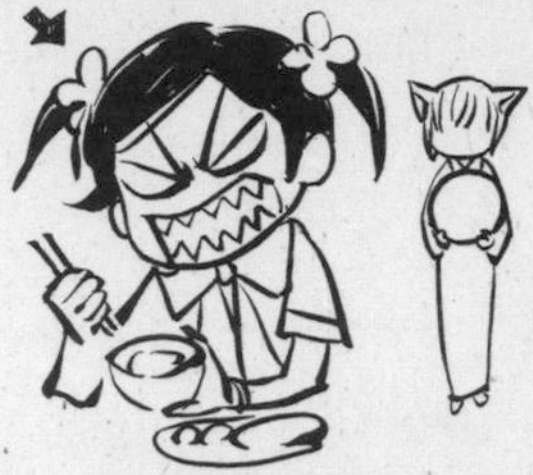

My master is her usual self today...

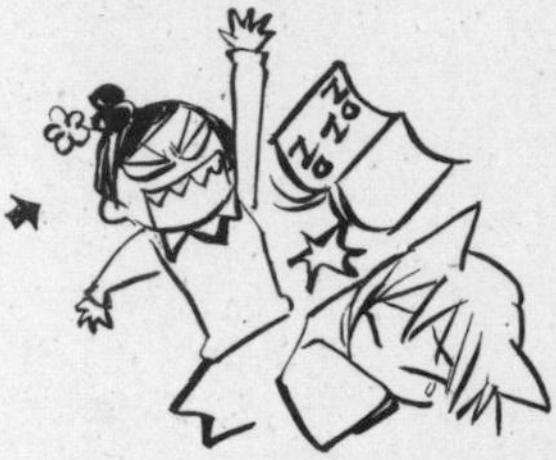
NO NO NO

I endure her violent behavior, but how long will it go on?

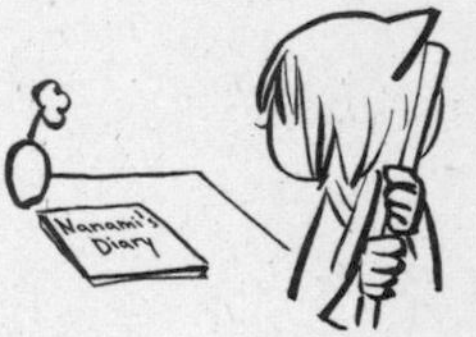
Nanami's Diary

I found master's diary while I was cleaning. I keep a blog, but she's pretty analog. To spite her, let's see what she's written in it.

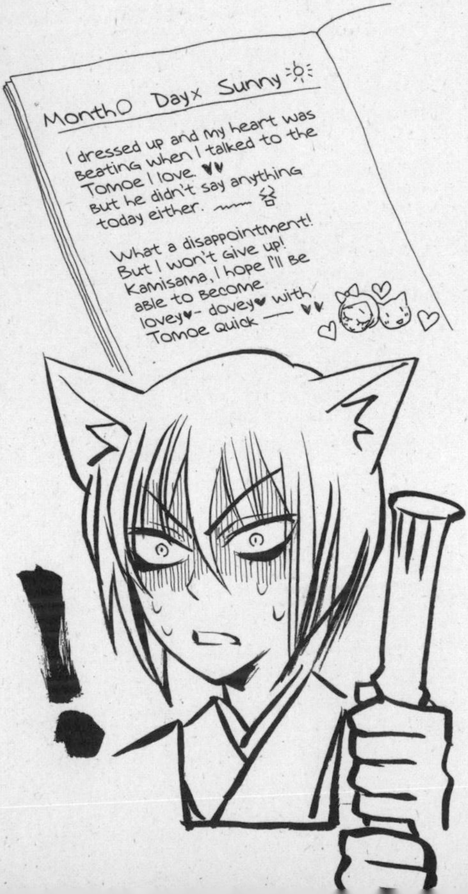
Month○ Day× Sunny
I dressed up and my heart was beating when I talked to the Tomoe I love. ♥♥
But he didn't say anything today either.
What a disappointment!
But I won't give up!
Kamisama, I hope I'll be able to become lovey♥-dovey♥ with Tomoe quick—— ♥♥

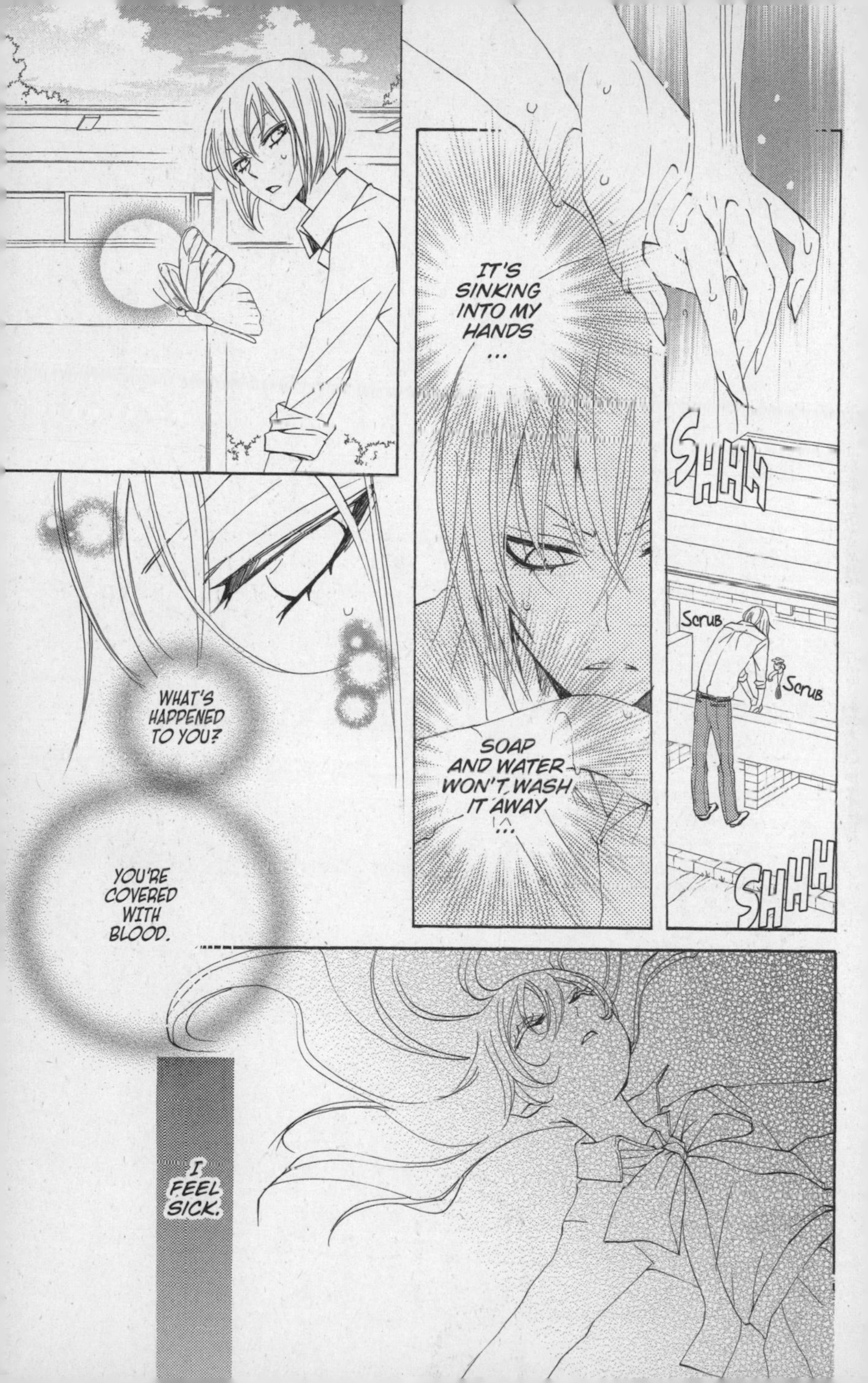
SHHH
Scrub
Scrub
SHHH
IT'S SINKING INTO MY HANDS...
SOAP AND WATER WON'T WASH IT AWAY...
WHAT'S HAPPENED TO YOU?
YOU'RE COVERED WITH BLOOD.
I FEEL SICK.

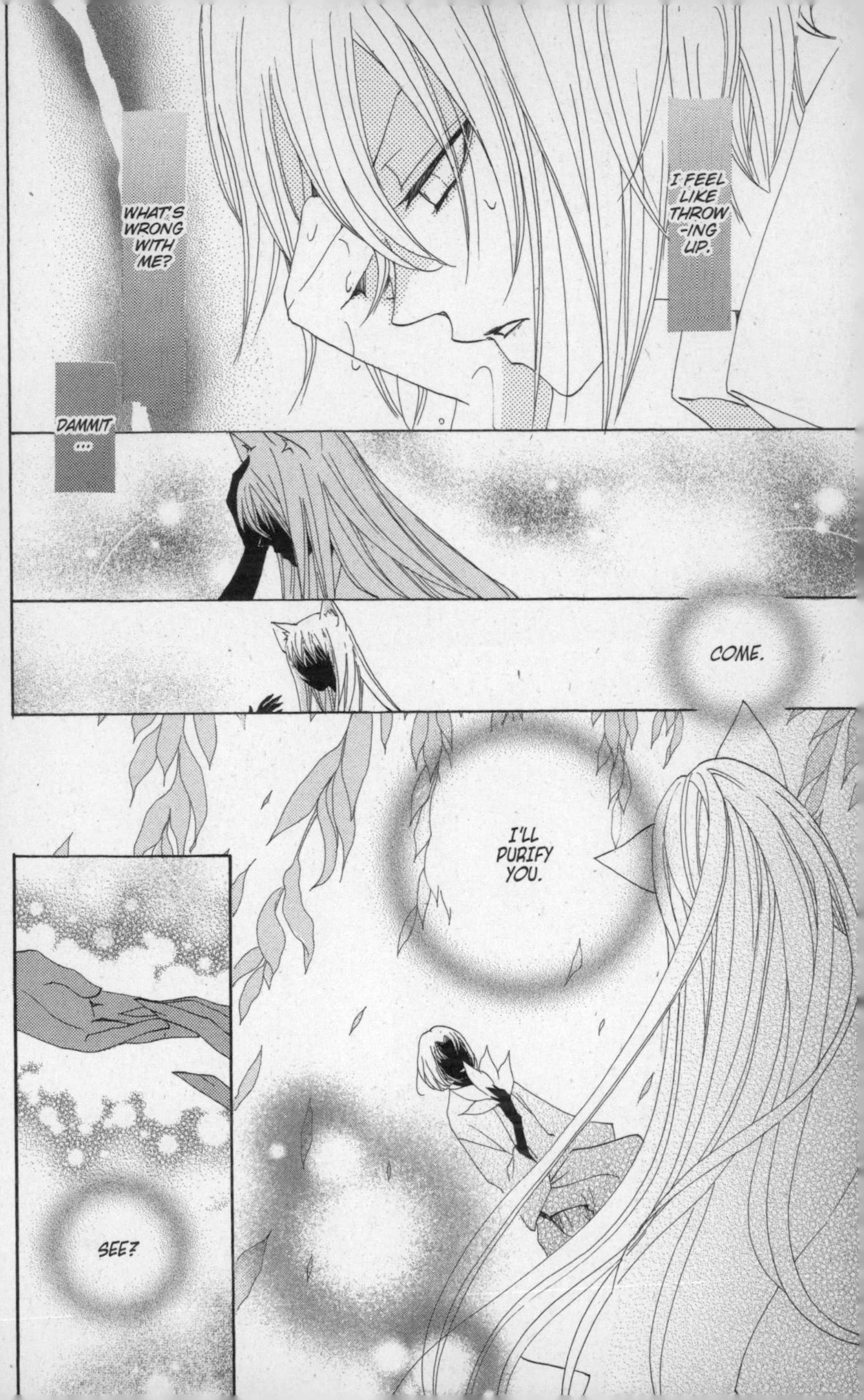
I FEEL LIKE THROW-ING UP.
WHAT'S WRONG WITH ME?
DAMMIT...
COME.
I'LL PURIFY YOU.
SEE?

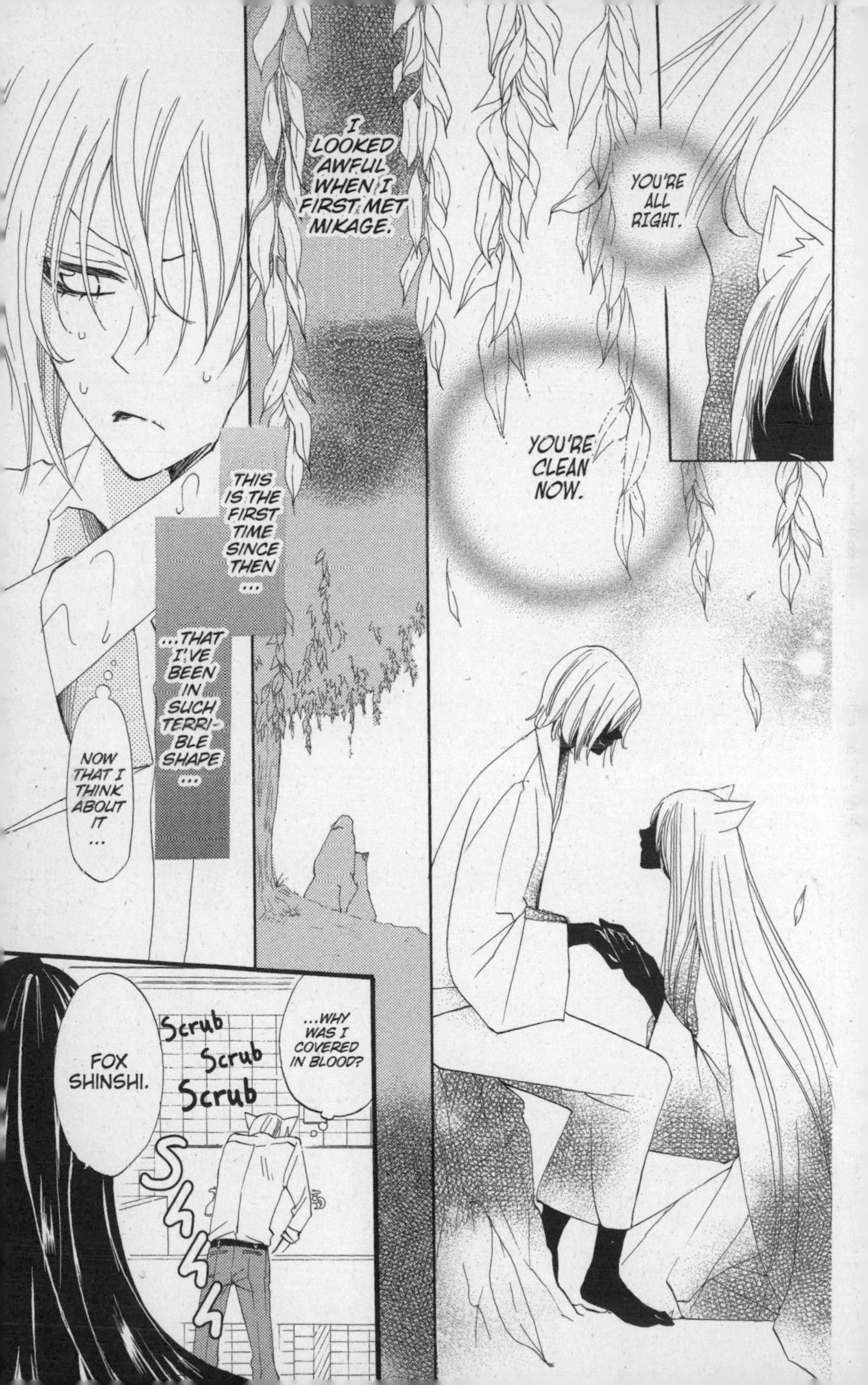
YOU'RE ALL RIGHT.
YOU'RE CLEAN NOW.
I LOOKED AWFUL WHEN I FIRST MET MIKAGE.
THIS IS THE FIRST TIME SINCE THEN...
...THAT I'VE BEEN IN SUCH TERRIBLE SHAPE...
NOW THAT I THINK ABOUT IT...
...WHY WAS I COVERED IN BLOOD?
Scrub
Scrub
Scrub
FOX SHINSHI.
Shhh

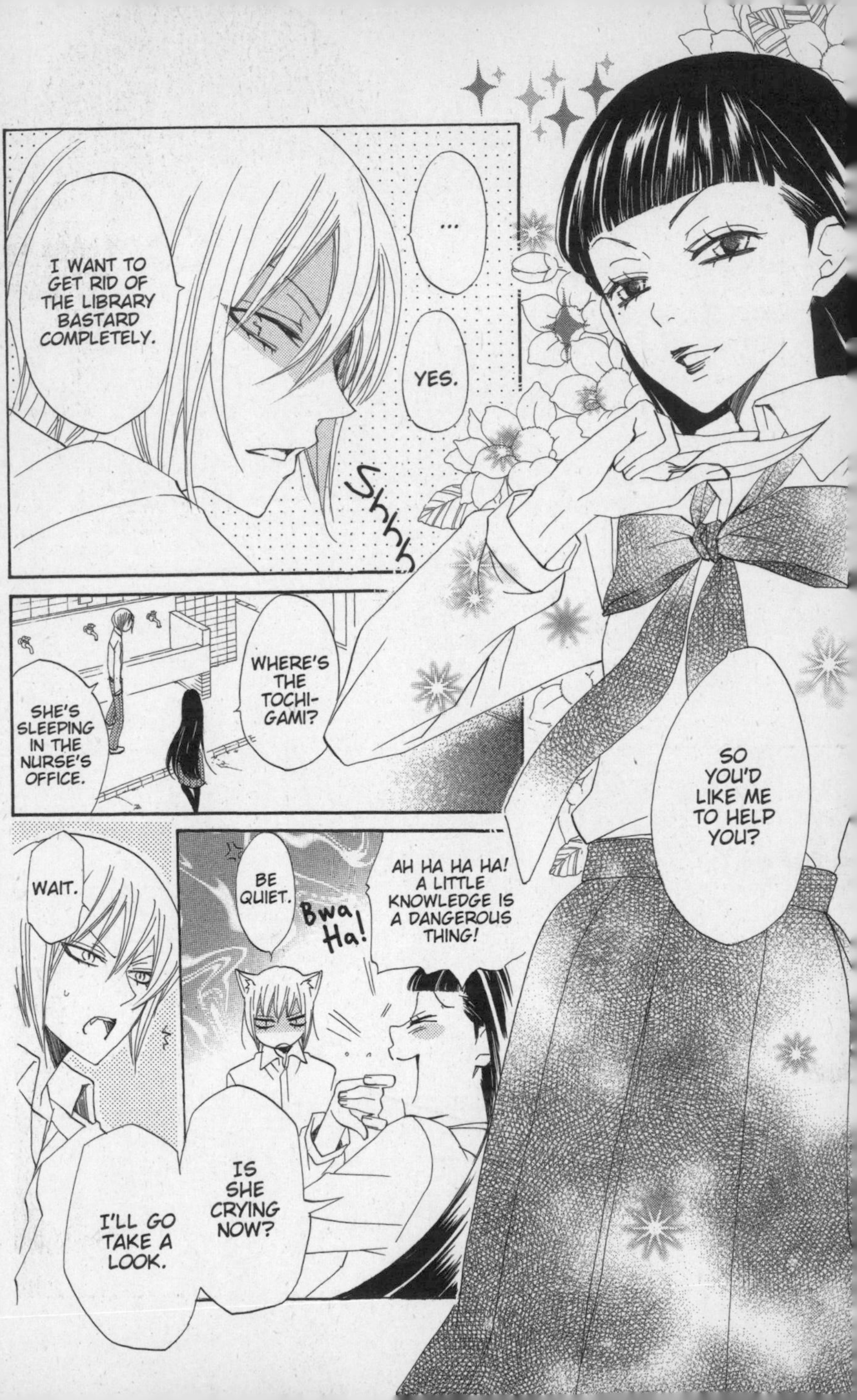
SO YOU'D LIKE ME TO HELP YOU?
...
YES.
I WANT TO GET RID OF THE LIBRARY BASTARD COMPLETELY.
Shhh
WHERE'S THE TOCHIGAMI?
SHE'S SLEEPING IN THE NURSE'S OFFICE.
AH HA HA HA! A LITTLE KNOWLEDGE IS A DANGEROUS THING!
Bwa Ha!
BE QUIET.
IS SHE CRYING NOW?
WAIT.
I'LL GO TAKE A LOOK.

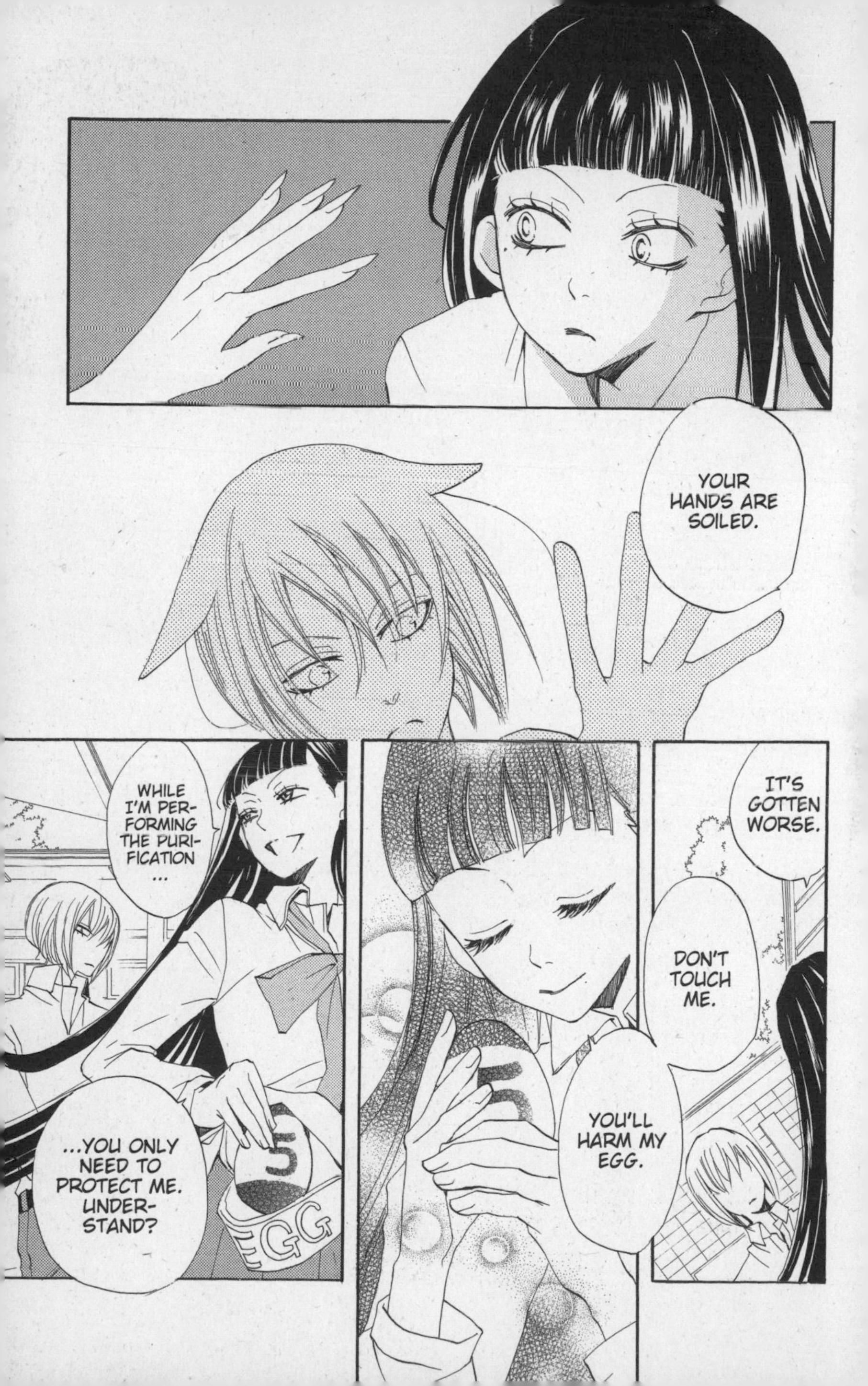
YOUR HANDS ARE SOILED.
IT'S GOTTEN WORSE.
DON'T TOUCH ME.
YOU'LL HARM MY EGG.
WHILE I'M PERFORMING THE PURIFICATION ...
...YOU ONLY NEED TO PROTECT ME. UNDERSTAND?
EGG

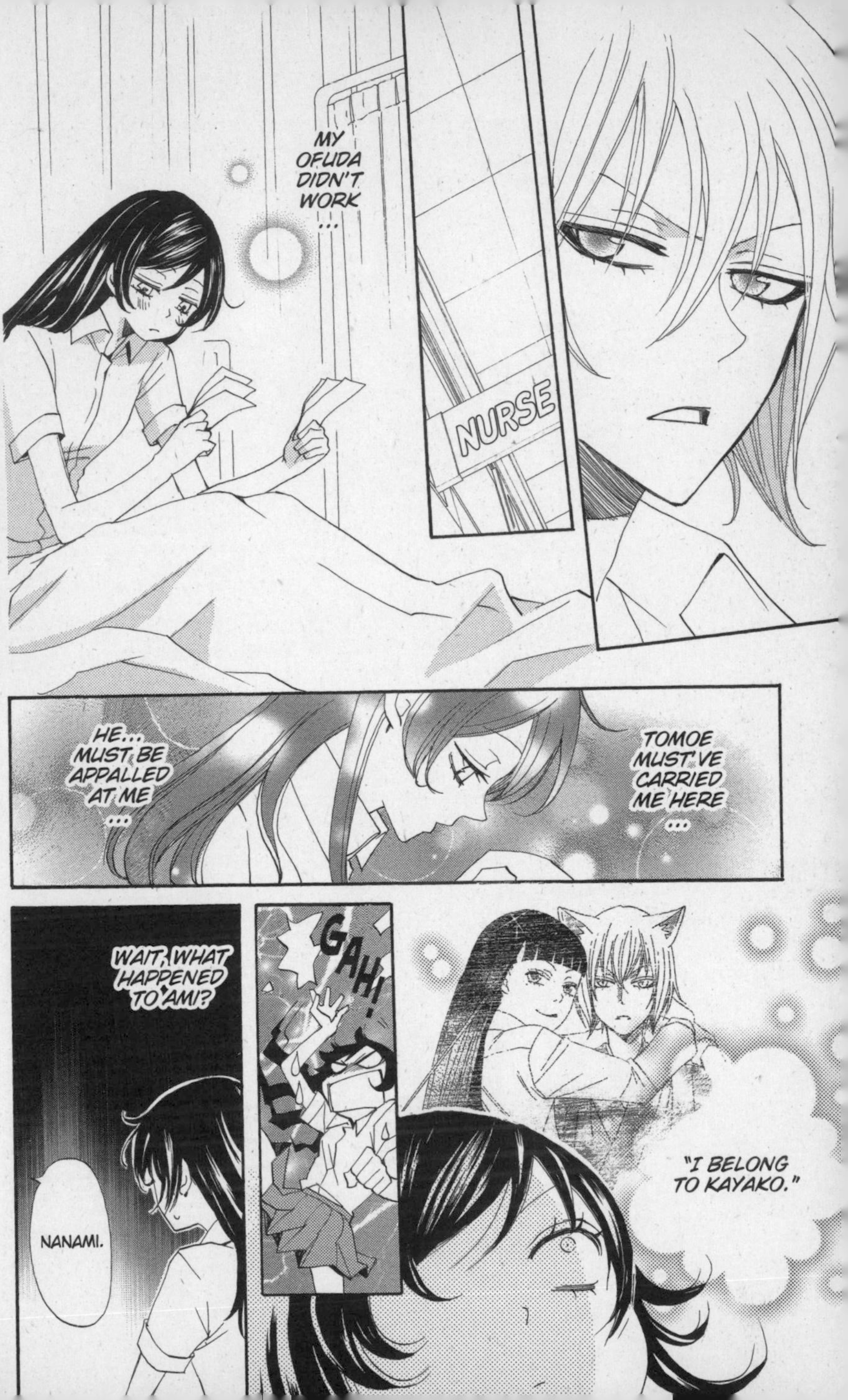
NURSE
MY OFUDA DIDN'T WORK ...
TOMOE MUST'VE CARRIED ME HERE ...
HE... MUST BE APPALLED AT ME ...
"I BELONG TO KAYAKO."
GAH!
WAIT, WHAT HAPPENED TO AMI?
NANAMI.

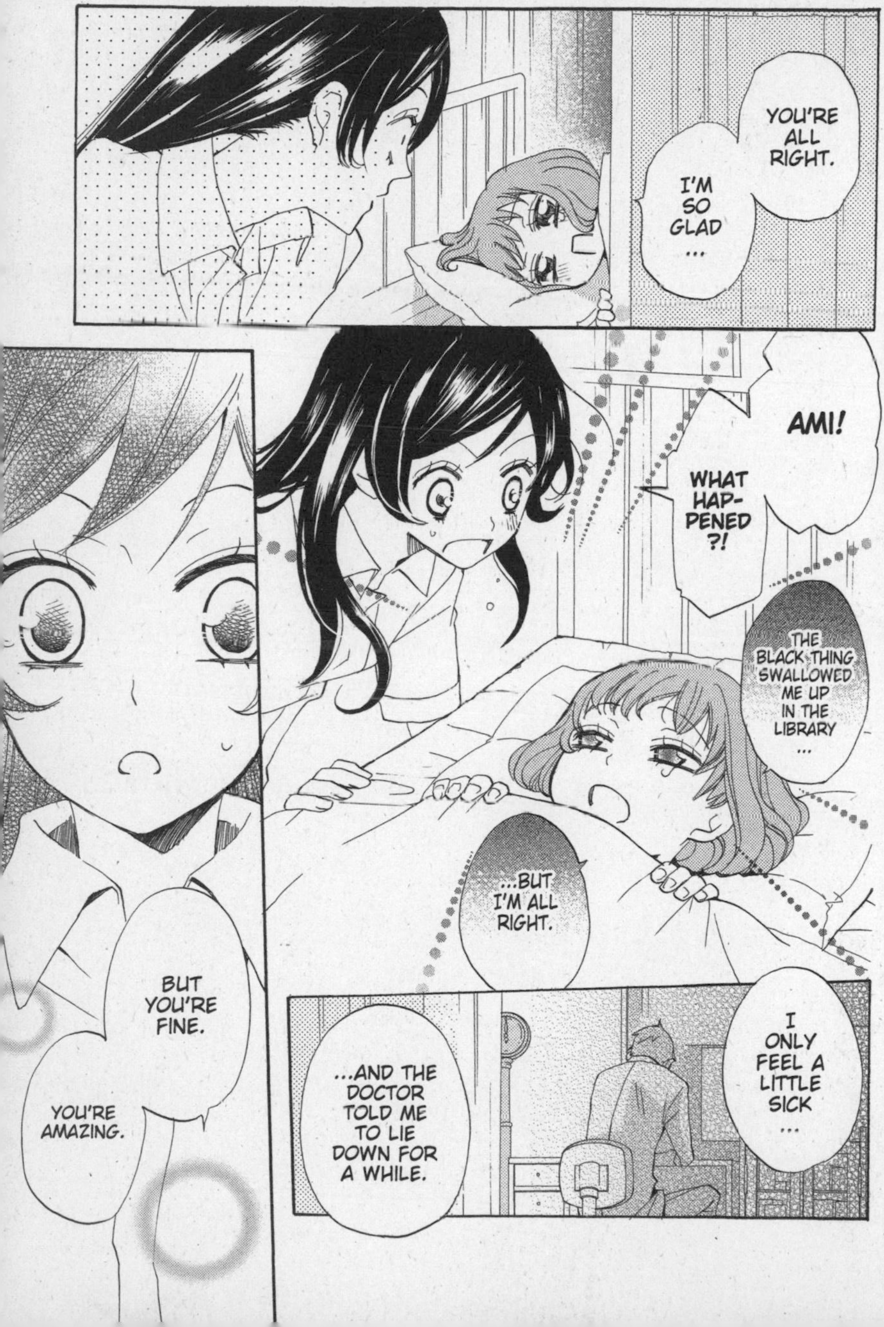
YOU'RE ALL RIGHT.
I'M SO GLAD ...
AMI!
WHAT HAP-PENED ?!
THE BLACK THING SWALLOWED ME UP IN THE LIBRARY ...
...BUT I'M ALL RIGHT.
I ONLY FEEL A LITTLE SICK ...
...AND THE DOCTOR TOLD ME TO LIE DOWN FOR A WHILE.
BUT YOU'RE FINE.
YOU'RE AMAZING.

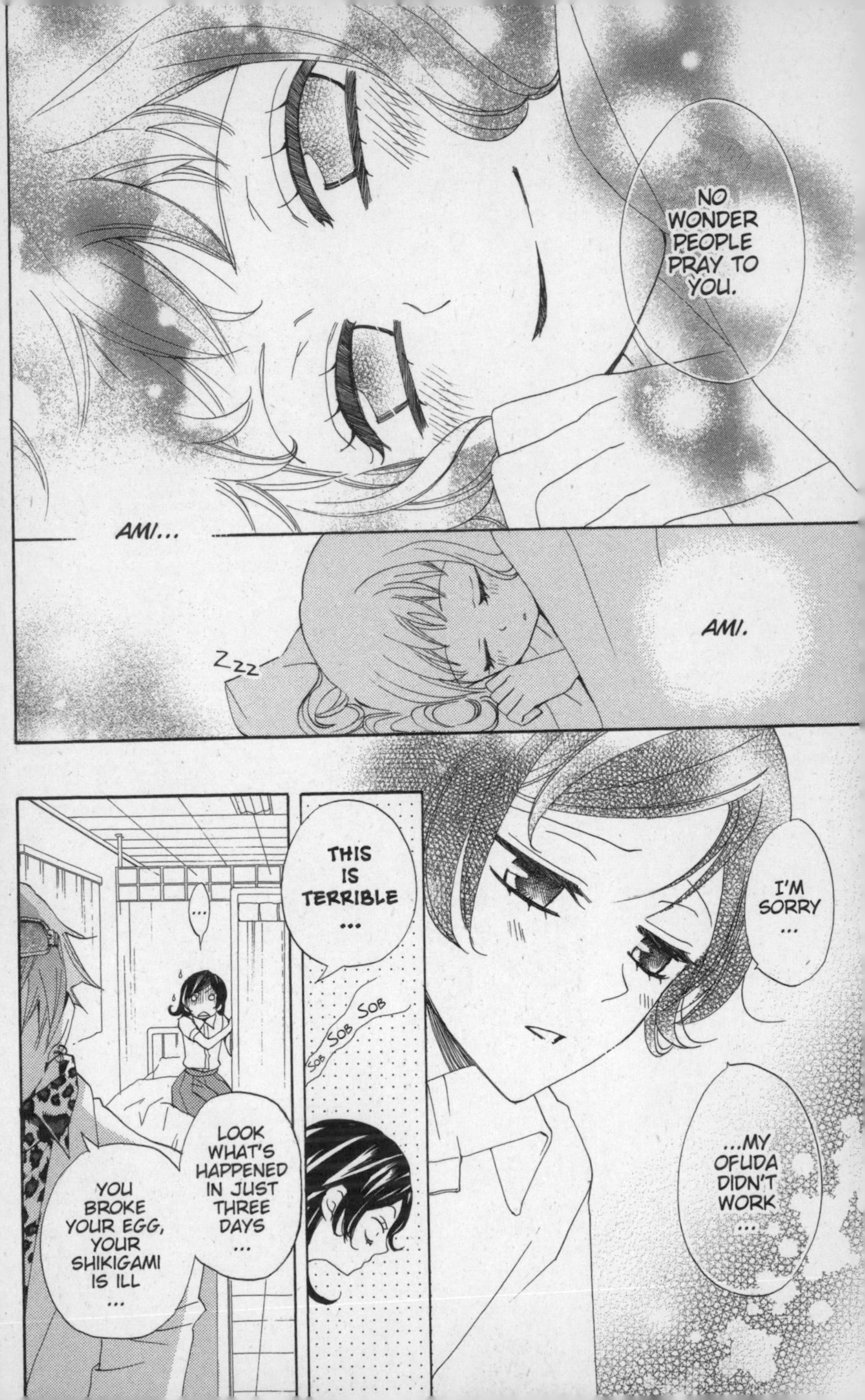
NO WONDER PEOPLE PRAY TO YOU.
AMI...
AMI.
Zzz
I'M SORRY...
...MY OFUDA DIDN'T WORK...
THIS IS TERRIBLE...
SOB SOB SOB
...
LOOK WHAT'S HAPPENED IN JUST THREE DAYS...
YOU BROKE YOUR EGG, YOUR SHIKIGAMI IS ILL...

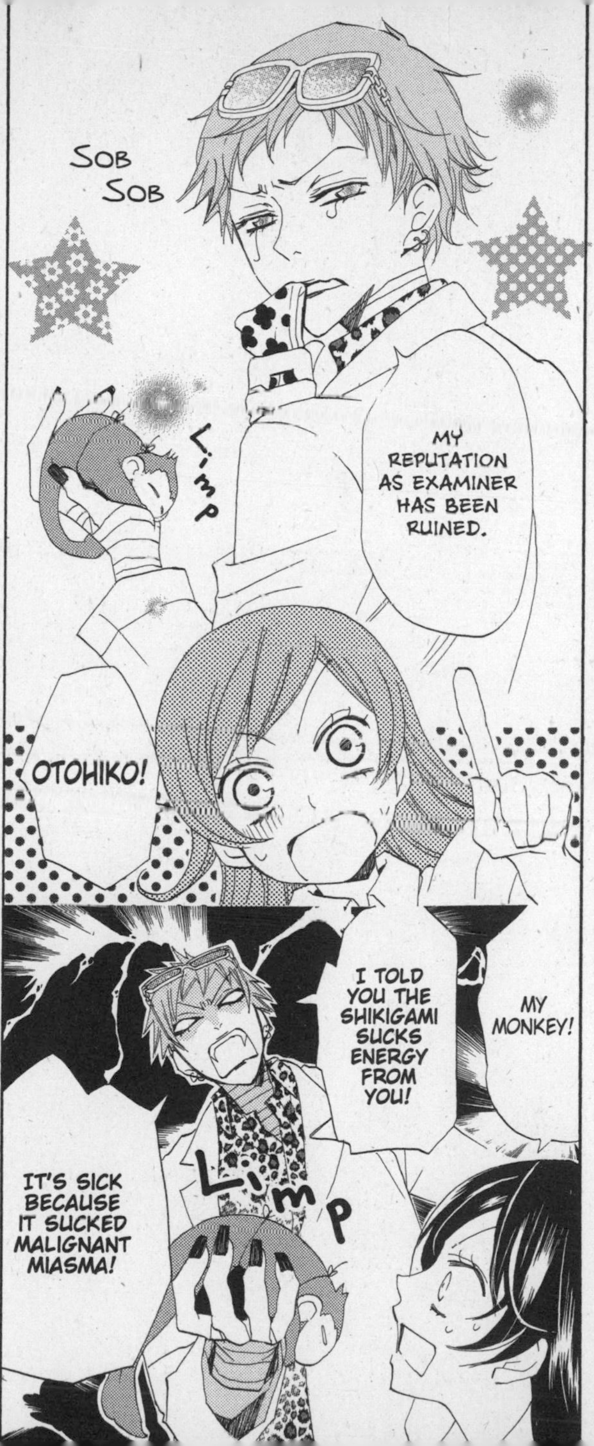
SOB
SOB
MY REPUTATION AS EXAMINER HAS BEEN RUINED.
LIMP
OTOHIKO!
MY MONKEY!
I TOLD YOU THE SHIKIGAMI SUCKS ENERGY FROM YOU!
IT'S SICK BECAUSE IT SUCKED MALIGNANT MIASMA!
LIMP

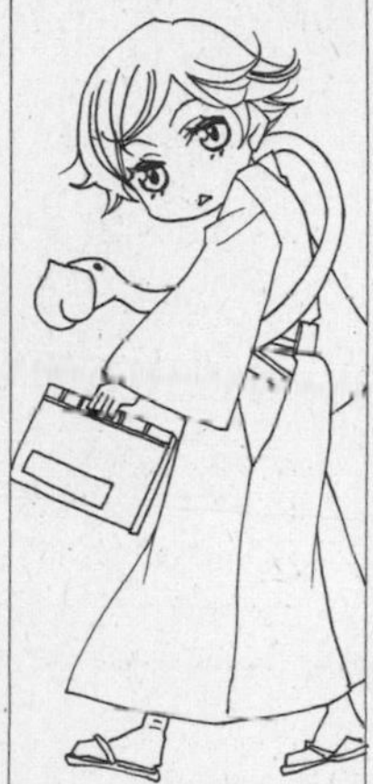

I've started tweeting! ✿

I'm @hiyokosweet.

I stop tweeting when I start feeling guilty about taking time away from work, but otherwise, I use it like a blog. So please follow me!

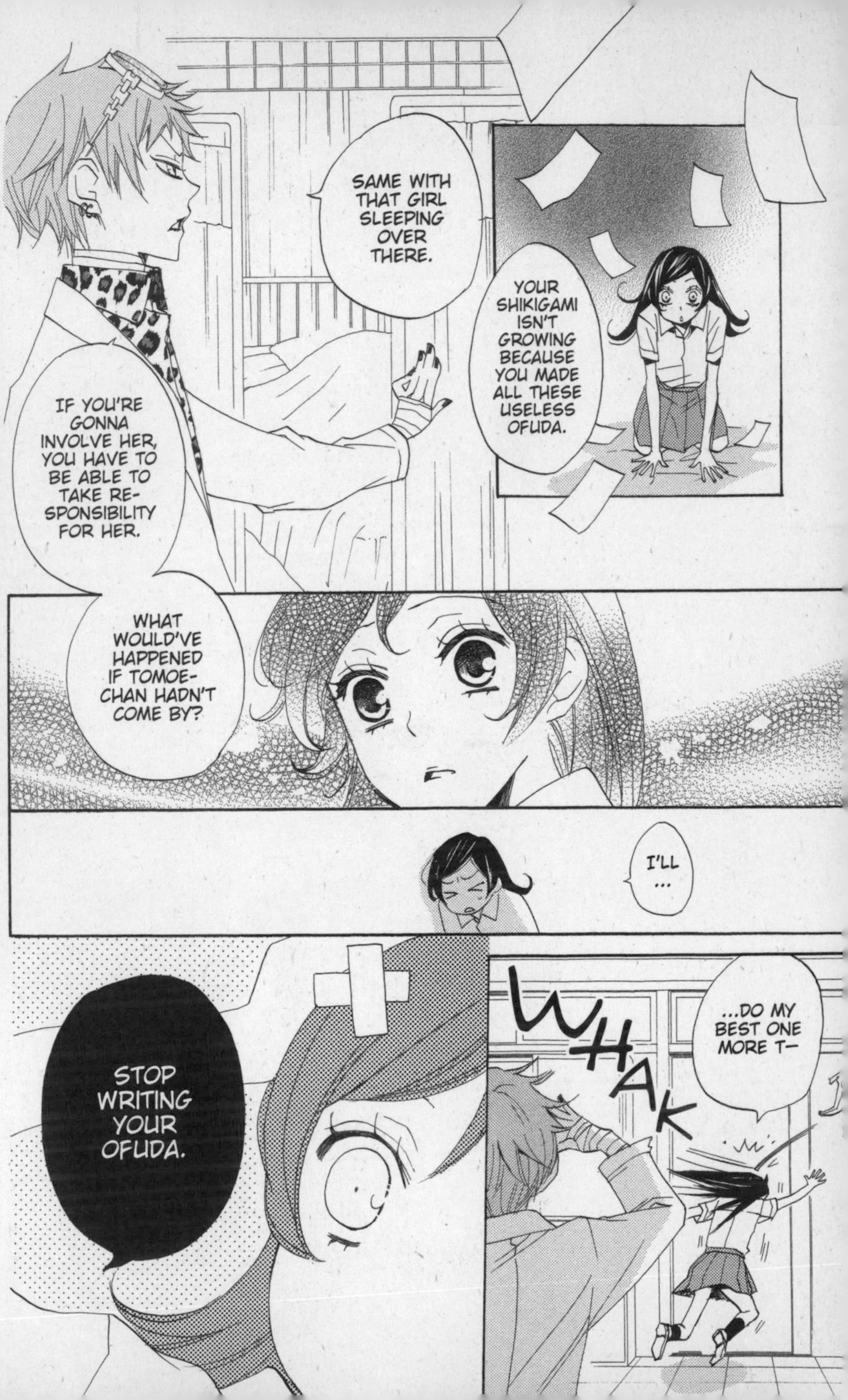
YOUR SHIKIGAMI ISN'T GROWING BECAUSE YOU MADE ALL THESE USELESS OFUDA.
SAME WITH THAT GIRL SLEEPING OVER THERE.
IF YOU'RE GONNA INVOLVE HER, YOU HAVE TO BE ABLE TO TAKE RE-SPONSIBILITY FOR HER.
WHAT WOULD'VE HAPPENED IF TOMOE-CHAN HADN'T COME BY?
I'LL ...
...DO MY BEST ONE MORE T—
WHAK
STOP WRITING YOUR OFUDA.

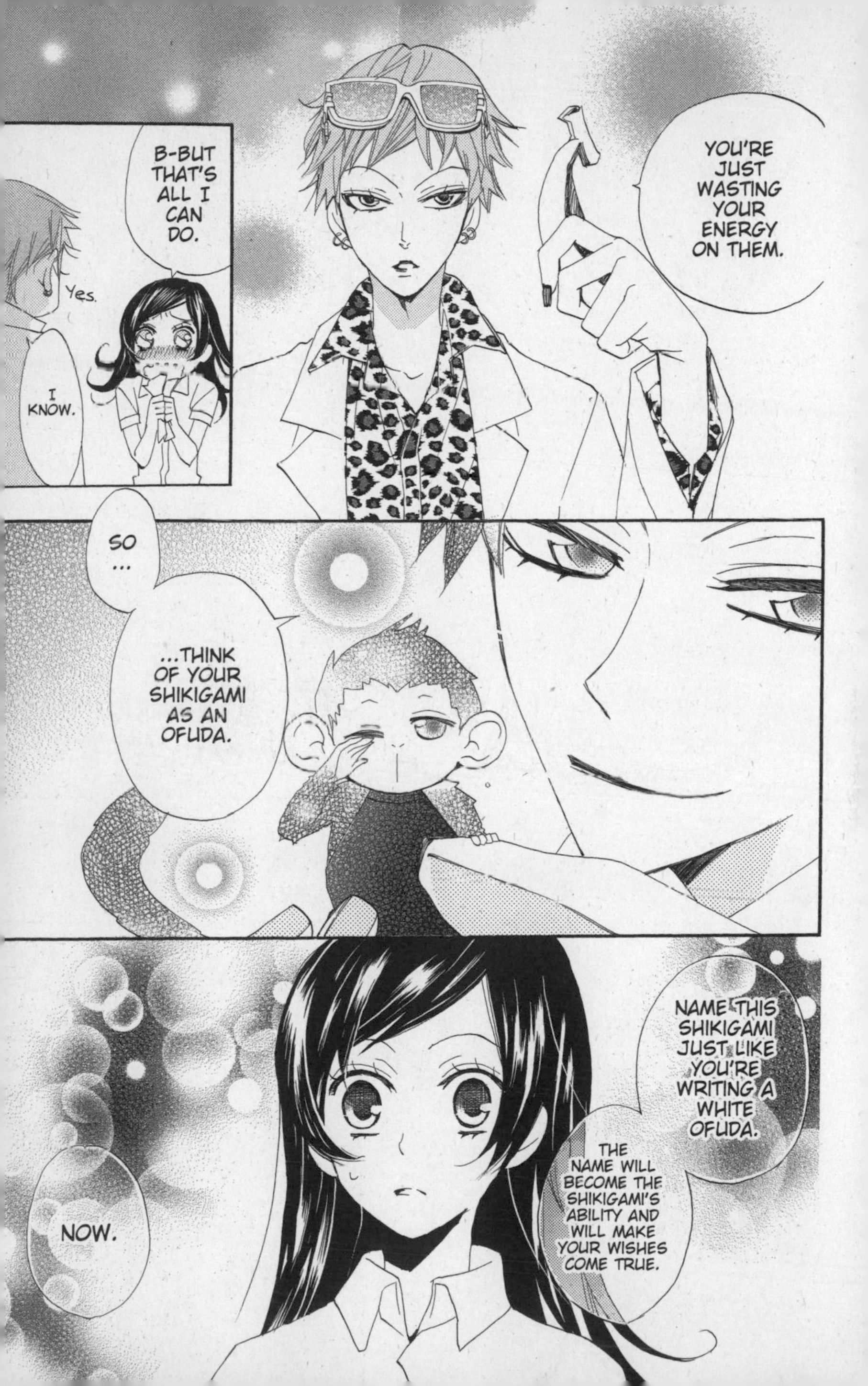
YOU'RE JUST WASTING YOUR ENERGY ON THEM.
B-BUT THAT'S ALL I CAN DO.
Yes.
I KNOW.
SO ...
...THINK OF YOUR SHIKIGAMI AS AN OFUDA.
NAME THIS SHIKIGAMI JUST LIKE YOU'RE WRITING A WHITE OFUDA.
THE NAME WILL BECOME THE SHIKIGAMI'S ABILITY AND WILL MAKE YOUR WISHES COME TRUE.
NOW.

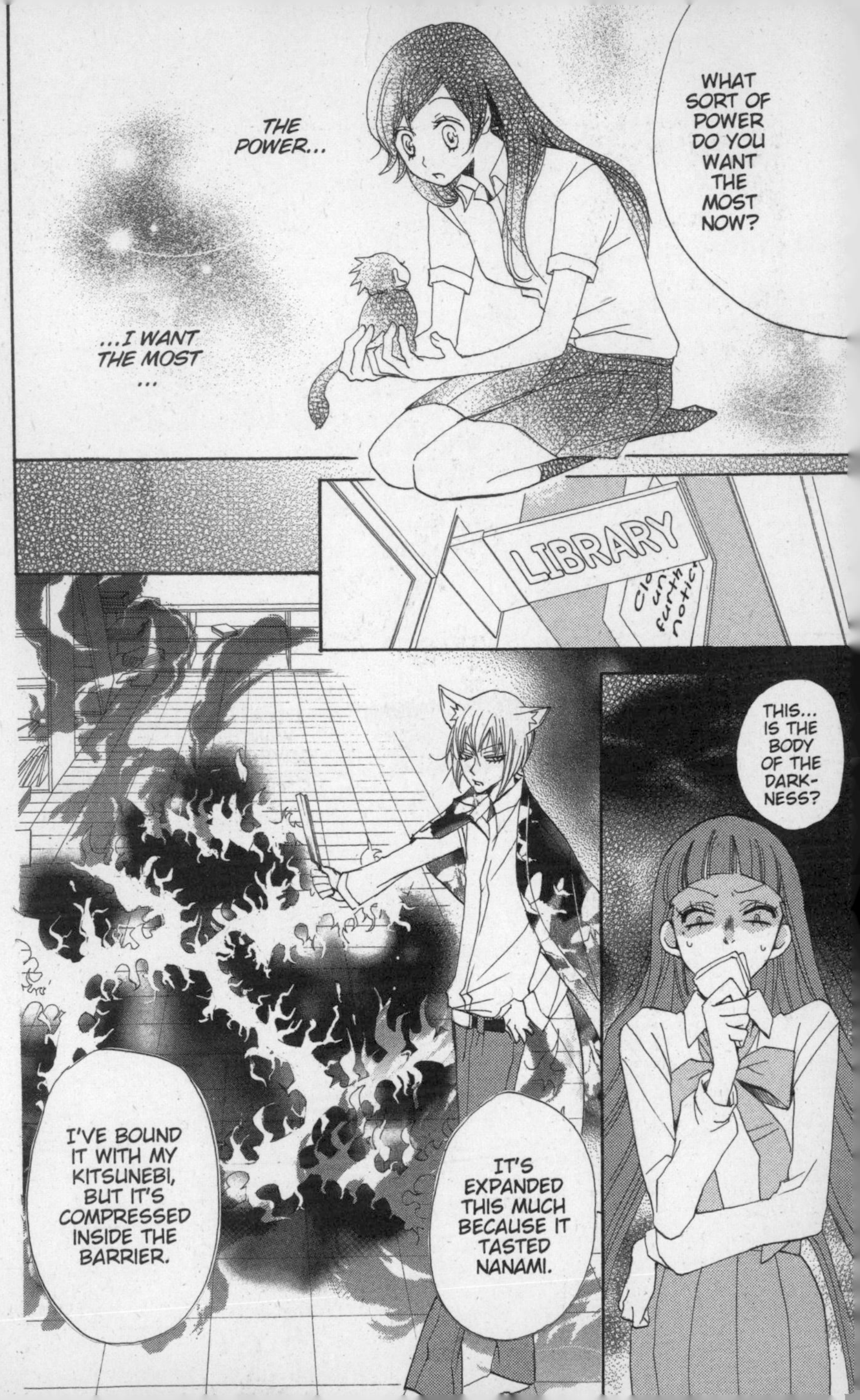
WHAT SORT OF POWER DO YOU WANT THE MOST NOW?
THE POWER...
...I WANT THE MOST ...
LIBRARY
THIS... IS THE BODY OF THE DARK-NESS?
IT'S EXPANDED THIS MUCH BECAUSE IT TASTED NANAMI.
I'VE BOUND IT WITH MY KITSUNEBI, BUT IT'S COMPRESSED INSIDE THE BARRIER.

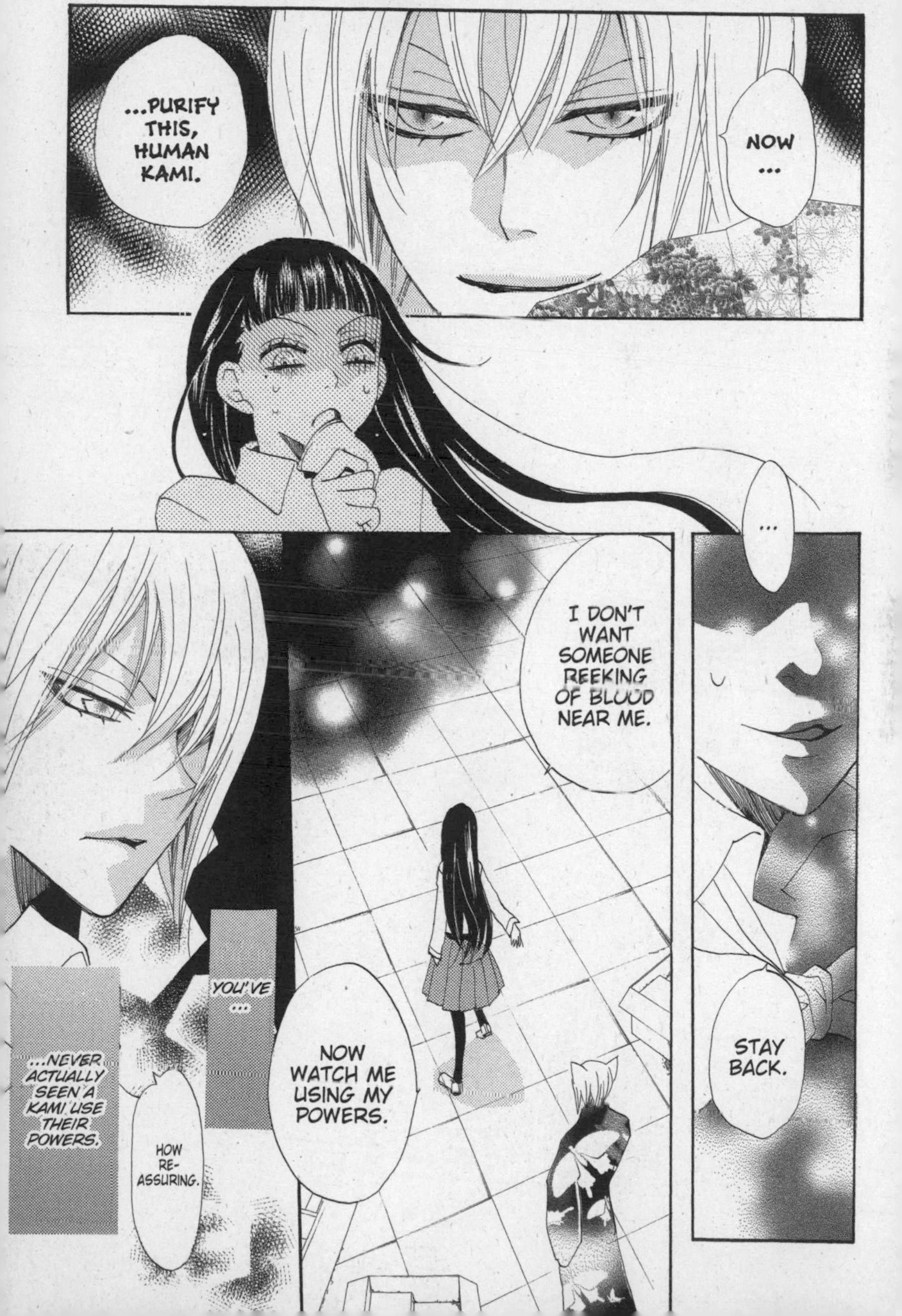
NOW ...
...PURIFY THIS, HUMAN KAMI.
...
STAY BACK.
I DON'T WANT SOMEONE REEKING OF BLOOD NEAR ME.
NOW WATCH ME USING MY POWERS.
YOU'VE ...
...NEVER ACTUALLY SEEN A KAMI USE THEIR POWERS.
HOW RE-ASSURING.

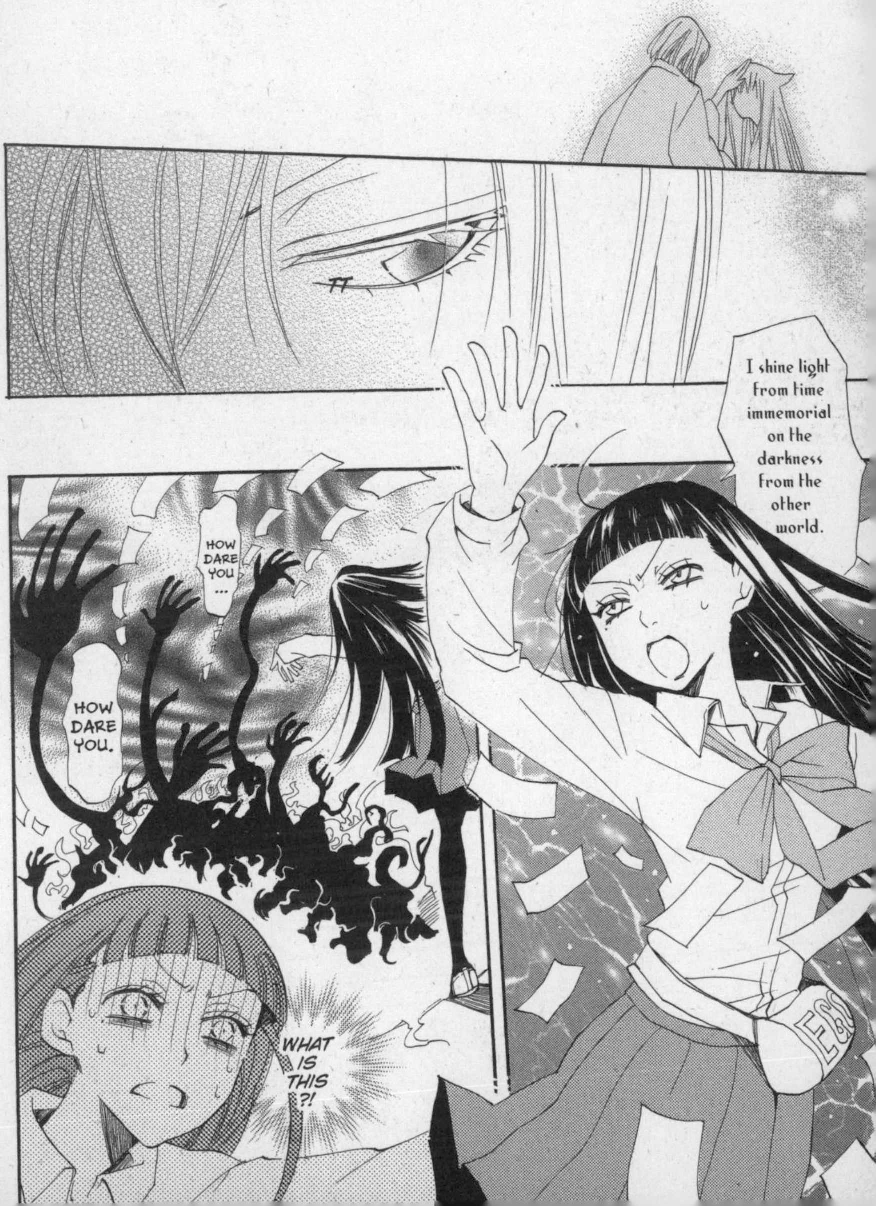
I shine light from time immemorial on the darkness from the other world.
HOW DARE YOU ...
HOW DARE YOU.
WHAT IS THIS ?!

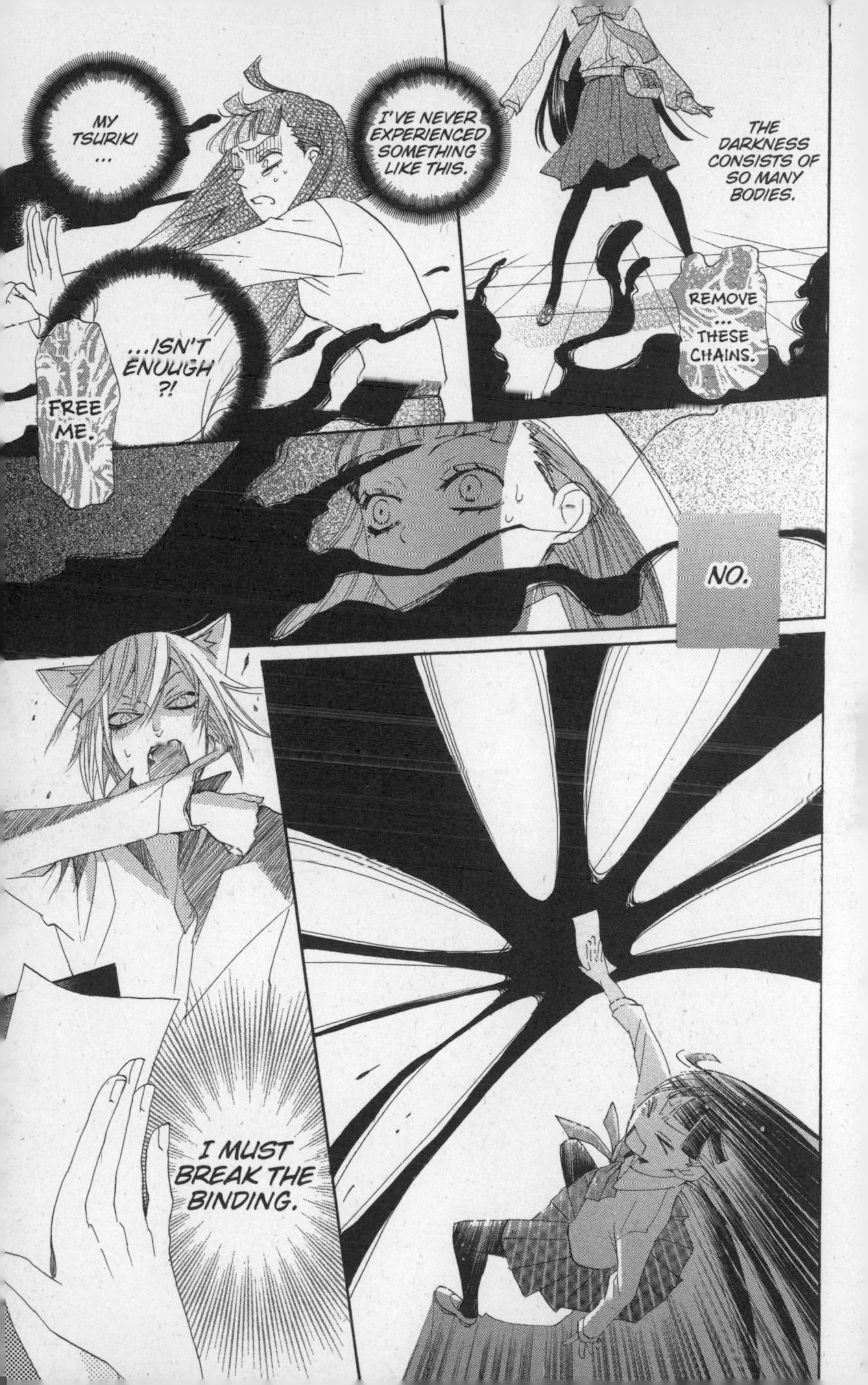
THE DARKNESS CONSISTS OF SO MANY BODIES.
REMOVE ... THESE CHAINS.
I'VE NEVER EXPERIENCED SOMETHING LIKE THIS.
MY TSURIKI ...
...ISN'T ENOUGH?!
FREE ME.
NO.
I MUST BREAK THE BINDING.

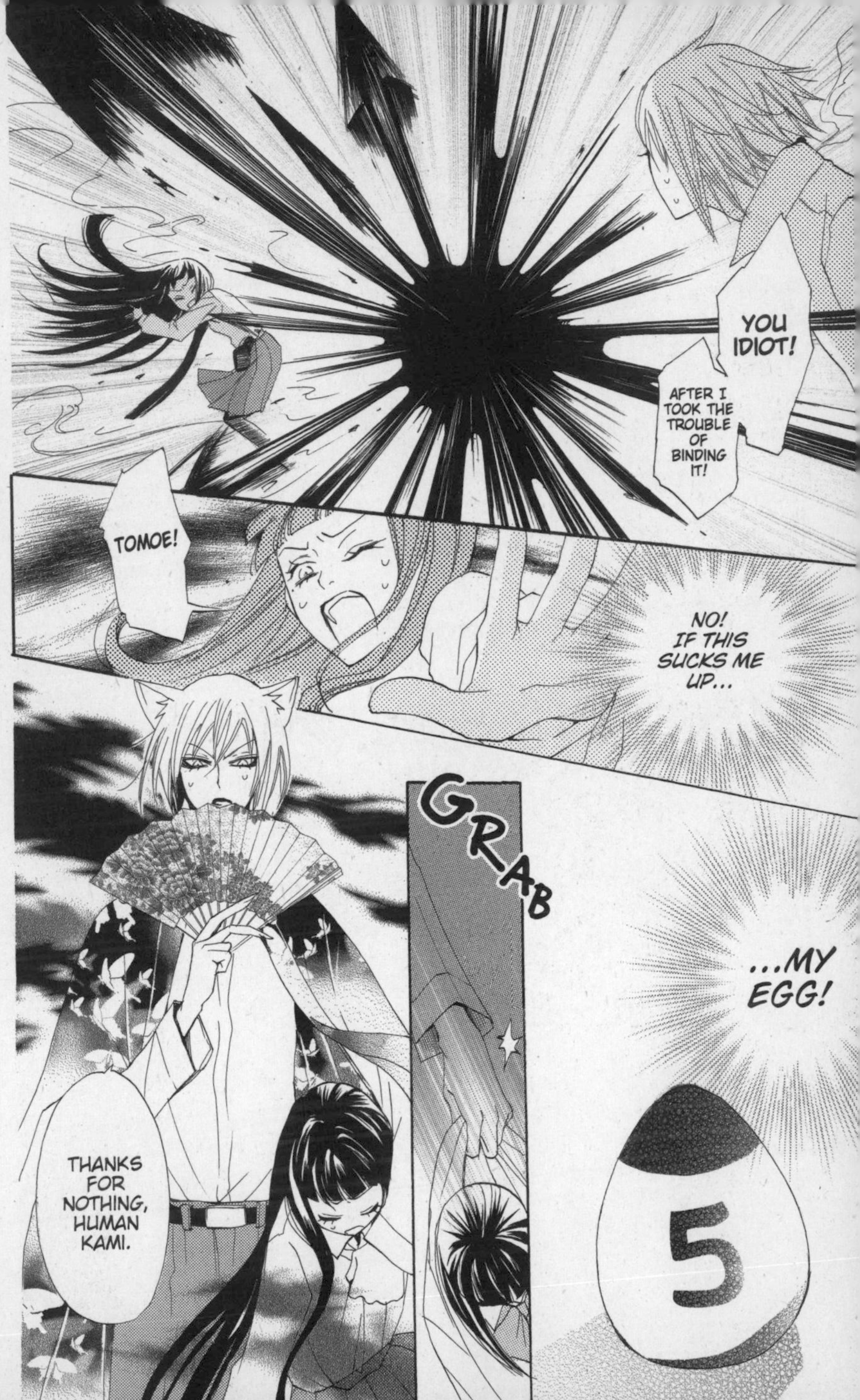
YOU IDIOT!
AFTER I TOOK THE TROUBLE OF BINDING IT!
NO! IF THIS SUCKS ME UP...
TOMOE!
...MY EGG!
5
GRAB
THANKS FOR NOTHING, HUMAN KAMI.

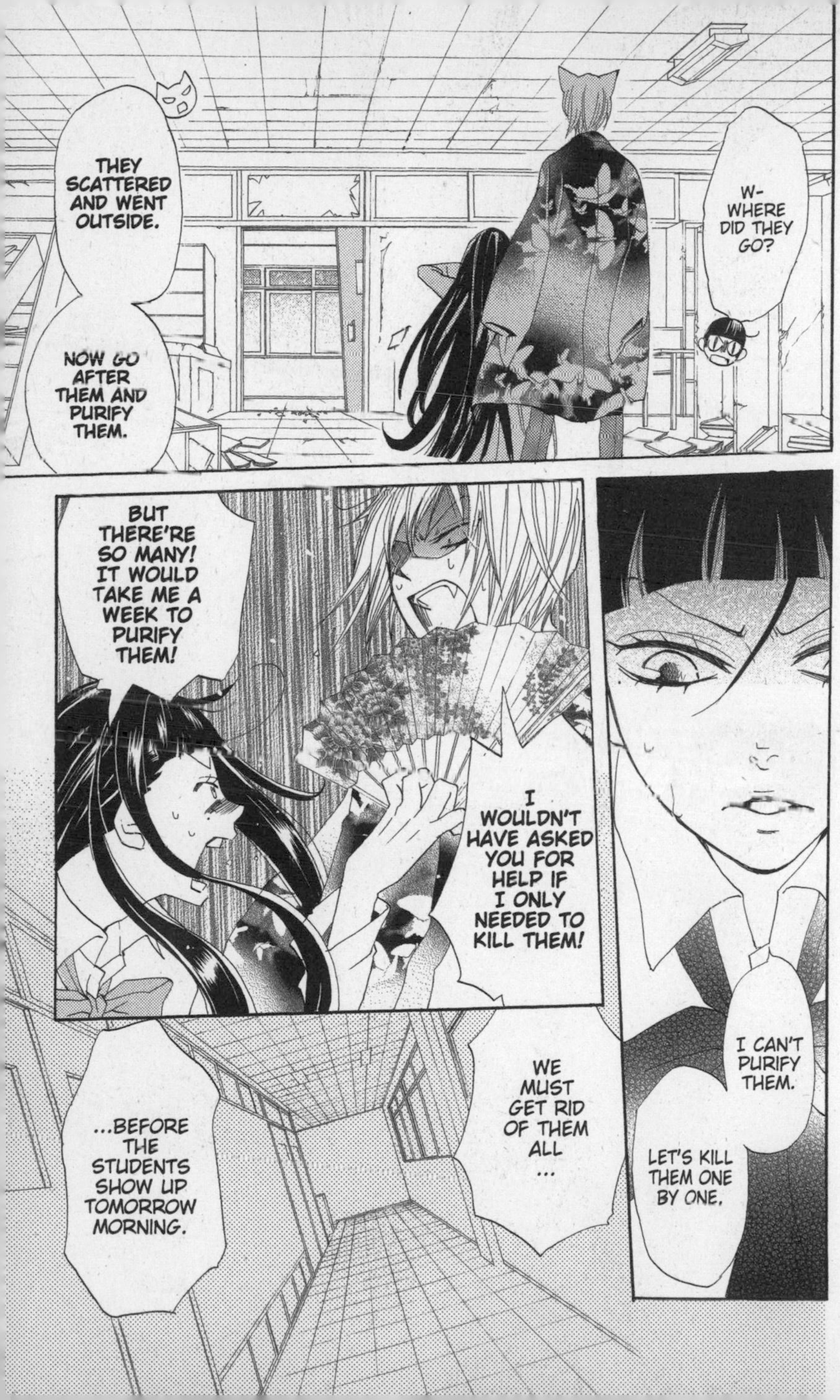
W-WHERE DID THEY GO?
THEY SCATTERED AND WENT OUTSIDE.
NOW GO AFTER THEM AND PURIFY THEM.
I CAN'T PURIFY THEM.
LET'S KILL THEM ONE BY ONE.
BUT THERE'RE SO MANY! IT WOULD TAKE ME A WEEK TO PURIFY THEM!
I WOULDN'T HAVE ASKED YOU FOR HELP IF I ONLY NEEDED TO KILL THEM!
WE MUST GET RID OF THEM ALL ...
...BEFORE THE STUDENTS SHOW UP TOMORROW MORNING.

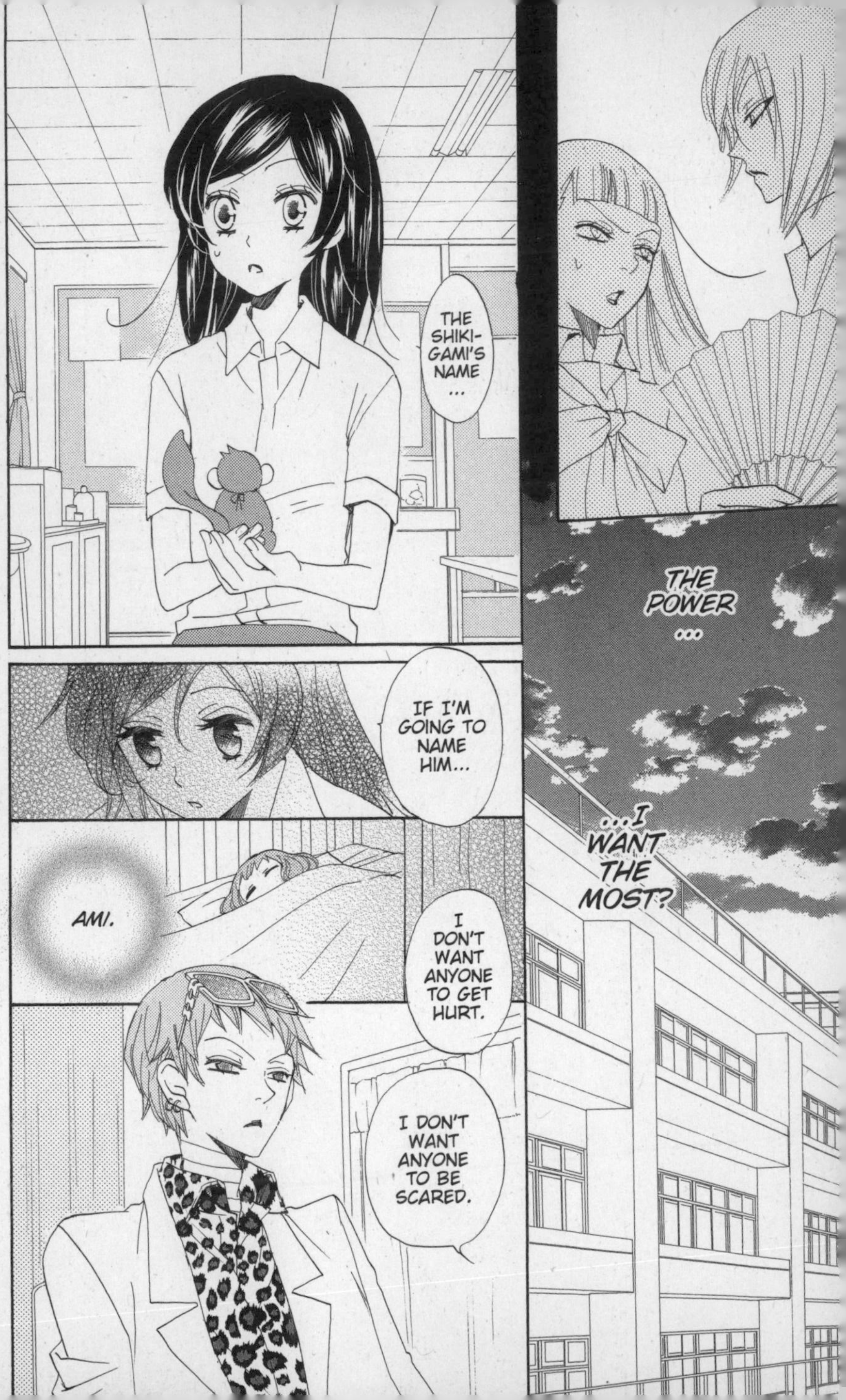
THE SHIKIGAMI'S NAME...
THE POWER...
...I WANT THE MOST?
IF I'M GOING TO NAME HIM...
AMI.
I DON'T WANT ANYONE TO GET HURT.
I DON'T WANT ANYONE TO BE SCARED.

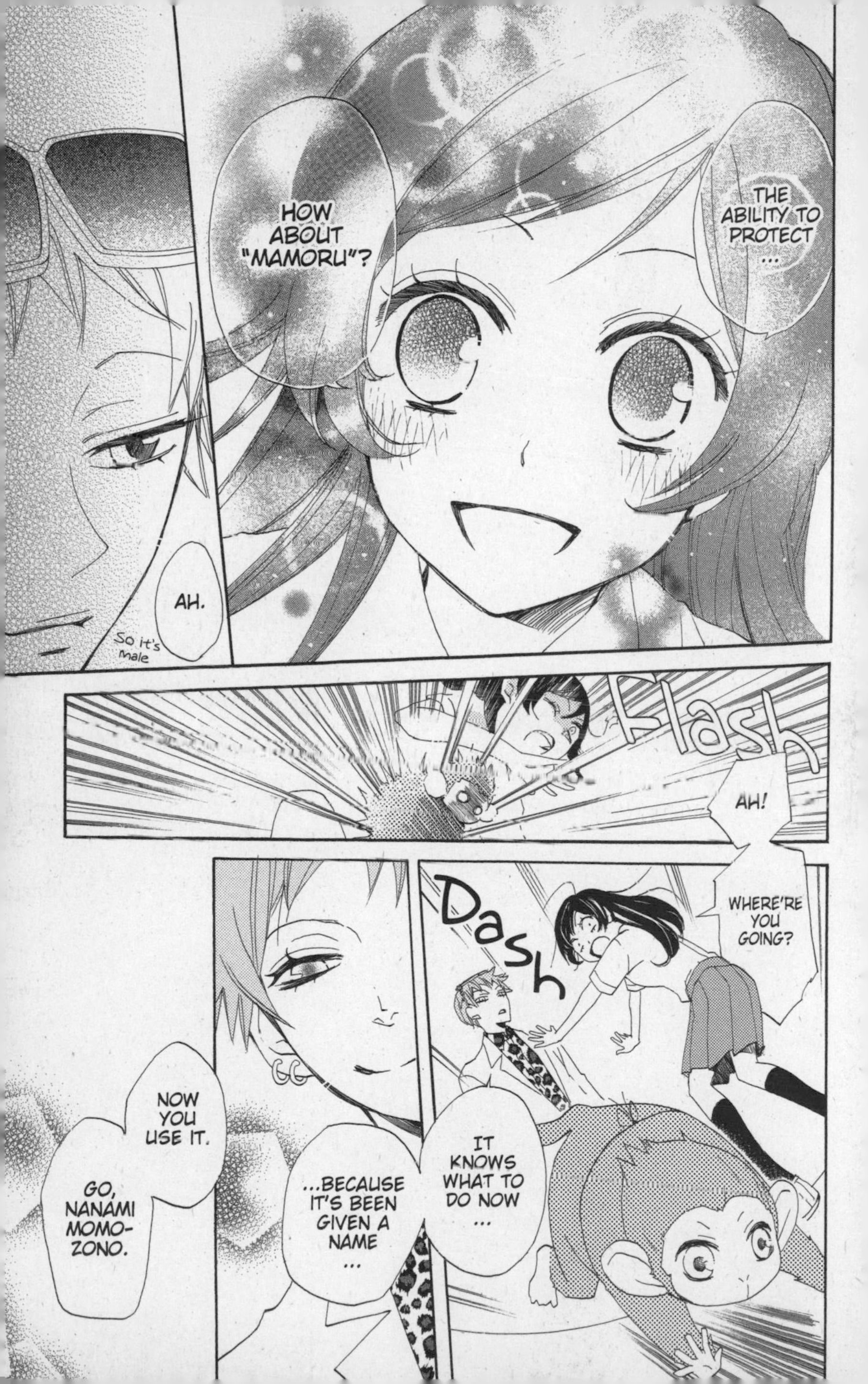
THE ABILITY TO PROTECT ...
HOW ABOUT "MAMORU"?
AH.
So it's male
Flash
AH!
Dash
WHERE'RE YOU GOING?
IT KNOWS WHAT TO DO NOW ...
...BECAUSE IT'S BEEN GIVEN A NAME ...
NOW YOU USE IT.
GO, NANAMI MOMO-ZONO.

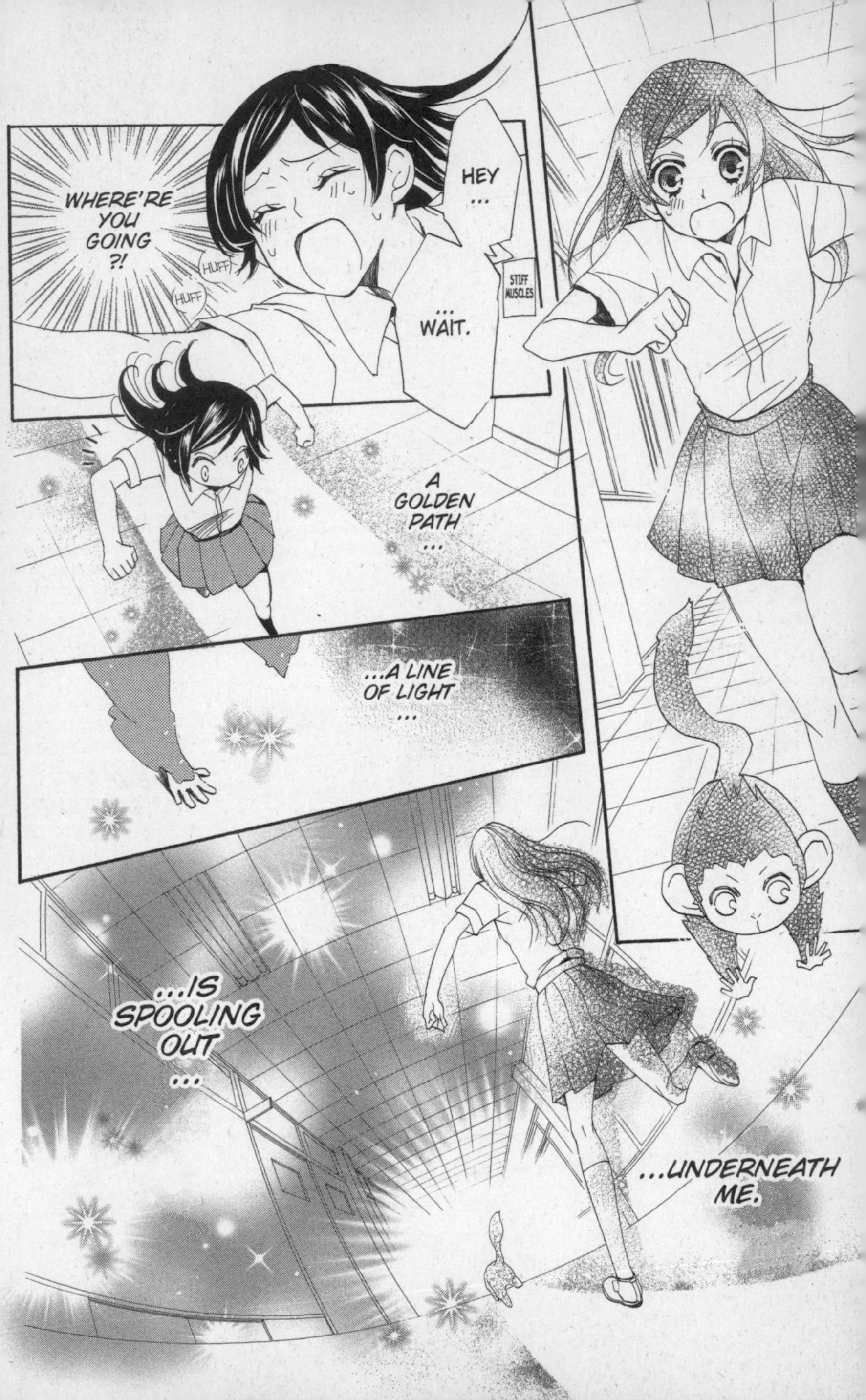
HEY ...
STIFF MUSCLES
... WAIT.
WHERE'RE YOU GOING ?!
HUFF
HUFF
A GOLDEN PATH ...
...A LINE OF LIGHT ...
...IS SPOOLING OUT ...
...UNDERNEATH ME.

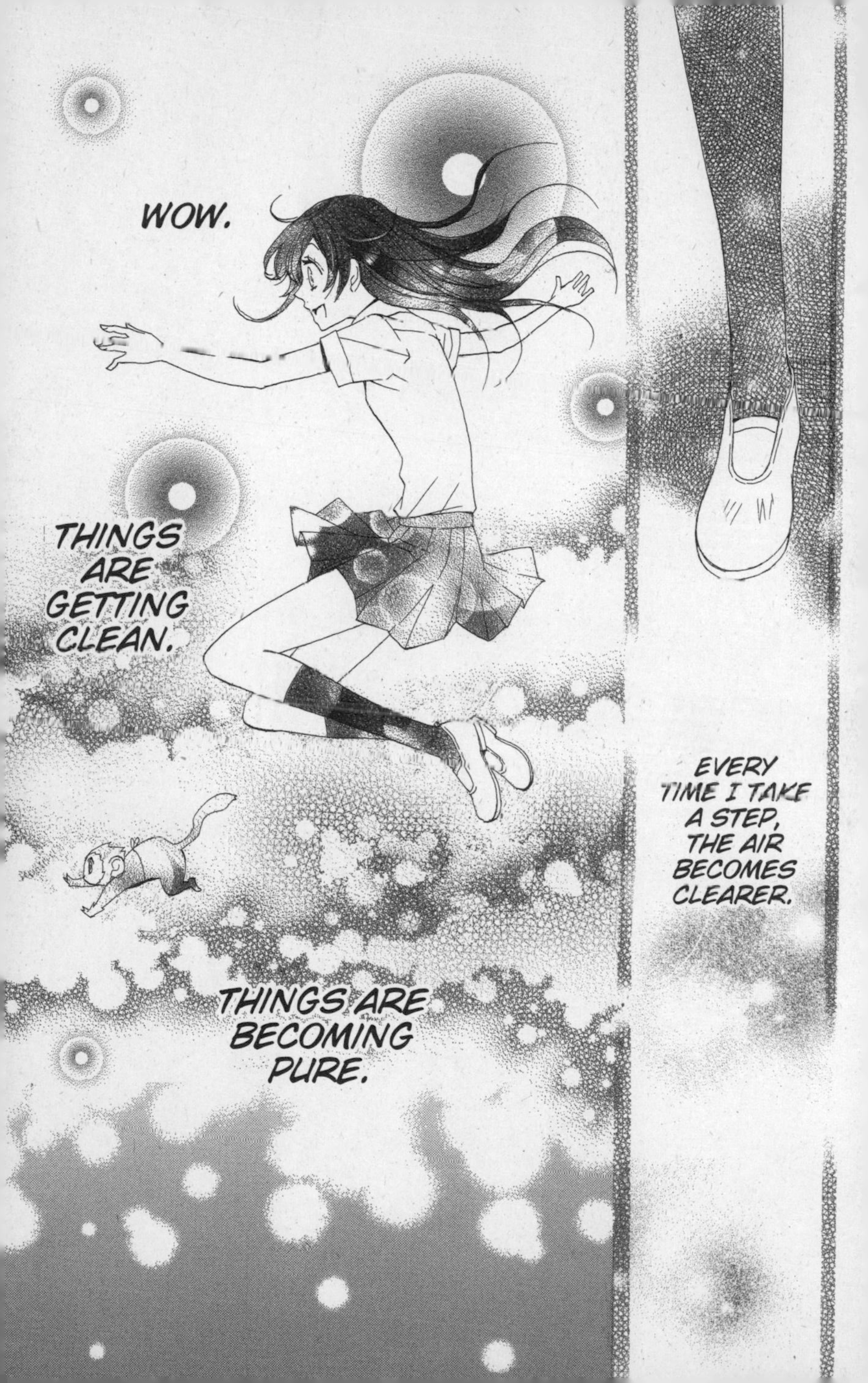
EVERY TIME I TAKE A STEP, THE AIR BECOMES CLEARER.
WOW.
THINGS ARE GETTING CLEAN.
THINGS ARE BECOMING PURE.

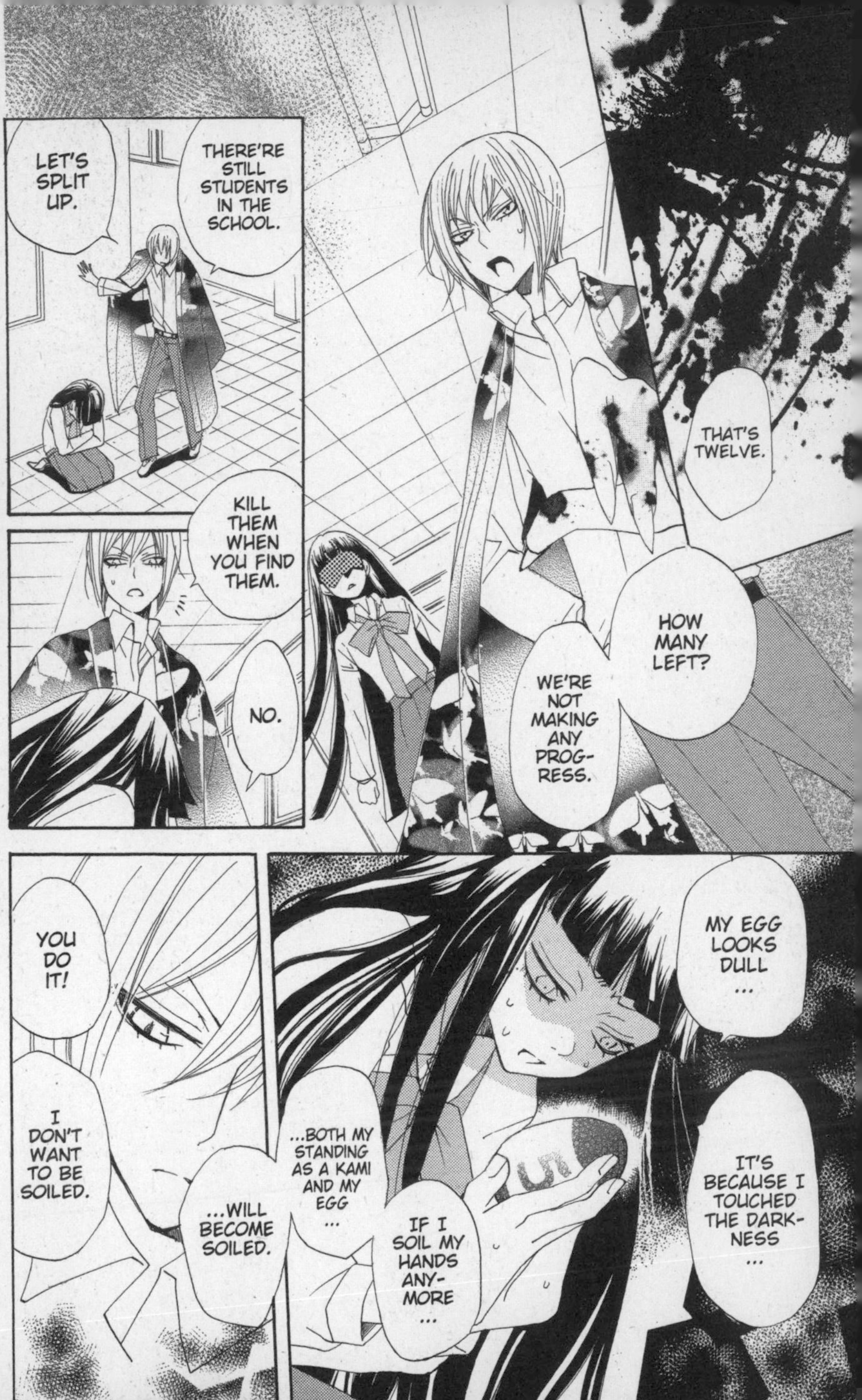
THAT'S TWELVE.
HOW MANY LEFT?
WE'RE NOT MAKING ANY PROG-RESS.
THERE'RE STILL STUDENTS IN THE SCHOOL.
LET'S SPLIT UP.
KILL THEM WHEN YOU FIND THEM.
NO.
MY EGG LOOKS DULL ...
IT'S BECAUSE I TOUCHED THE DARK-NESS ...
IF I SOIL MY HANDS ANY-MORE ...
...BOTH MY STANDING AS A KAMI AND MY EGG ...
...WILL BECOME SOILED.
YOU DO IT!
I DON'T WANT TO BE SOILED.

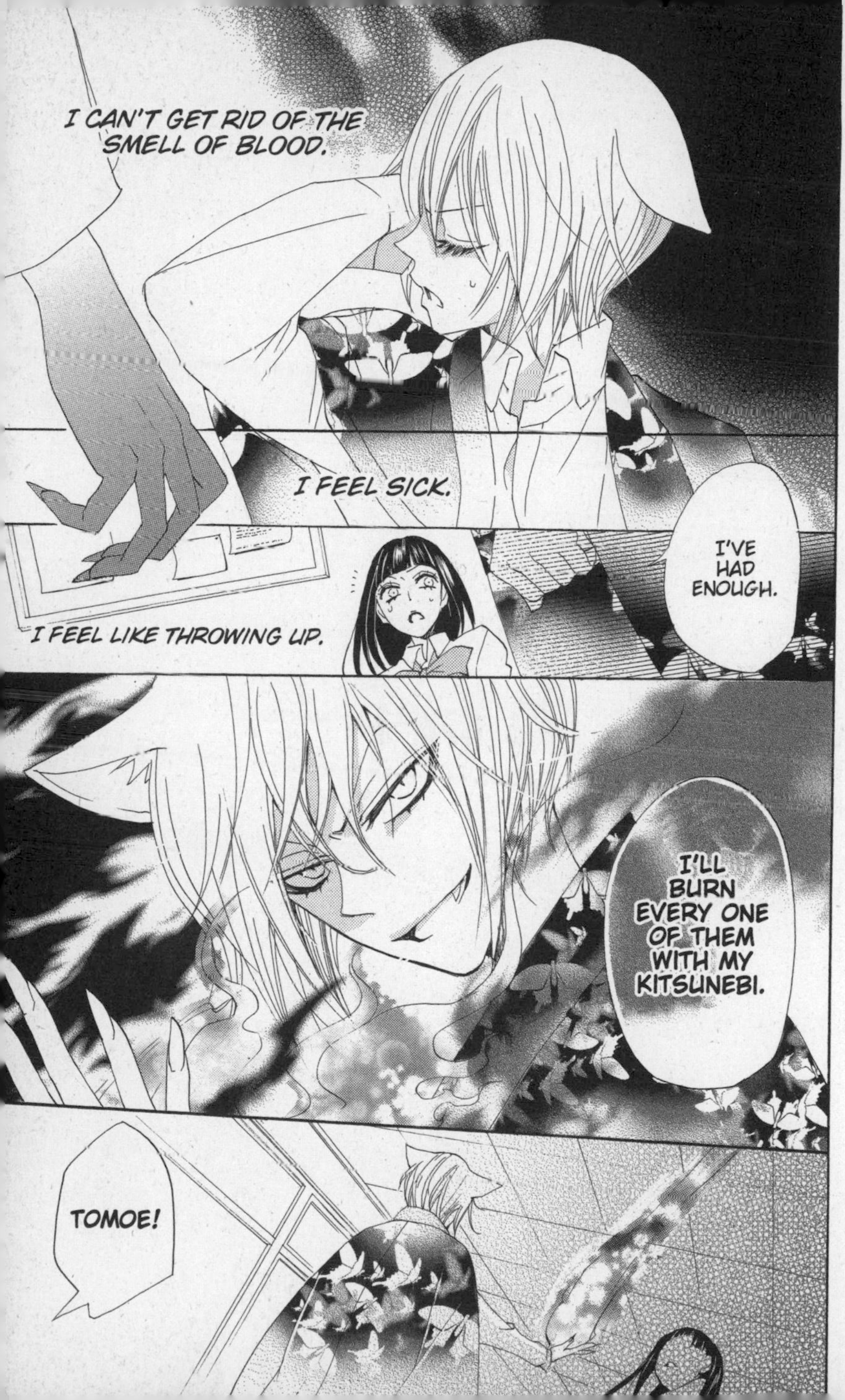
I CAN'T GET RID OF THE SMELL OF BLOOD.
I FEEL SICK.
I'VE HAD ENOUGH.
I FEEL LIKE THROWING UP.
I'LL BURN EVERY ONE OF THEM WITH MY KITSUNEBI.
TOMOE!

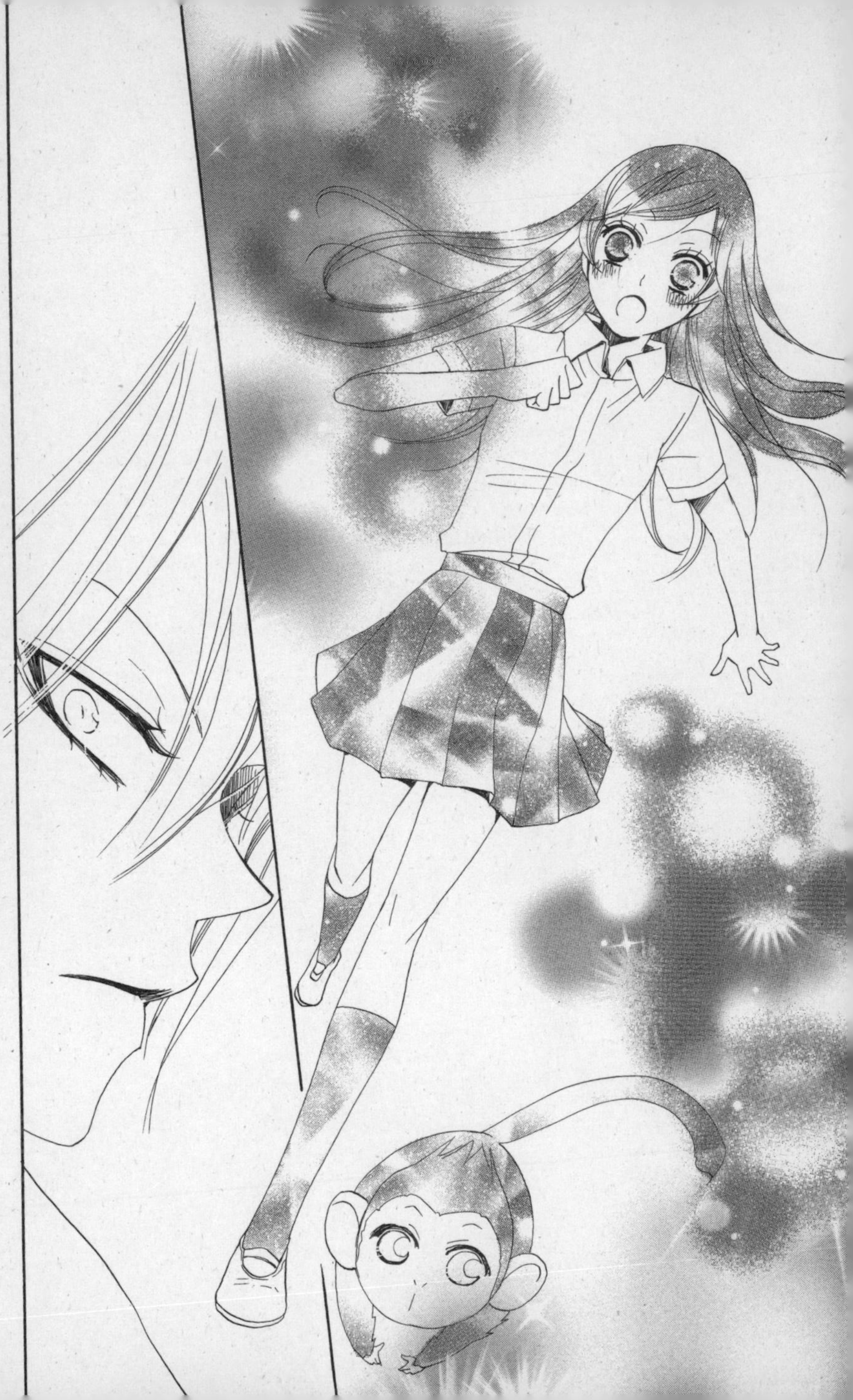

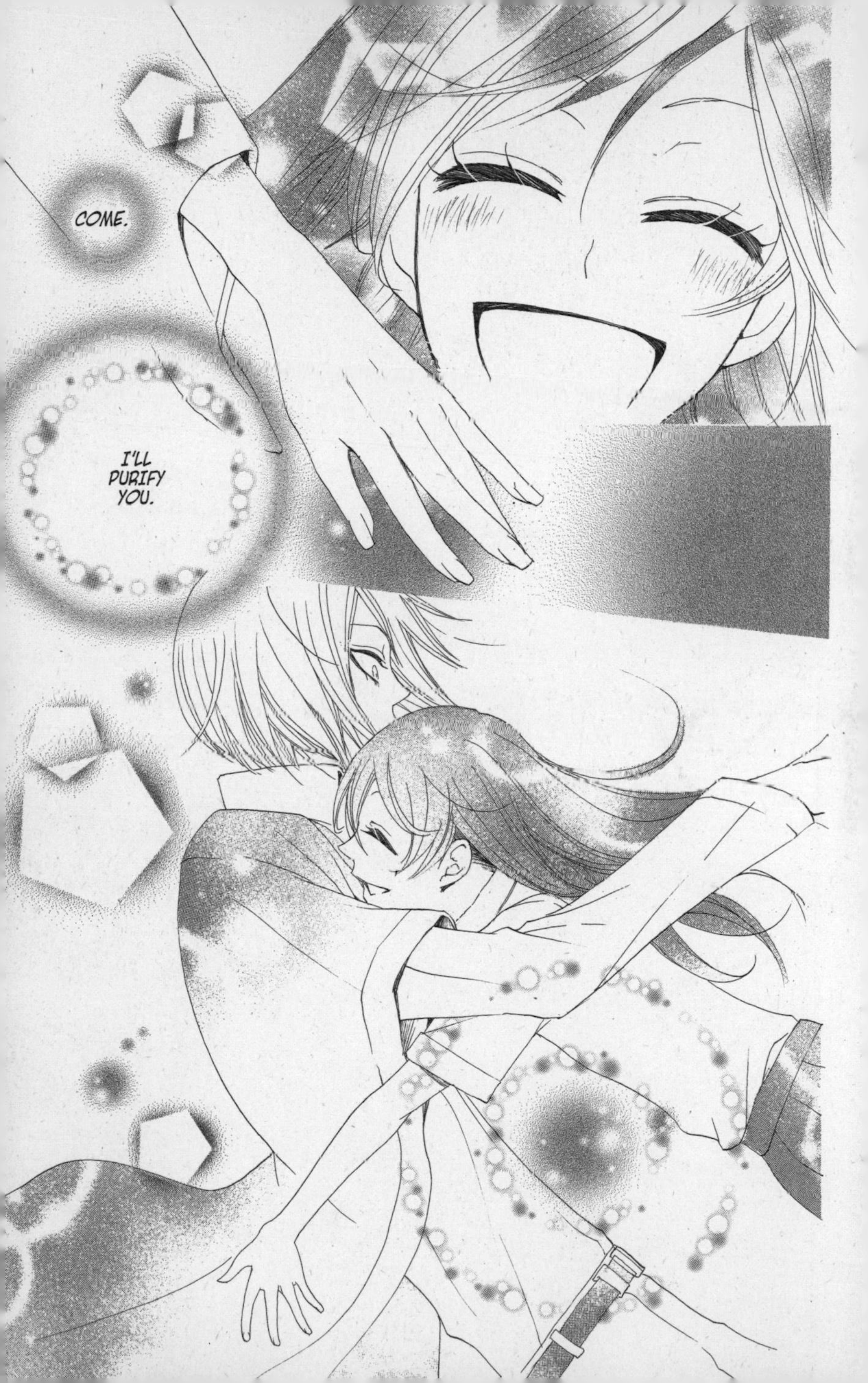
COME.
I'LL PURIFY YOU.

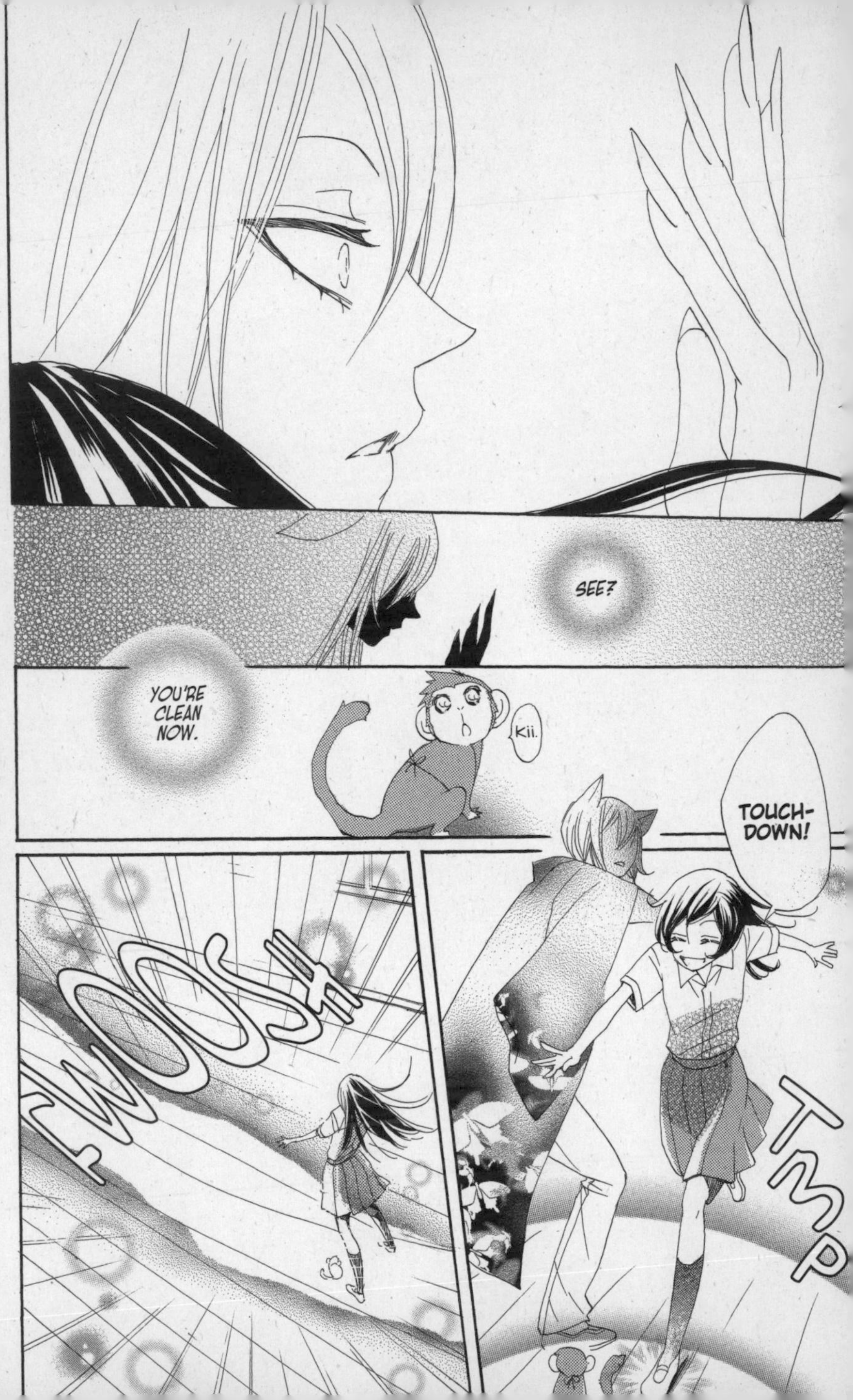
SEE?
YOU'RE CLEAN NOW.
Kii.
TOUCH-DOWN!
TMP
FWOOSH

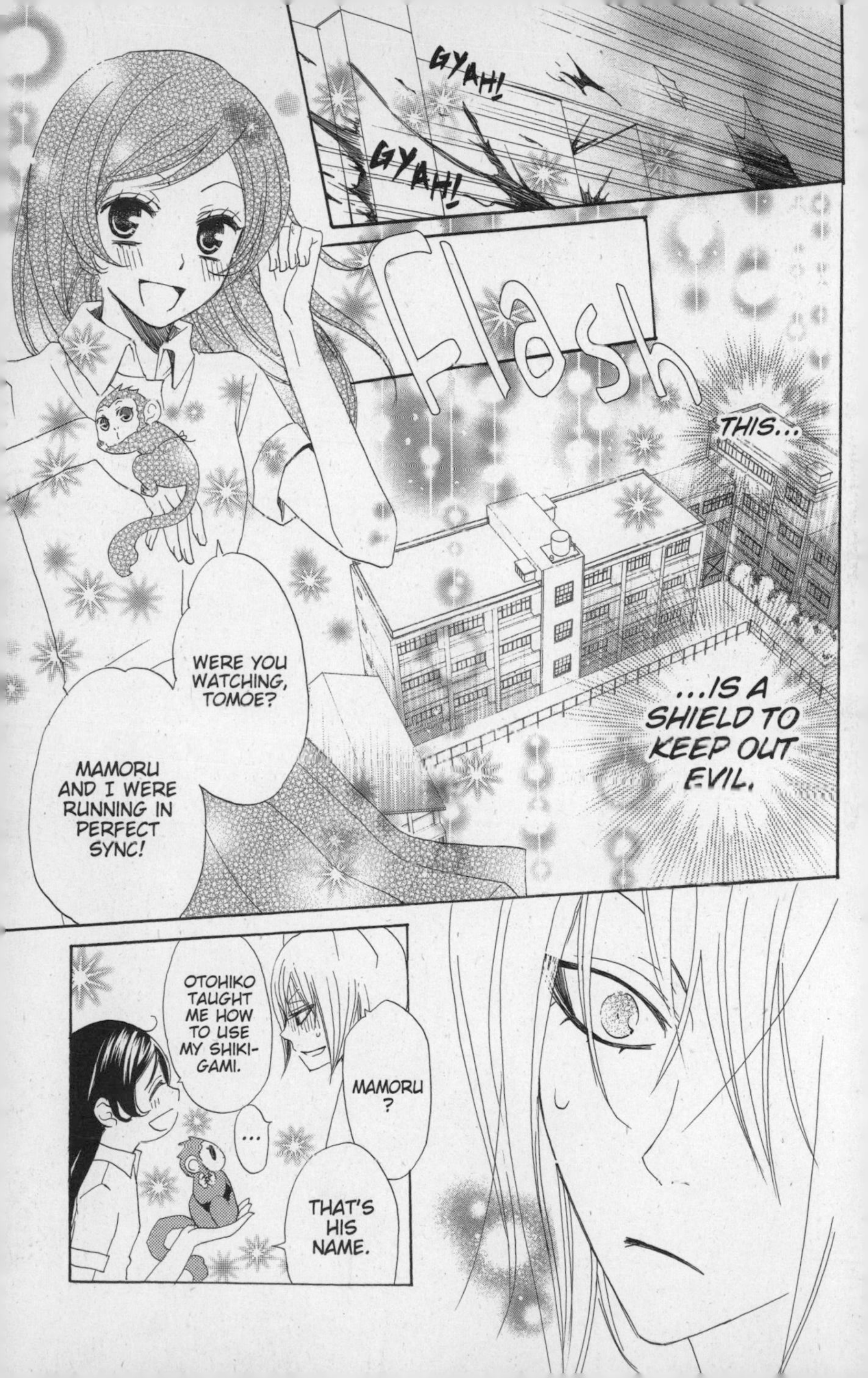
GYAH!
GYAH!
Flash
THIS...
...IS A SHIELD TO KEEP OUT EVIL.
WERE YOU WATCHING, TOMOE?
MAMORU AND I WERE RUNNING IN PERFECT SYNC!
OTOHIKO TAUGHT ME HOW TO USE MY SHIKI-GAMI.
MAMORU?
...
THAT'S HIS NAME.

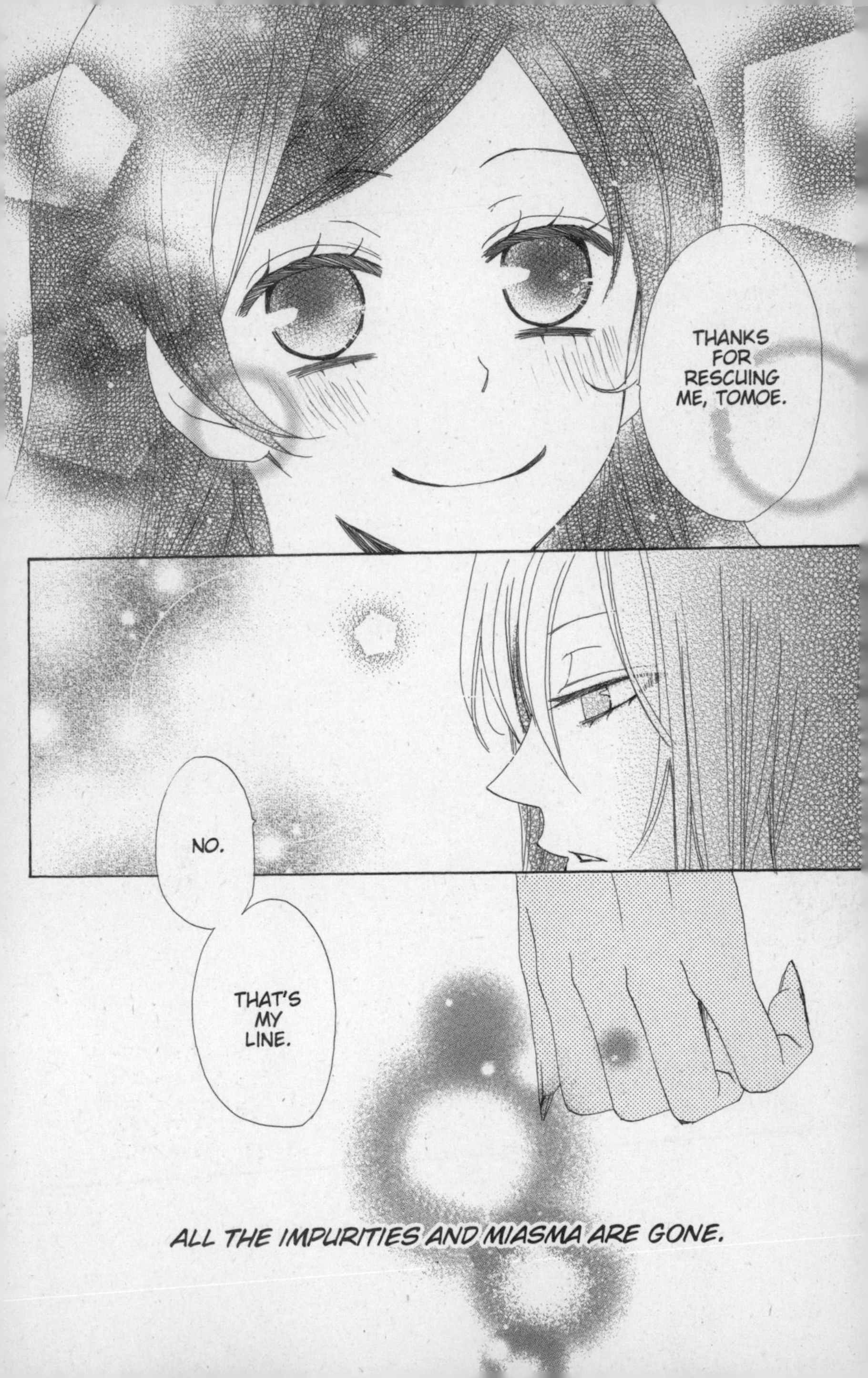
THANKS FOR RESCUING ME, TOMOE.
NO.
THAT'S MY LINE.
ALL THE IMPURITIES AND MIASMA ARE GONE.

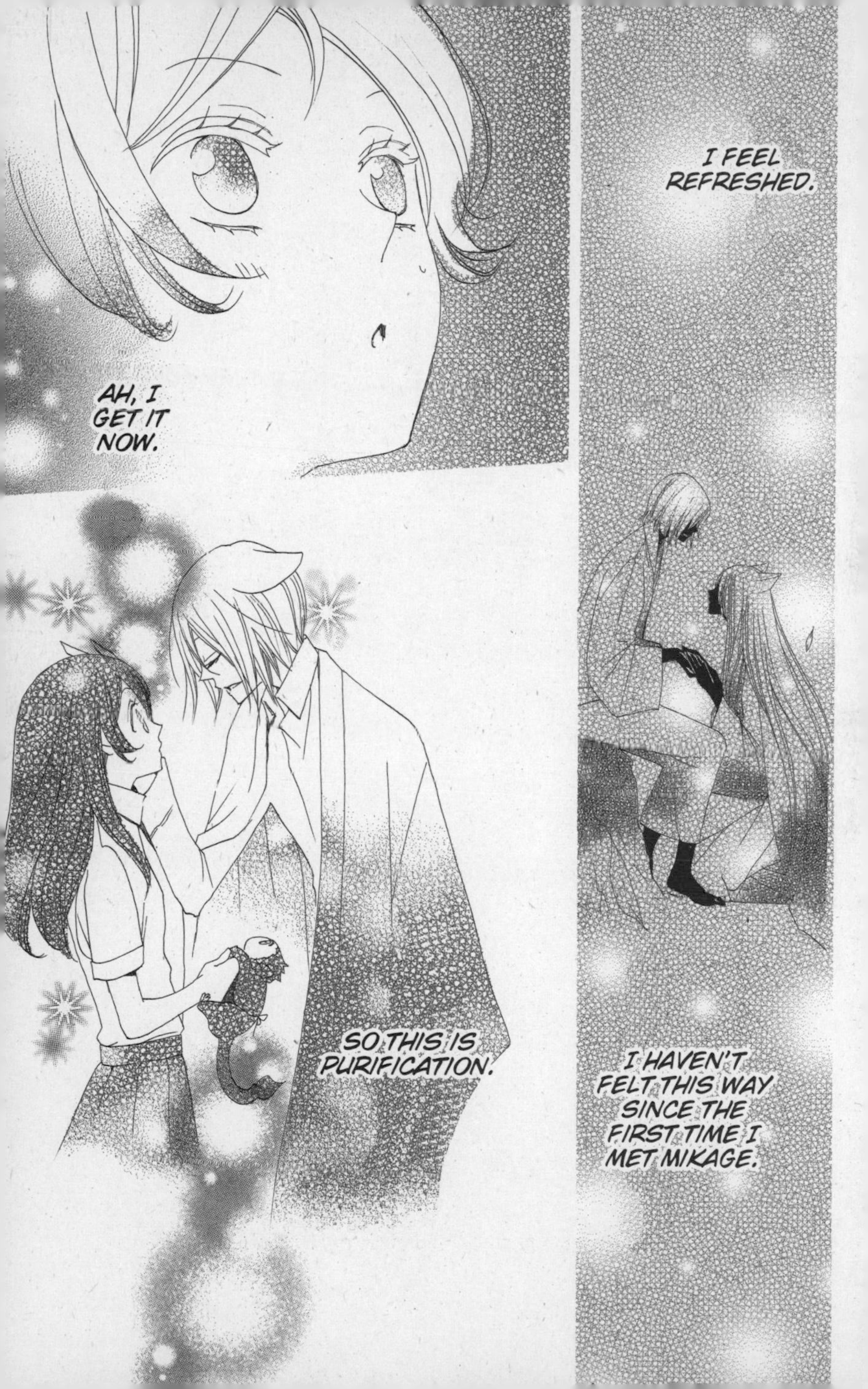
I FEEL REFRESHED.
I HAVEN'T FELT THIS WAY SINCE THE FIRST TIME I MET MIKAGE.
AH, I GET IT NOW.
SO THIS IS PURIFICATION.

THE MIASMA IN THE SCHOOL DISAPPEARED IN A FLASH.

WHEN DID THAT WOMAN ...?

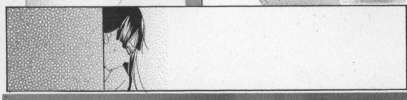

SO, OTOHIKO ASSISTED HER.

WHY?

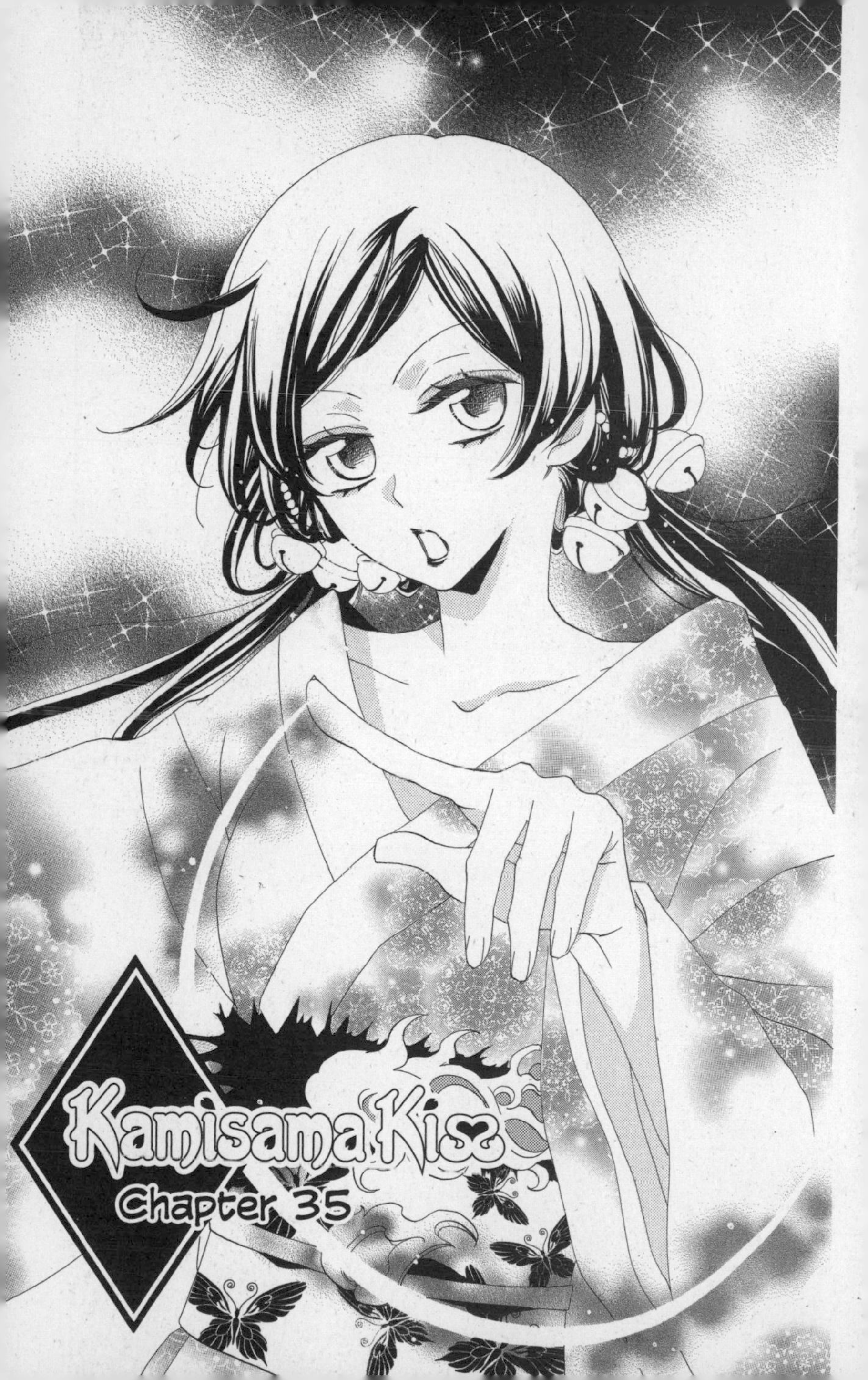
Kamisama Kiss
Chapter 35

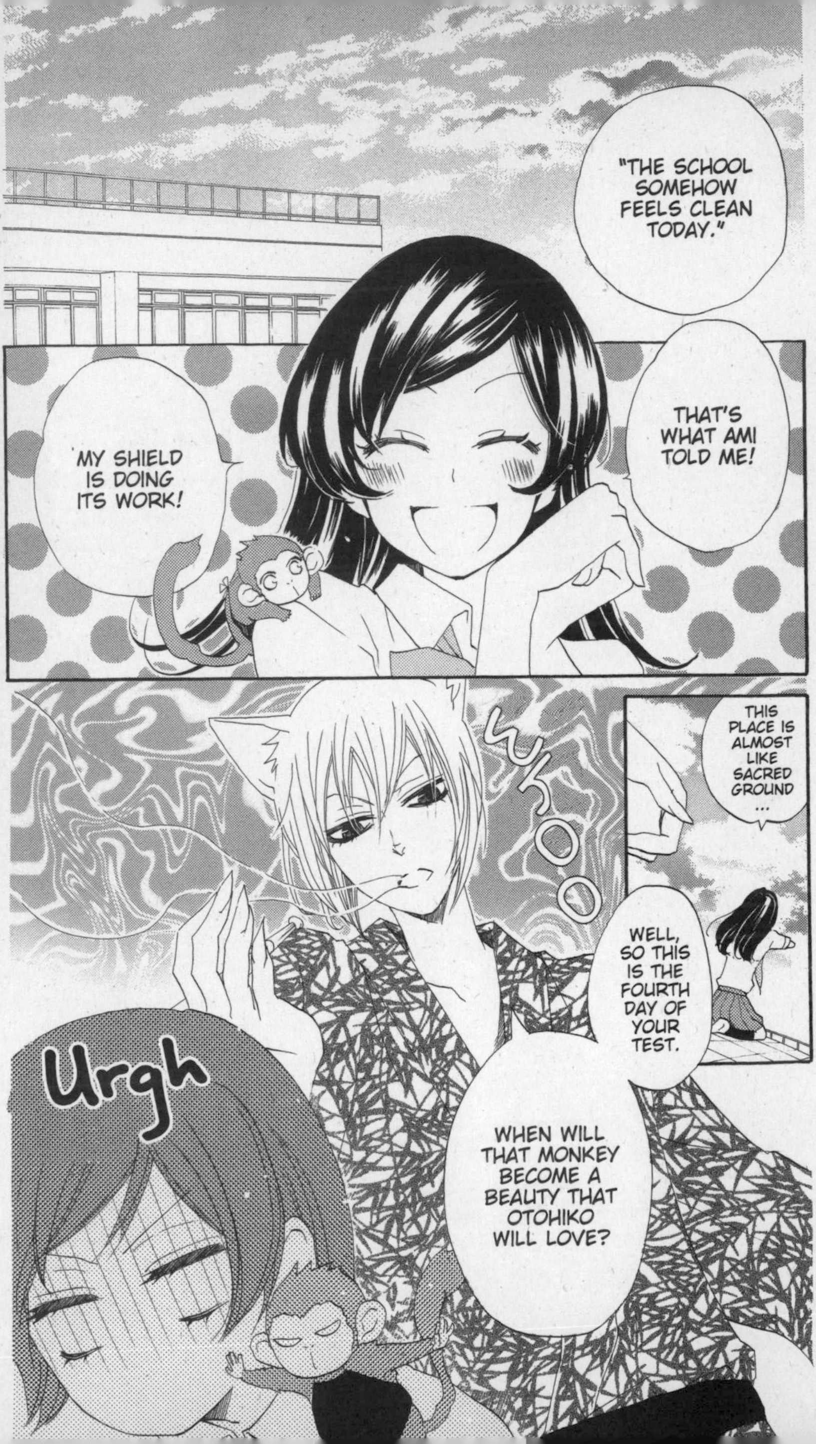
"THE SCHOOL SOMEHOW FEELS CLEAN TODAY."
THAT'S WHAT AMI TOLD ME!
MY SHIELD IS DOING ITS WORK!
THIS PLACE IS ALMOST LIKE SACRED GROUND...
WHOO
WELL, SO THIS IS THE FOURTH DAY OF YOUR TEST.
WHEN WILL THAT MONKEY BECOME A BEAUTY THAT OTOHIKO WILL LOVE?
Urgh

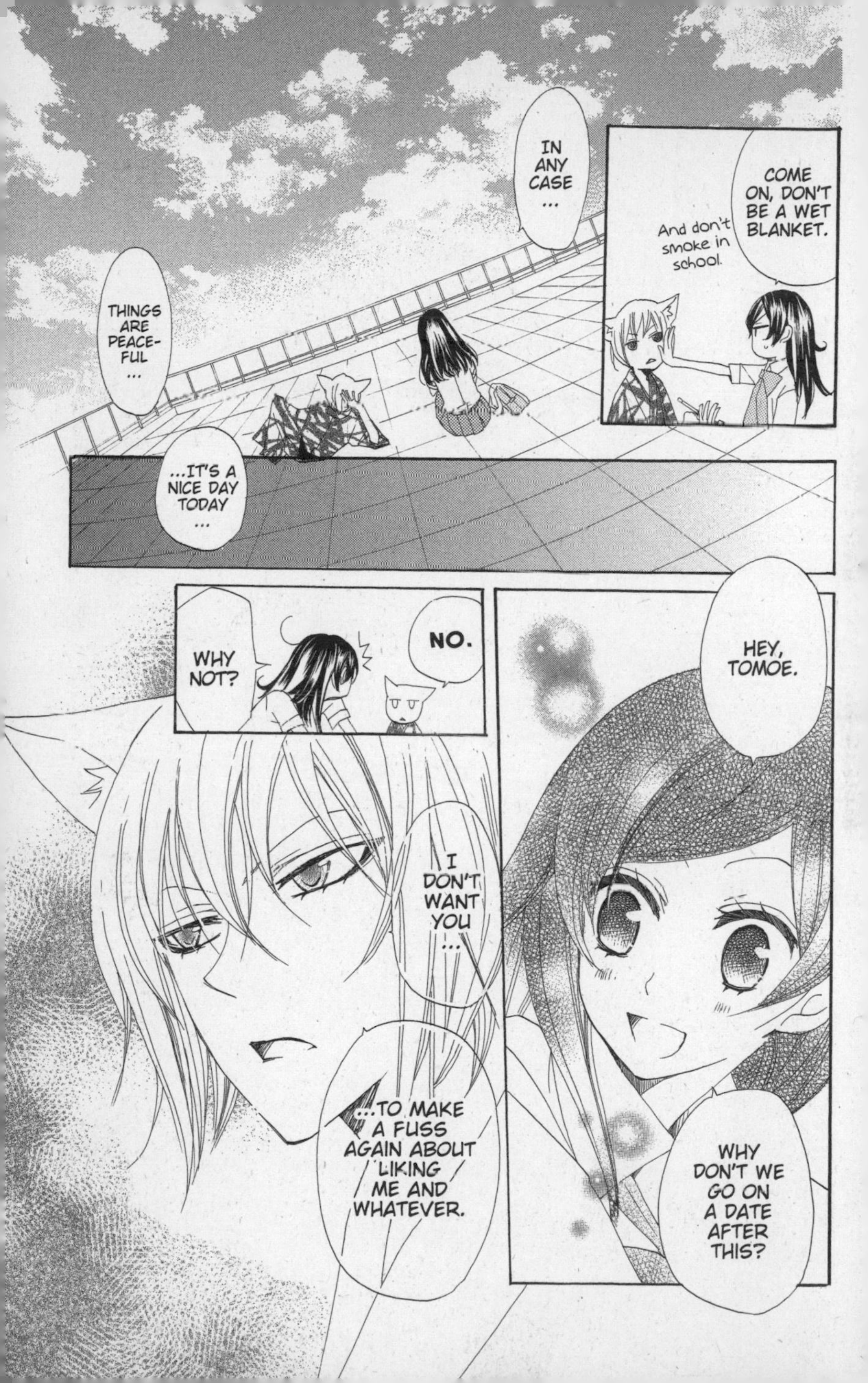
COME ON, DON'T BE A WET BLANKET.
And don't smoke in school.
IN ANY CASE...
THINGS ARE PEACEFUL...
...IT'S A NICE DAY TODAY...
HEY, TOMOE.
WHY DON'T WE GO ON A DATE AFTER THIS?
NO.
WHY NOT?
I DON'T WANT YOU...
...TO MAKE A FUSS AGAIN ABOUT LIKING ME AND WHATEVER.

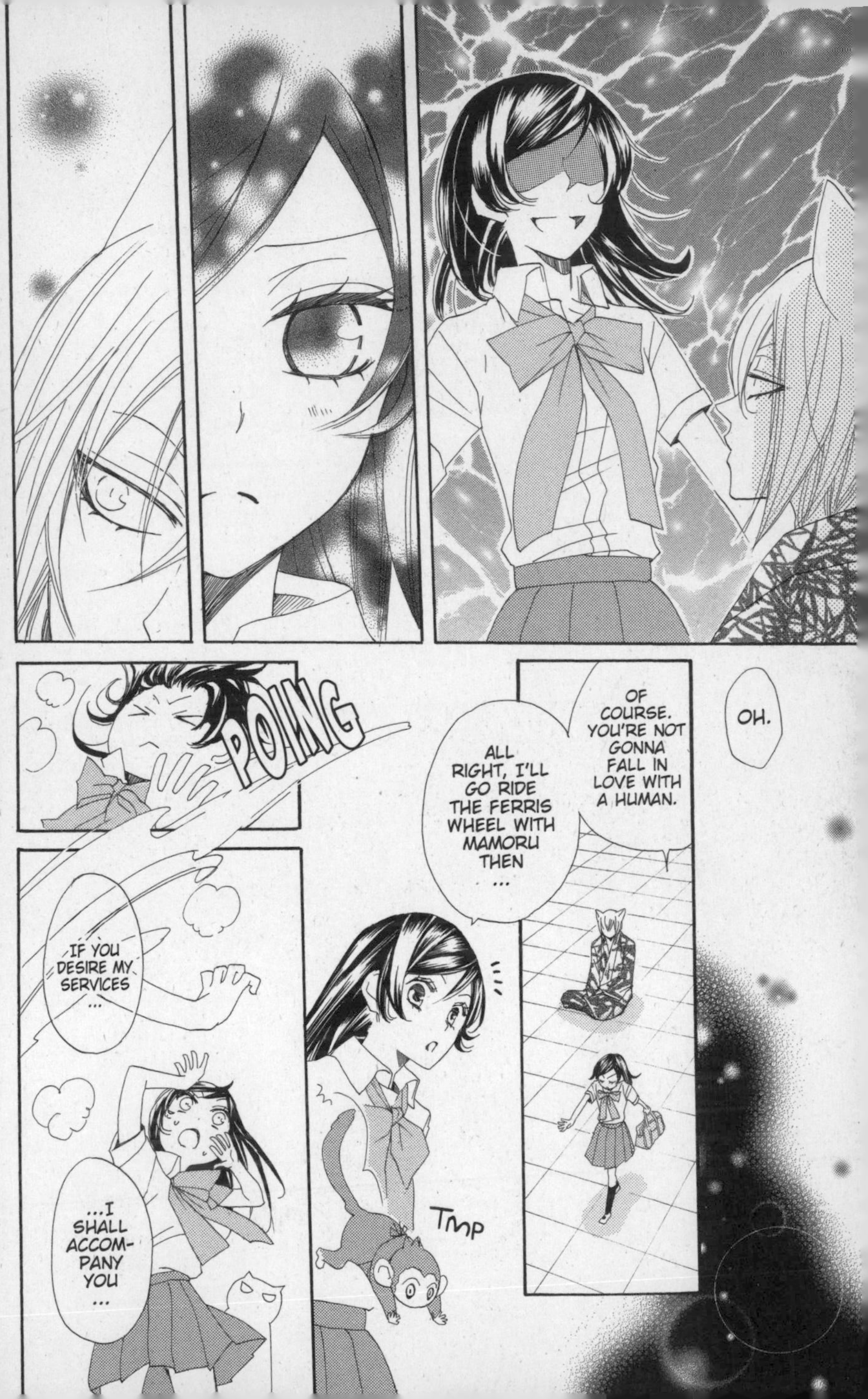
OH.
OF COURSE. YOU'RE NOT GONNA FALL IN LOVE WITH A HUMAN.
ALL RIGHT, I'LL GO RIDE THE FERRIS WHEEL WITH MAMORU THEN ...
POING
TMP
IF YOU DESIRE MY SERVICES ...
...I SHALL ACCOMPANY YOU ...

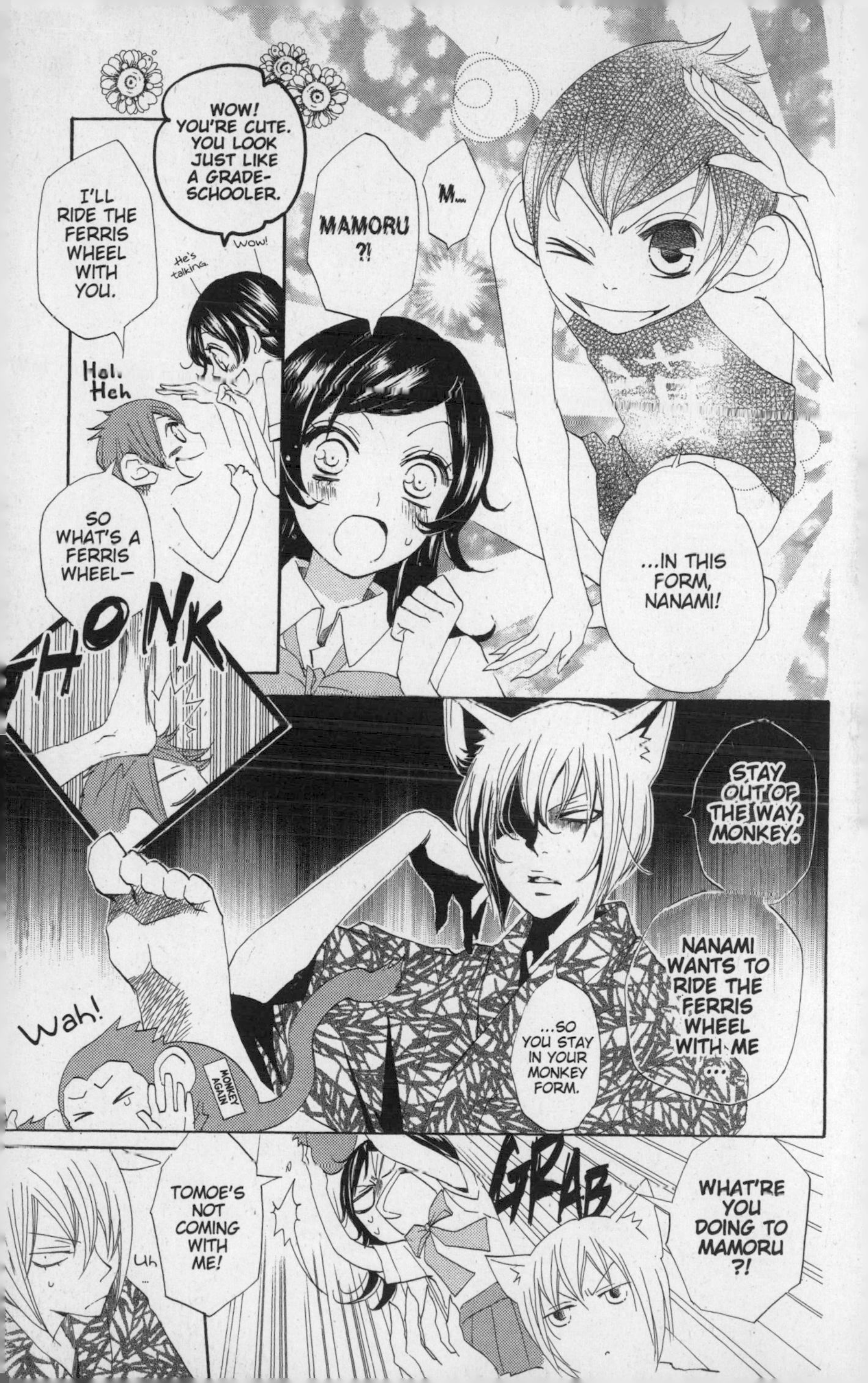
M...
MAMORU ?!
...IN THIS FORM, NANAMI!
WOW! YOU'RE CUTE. YOU LOOK JUST LIKE A GRADE-SCHOOLER.
I'LL RIDE THE FERRIS WHEEL WITH YOU.
Wow!
He's talking
Heh Heh
SO WHAT'S A FERRIS WHEEL—
THONK
STAY OUT OF THE WAY, MONKEY.
NANAMI WANTS TO RIDE THE FERRIS WHEEL WITH ME ...
...SO YOU STAY IN YOUR MONKEY FORM.
Wah!
MONKEY AGAIN
WHAT'RE YOU DOING TO MAMORU ?!
GRAB
TOMOE'S NOT COMING WITH ME!
Uh ...

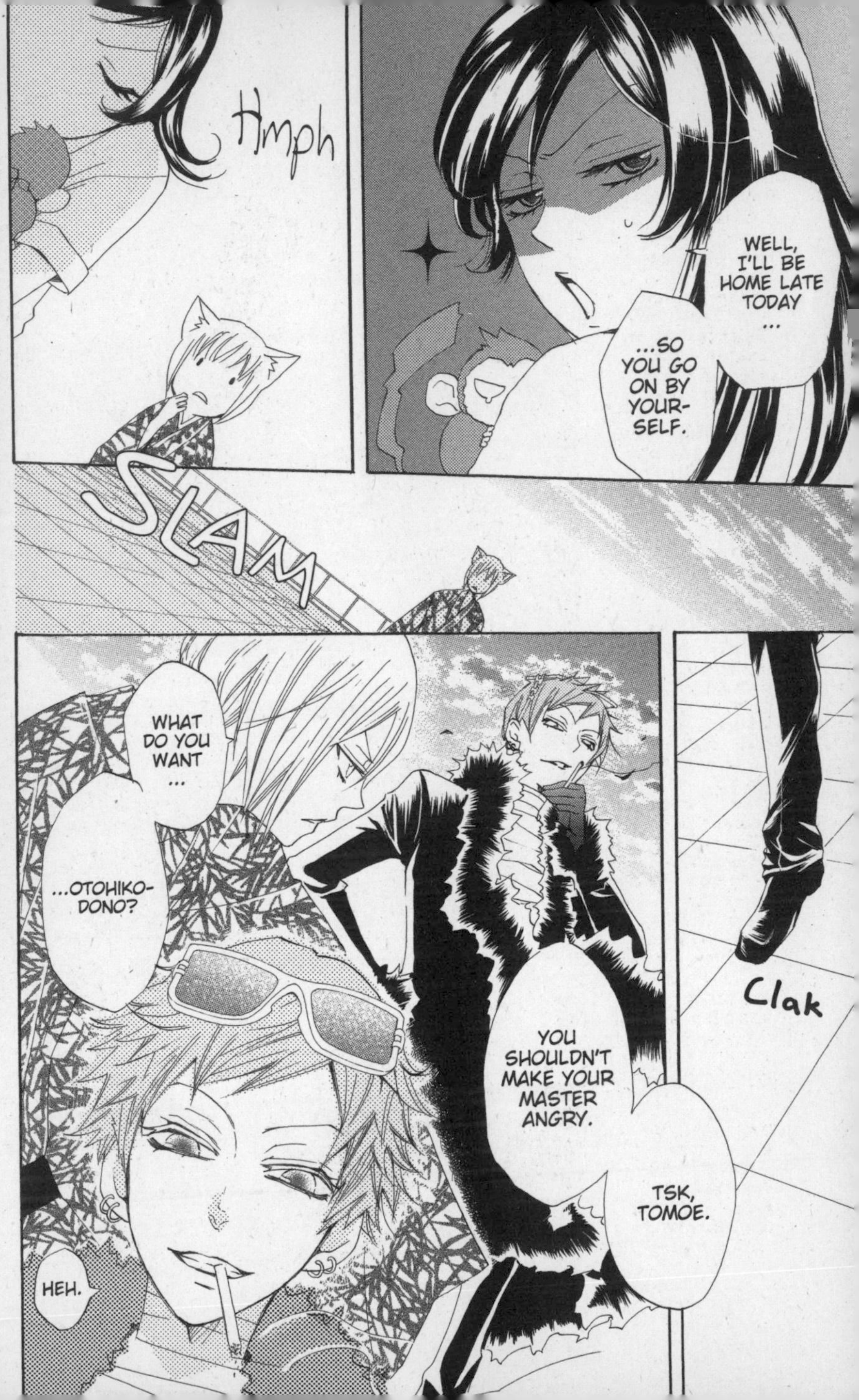
WELL, I'LL BE HOME LATE TODAY ...
...SO YOU GO ON BY YOURSELF.
Hmph
SLAM
Clak
WHAT DO YOU WANT ...
...OTOHIKO-DONO?
HEH.
TSK, TOMOE.
YOU SHOULDN'T MAKE YOUR MASTER ANGRY.

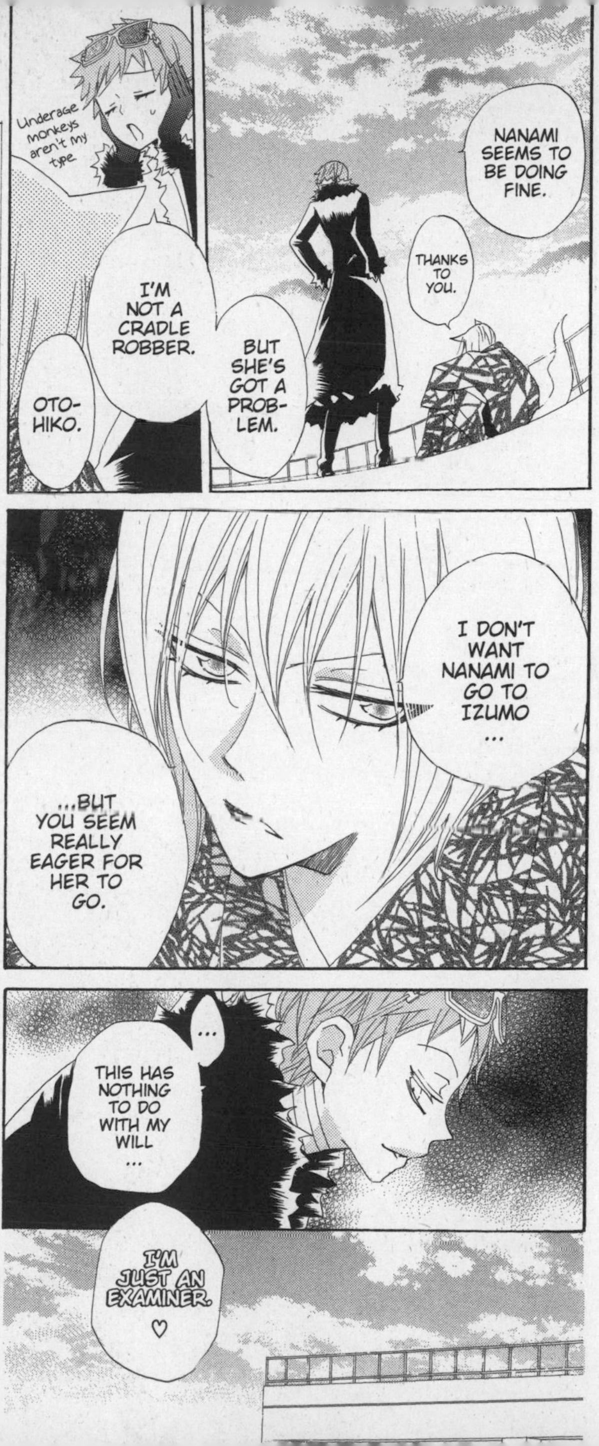
NANAMI SEEMS TO BE DOING FINE.
THANKS TO YOU.
BUT SHE'S GOT A PROBLEM.
Underage monkeys aren't my type
I'M NOT A CRADLE ROBBER.
OTO-HIKO.
I DON'T WANT NANAMI TO GO TO IZUMO ...
...BUT YOU SEEM REALLY EAGER FOR HER TO GO.
...
THIS HAS NOTHING TO DO WITH MY WILL ...
I'M JUST AN EXAMINER. ♡

My family didn't believe me at all when I told them I tend to get headaches before a rainy day. I think I heard something about blood vessels in your head being affected by changes in air pressure, but I wonder what the truth is. And so I now have a really bad headache. It must rain tomorrow for sure!

During the spring I travelled to Nagasaki. I saw lots of things from Nagasaki to Sasebo. Nagasaki is amazing! It was a real tourist spot. I'm from Fukuoka, but I can't really recommend it to friends from other prefectures because there's not much to see, considering the distance you have to travel to get there. Dazaifu is far away. It's a good place to live though, and the food is very very good. But I can't tell people

Come visit!

Uh, they won't come, so I'm amazed at Nagasaki! I envy the place. Let's all go to Nagasaki! And to Fukuoka too!

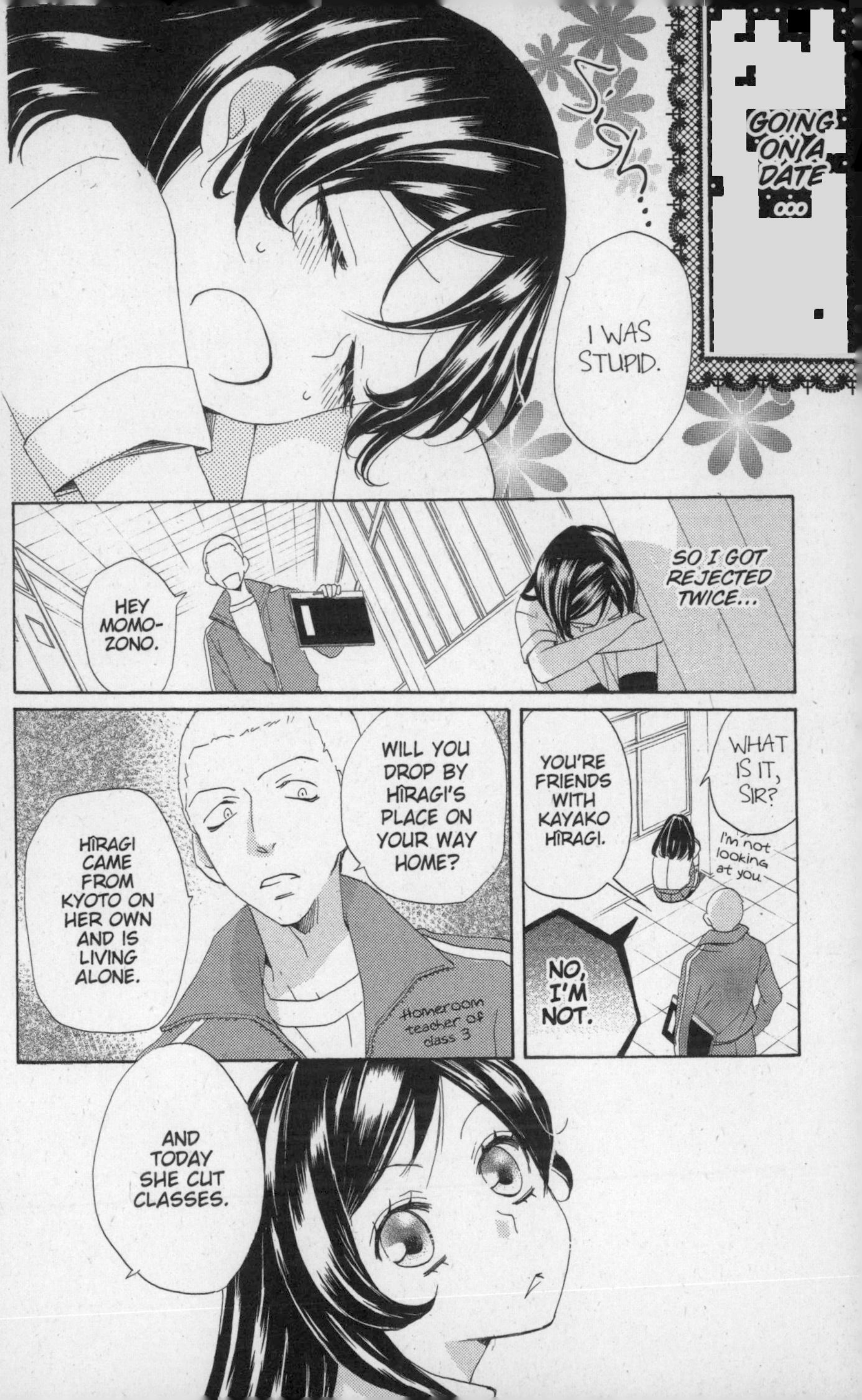

GOING ON A DATE...
Sigh...
I WAS STUPID.
SO I GOT REJECTED TWICE...
HEY MOMO-ZONO.
WHAT IS IT, SIR?
I'm not looking at you
YOU'RE FRIENDS WITH KAYAKO HĪRAGI.
NO, I'M NOT.
WILL YOU DROP BY HĪRAGI'S PLACE ON YOUR WAY HOME?
HĪRAGI CAME FROM KYOTO ON HER OWN AND IS LIVING ALONE.
Homeroom teacher of class 3
AND TODAY SHE CUT CLASSES.

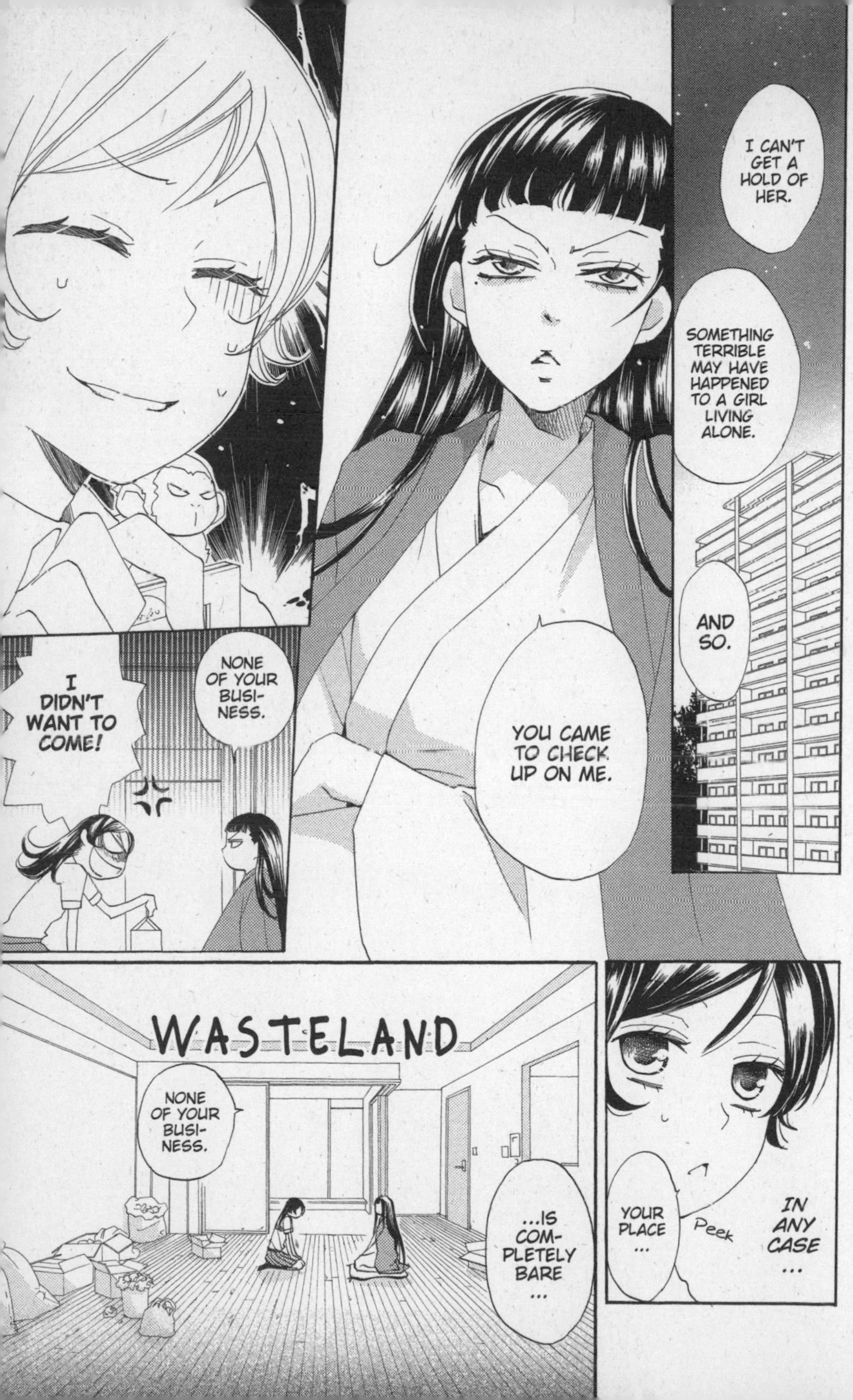
I CAN'T GET A HOLD OF HER.
SOMETHING TERRIBLE MAY HAVE HAPPENED TO A GIRL LIVING ALONE.
AND SO.
YOU CAME TO CHECK UP ON ME.
NONE OF YOUR BUSI-NESS.
I DIDN'T WANT TO COME!
IN ANY CASE...
Peek
YOUR PLACE...
...IS COM-PLETELY BARE...
WASTELAND
NONE OF YOUR BUSI-NESS.

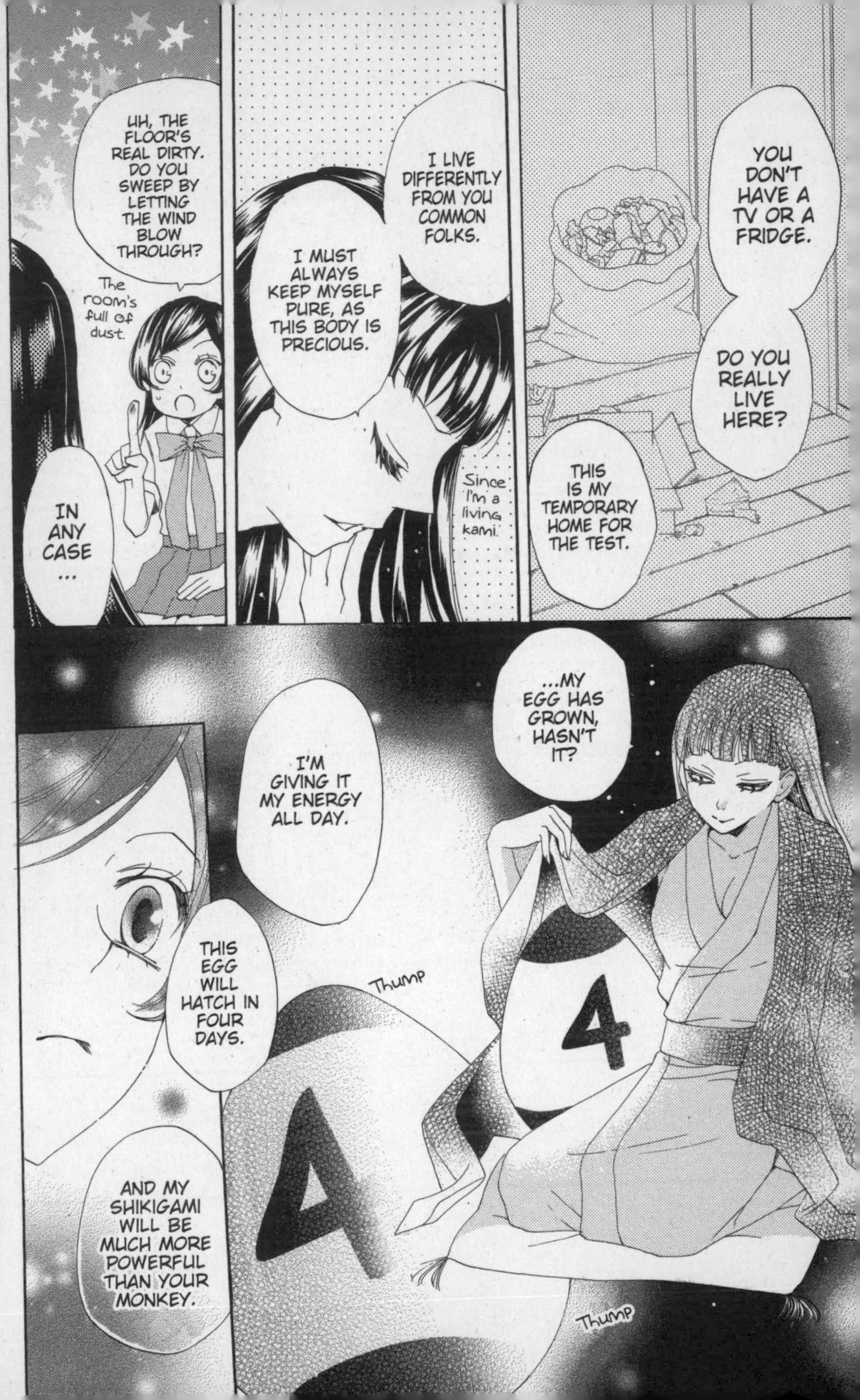
YOU DON'T HAVE A TV OR A FRIDGE.
DO YOU REALLY LIVE HERE?
THIS IS MY TEMPORARY HOME FOR THE TEST.
I LIVE DIFFERENTLY FROM YOU COMMON FOLKS.
I MUST ALWAYS KEEP MYSELF PURE, AS THIS BODY IS PRECIOUS.
Since I'm a living kami.
UH, THE FLOOR'S REAL DIRTY. DO YOU SWEEP BY LETTING THE WIND BLOW THROUGH?
The room's full of dust.
IN ANY CASE ...
...MY EGG HAS GROWN, HASN'T IT?
I'M GIVING IT MY ENERGY ALL DAY.
4
Thump
THIS EGG WILL HATCH IN FOUR DAYS.
4
AND MY SHIKIGAMI WILL BE MUCH MORE POWERFUL THAN YOUR MONKEY.
Thump

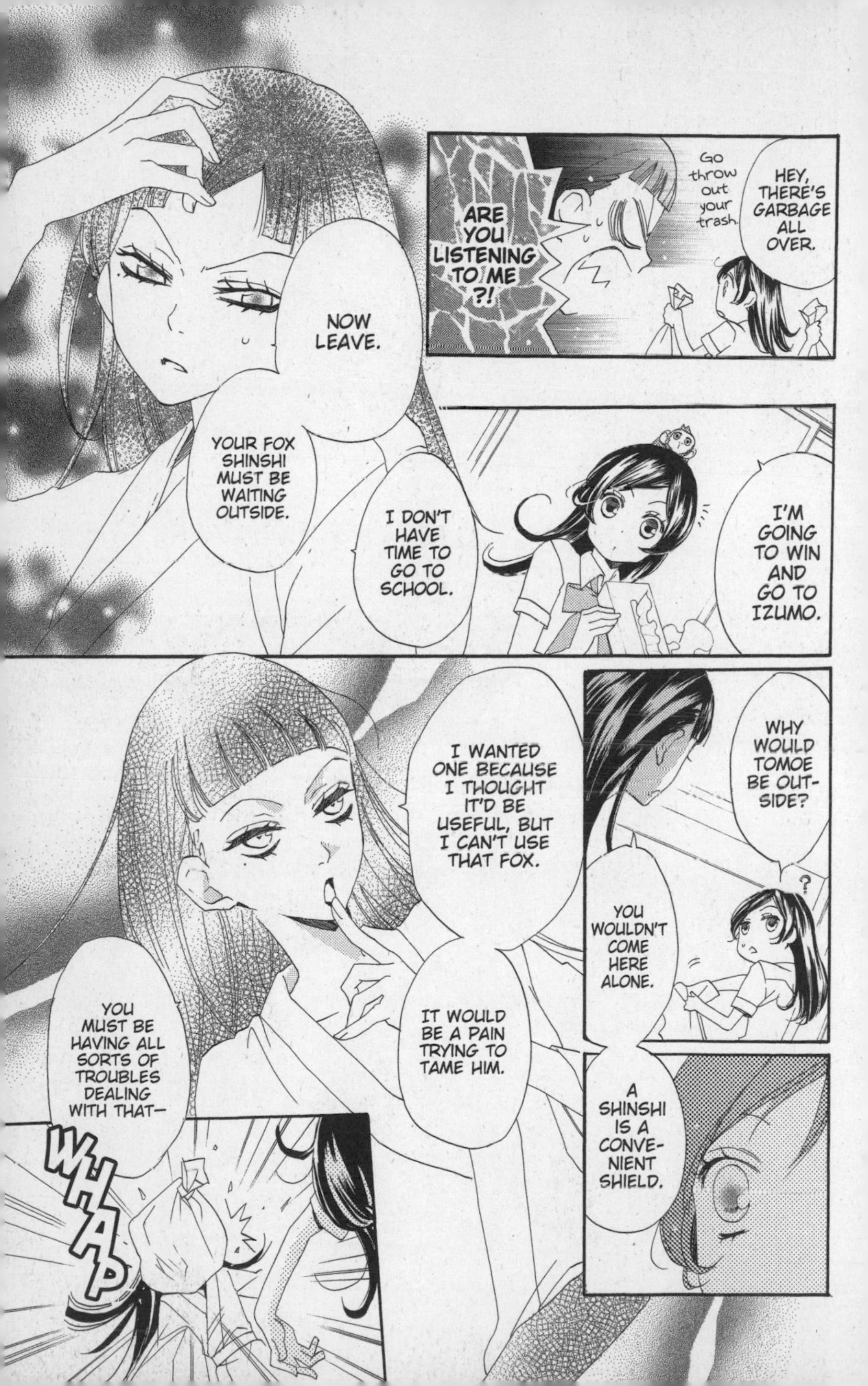
HEY, THERE'S GARBAGE ALL OVER.
Go throw out your trash.
ARE YOU LISTENING TO ME ?!
NOW LEAVE.
I'M GOING TO WIN AND GO TO IZUMO.
I DON'T HAVE TIME TO GO TO SCHOOL.
YOUR FOX SHINSHI MUST BE WAITING OUTSIDE.
WHY WOULD TOMOE BE OUT-SIDE?
YOU WOULDN'T COME HERE ALONE.
A SHINSHI IS A CONVE-NIENT SHIELD.
I WANTED ONE BECAUSE I THOUGHT IT'D BE USEFUL, BUT I CAN'T USE THAT FOX.
IT WOULD BE A PAIN TRYING TO TAME HIM.
YOU MUST BE HAVING ALL SORTS OF TROUBLES DEALING WITH THAT—
WHAP

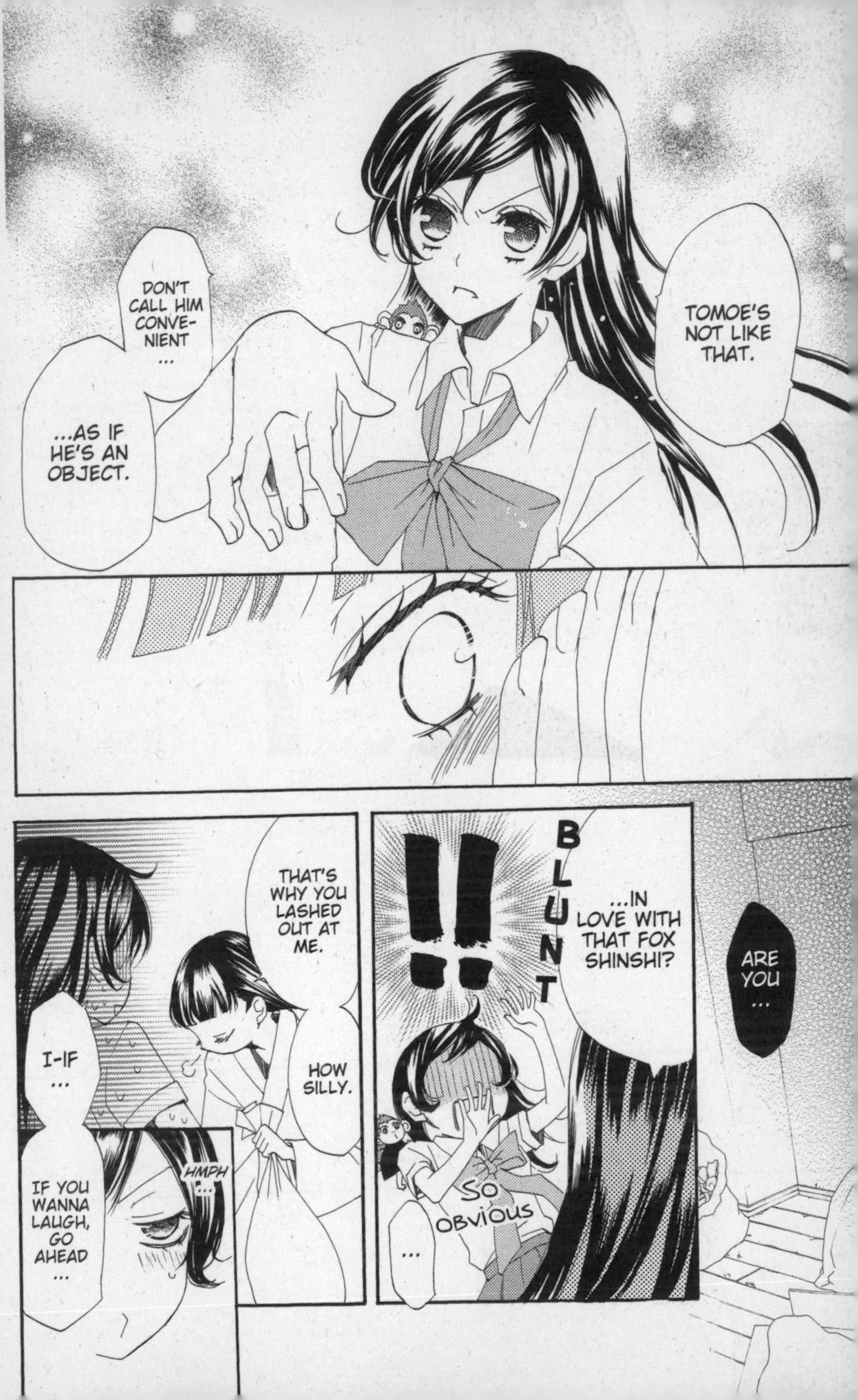
TOMOE'S NOT LIKE THAT.
DON'T CALL HIM CONVENIENT ...
...AS IF HE'S AN OBJECT.
ARE YOU ...
...IN LOVE WITH THAT FOX SHINSHI?
BLUNT
!!
SO OBVIOUS
...
THAT'S WHY YOU LASHED OUT AT ME.
HOW SILLY.
I-IF ...
HMPH ...
IF YOU WANNA LAUGH, GO AHEAD ...

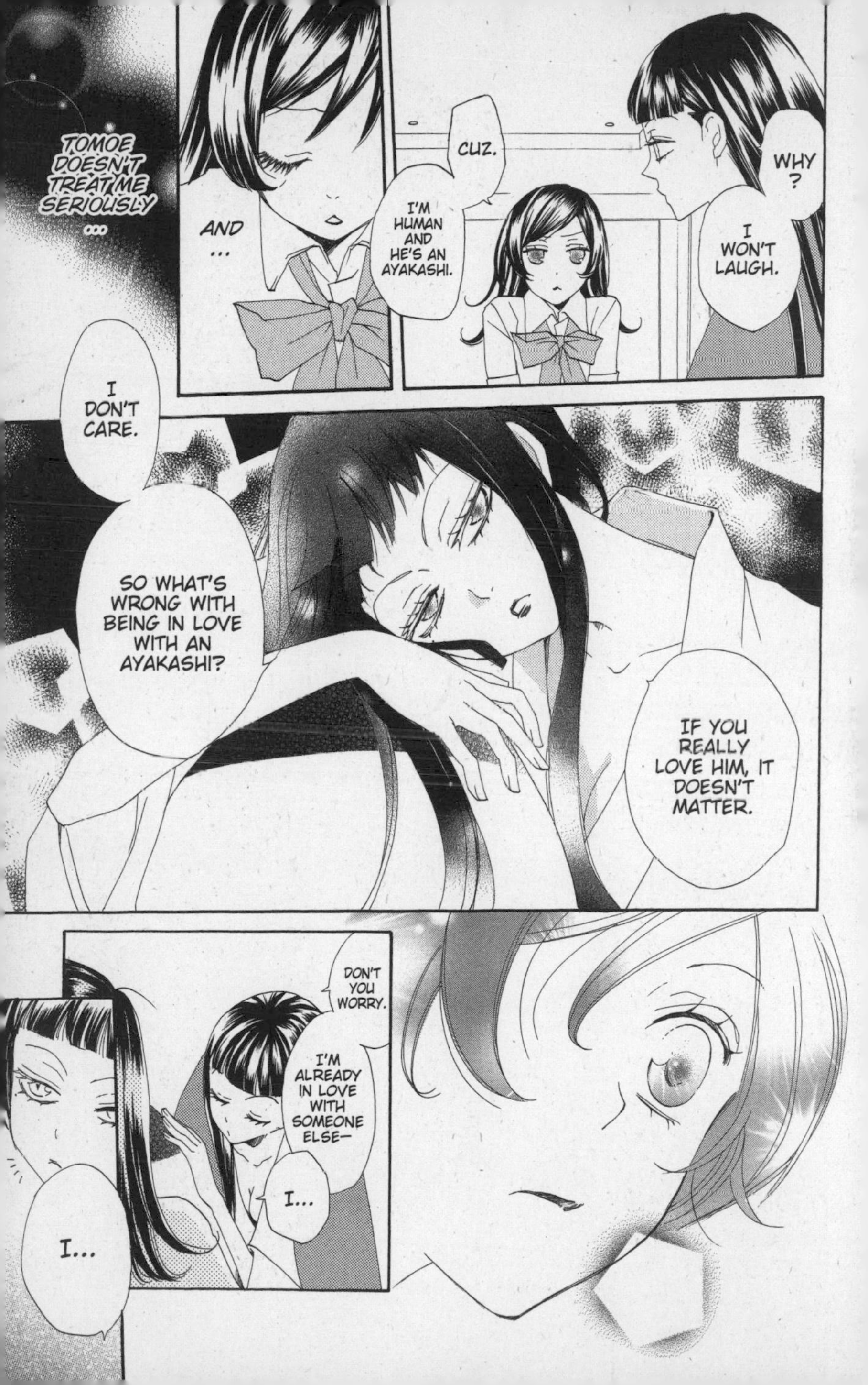
WHY?
I WON'T LAUGH.
CUZ.
I'M HUMAN AND HE'S AN AYAKASHI.
AND...
TOMOE DOESN'T TREAT ME SERIOUSLY...
I DON'T CARE.
SO WHAT'S WRONG WITH BEING IN LOVE WITH AN AYAKASHI?
IF YOU REALLY LOVE HIM, IT DOESN'T MATTER.
DON'T YOU WORRY.
I'M ALREADY IN LOVE WITH SOMEONE ELSE—
I...
I...

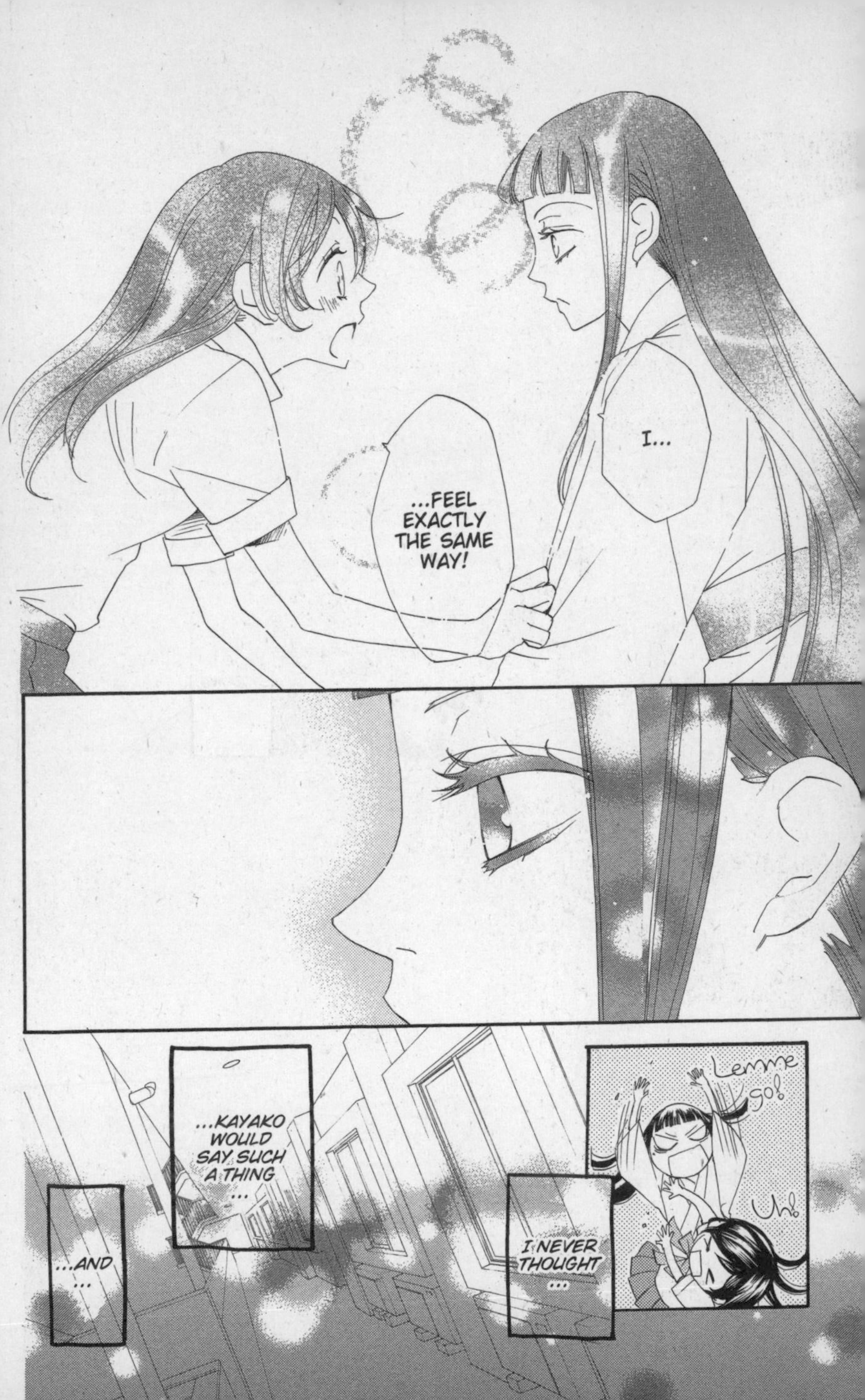
I...
...FEEL EXACTLY THE SAME WAY!
Lemme go!
Uh!
I NEVER THOUGHT ...
...KAYAKO WOULD SAY SUCH A THING ...
...AND ...

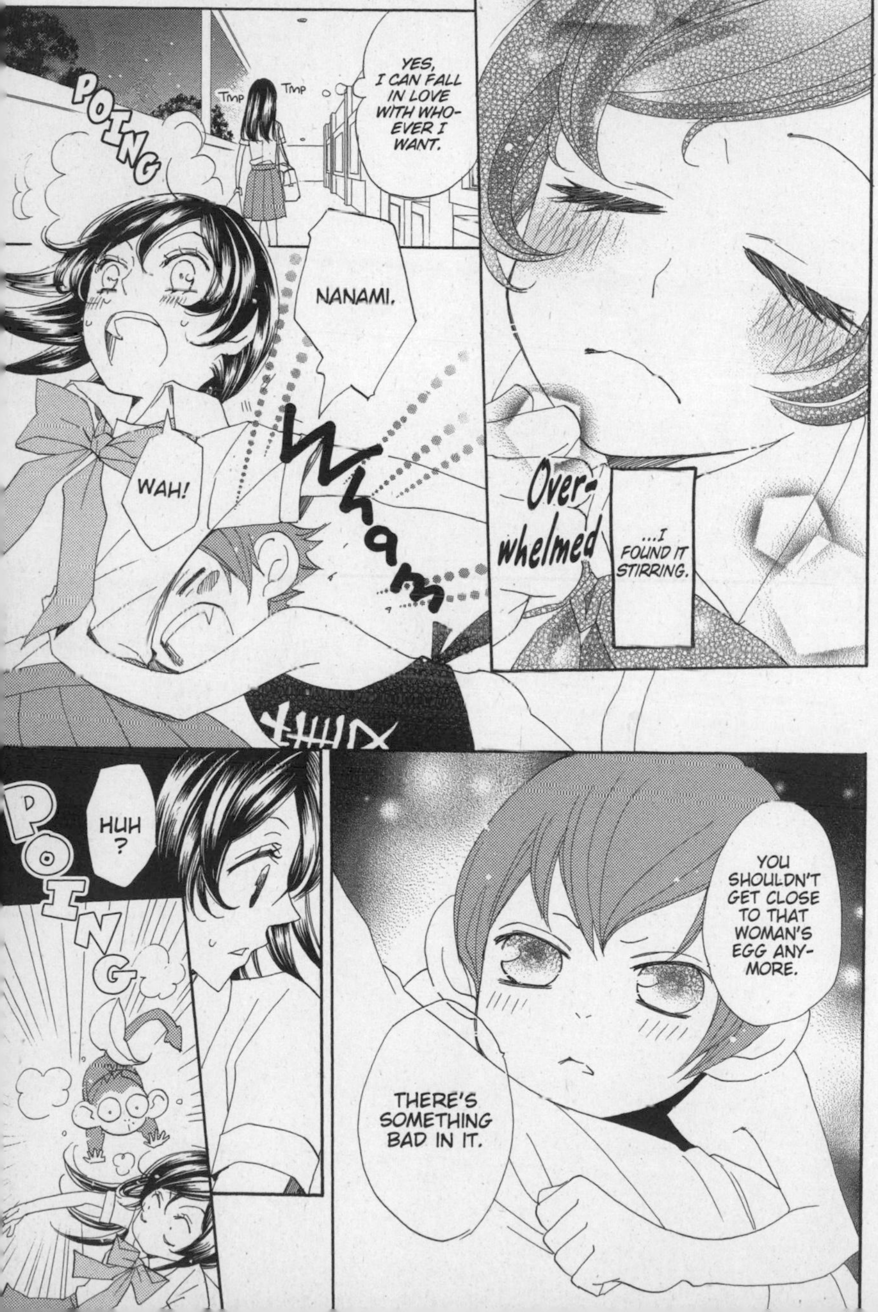
Over-whelmed
...I FOUND IT STIRRING.
YES, I CAN FALL IN LOVE WITH WHO-EVER I WANT.
Tmp Tmp
POING
NANAMI.
WAH!
Wham
YOU SHOULDN'T GET CLOSE TO THAT WOMAN'S EGG ANY-MORE.
THERE'S SOMETHING BAD IN IT.
HUH?
POING

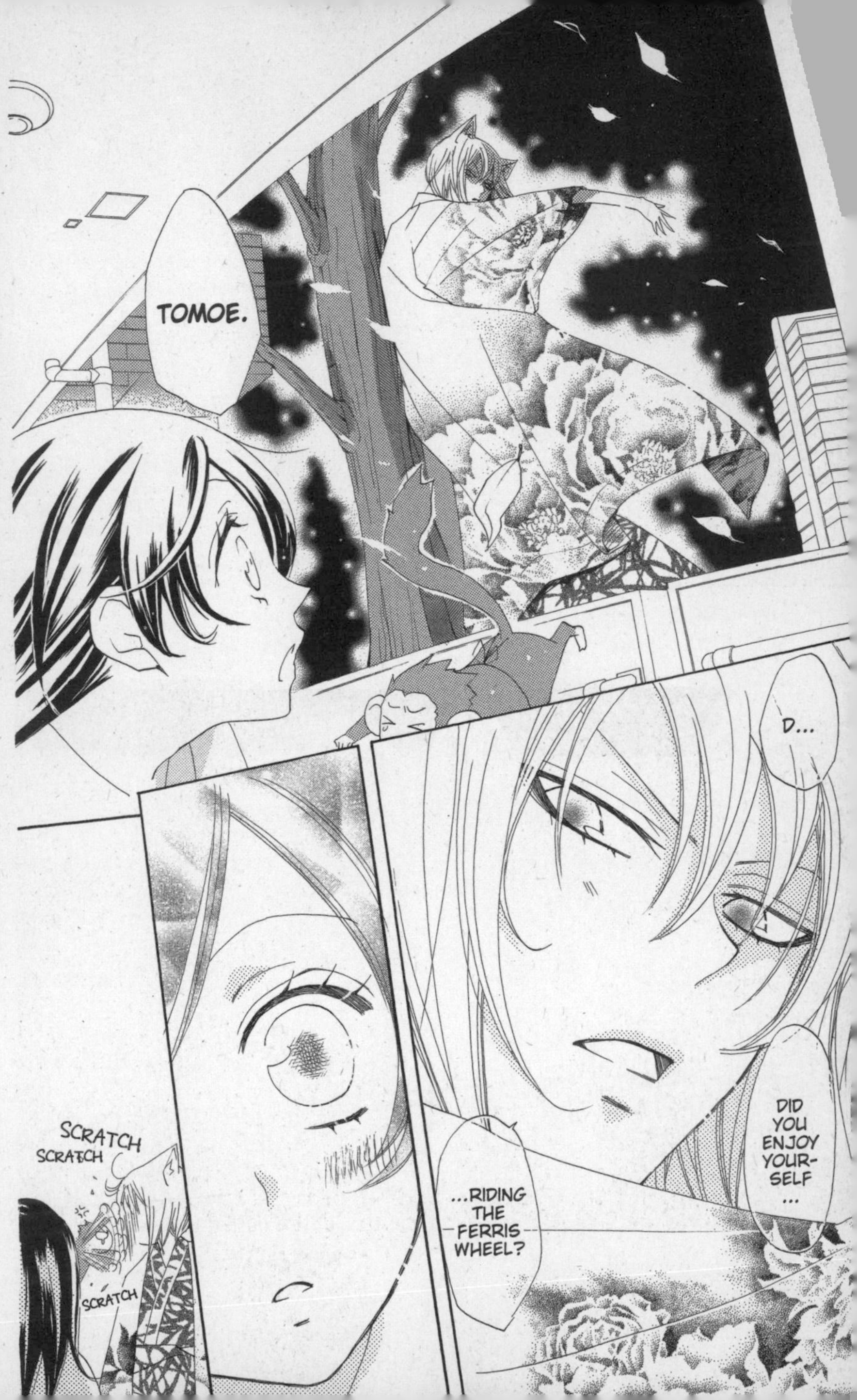
TOMOE.
D...
DID YOU ENJOY YOURSELF...
...RIDING THE FERRIS WHEEL?
SCRATCH
SCRATCH
SCRATCH

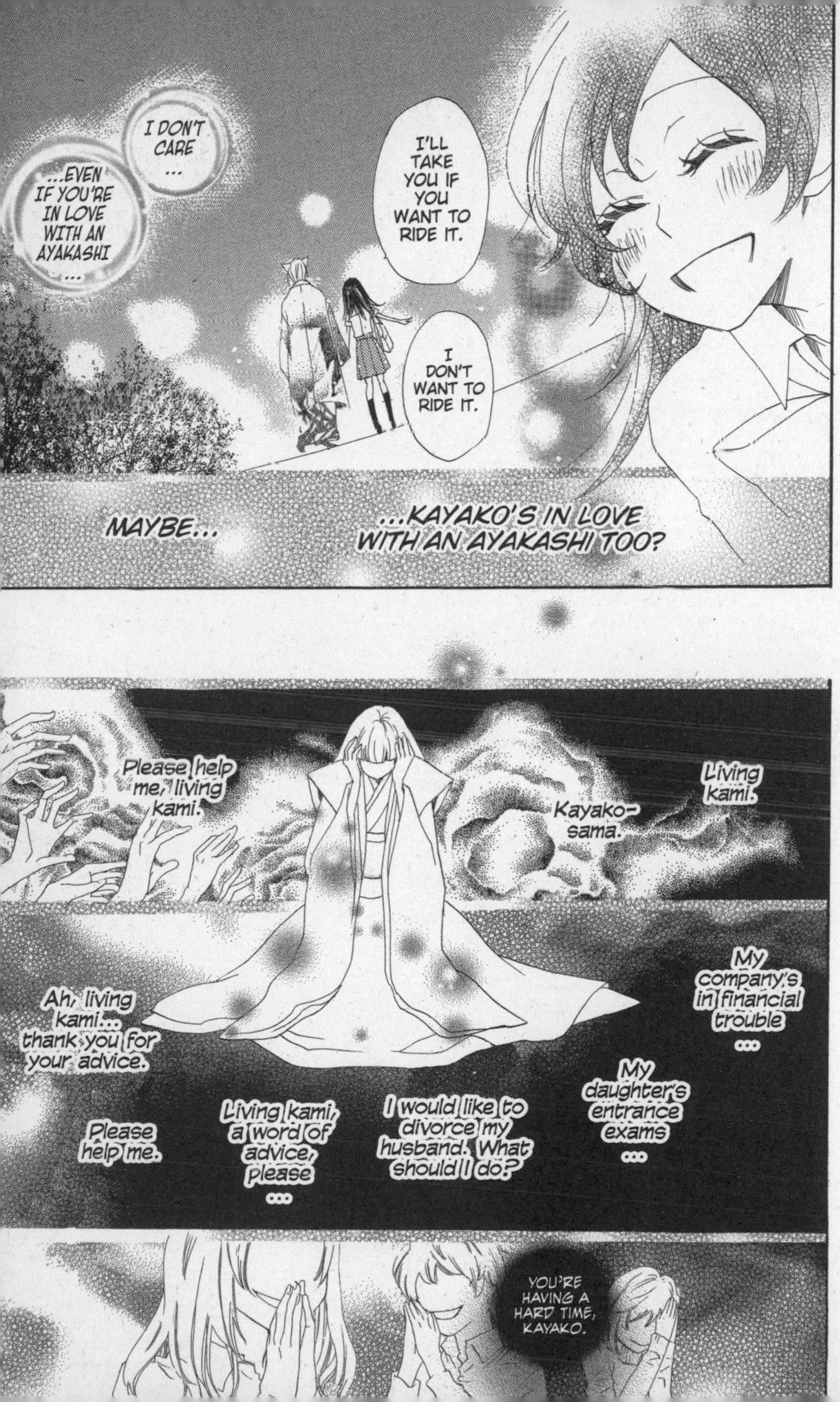
I'LL TAKE YOU IF YOU WANT TO RIDE IT.
I DON'T WANT TO RIDE IT.
I DON'T CARE ...
...EVEN IF YOU'RE IN LOVE WITH AN AYAKASHI ...
MAYBE...
...KAYAKO'S IN LOVE WITH AN AYAKASHI TOO?
Living kami.
Kayako-sama.
Please help me, living kami.
My company's in financial trouble ...
My daughter's entrance exams ...
I would like to divorce my husband. What should I do?
Living kami, a word of advice, please ...
Ah, living kami... thank you for your advice.
Please help me.
YOU'RE HAVING A HARD TIME, KAYAKO.

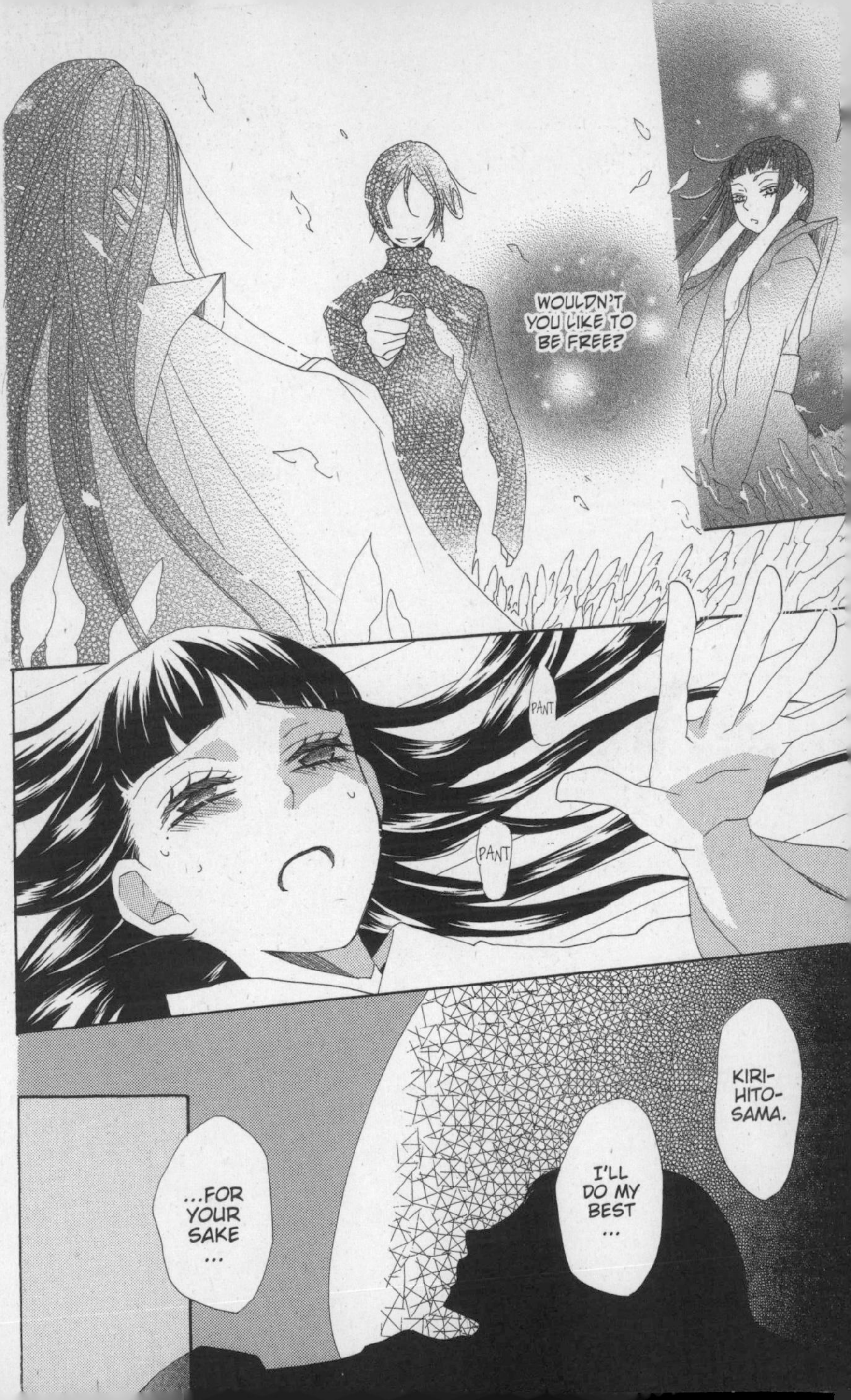
WOULDN'T YOU LIKE TO BE FREE?
PANT
PANT
KIRI-HITO-SAMA.
I'LL DO MY BEST ...
...FOR YOUR SAKE ...

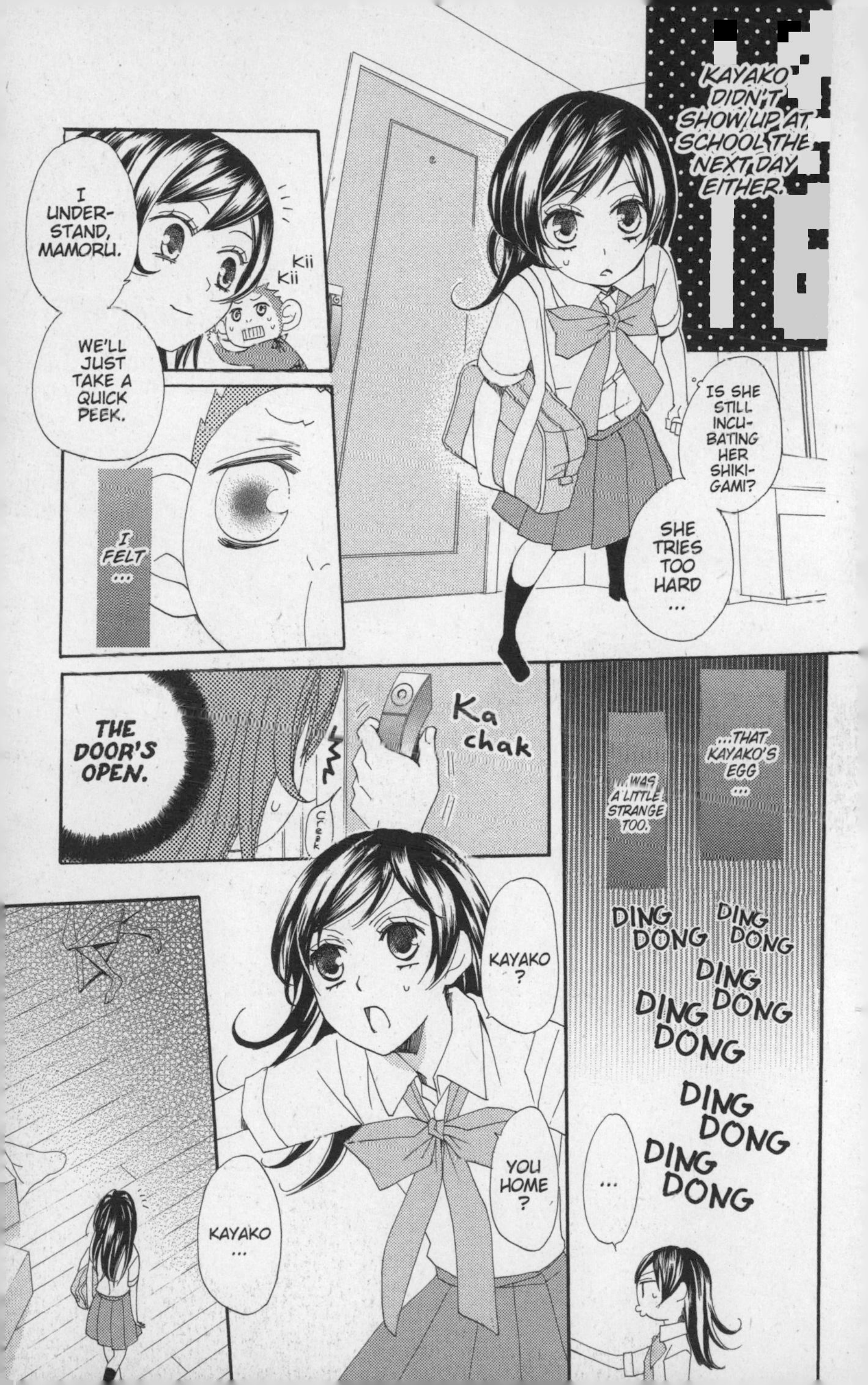

16
KAYAKO DIDN'T SHOW UP AT SCHOOL THE NEXT DAY EITHER.
IS SHE STILL INCUBATING HER SHIKIGAMI?
SHE TRIES TOO HARD ...
I UNDERSTAND, MAMORU.
kii kii
WE'LL JUST TAKE A QUICK PEEK.
I FELT ...
...THAT KAYAKO'S EGG ...
WAS A LITTLE STRANGE TOO.
DING DONG DING DONG
DING DONG
DING DONG
DING DONG
DING DONG
...
Ka chak
Creak
THE DOOR'S OPEN.
KAYAKO?
YOU HOME?
KAYAKO ...

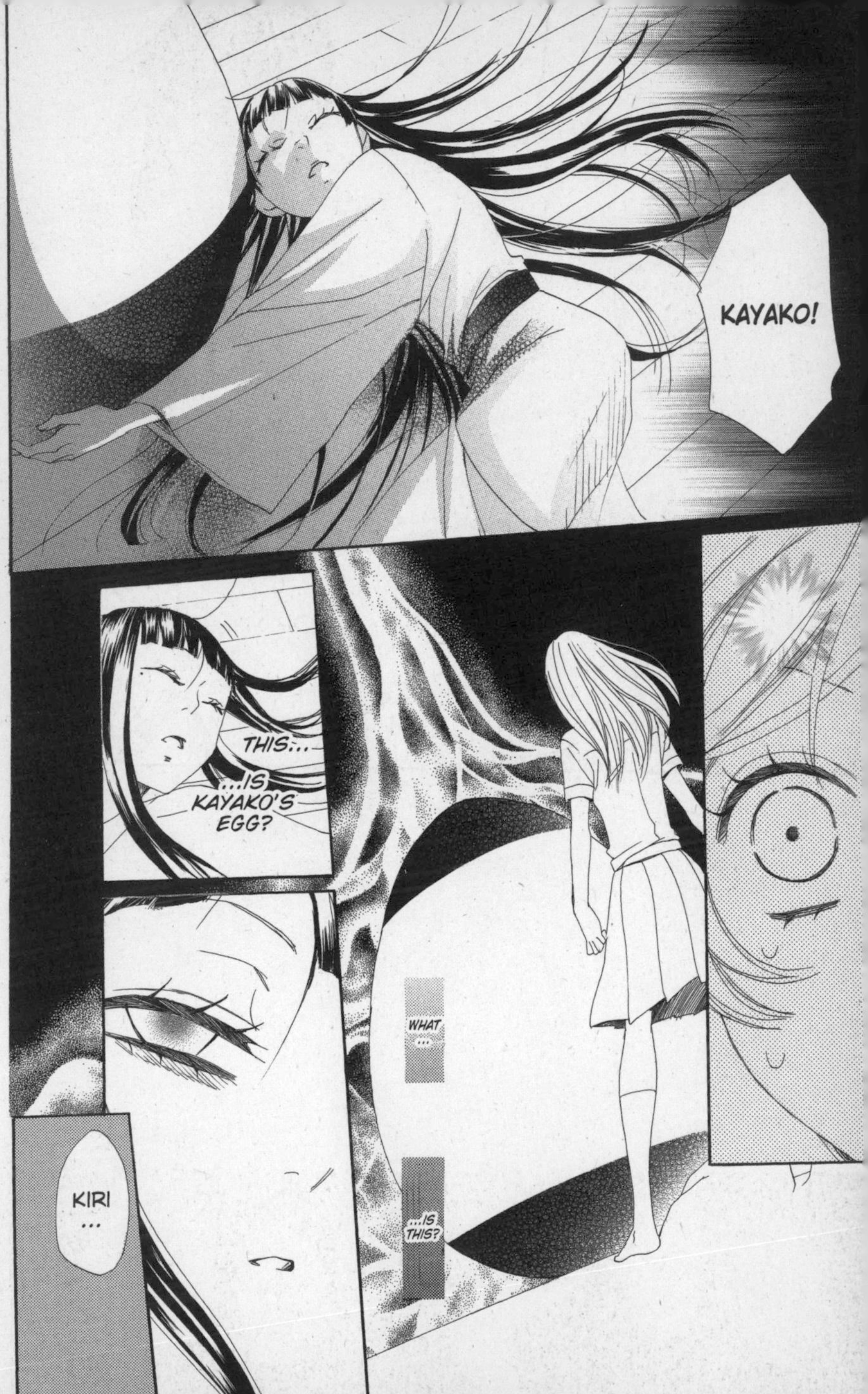
KAYAKO!
WHAT...
...IS THIS?
THIS...
...IS KAYAKO'S EGG?
KIRI...

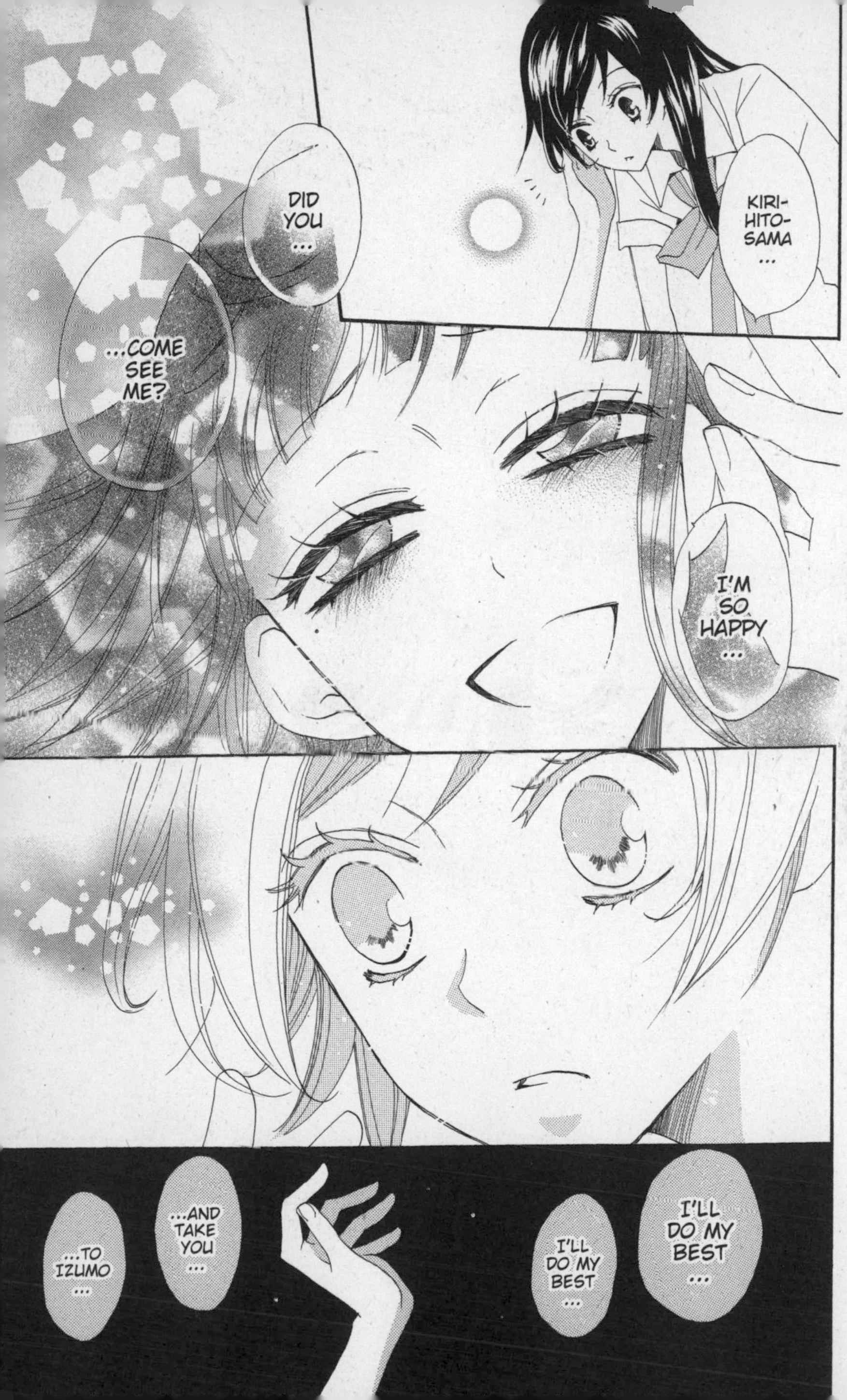
KIRI-HITO-SAMA...
DID YOU...
...COME SEE ME?
I'M SO HAPPY...
I'LL DO MY BEST...
I'LL DO MY BEST...
...AND TAKE YOU...
...TO IZUMO...

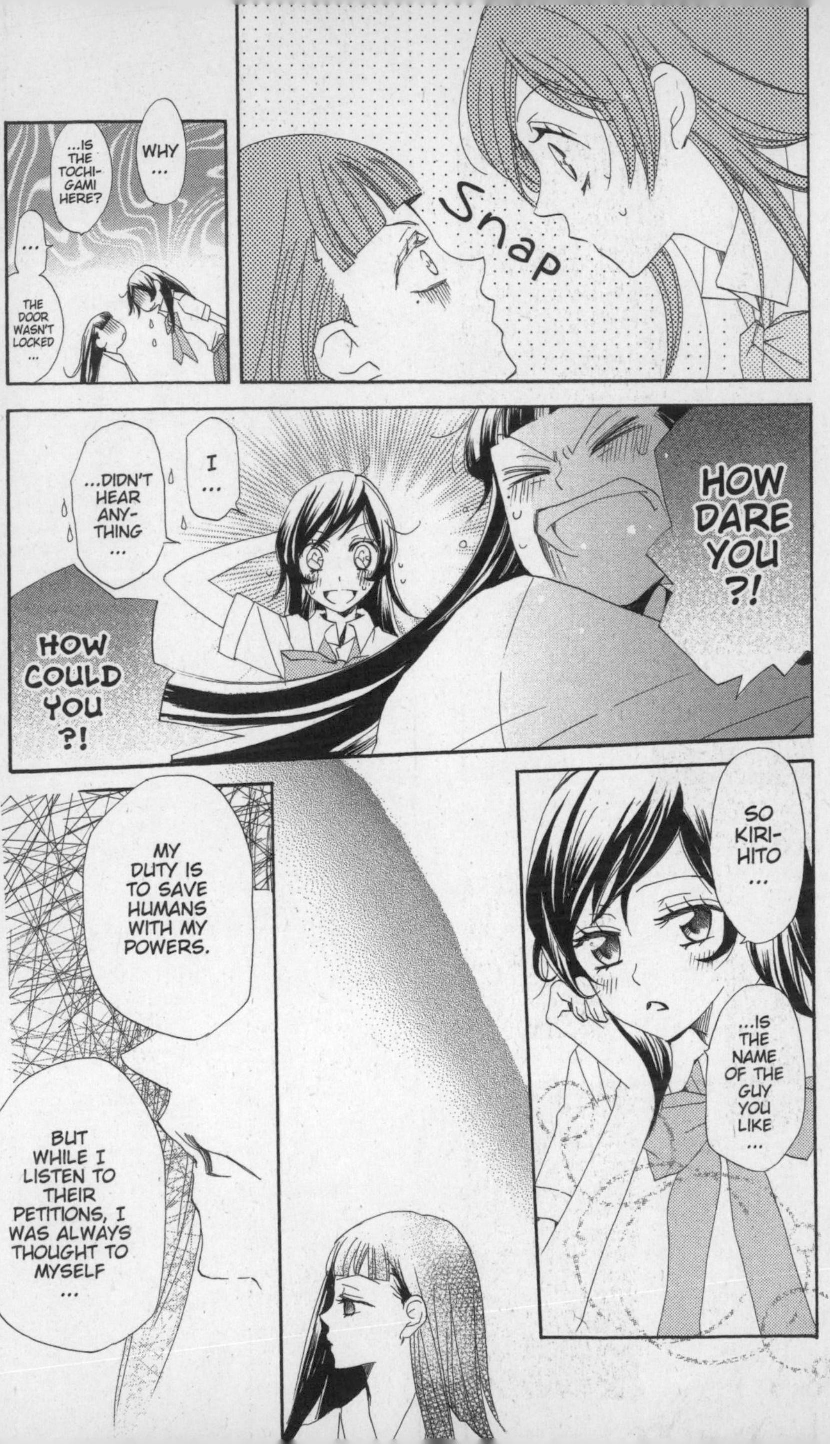
Snap
WHY ...
...IS THE TOCHI-GAMI HERE?
...
THE DOOR WASN'T LOCKED ...
HOW DARE YOU?!
I ...
...DIDN'T HEAR ANY-THING ...
HOW COULD YOU?!
SO KIRI-HITO ...
...IS THE NAME OF THE GUY YOU LIKE ...
MY DUTY IS TO SAVE HUMANS WITH MY POWERS.
BUT WHILE I LISTEN TO THEIR PETITIONS, I WAS ALWAYS THOUGHT TO MYSELF ...

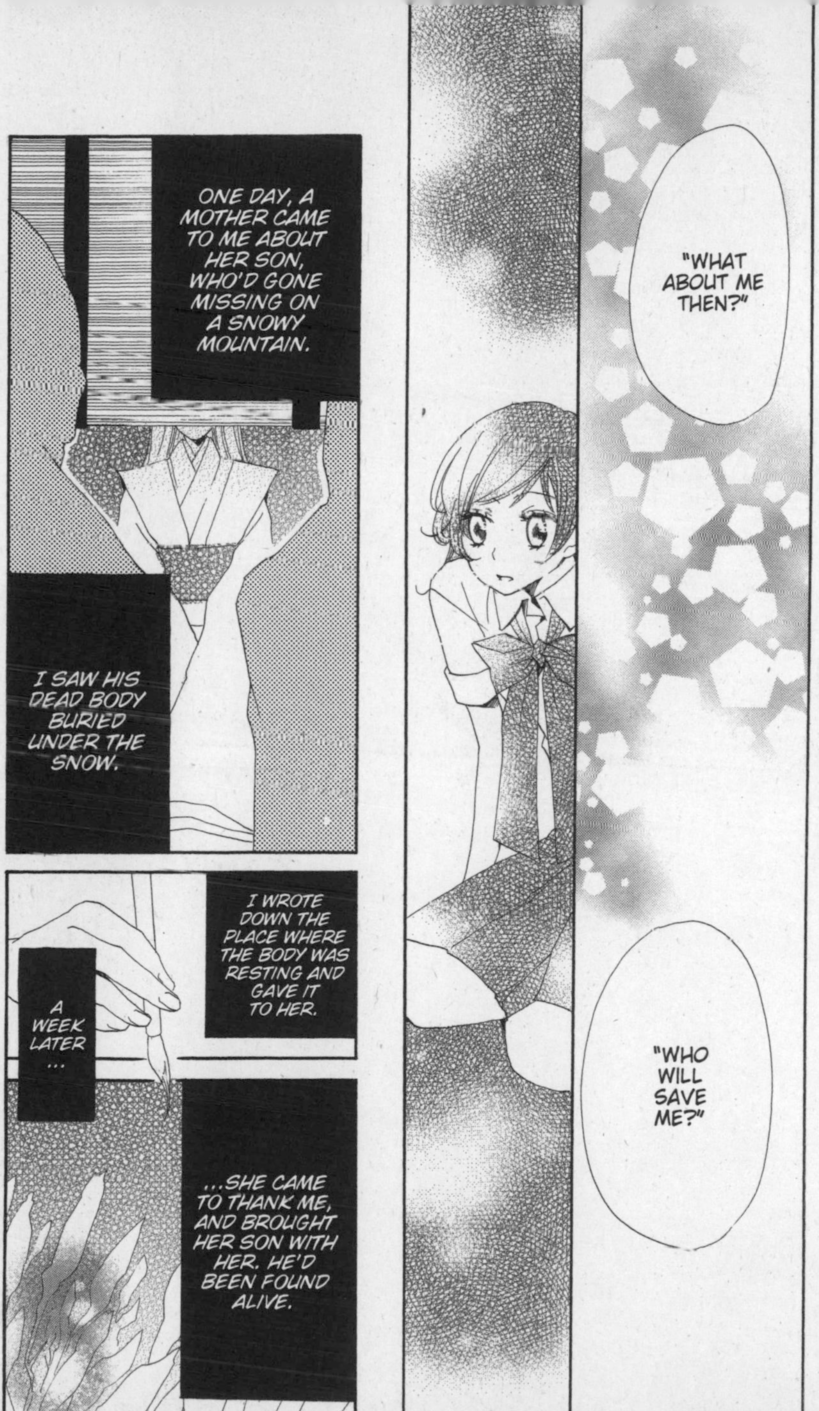
"WHAT ABOUT ME THEN?"
"WHO WILL SAVE ME?"
ONE DAY, A MOTHER CAME TO ME ABOUT HER SON, WHO'D GONE MISSING ON A SNOWY MOUNTAIN.
I SAW HIS DEAD BODY BURIED UNDER THE SNOW.
I WROTE DOWN THE PLACE WHERE THE BODY WAS RESTING AND GAVE IT TO HER.
A WEEK LATER...
...SHE CAME TO THANK ME, AND BROUGHT HER SON WITH HER. HE'D BEEN FOUND ALIVE.

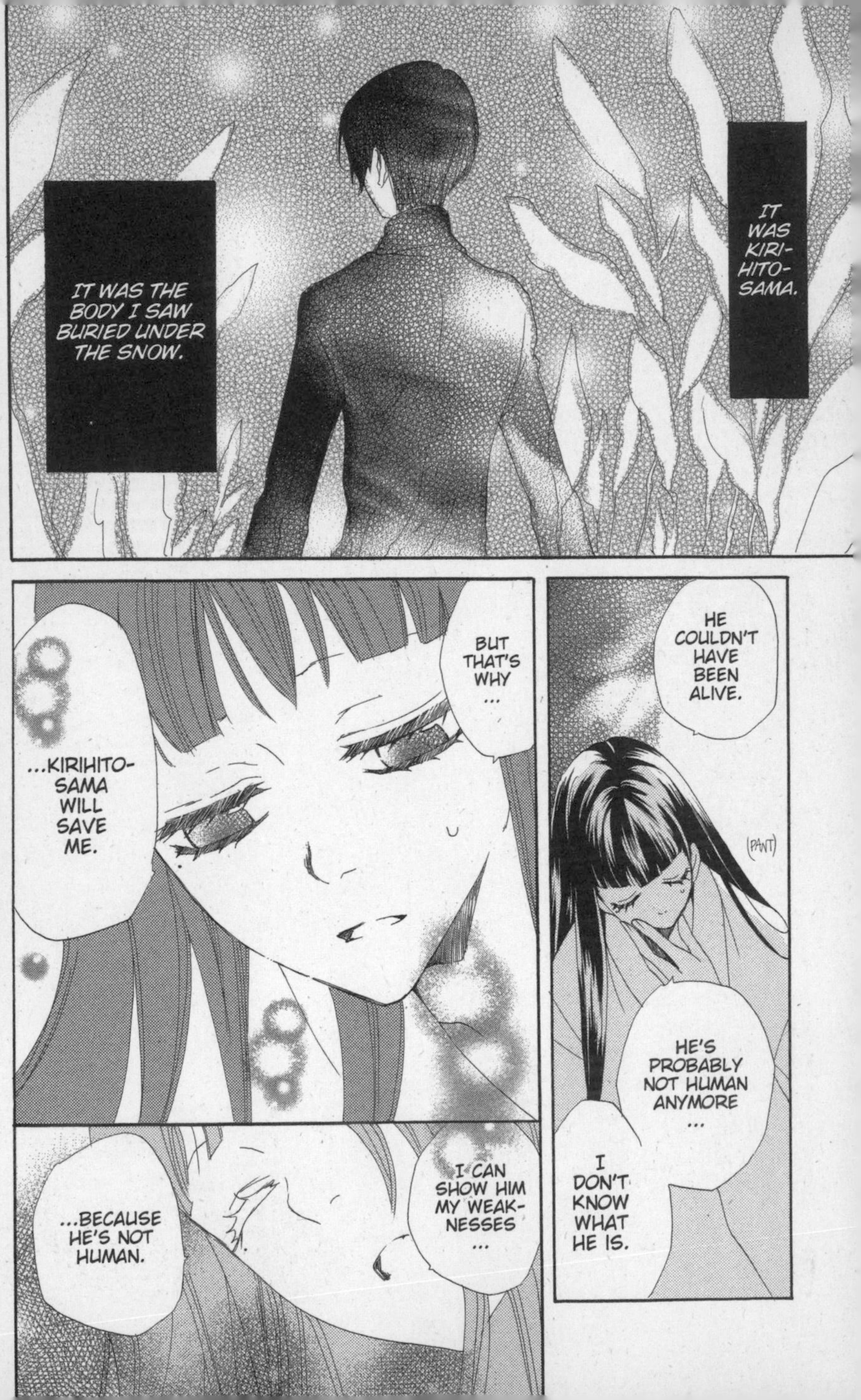
IT WAS KIRI-HITO-SAMA.
IT WAS THE BODY I SAW BURIED UNDER THE SNOW.
HE COULDN'T HAVE BEEN ALIVE.
(PANT)
HE'S PROBABLY NOT HUMAN ANYMORE ...
I DON'T KNOW WHAT HE IS.
BUT THAT'S WHY ...
...KIRIHITO-SAMA WILL SAVE ME.
I CAN SHOW HIM MY WEAK-NESSES ...
...BECAUSE HE'S NOT HUMAN.

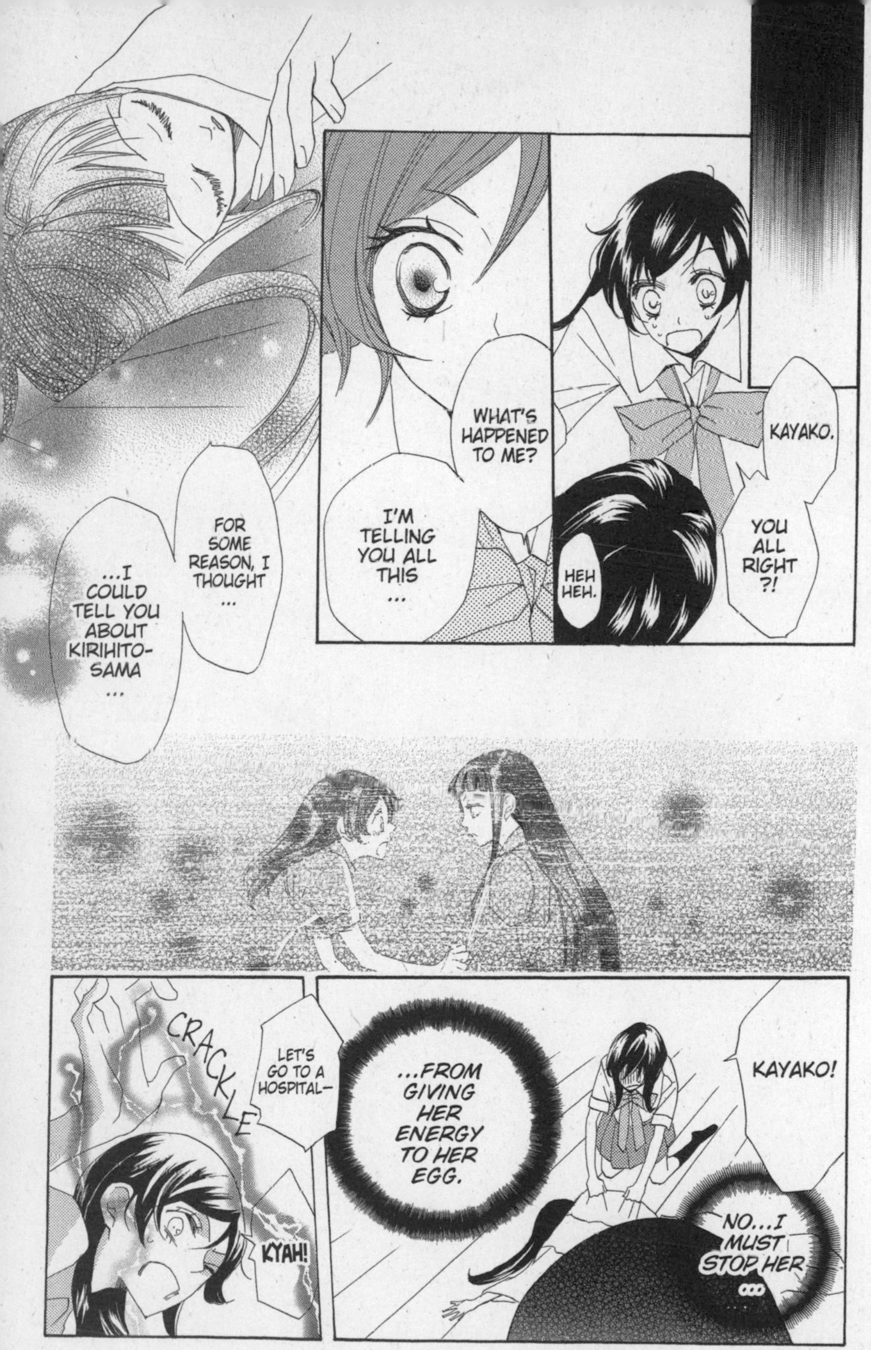
KAYAKO.
YOU ALL RIGHT?!
HEH HEH.
WHAT'S HAPPENED TO ME?
I'M TELLING YOU ALL THIS...
FOR SOME REASON, I THOUGHT...
...I COULD TELL YOU ABOUT KIRIHITO-SAMA...
KAYAKO!
NO...I MUST STOP HER...
...FROM GIVING HER ENERGY TO HER EGG.
LET'S GO TO A HOSPITAL—
CRACKLE
KYAH!

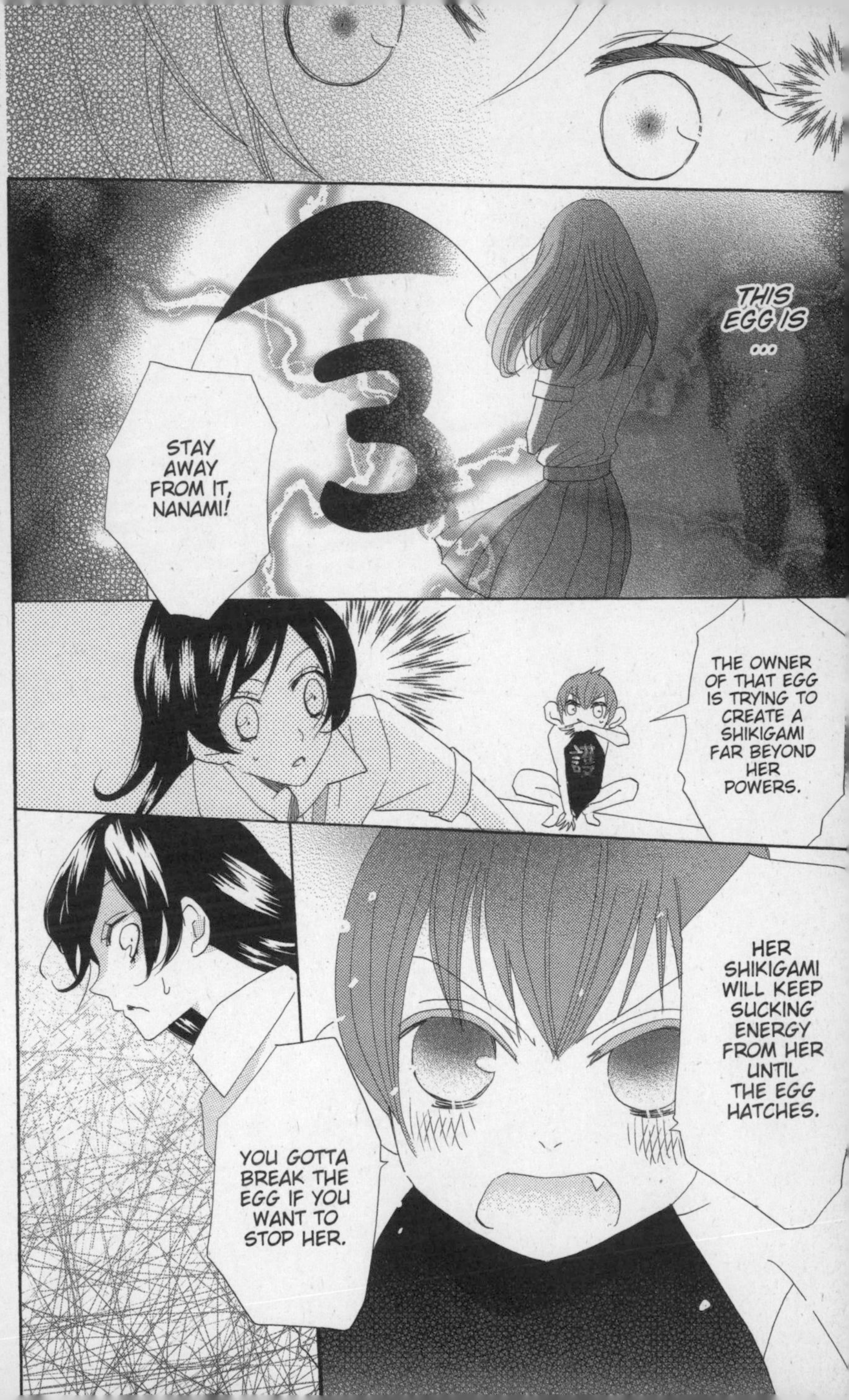
THIS EGG IS ...
3
STAY AWAY FROM IT, NANAMI!
THE OWNER OF THAT EGG IS TRYING TO CREATE A SHIKIGAMI FAR BEYOND HER POWERS.
HER SHIKIGAMI WILL KEEP SUCKING ENERGY FROM HER UNTIL THE EGG HATCHES.
YOU GOTTA BREAK THE EGG IF YOU WANT TO STOP HER.

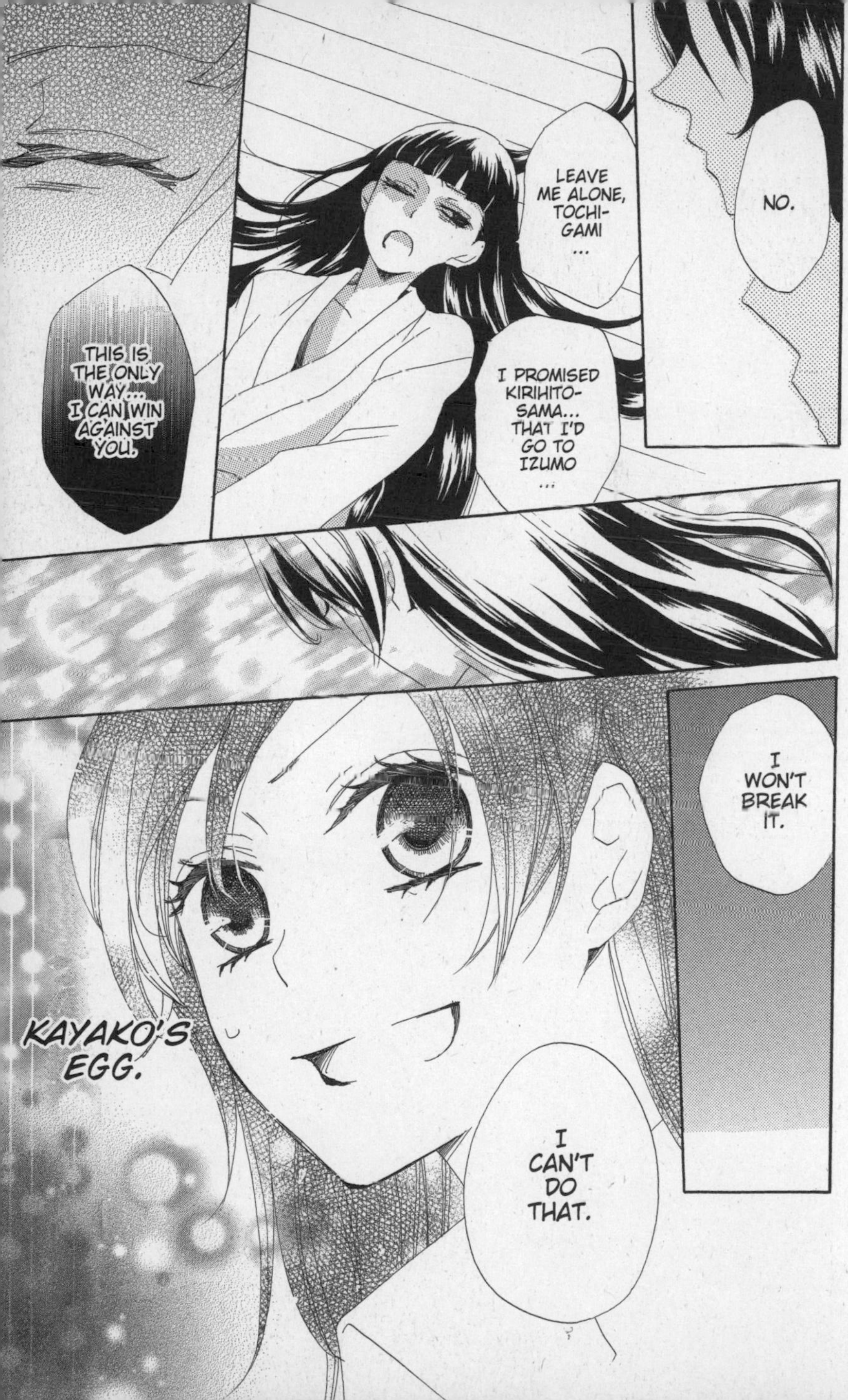
NO.
LEAVE ME ALONE, TOCHIGAMI ...
I PROMISED KIRIHITO-SAMA... THAT I'D GO TO IZUMO ...
THIS IS THE ONLY WAY... I CAN WIN AGAINST YOU.
I WON'T BREAK IT.
I CAN'T DO THAT.
KAYAKO'S EGG.

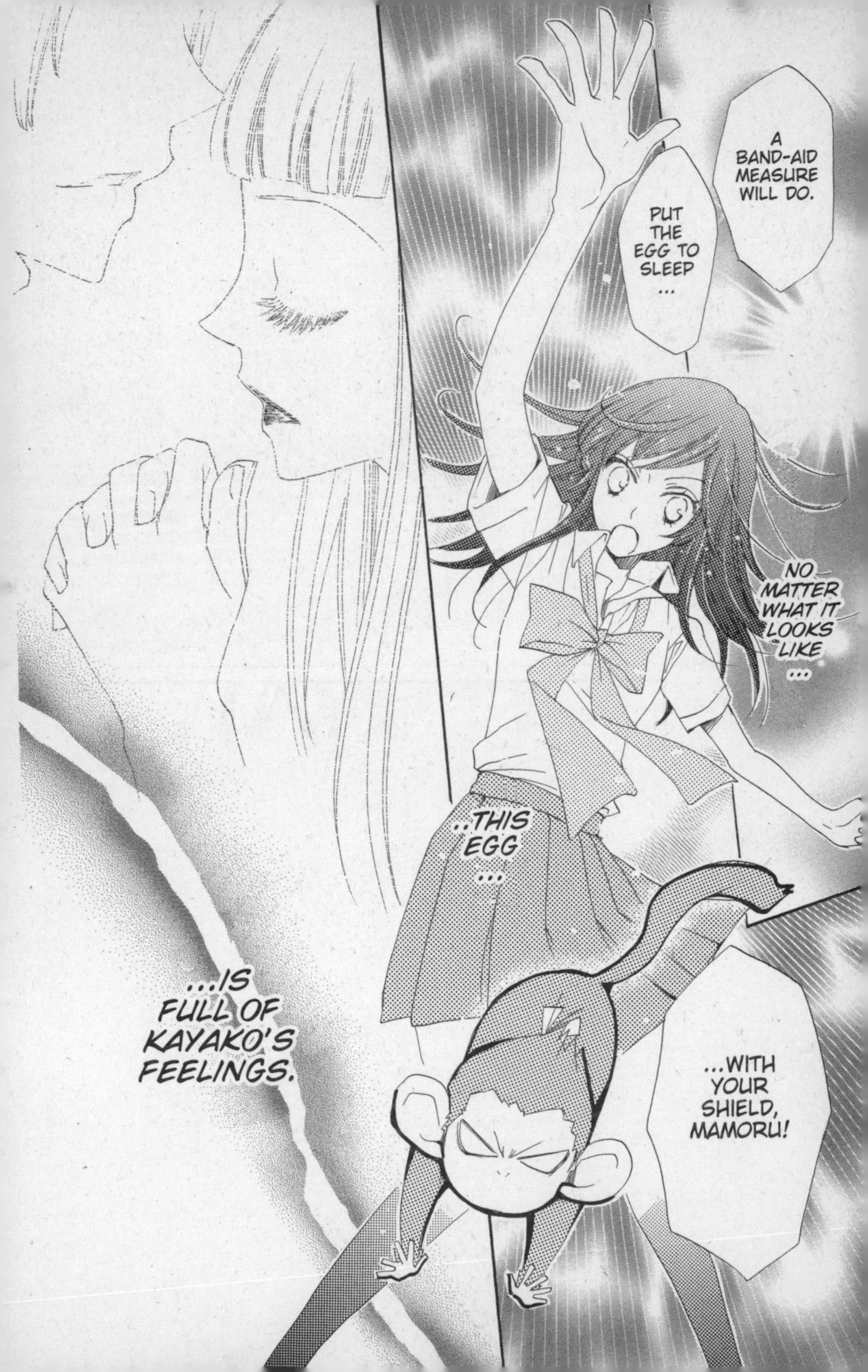
A BAND-AID MEASURE WILL DO.
PUT THE EGG TO SLEEP...
...WITH YOUR SHIELD, MAMORU!
NO MATTER WHAT IT LOOKS LIKE...
...THIS EGG...
...IS FULL OF KAYAKO'S FEELINGS.

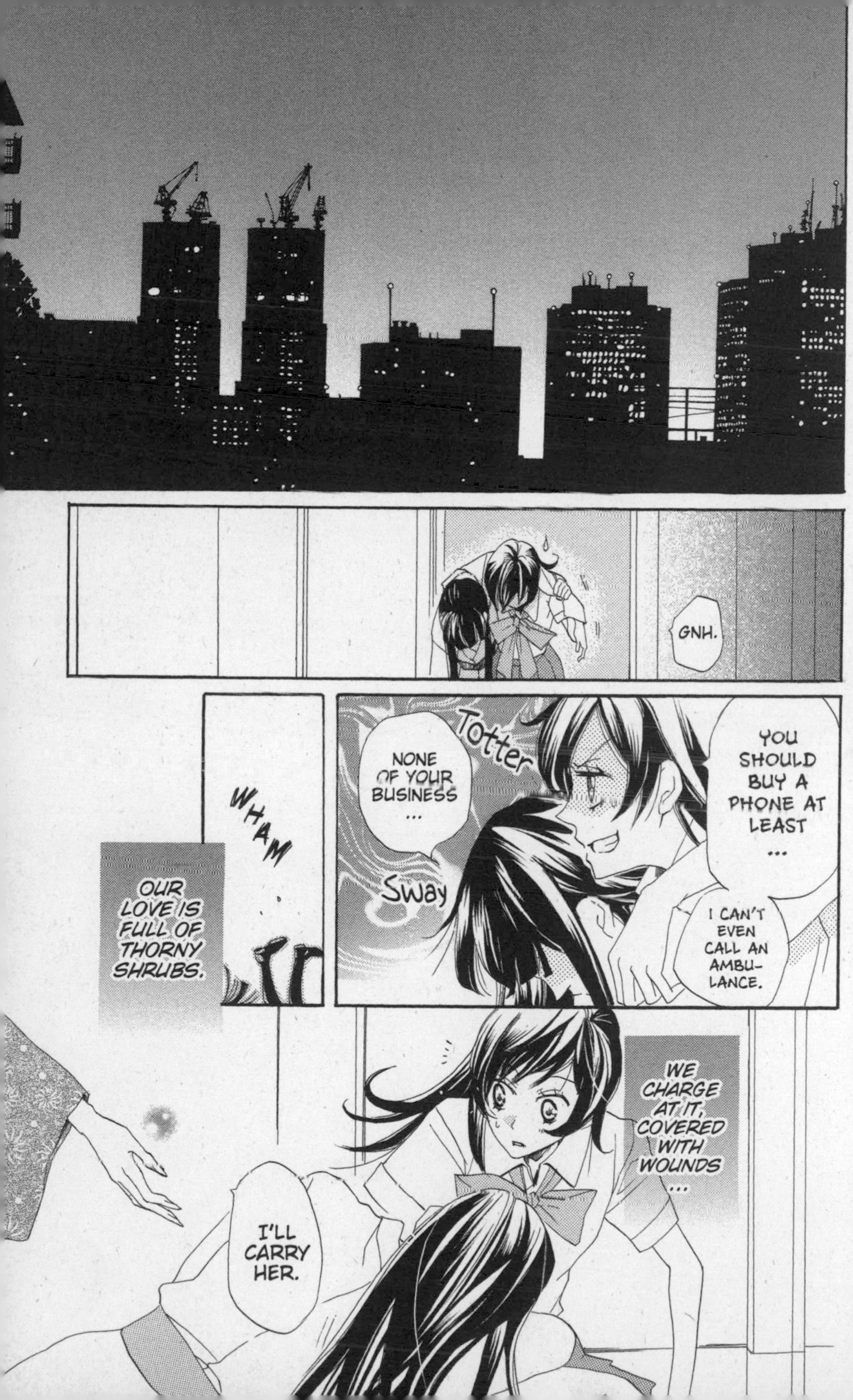
GNH.
YOU SHOULD BUY A PHONE AT LEAST ...
Totter
NONE OF YOUR BUSINESS ...
I CAN'T EVEN CALL AN AMBU-LANCE.
Sway
WHAM
OUR LOVE IS FULL OF THORNY SHRUBS.
WE CHARGE AT IT, COVERED WITH WOUNDS ...
I'LL CARRY HER.

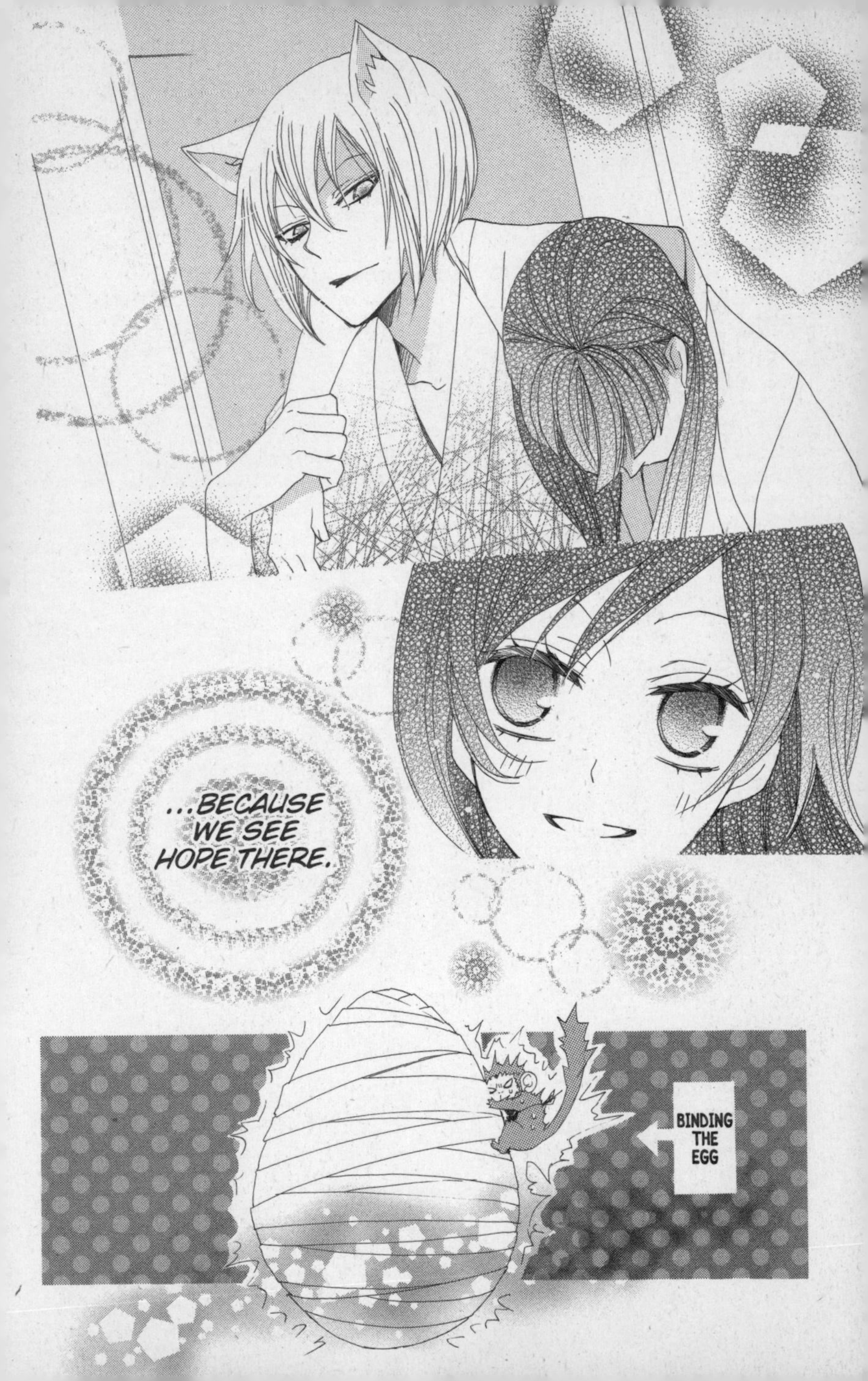
...BECAUSE WE SEE HOPE THERE.
BINDING THE EGG

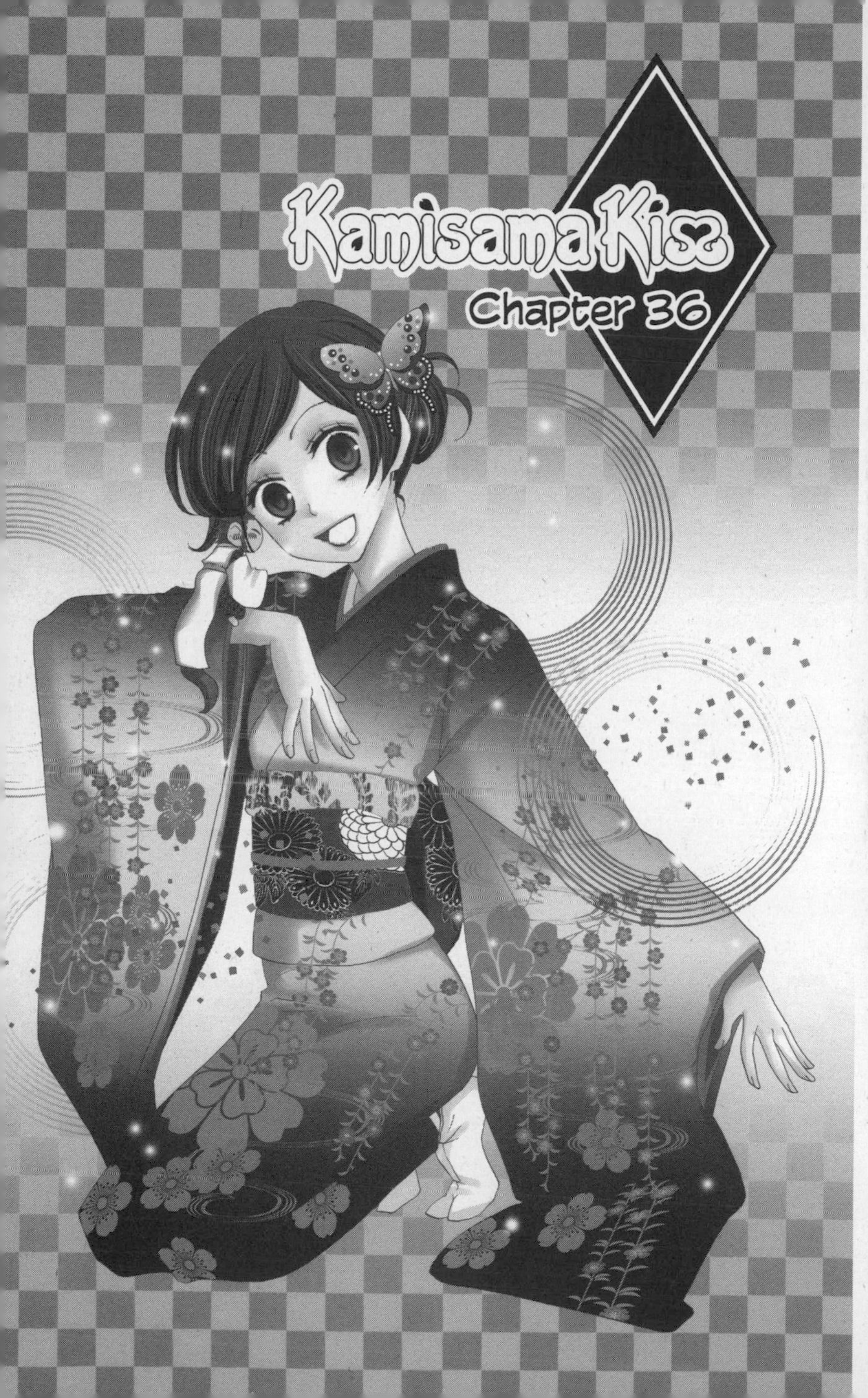

Kamisama Kiss
Chapter 36

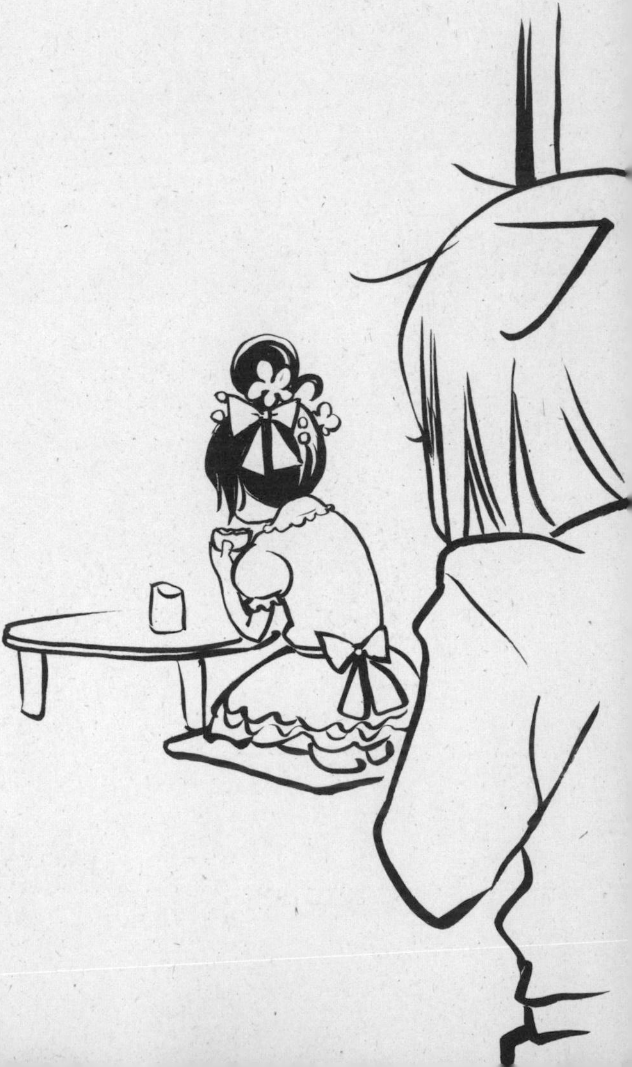

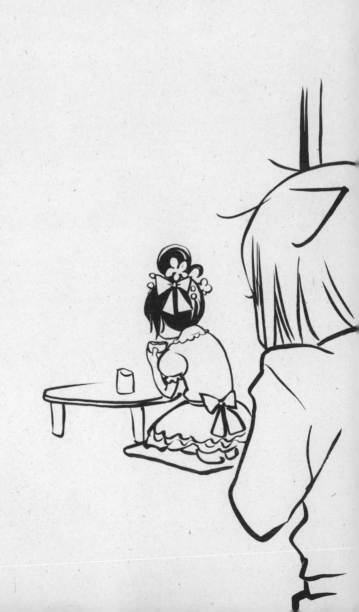

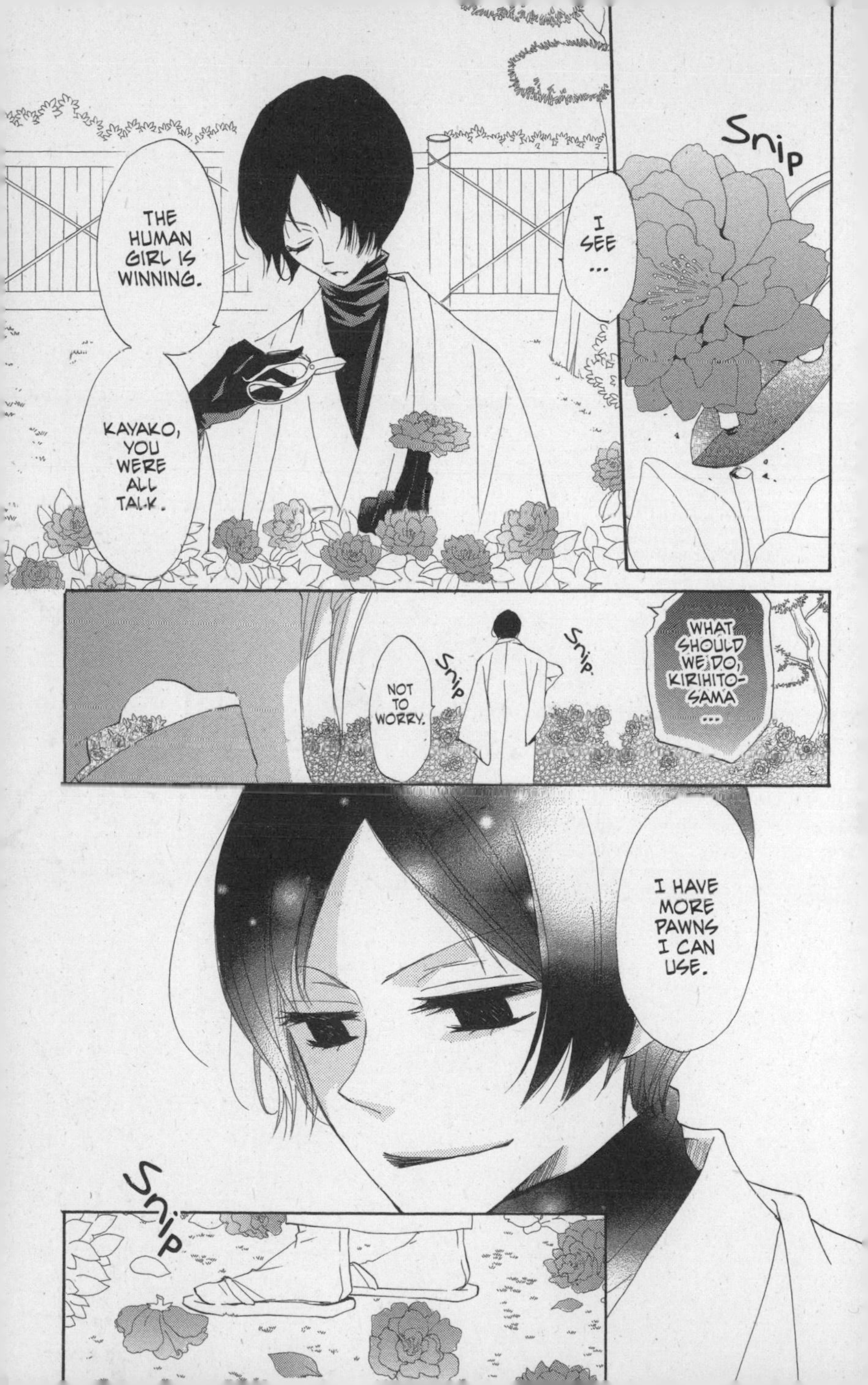
Snip
I SEE ...
THE HUMAN GIRL IS WINNING.
KAYAKO, YOU WERE ALL TALK.
WHAT SHOULD WE DO, KIRIHITO-SAMA ...
Snip
Snip
NOT TO WORRY.
I HAVE MORE PAWNS I CAN USE.
Snip

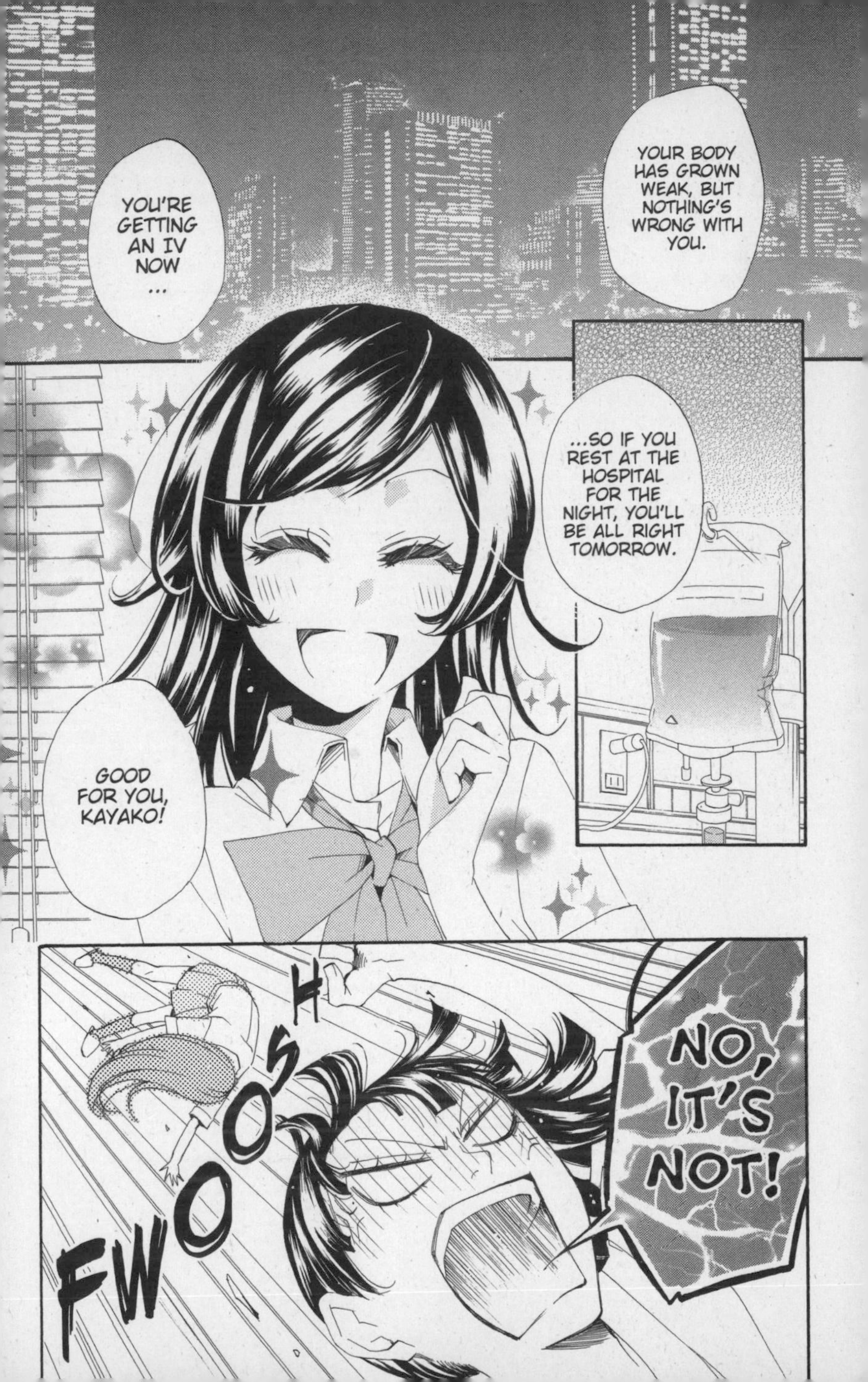
YOUR BODY HAS GROWN WEAK, BUT NOTHING'S WRONG WITH YOU.
YOU'RE GETTING AN IV NOW ...
...SO IF YOU REST AT THE HOSPITAL FOR THE NIGHT, YOU'LL BE ALL RIGHT TOMORROW.
GOOD FOR YOU, KAYAKO!
NO, IT'S NOT!
FWOOOSH

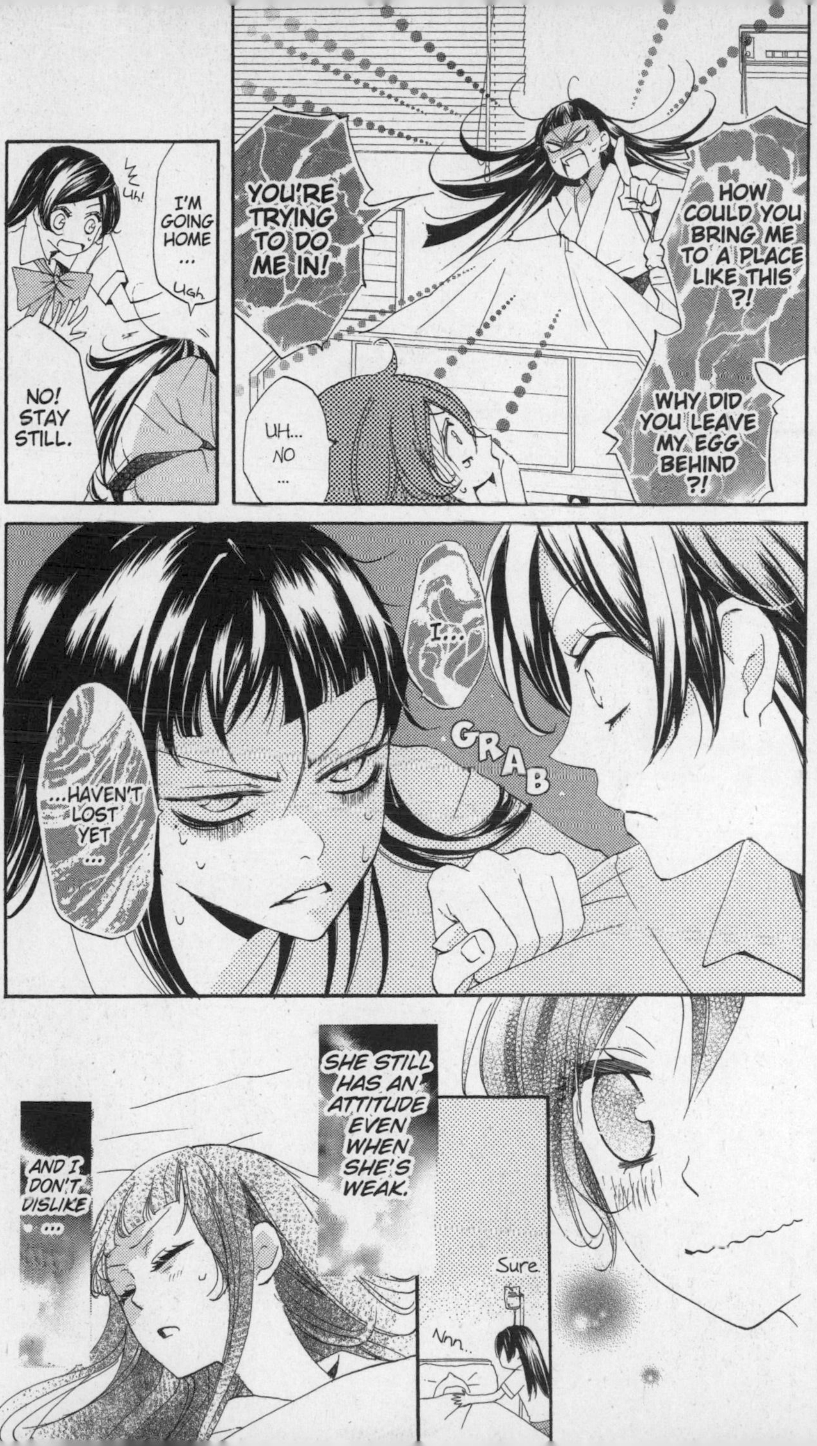
HOW COULD YOU BRING ME TO A PLACE LIKE THIS?!
YOU'RE TRYING TO DO ME IN!
WHY DID YOU LEAVE MY EGG BEHIND?!
UH... NO ...
Uh!
I'M GOING HOME ...
Ugh.
NO! STAY STILL.
I...
GRAB
...HAVEN'T LOST YET ...
Sure.
Nnn..
SHE STILL HAS AN ATTITUDE EVEN WHEN SHE'S WEAK.
AND I DON'T DISLIKE ♥ ...

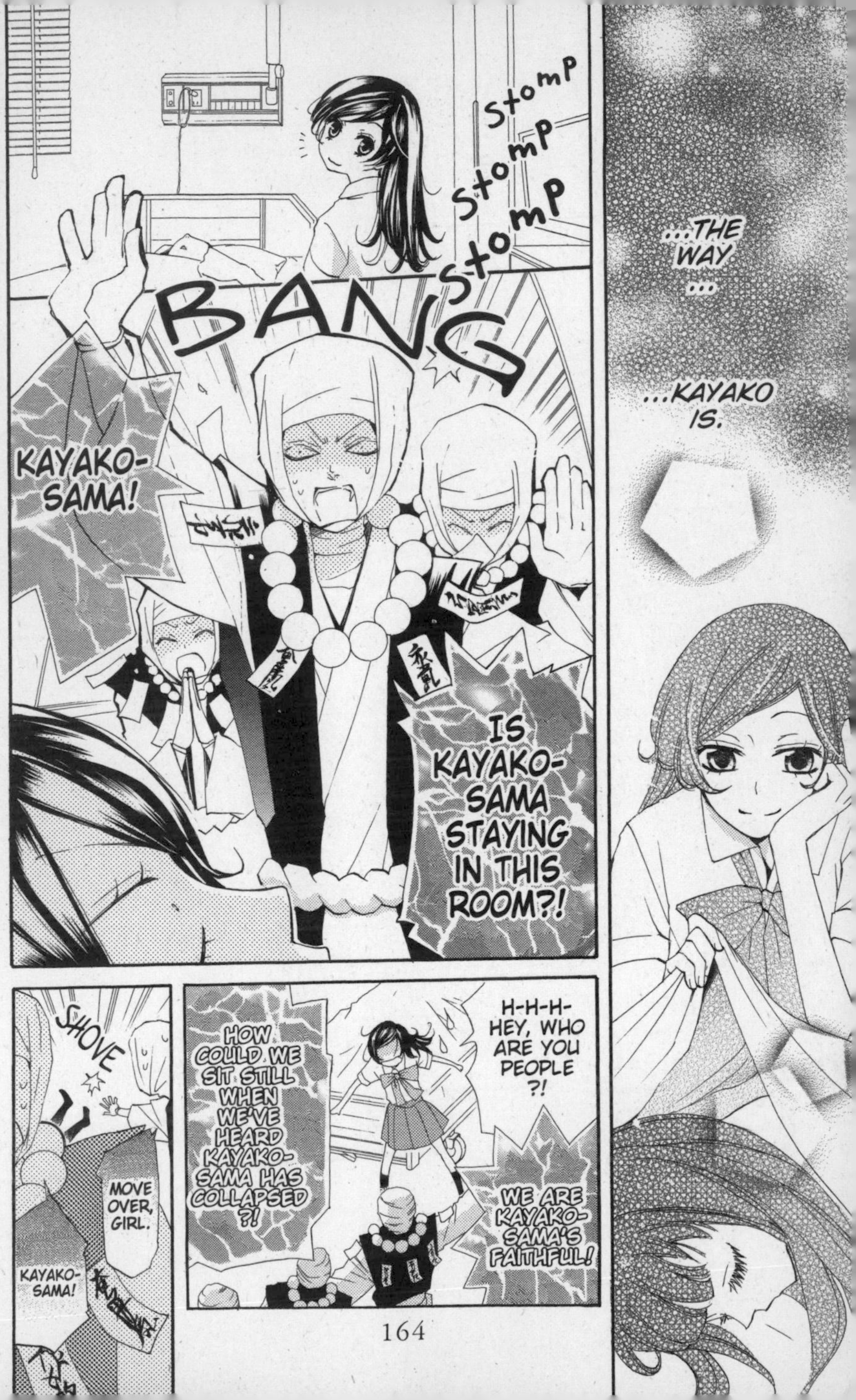
...THE WAY ...
...KAYAKO IS.
Stomp Stomp Stomp
BANG
KAYAKO-SAMA!
IS KAYAKO-SAMA STAYING IN THIS ROOM?!
H-H-H-HEY, WHO ARE YOU PEOPLE ?!
HOW COULD WE SIT STILL WHEN WE'VE HEARD KAYAKO-SAMA HAS COLLAPSED ?!
WE ARE KAYAKO-SAMA'S FAITHFUL!
SHOVE
MOVE OVER, GIRL.
KAYAKO-SAMA!

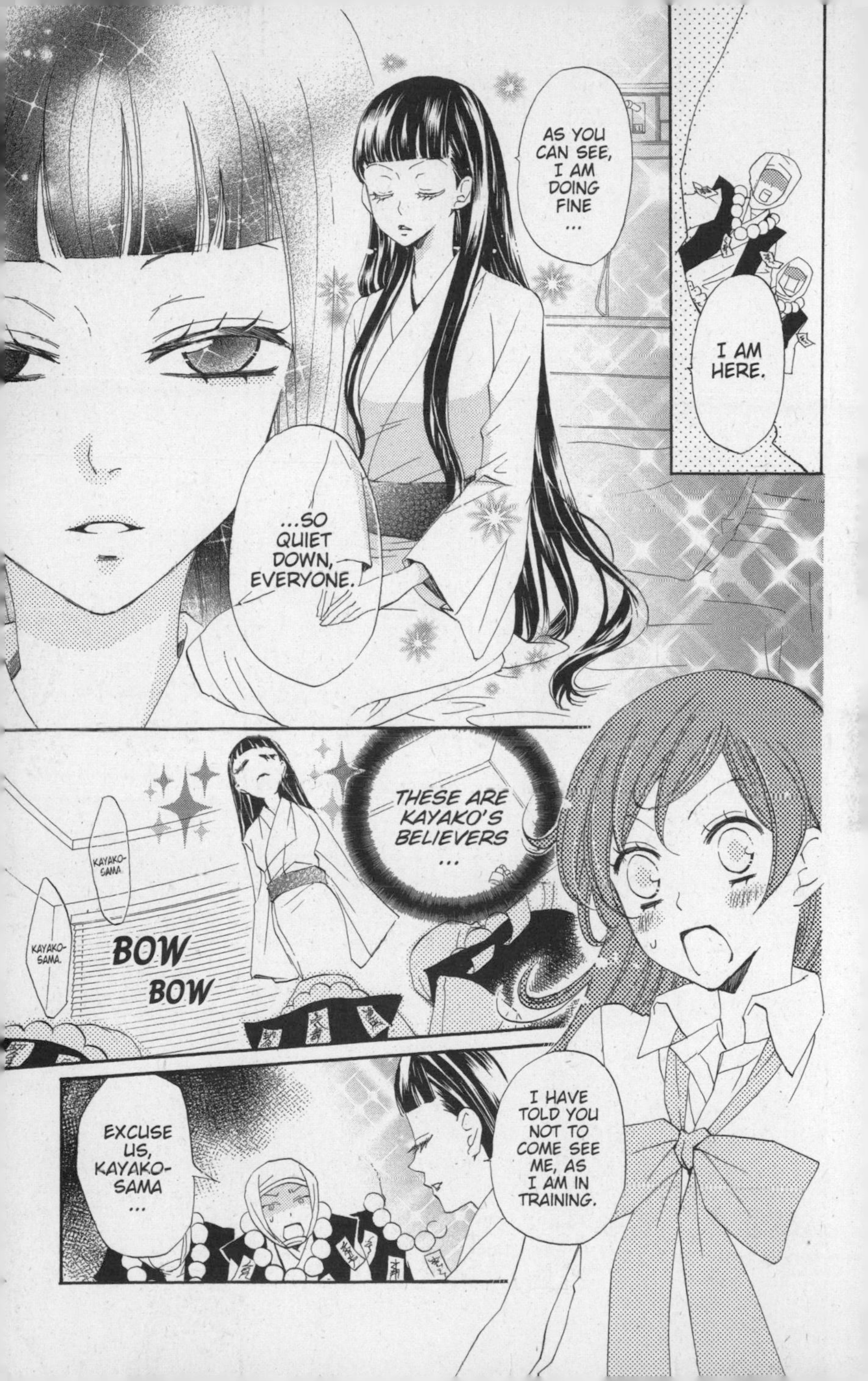
I AM HERE.
AS YOU CAN SEE, I AM DOING FINE ...
...SO QUIET DOWN, EVERYONE.
THESE ARE KAYAKO'S BELIEVERS ...
KAYAKO-SAMA.
KAYAKO-SAMA.
BOW BOW
I HAVE TOLD YOU NOT TO COME SEE ME, AS I AM IN TRAINING.
EXCUSE US, KAYAKO-SAMA ...

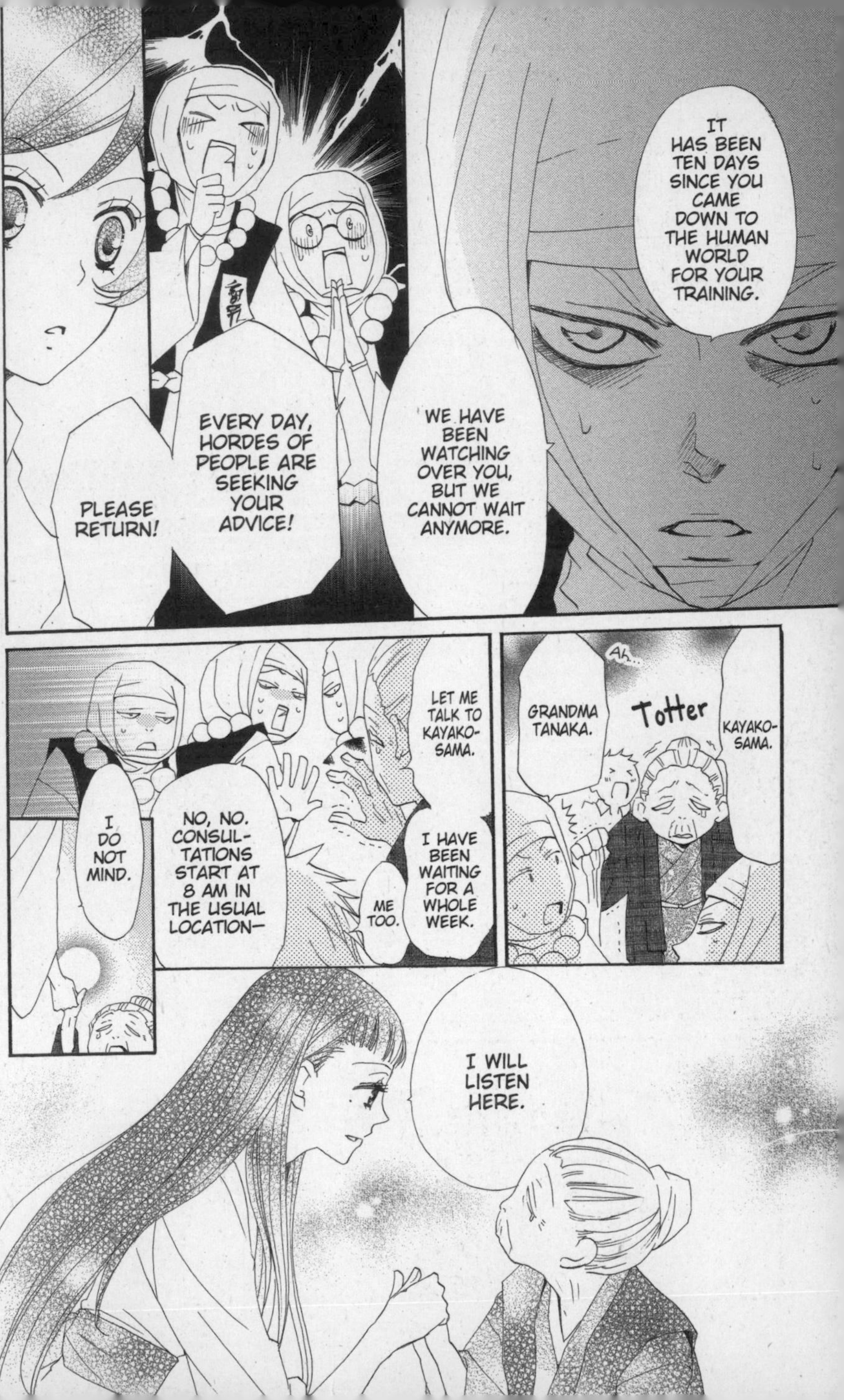
IT HAS BEEN TEN DAYS SINCE YOU CAME DOWN TO THE HUMAN WORLD FOR YOUR TRAINING.
WE HAVE BEEN WATCHING OVER YOU, BUT WE CANNOT WAIT ANYMORE.
EVERY DAY, HORDES OF PEOPLE ARE SEEKING YOUR ADVICE!
PLEASE RETURN!
Ah...
KAYAKO-SAMA.
Totter
GRANDMA TANAKA.
LET ME TALK TO KAYAKO-SAMA.
I HAVE BEEN WAITING FOR A WHOLE WEEK.
ME TOO.
NO, NO. CONSULTATIONS START AT 8 AM IN THE USUAL LOCATION—
I DO NOT MIND.
I WILL LISTEN HERE.

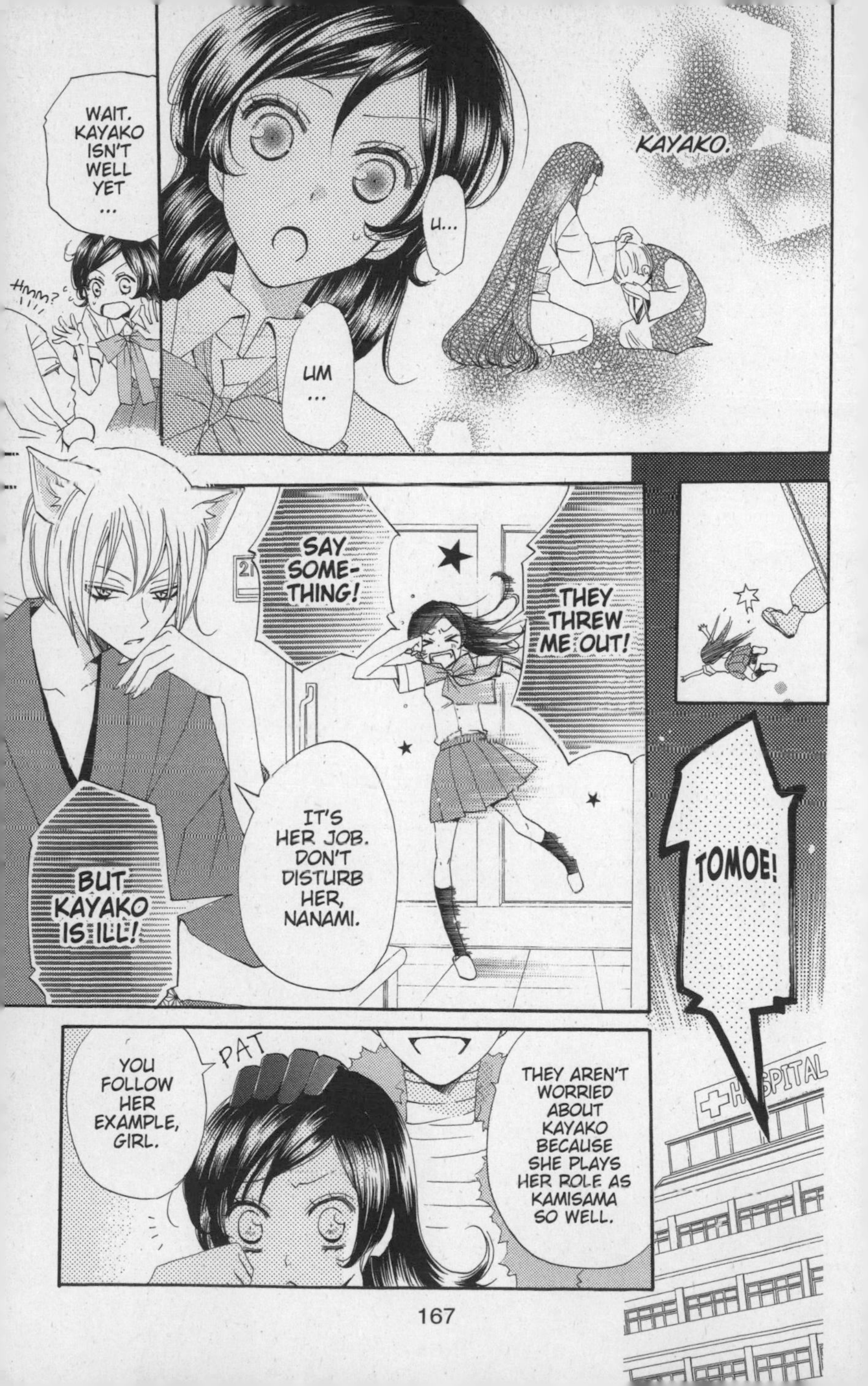

KAYAKO.
U...
UM ...
WAIT. KAYAKO ISN'T WELL YET ...
Hmm?
TOMOE!
HOSPITAL
THEY THREW ME OUT!
SAY SOME-THING!
IT'S HER JOB. DON'T DISTURB HER, NANAMI.
BUT KAYAKO IS ILL!
THEY AREN'T WORRIED ABOUT KAYAKO BECAUSE SHE PLAYS HER ROLE AS KAMISAMA SO WELL.
PAT
YOU FOLLOW HER EXAMPLE, GIRL.

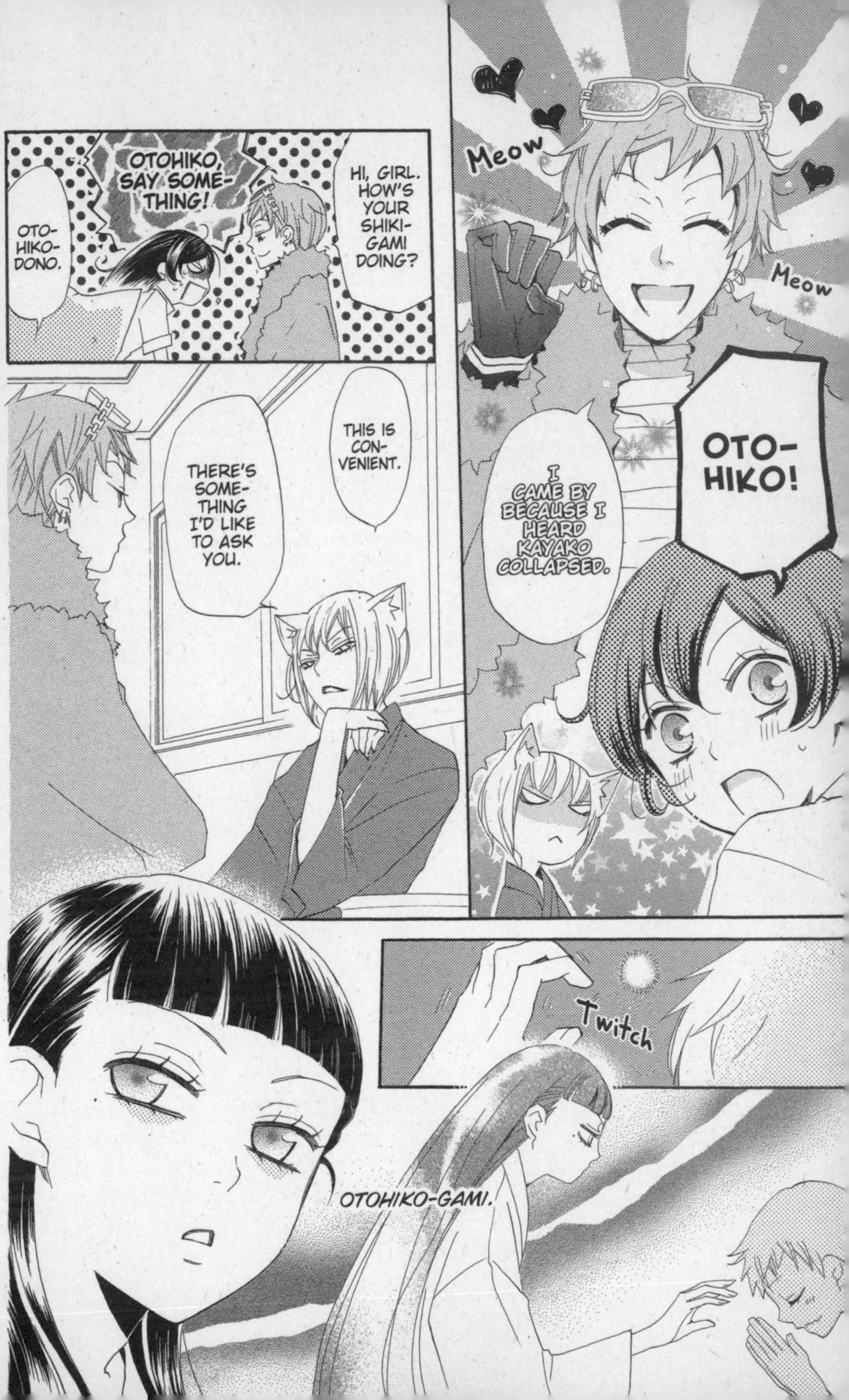
Meow
Meow
OTO-HIKO!
I CAME BY BECAUSE I HEARD KAYAKO COLLAPSED.
HI, GIRL. HOW'S YOUR SHIKI-GAMI DOING?
OTOHIKO, SAY SOME-THING!
OTO-HIKO-DONO.
THIS IS CON-VENIENT.
THERE'S SOME-THING I'D LIKE TO ASK YOU.
Twitch
OTOHIKO-GAMI.

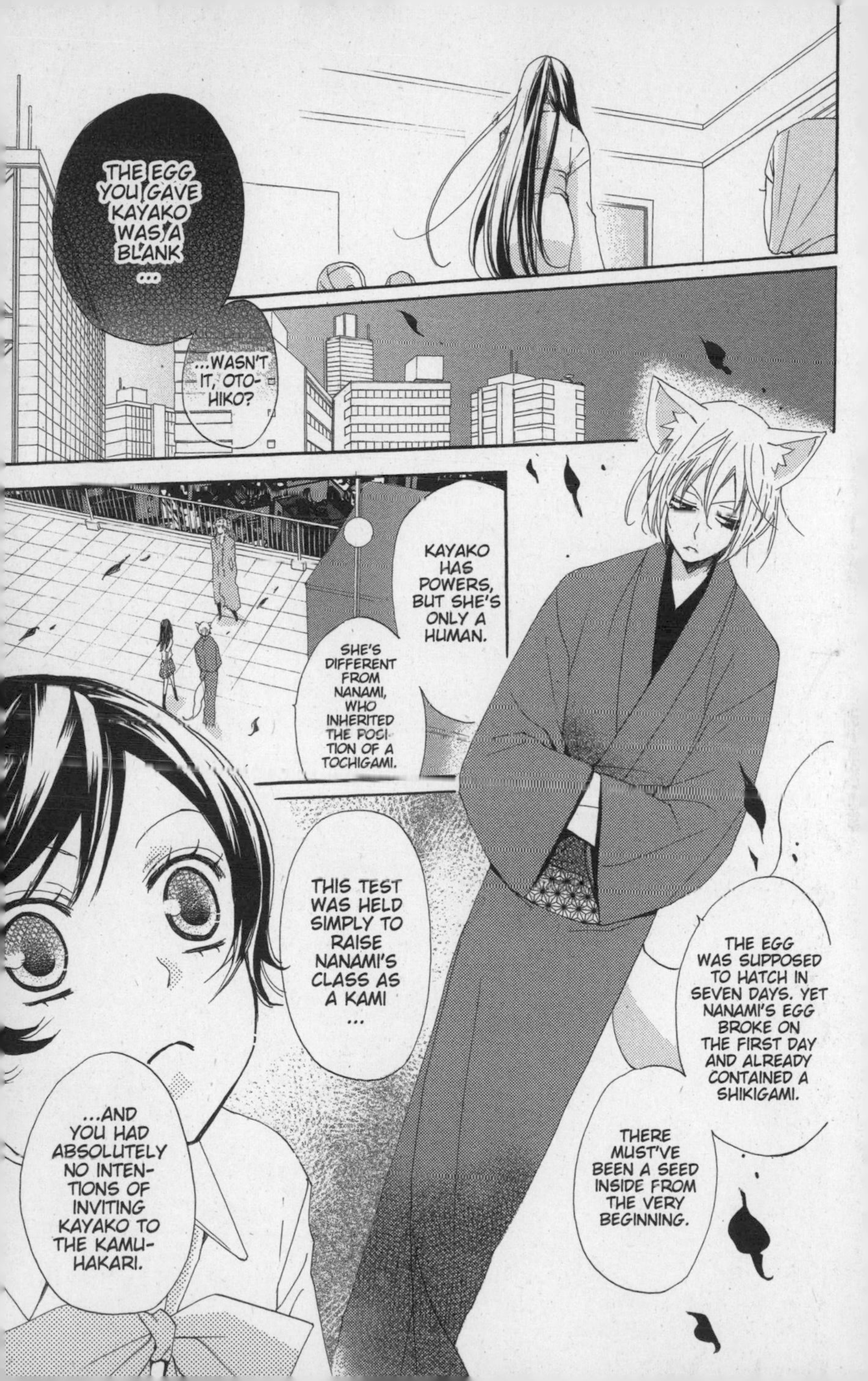
THE EGG YOU GAVE KAYAKO WAS A BLANK...
...WASN'T IT, OTO-HIKO?
KAYAKO HAS POWERS, BUT SHE'S ONLY A HUMAN.
SHE'S DIFFERENT FROM NANAMI, WHO INHERITED THE POSITION OF A TOCHIGAMI.
THE EGG WAS SUPPOSED TO HATCH IN SEVEN DAYS. YET NANAMI'S EGG BROKE ON THE FIRST DAY AND ALREADY CONTAINED A SHIKIGAMI.
THERE MUST'VE BEEN A SEED INSIDE FROM THE VERY BEGINNING.
THIS TEST WAS HELD SIMPLY TO RAISE NANAMI'S CLASS AS A KAMI...
...AND YOU HAD ABSOLUTELY NO INTEN-TIONS OF INVITING KAYAKO TO THE KAMU-HAKARI.

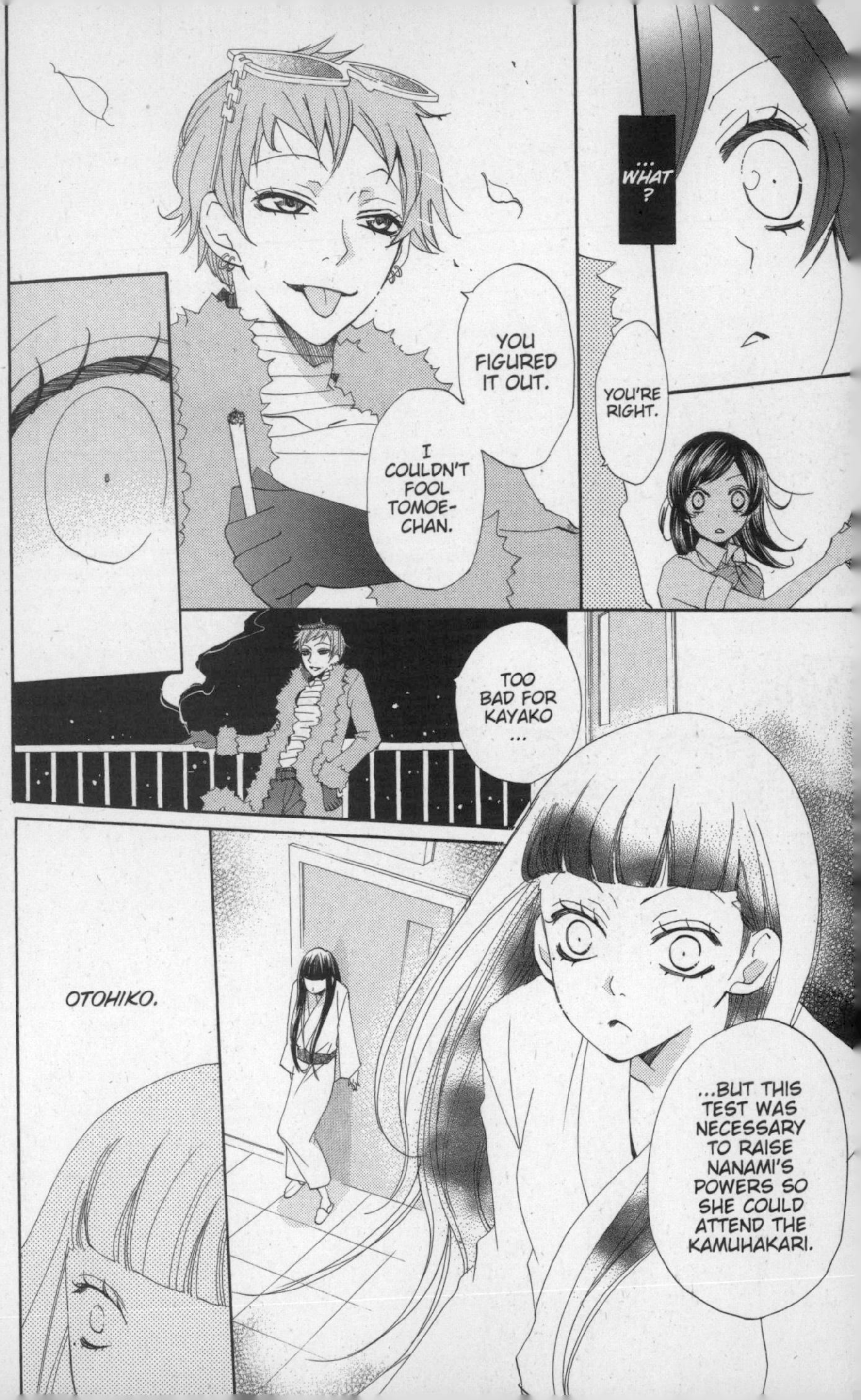

...WHAT?
YOU'RE RIGHT.
YOU FIGURED IT OUT.
I COULDN'T FOOL TOMOE-CHAN.
TOO BAD FOR KAYAKO...
...BUT THIS TEST WAS NECESSARY TO RAISE NANAMI'S POWERS SO SHE COULD ATTEND THE KAMUHAKARI.
OTOHIKO.

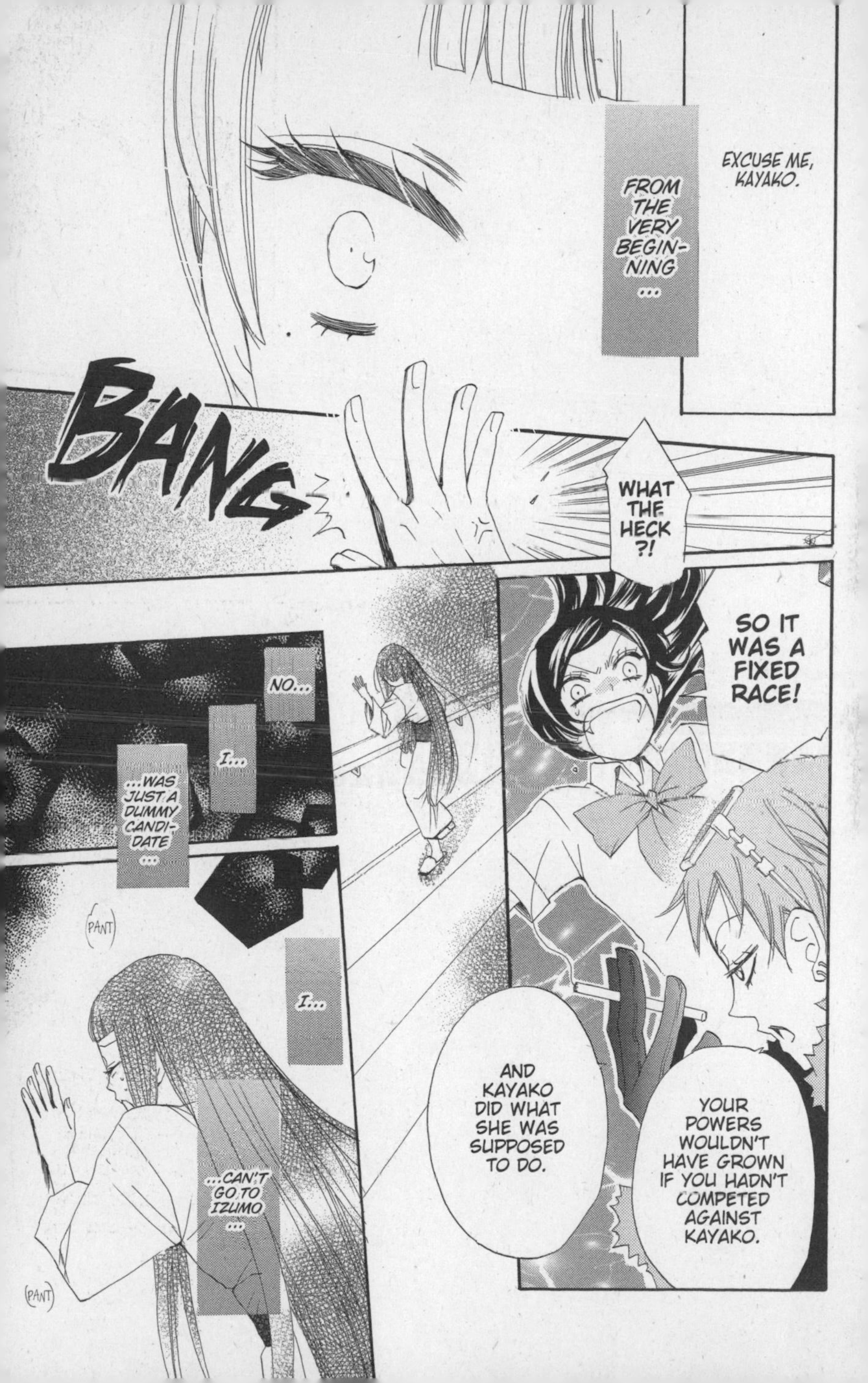
EXCUSE ME, KAYAKO.
FROM THE VERY BEGIN-NING...
BANG
WHAT THE HECK?!
SO IT WAS A FIXED RACE!
YOUR POWERS WOULDN'T HAVE GROWN IF YOU HADN'T COMPETED AGAINST KAYAKO.
AND KAYAKO DID WHAT SHE WAS SUPPOSED TO DO.
NO...
I...
...WAS JUST A DUMMY CANDI-DATE...
PANT
I...
...CAN'T GO TO IZUMO...
PANT

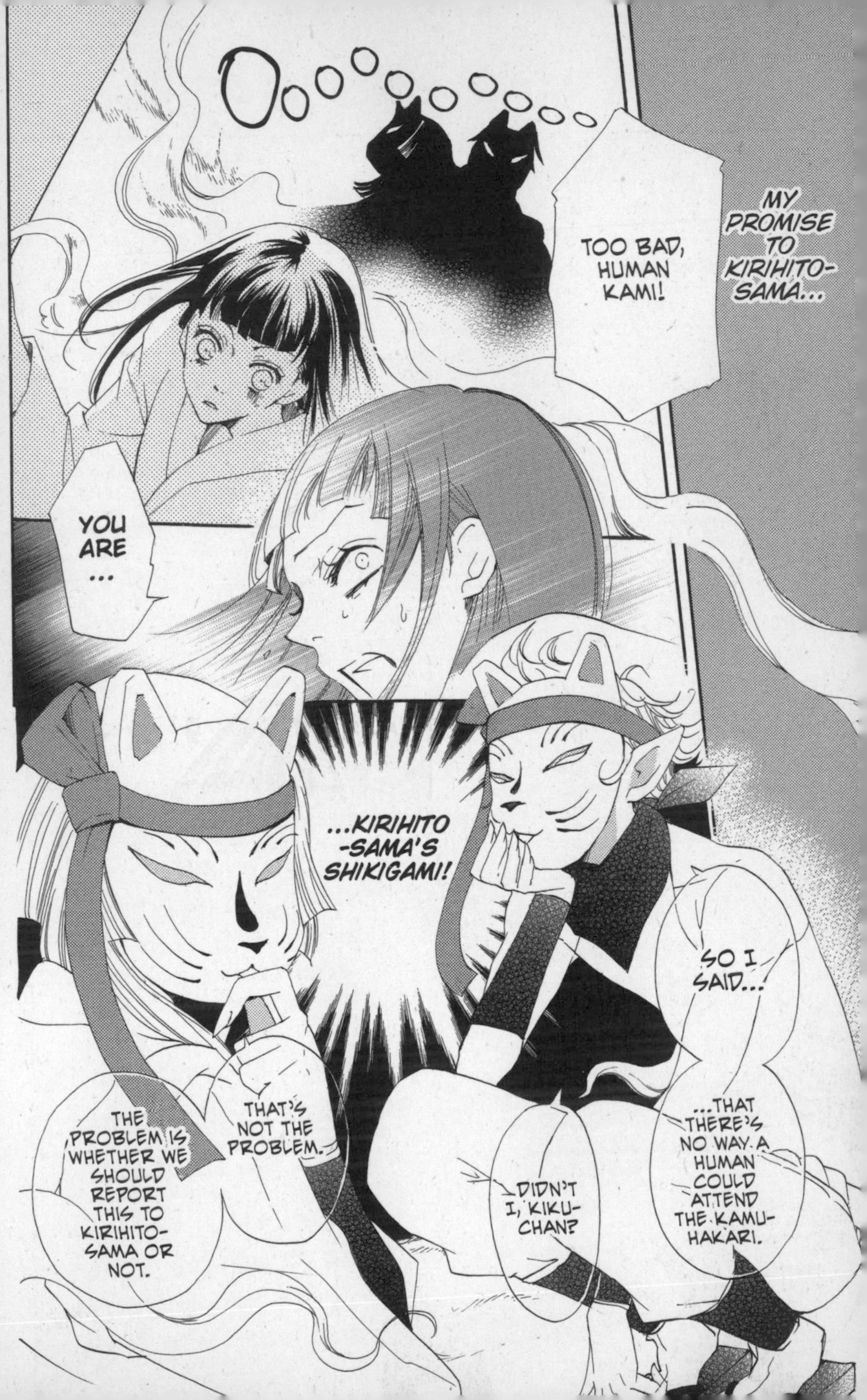
MY PROMISE TO KIRIHITO-SAMA...
OOOOOOOOOOO...
TOO BAD, HUMAN KAMI!
YOU ARE ...
...KIRIHITO-SAMA'S SHIKIGAMI!
SO I SAID...
...THAT THERE'S NO WAY A HUMAN COULD ATTEND THE KAMUHAKARI.
DIDN'T I, KIKU-CHAN?
THAT'S NOT THE PROBLEM.
THE PROBLEM IS WHETHER WE SHOULD REPORT THIS TO KIRIHITO-SAMA OR NOT.

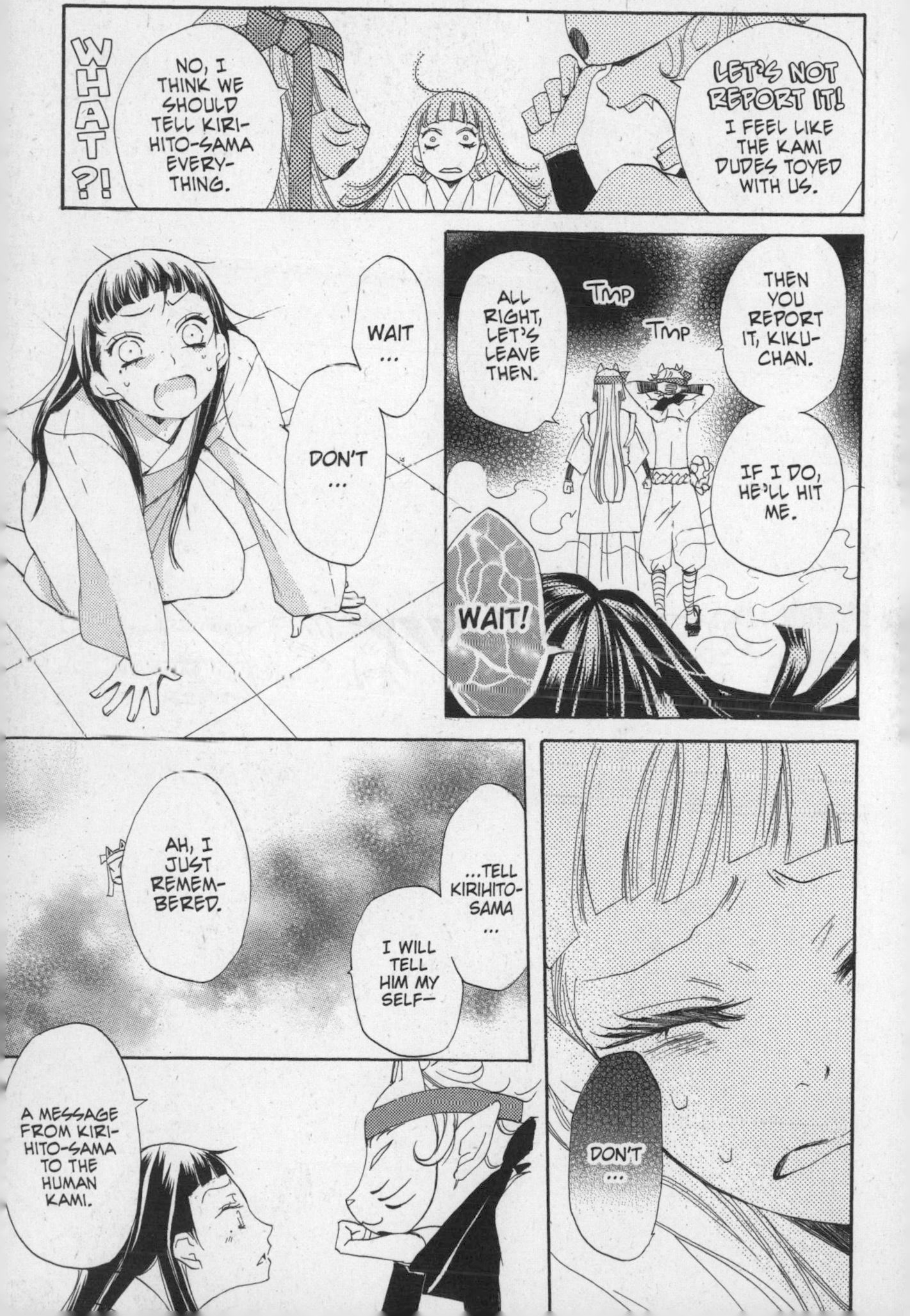
LET'S NOT REPORT IT! I FEEL LIKE THE KAMI DUDES TOYED WITH US.
NO, I THINK WE SHOULD TELL KIRI-HITO-SAMA EVERY-THING.
WHAT?!
THEN YOU REPORT IT, KIKU-CHAN.
IF I DO, HE'LL HIT ME.
Tmp
Tmp
ALL RIGHT, LET'S LEAVE THEN.
WAIT!
WAIT ...
DON'T ...
DON'T ...
...TELL KIRIHITO-SAMA ...
I WILL TELL HIM MY SELF—
AH, I JUST REMEMBERED.
A MESSAGE FROM KIRI-HITO-SAMA TO THE HUMAN KAMI.

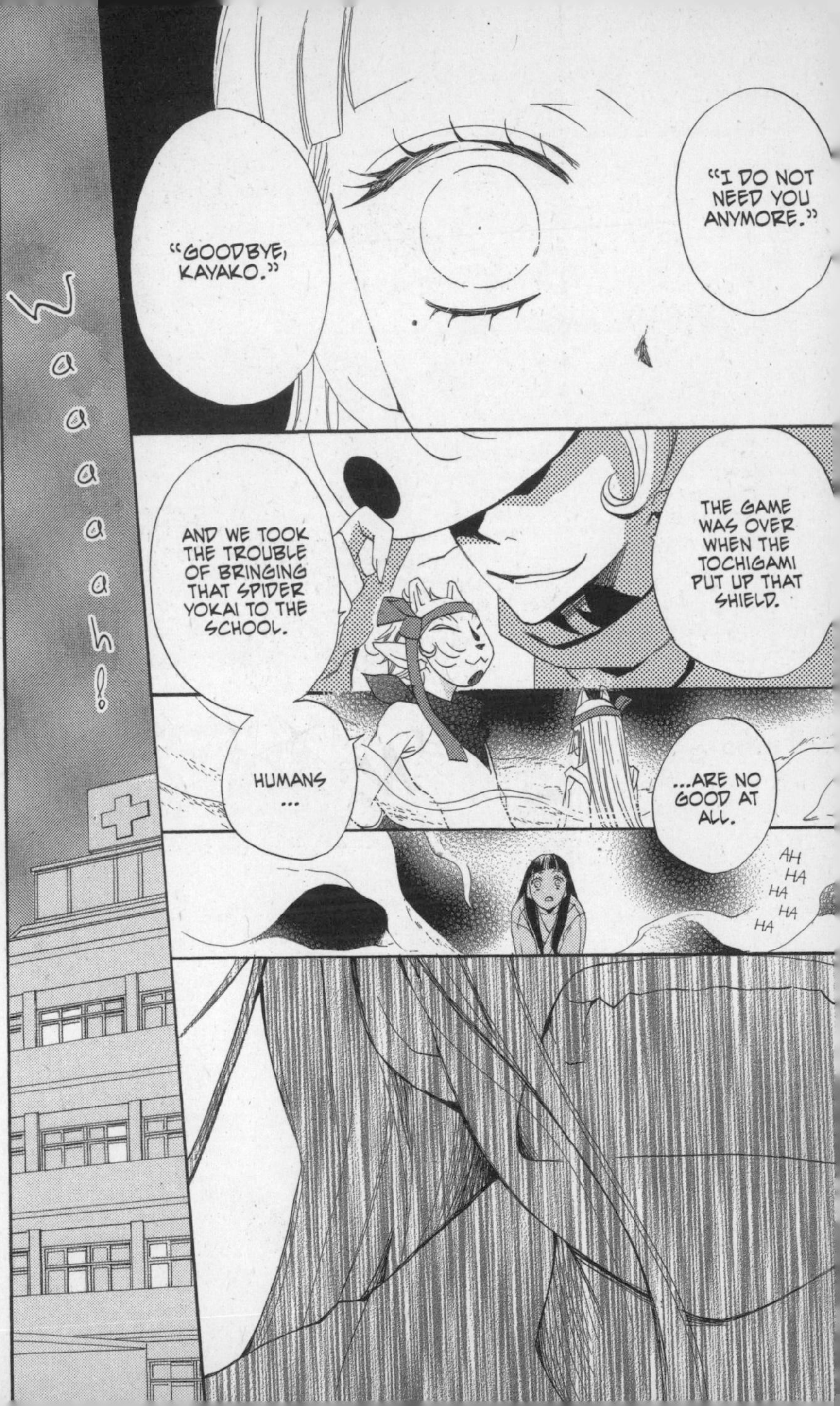
"I DO NOT NEED YOU ANYMORE."
"GOODBYE, KAYAKO."
THE GAME WAS OVER WHEN THE TOCHIGAMI PUT UP THAT SHIELD.
AND WE TOOK THE TROUBLE OF BRINGING THAT SPIDER YOKAI TO THE SCHOOL.
HUMANS ...
...ARE NO GOOD AT ALL.
AH HA HA HA HA
Waaaaah!

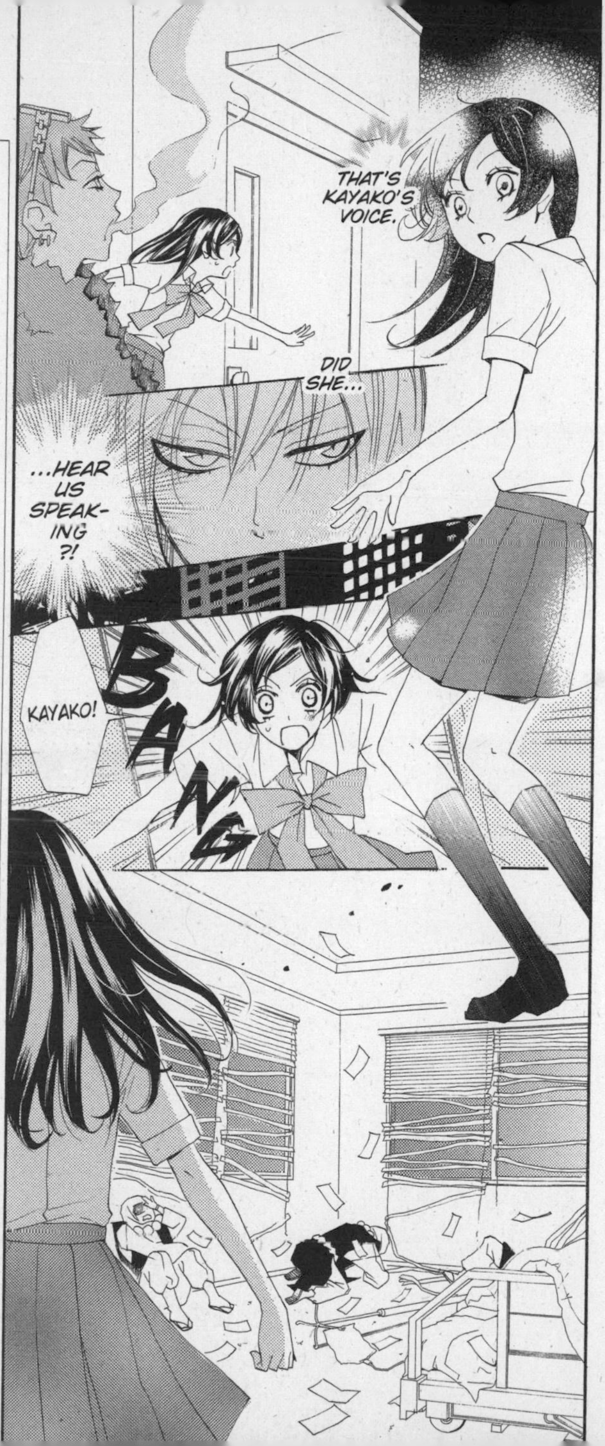
THAT'S KAYAKO'S VOICE.
DID SHE...
...HEAR US SPEAK-ING ?!
BANG
KAYAKO!

Thank you for reading this far. ✿

Nanami will go to Izumo in the next volume. I love Izumo. I'd like to go on a trip there again.

The next volume is Volume 7. Wow! It's a happy Volume 7. I hope you read the next volume too. ✿

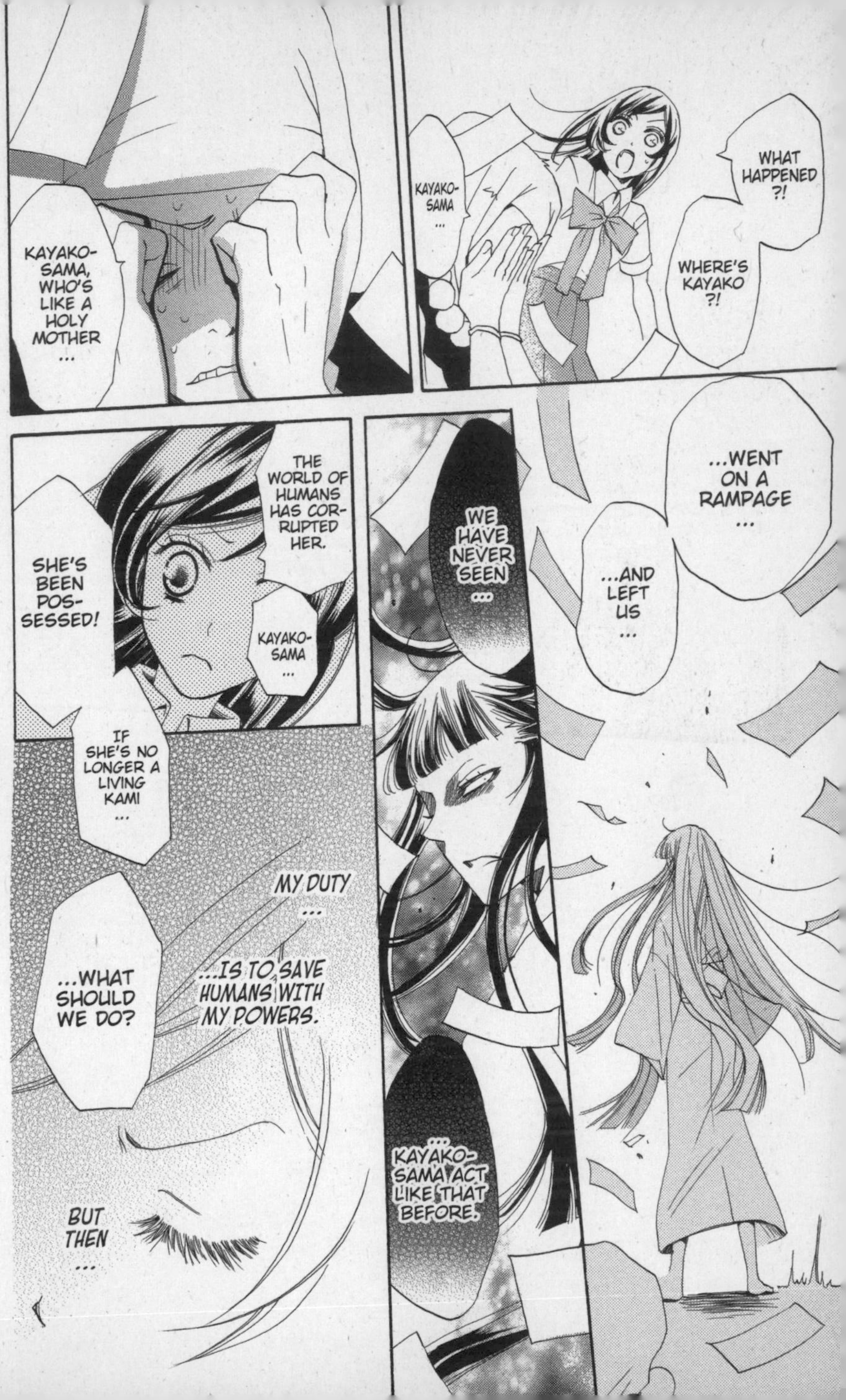
WHAT HAPPENED?!
WHERE'S KAYAKO?!
KAYAKO-SAMA ...
KAYAKO-SAMA, WHO'S LIKE A HOLY MOTHER ...
...WENT ON A RAMPAGE ...
...AND LEFT US ...
WE HAVE NEVER SEEN ...
...KAYAKO-SAMA ACT LIKE THAT BEFORE.
THE WORLD OF HUMANS HAS COR-RUPTED HER.
SHE'S BEEN POS-SESSED!
KAYAKO-SAMA ...
IF SHE'S NO LONGER A LIVING KAMI ...
MY DUTY ...
...IS TO SAVE HUMANS WITH MY POWERS.
...WHAT SHOULD WE DO?
BUT THEN ...

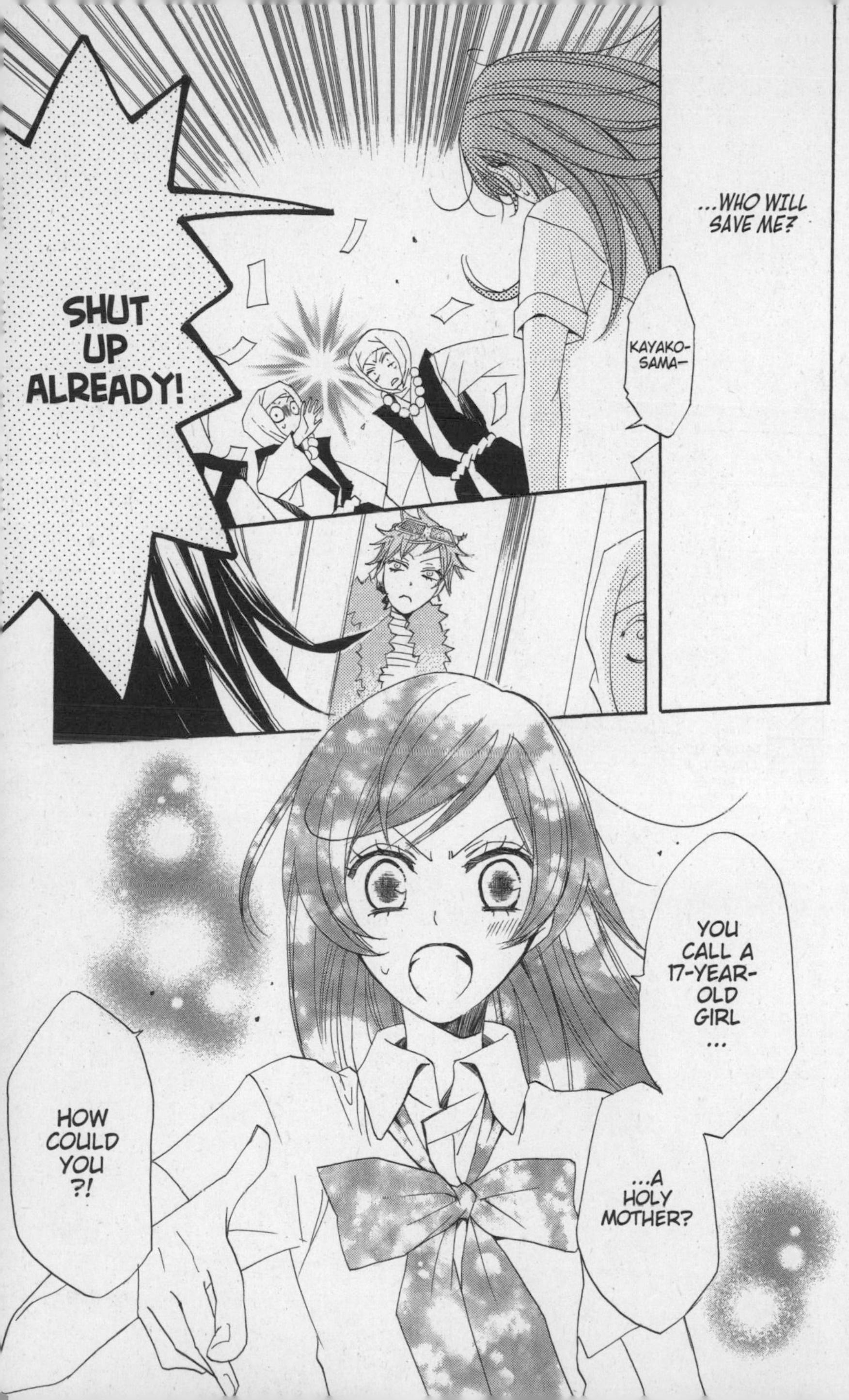
...WHO WILL SAVE ME?
KAYAKO-SAMA-
SHUT UP ALREADY!
YOU CALL A 17-YEAR-OLD GIRL ...
...A HOLY MOTHER?
HOW COULD YOU?!

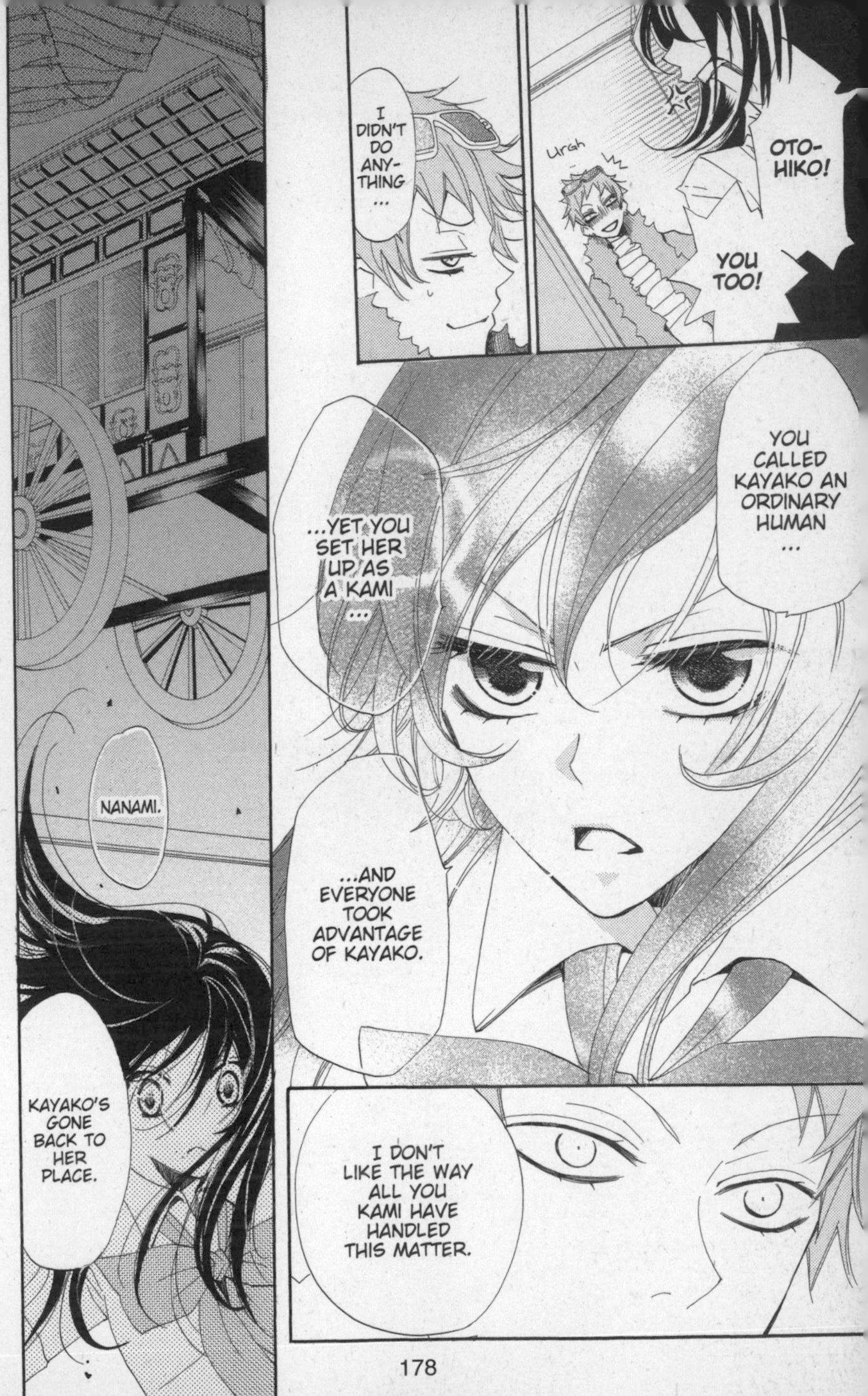
OTO-HIKO!
YOU TOO!
Urgh
I DIDN'T DO ANYTHING...
YOU CALLED KAYAKO AN ORDINARY HUMAN...
...YET YOU SET HER UP AS A KAMI...
...AND EVERYONE TOOK ADVANTAGE OF KAYAKO.
I DON'T LIKE THE WAY ALL YOU KAMI HAVE HANDLED THIS MATTER.
NANAMI.
KAYAKO'S GONE BACK TO HER PLACE.

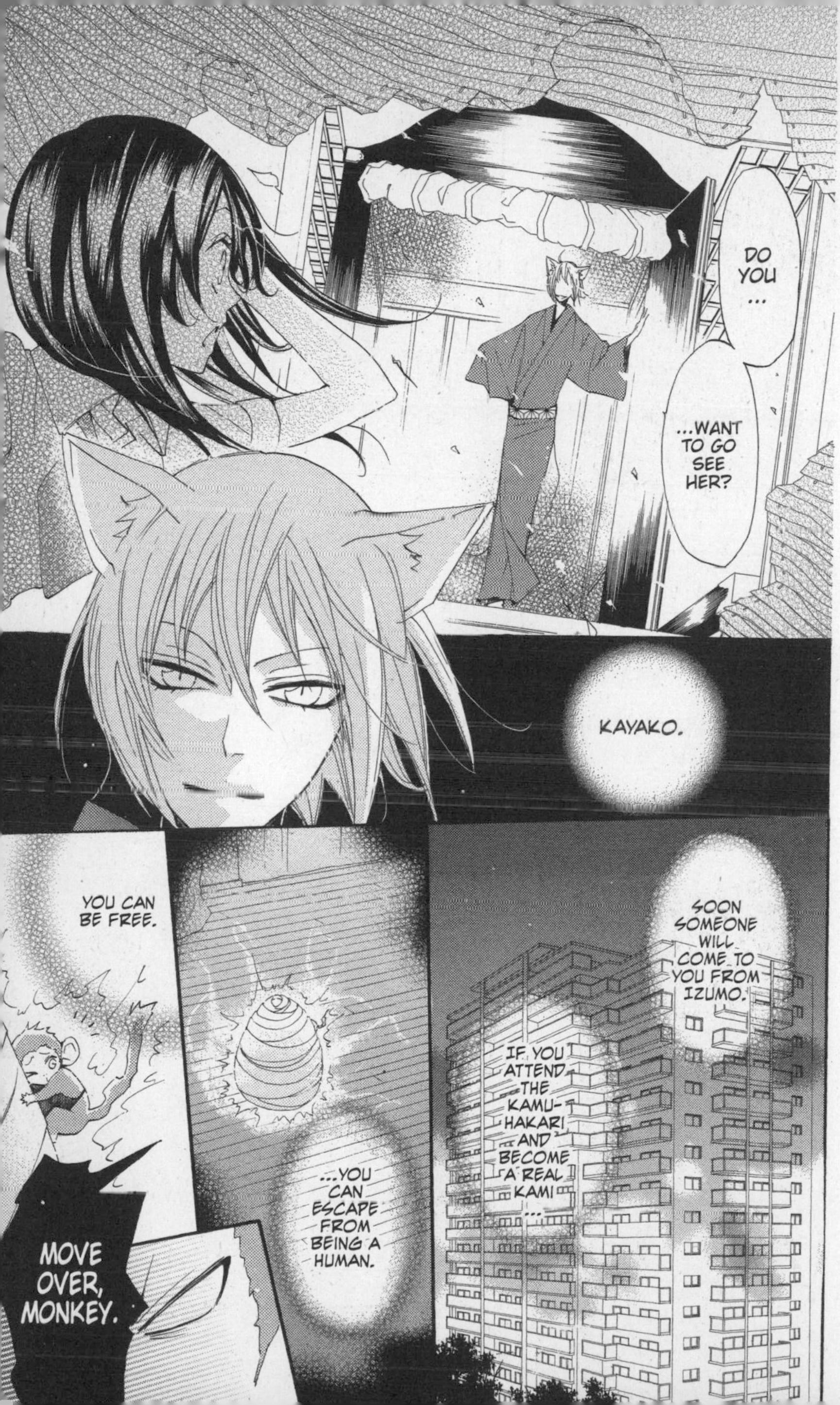
DO YOU ...
...WANT TO GO SEE HER?
KAYAKO.
SOON SOMEONE WILL COME TO YOU FROM IZUMO.
IF YOU ATTEND THE KAMU-HAKARI AND BECOME A REAL KAMI ...
...YOU CAN ESCAPE FROM BEING A HUMAN.
YOU CAN BE FREE.
MOVE OVER, MONKEY.

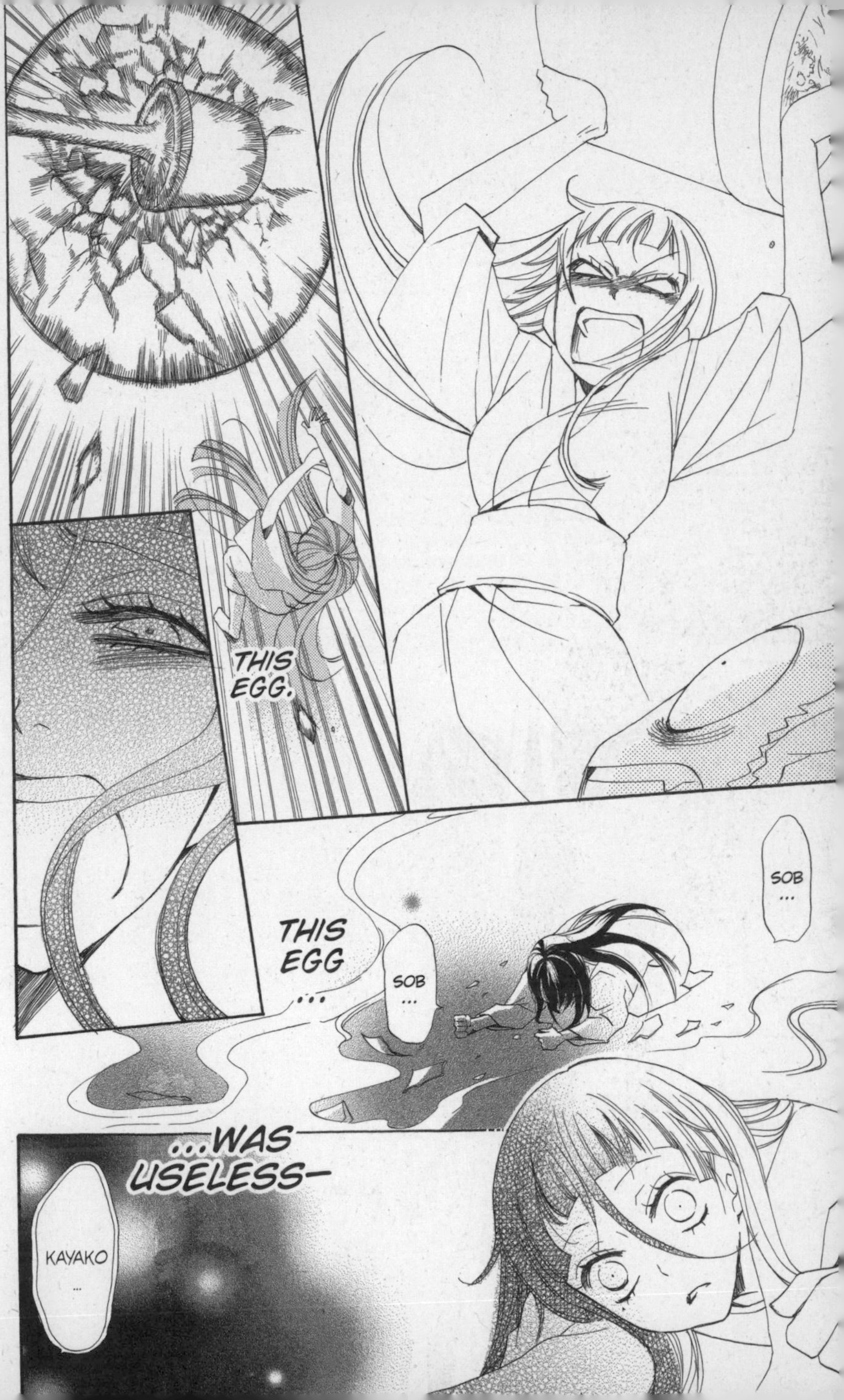
THIS EGG.
SOB ...
THIS EGG ...
SOB ...
...WAS USELESS—
KAYAKO ...

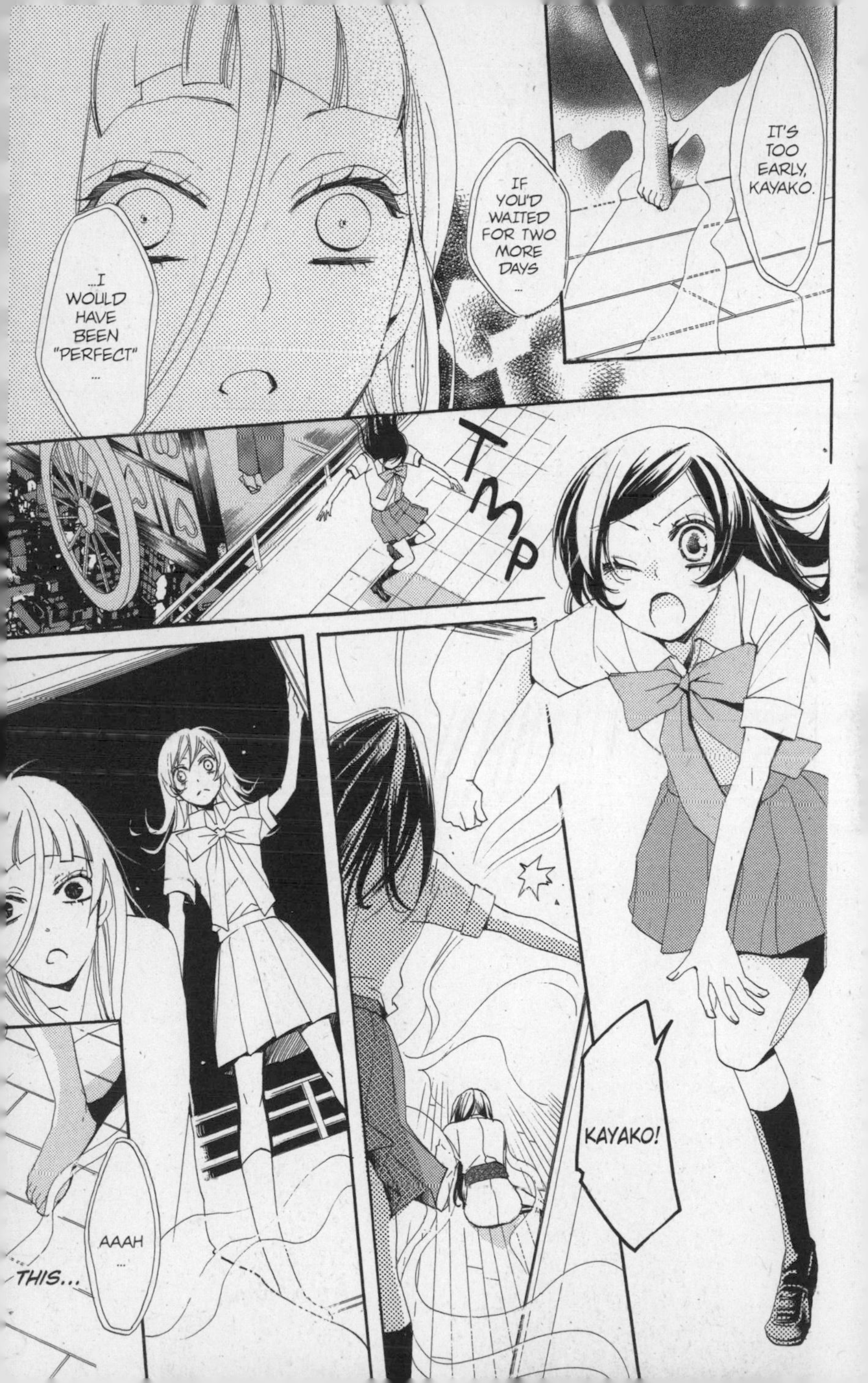
IT'S TOO EARLY, KAYAKO.
IF YOU'D WAITED FOR TWO MORE DAYS ...
...I WOULD HAVE BEEN "PERFECT" ...
TMP
KAYAKO!
AAAH ...
THIS...

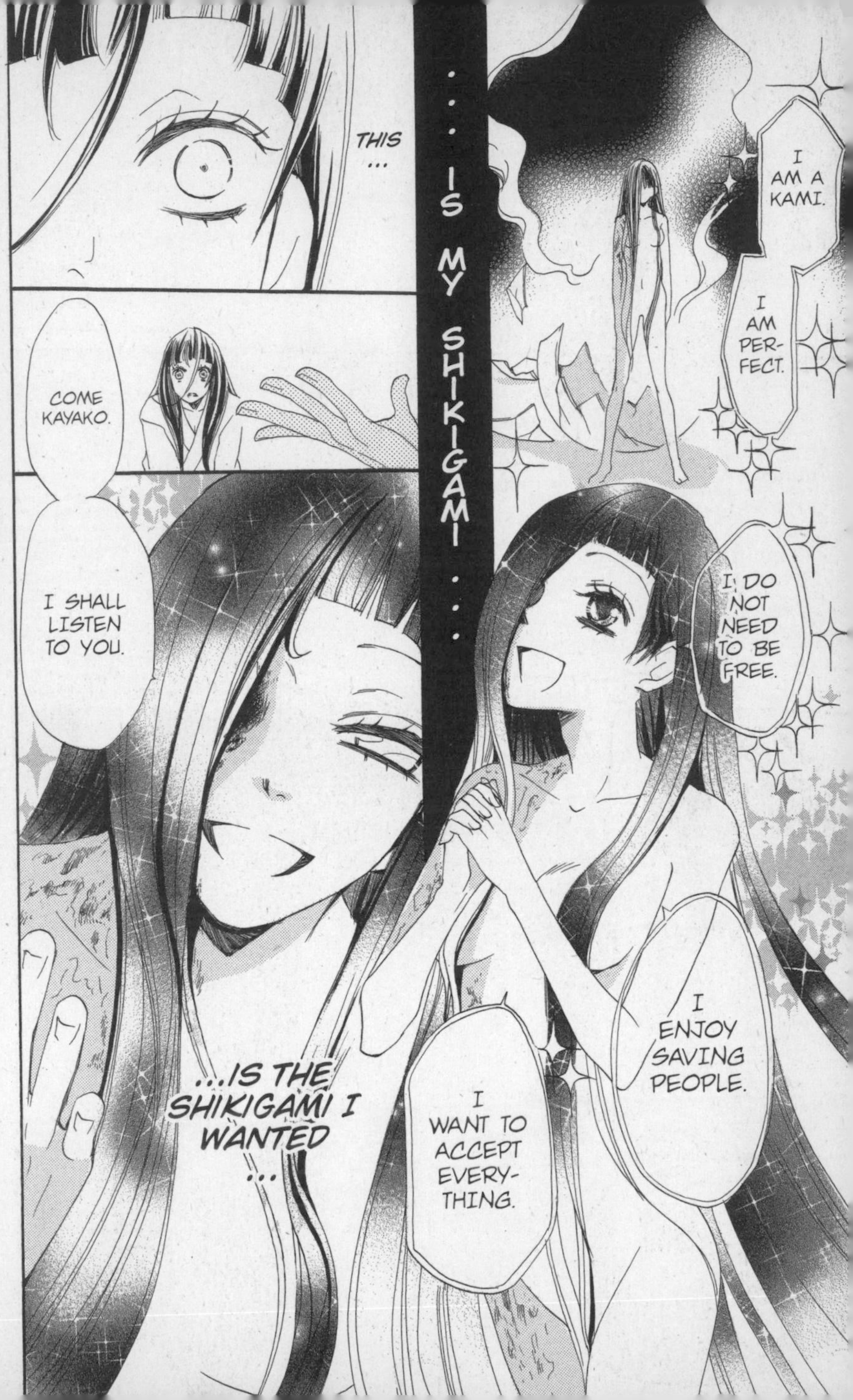
I AM A KAMI.
I AM PER-FECT.
I DO NOT NEED TO BE FREE.
I ENJOY SAVING PEOPLE.
I WANT TO ACCEPT EVERY-THING.
THIS ...
... IS MY SHIKIGAMI ...
COME KAYAKO.
I SHALL LISTEN TO YOU.
...IS THE SHIKIGAMI I WANTED ...

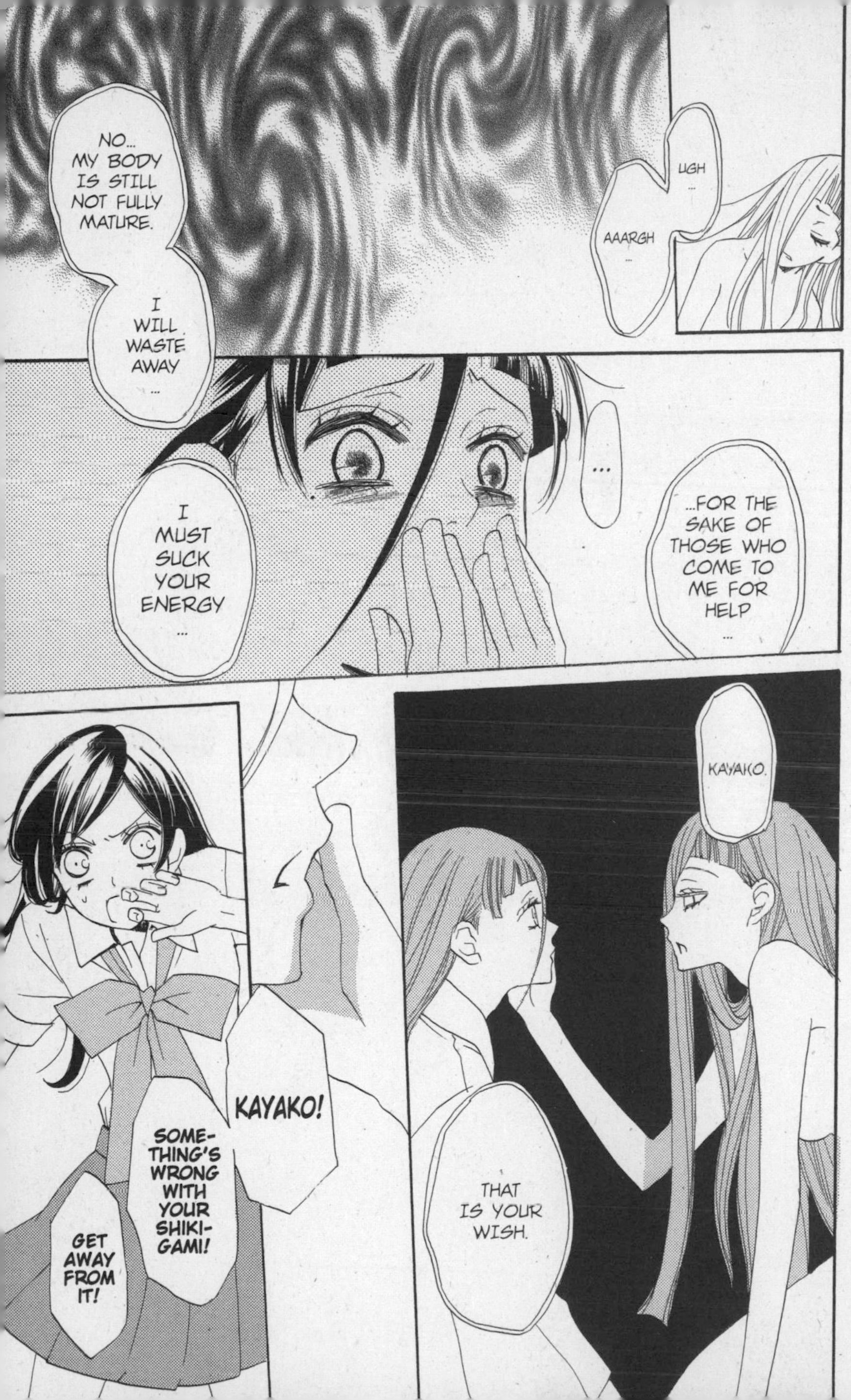
UGH...
AAARGH...
NO... MY BODY IS STILL NOT FULLY MATURE.
I WILL WASTE AWAY...
...
...FOR THE SAKE OF THOSE WHO COME TO ME FOR HELP...
I MUST SUCK YOUR ENERGY...
KAYAKO.
THAT IS YOUR WISH.
KAYAKO!
SOMETHING'S WRONG WITH YOUR SHIKIGAMI!
GET AWAY FROM IT!

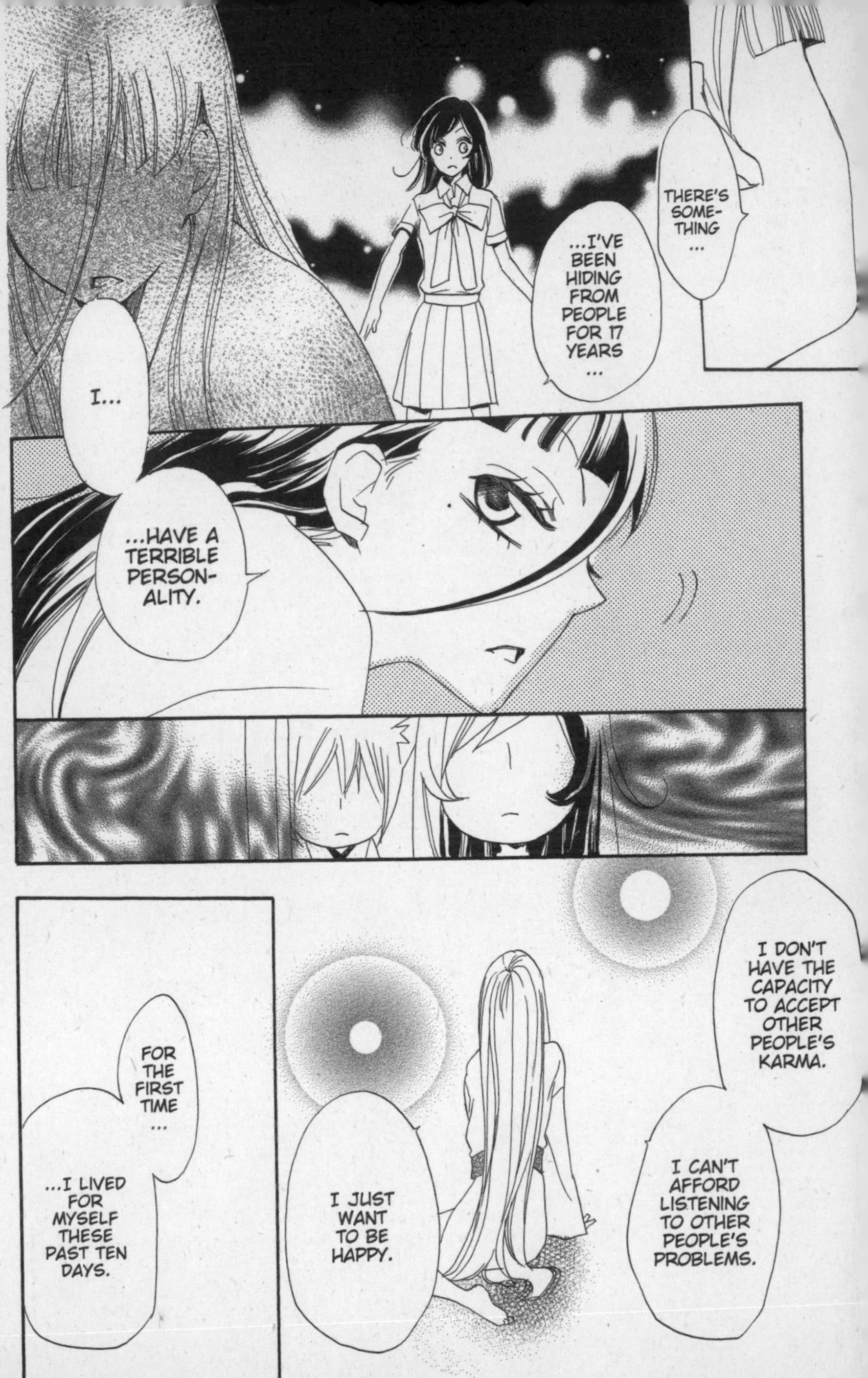
THERE'S SOMETHING...
...I'VE BEEN HIDING FROM PEOPLE FOR 17 YEARS...
I...
...HAVE A TERRIBLE PERSONALITY.
I DON'T HAVE THE CAPACITY TO ACCEPT OTHER PEOPLE'S KARMA.
I CAN'T AFFORD LISTENING TO OTHER PEOPLE'S PROBLEMS.
I JUST WANT TO BE HAPPY.
FOR THE FIRST TIME...
...I LIVED FOR MYSELF THESE PAST TEN DAYS.

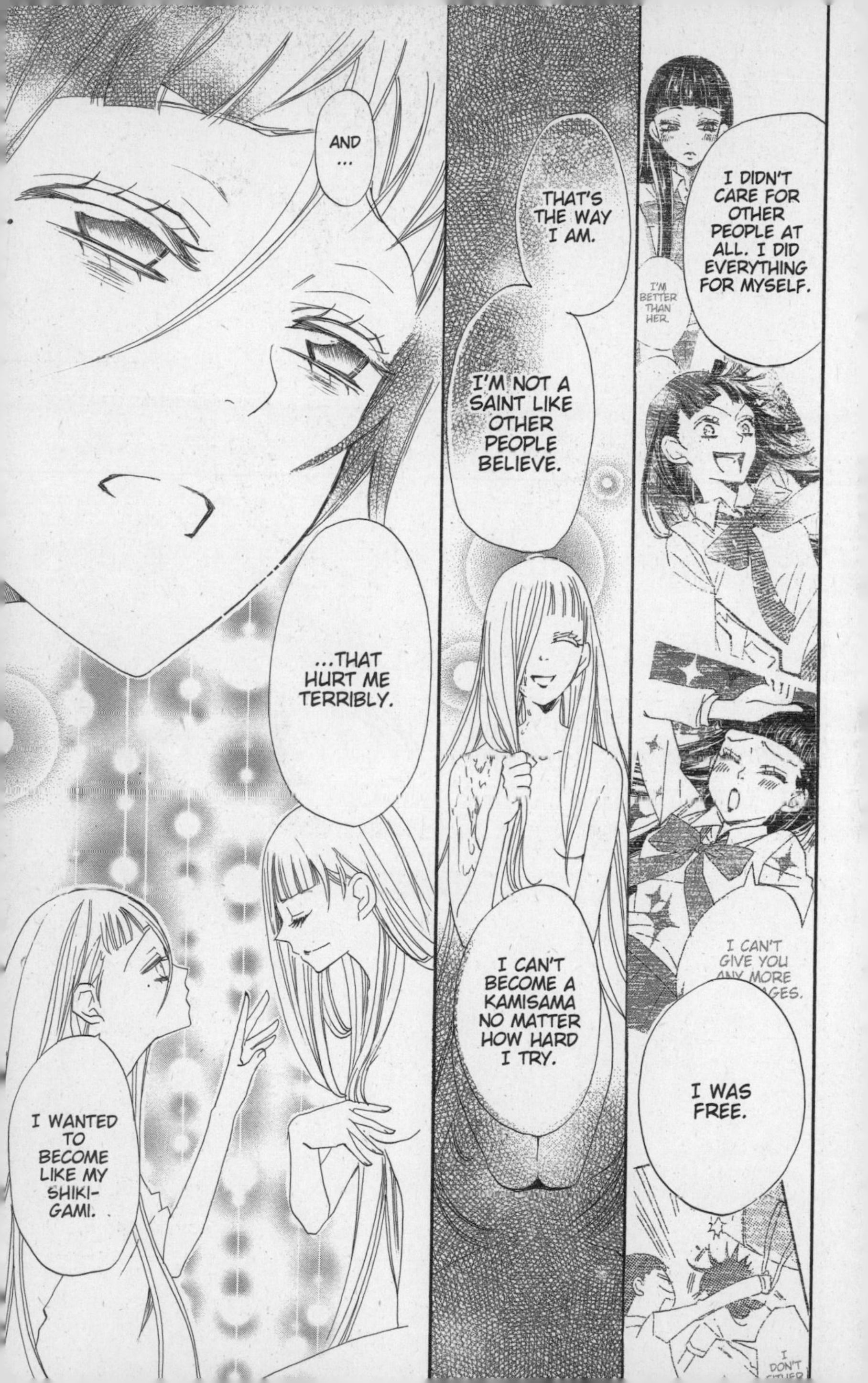
I DIDN'T CARE FOR OTHER PEOPLE AT ALL. I DID EVERYTHING FOR MYSELF.
I'M BETTER THAN HER.
I CAN'T GIVE YOU
I WAS FREE.
I DON'T
THAT'S THE WAY I AM.
I'M NOT A SAINT LIKE OTHER PEOPLE BELIEVE.
I CAN'T BECOME A KAMISAMA NO MATTER HOW HARD I TRY.
AND ...
...THAT HURT ME TERRIBLY.
I WANTED TO BECOME LIKE MY SHIKI-GAMI.

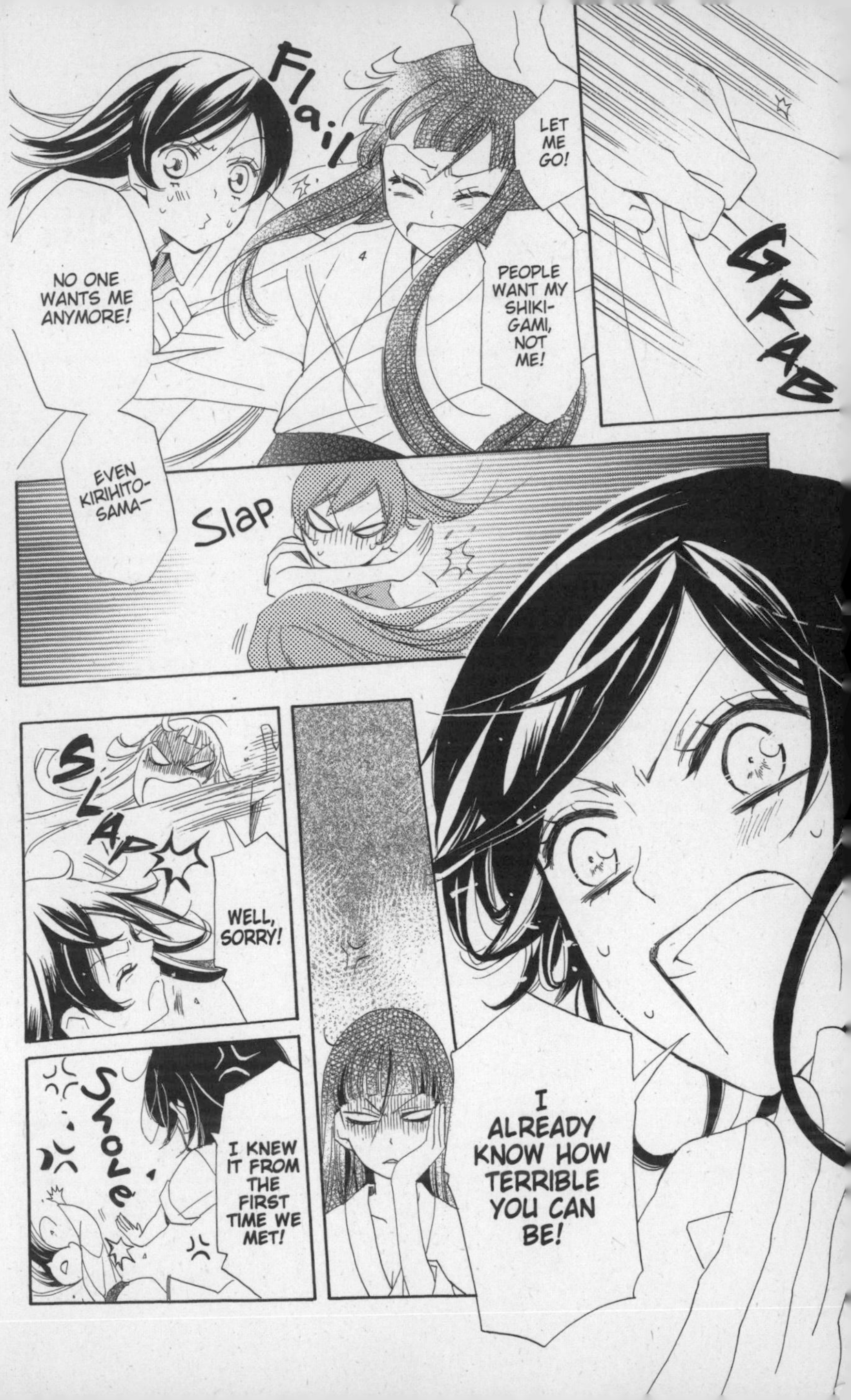
GRAB
LET ME GO!
Flail
PEOPLE WANT MY SHIKI-GAMI, NOT ME!
NO ONE WANTS ME ANYMORE!
EVEN KIRIHITO-SAMA—
I ALREADY KNOW HOW TERRIBLE YOU CAN BE!
Slap
SLAP
WELL, SORRY!
Shove
I KNEW IT FROM THE FIRST TIME WE MET!

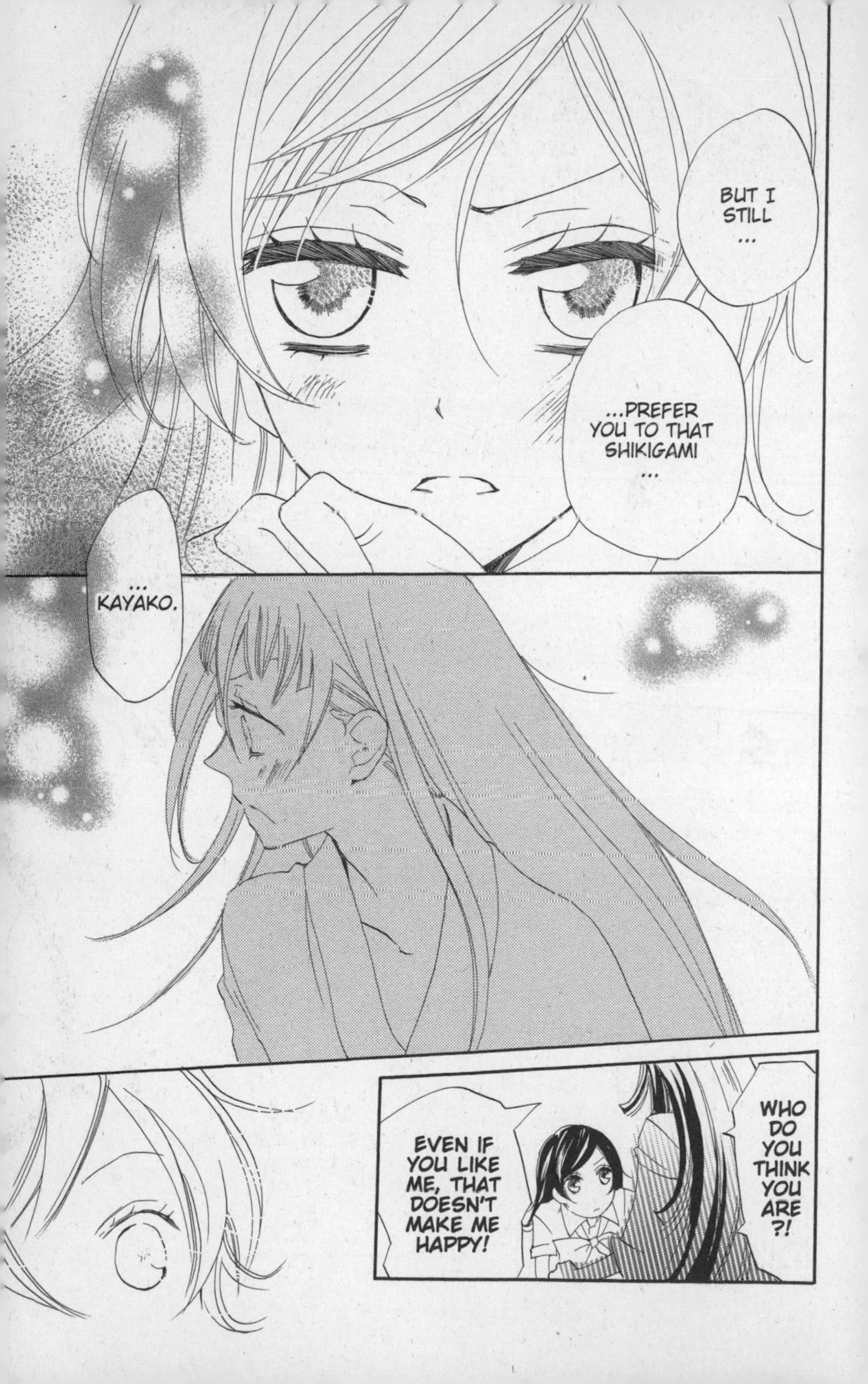
BUT I STILL ...
...PREFER YOU TO THAT SHIKIGAMI ...
... KAYAKO.
WHO DO YOU THINK YOU ARE?!
EVEN IF YOU LIKE ME, THAT DOESN'T MAKE ME HAPPY!

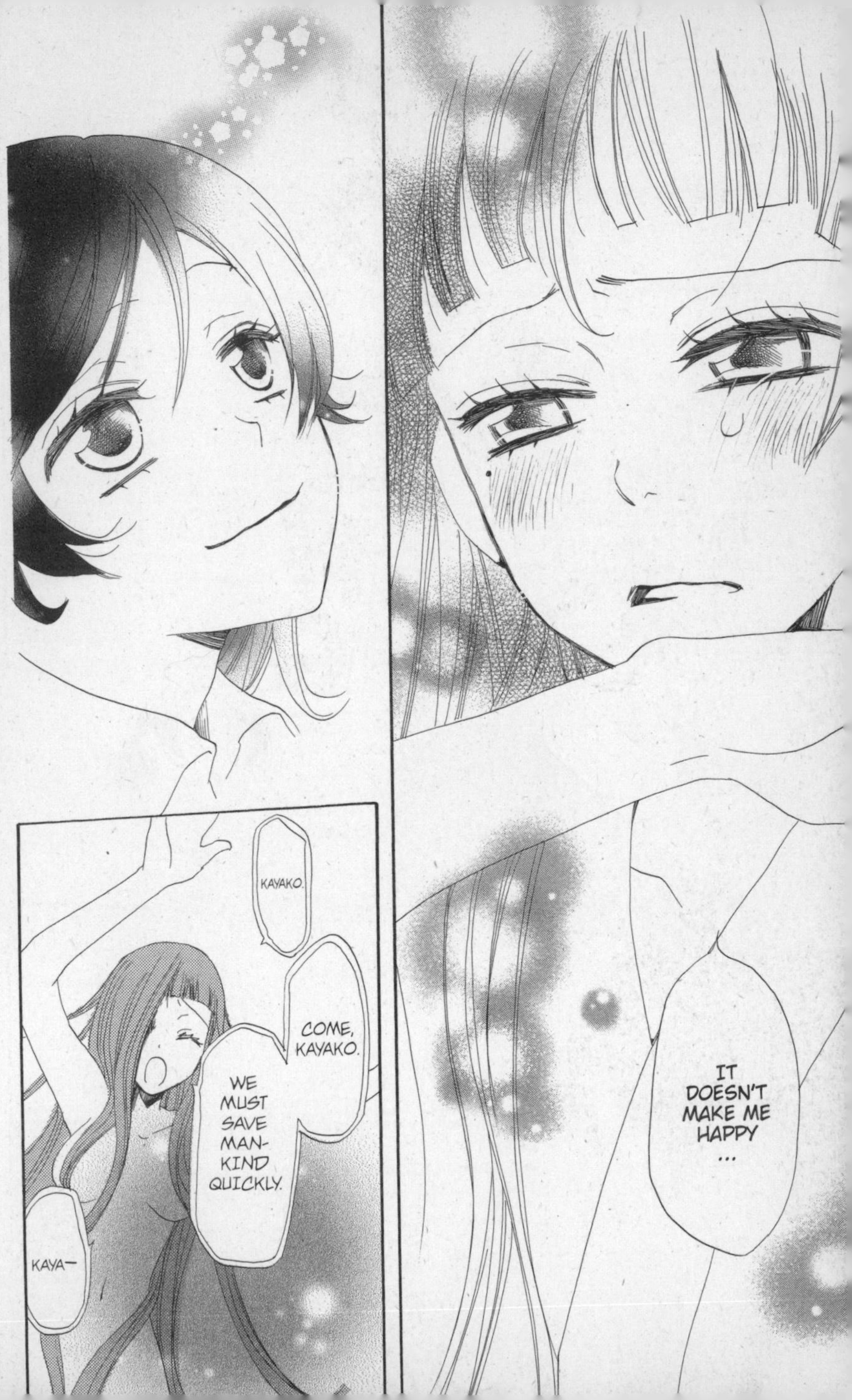
IT DOESN'T MAKE ME HAPPY ...
KAYAKO.
COME, KAYAKO.
WE MUST SAVE MAN-KIND QUICKLY.
KAYA—

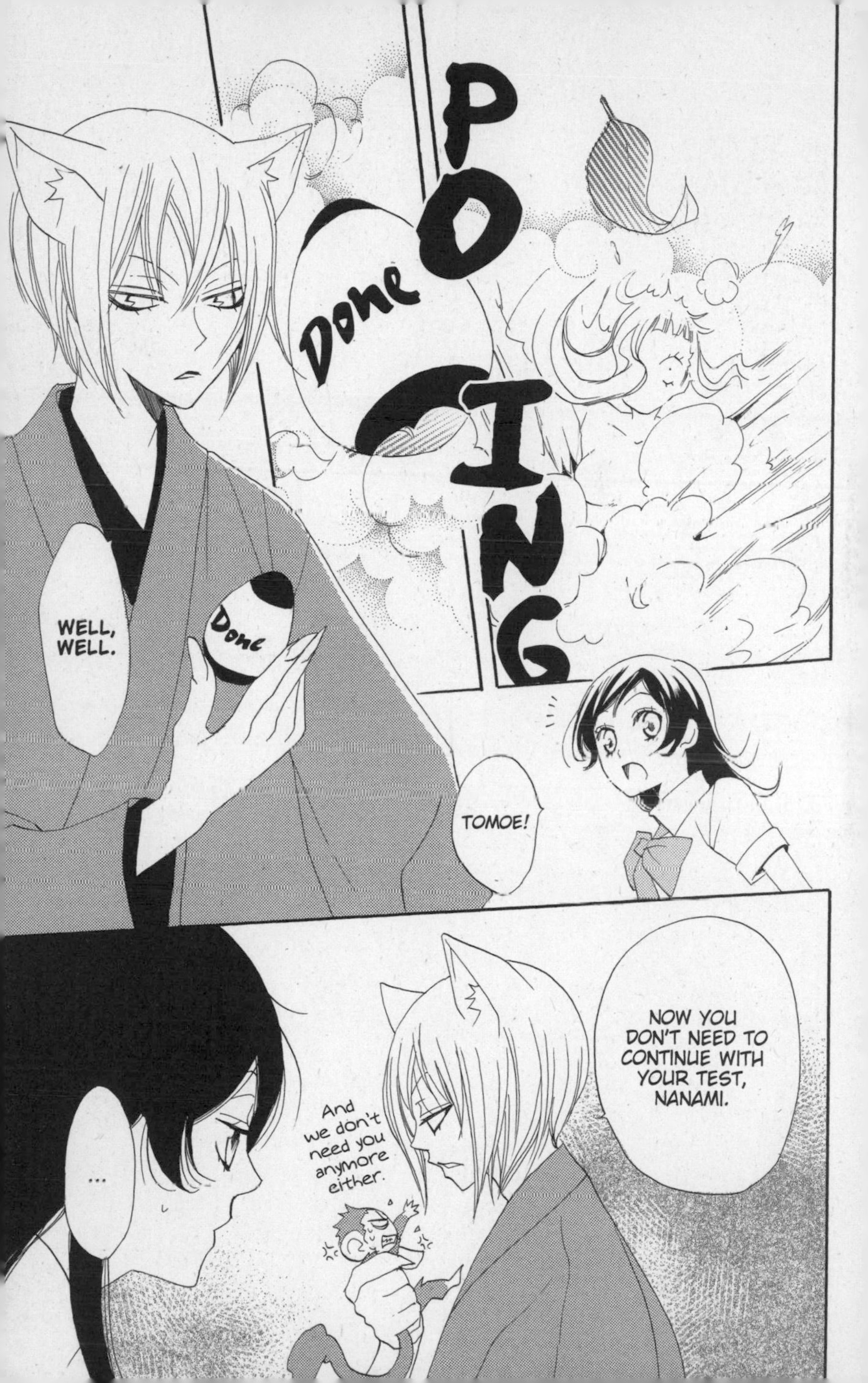
POING
Done
TOMOE!
WELL, WELL.
Done
NOW YOU DON'T NEED TO CONTINUE WITH YOUR TEST, NANAMI.
And we don't need you anymore either.
...

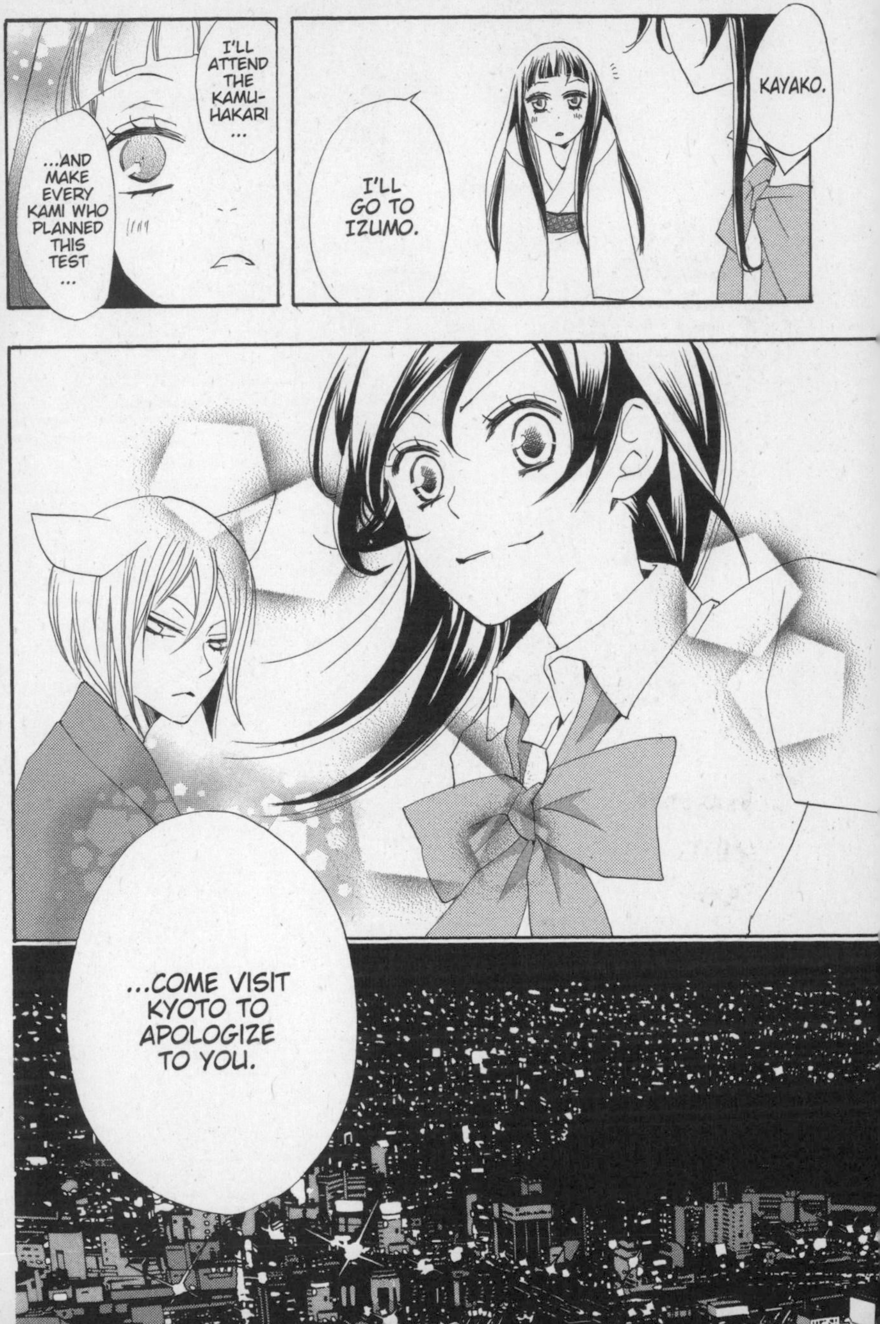
KAYAKO.
I'LL GO TO IZUMO.
I'LL ATTEND THE KAMU-HAKARI ...
...AND MAKE EVERY KAMI WHO PLANNED THIS TEST ...
...COME VISIT KYOTO TO APOLOGIZE TO YOU.

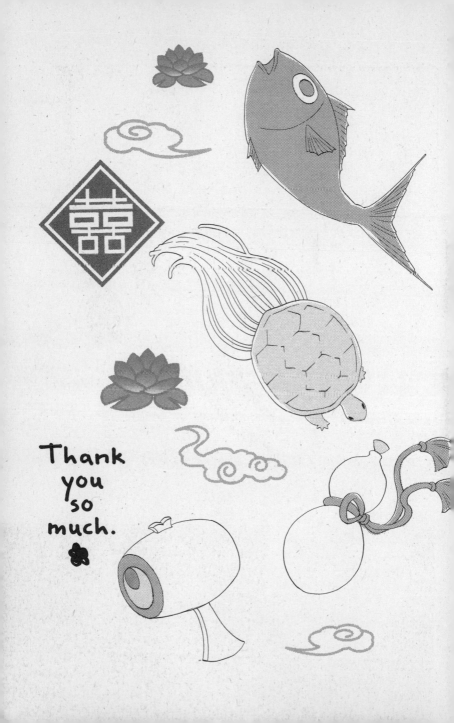

Thank
you
so
much.

The Otherworld

Ayakashi is an archaic term for yokai.

Kami are Shinto deities or spirits. The word can be used for a range of creatures, from nature spirits to strong and dangerous gods.

Shikigami are spirits that are summoned and employed by *onmyoji* (Yin-Yang sorcerers).

Shinshi are birds, beasts, insects or fish that have a special relationship with a kami.

Tengu are a type of yokai. They are sometimes associated with excess pride.

Tochigami (or jinushigami) are deities of a specific area of land.

Honorifics

-chan is a diminutive most often used with babies, children or teenage girls.

-dono roughly means "my lord," although not in the aristocratic sense.

-kun is used by persons of superior rank to their juniors. It can sometimes have a familiar connotation.

-sama is used with people of much higher rank.

Notes

Page 12, panel 3: Izumo
A city in Shimane Prefecture and home to Izumo Oyashiro shrine,
one of the most sacred sites in Shinto. Ookuninushi (Daikokuten)
is the kami enshrined in Izumo Oyashiro.

Page 14, panel 2: Kamuhakari
In October of the lunar calendar, all the kami in Japan gather at
Izumo Oyashiro shrine for a one-week convocation. Therefore
in the lunar calendar, October is called *Kamiarizuki* (month-
with-kami) in Izumo, and *Kannazuki* (month-without-kami) in
other regions. Festivals are held at Izumo Oyashiro during the
Kamuhakari.

Page 68, panel 2: Ofuda
A strip of paper or a small wooden tablet that acts as a spell.

Page 117, panel 1: Mamoru
The kanji for *Mamoru* means "to protect" (護).

Julietta Suzuki's debut manga *Hoshi ni Naru Hi* (The Day One Becomes a Star) appeared in the 2004 *Hana to Yume Plus*. Her other books include *Akuma to Dolce* (The Devil and Sweets) and *Karakuri Odette*. Born in December in Fukuoka Prefecture, she enjoys having movies play in the background while she works on her manga.

KAMISAMA KISS
VOL. 6
Shojo Beat Edition

STORY AND ART BY
Julietta Suzuki

English Translation & Adaptation/Tomo Kimura
Touch-up Art & Lettering/Joanna Estep
Design/Yukiko Whitley
Editor/Pancha Diaz

KAMISAMA HAJIMEMASHITA by Julietta Suzuki
© Julietta Suzuki 2010
All rights reserved.
First published in Japan in 2010 by HAKUSENSHA, Inc., Tokyo.
English language translation rights arranged with
HAKUSENSHA, Inc., Tokyo.

Printed in Canada

Published by VIZ Media, LLC
P.O. Box 77010
San Francisco, CA 94107

10 9 8 7 6 5 4 3 2 1
First printing, December 2011

VIZ MEDIA
www.viz.com

www.shojobeat.com

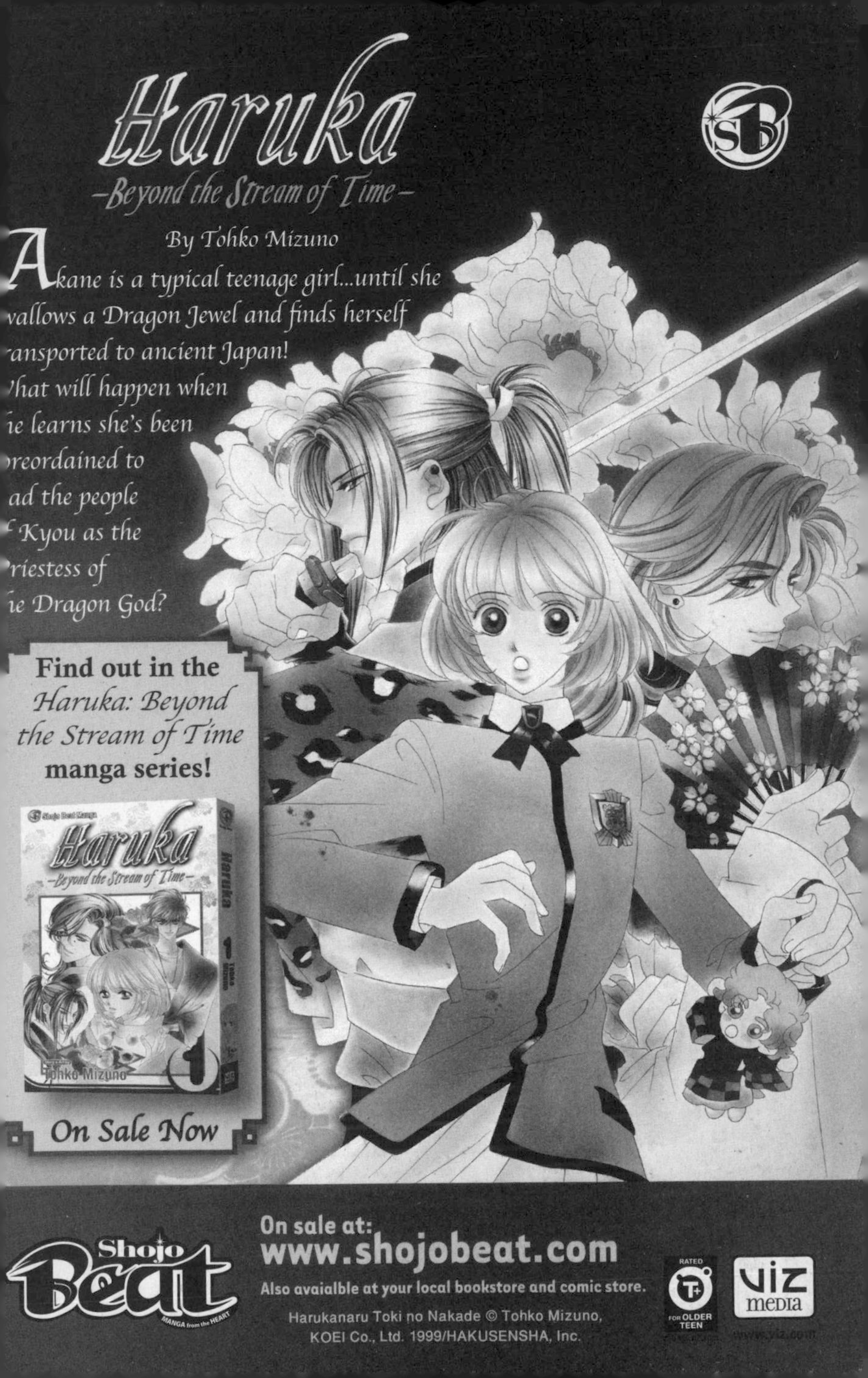
Haruka
-Beyond the Stream of Time-
By Tohko Mizuno
Akane is a typical teenage girl...until she
vallows a Dragon Jewel and finds herself
ansported to ancient Japan!
/hat will happen when
ie learns she's been
oreordained to
ad the people
Kyou as the
riestess of
ie Dragon God?
Find out in the
Haruka: Beyond
the Stream of Time
manga series!
Shojo Beat Manga
Haruka
-Beyond the Stream of Time-
Haruka
Tohko Mizuno
1
On Sale Now
Shojo Beat
MANGA from the HEART
On sale at:
www.shojobeat.com
Also avaialble at your local bookstore and comic store.
Harukanaru Toki no Nakade © Tohko Mizuno,
KOEI Co., Ltd. 1999/HAKUSENSHA, Inc.
RATED
T+
FOR OLDER TEEN
viz media

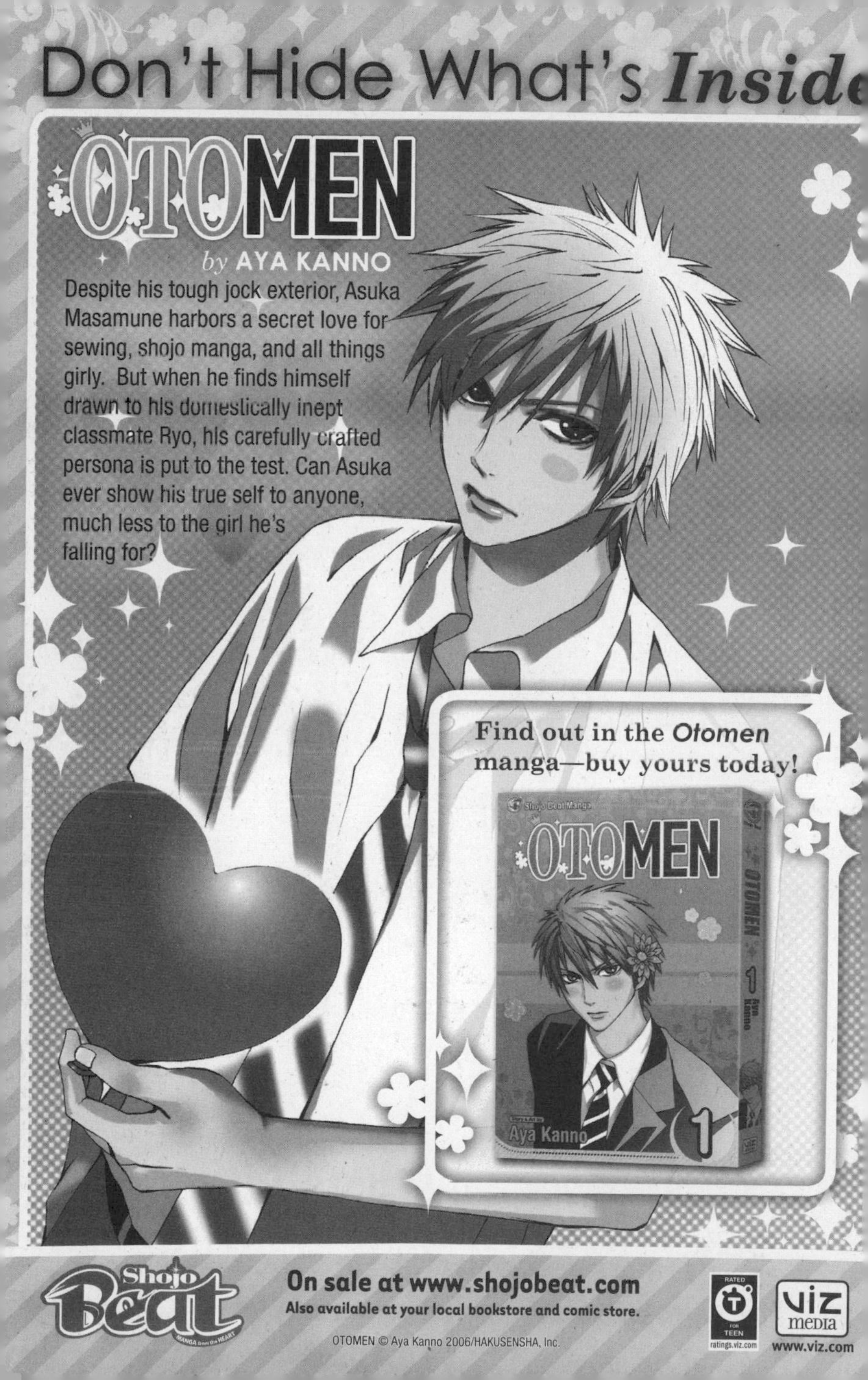
Don't Hide What's Inside
OTOMEN
by AYA KANNO
Despite his tough jock exterior, Asuka Masamune harbors a secret love for sewing, shojo manga, and all things girly. But when he finds himself drawn to his domestically inept classmate Ryo, his carefully crafted persona is put to the test. Can Asuka ever show his true self to anyone, much less to the girl he's falling for?
Find out in the Otomen manga—buy yours today!
Shojo Beat Manga
OTOMEN
Story & Art by Aya Kanno
1
Shojo Beat
MANGA from the HEART
On sale at www.shojobeat.com
Also available at your local bookstore and comic store.
OTOMEN © Aya Kanno 2006/HAKUSENSHA, Inc.
RATED T FOR TEEN
ratings.viz.com
VIZ MEDIA
www.viz.com